Library of
Davidson College

OXFORD HISTORICAL MONOGRAPHS

Editors

BARBARA HARVEY   A. D. MACINTYRE
R. W. SOUTHERN   A. F. THOMPSON
H. R. TREVOR-ROPER

NOTE

Oxford Historical Monographs will consist of books which would formerly have been published in the Oxford Historical Series. As with the previous series, they will be carefully selected studies which have been submitted, or are based upon theses submitted, for higher degrees in this University. The works listed below are those still in print in the Oxford Historical Series.

The Medieval Administration of the Channel Islands, 1199–1399.
By J. H. LE PATOUREL. 1937

The Corporation of Leicester, 1689–1836. By R. W. GREAVES. 1939

Durham Jurisdictional Peculiars. By FRANK BARLOW. 1950

English Monasteries and their Patrons in the Thirteenth Century.
By SUSAN WOOD 1955

The Estates of the Percy Family, 1416–1537. By J. M. W. BEAN. 1958

The Radical Duke. Career and Correspondence of Charles Lennox, third Duke of Richmond. By ALISON GILBERT OLSON. 1961

The Norman Monasteries and their English Possessions.
By DONALD MATTHEW. 1962

Edward III and the Scots. The Formative Years of a Military Career, 1327–1335. By RANALD NICHOLSON. 1965

A Medieval Oxfordshire Village: Cuxham: 1240 to 1400.
By P. D. A. HARVEY. 1965

Cardinal Bainbridge in the Court of Rome, 1509–1514.
By D. S. CHAMBERS. 1965

The Later Lollards, 1414–1520. By JOHN A. F. THOMSON. 1965

The Impeachment of Warren Hastings. By P. J. MARSHALL. 1965

The Passing of the Irish Act of Union. By G. C. BOLTON. 1966

The Miners and British Politics, 1906–1914. By ROY GREGORY. 1968

The General Election of 1880. By TREVOR LLOYD. 1968

From Joseph II to the Jacobin Trials, second edition.
By ERNST WANGERMANN. 1969

The Pauper Press. By PATRICIA HOLLIS. 1970

Victorian Quakers. By ELIZABETH ISICHEI. 1970

English Gascony, 1399–1453. By M. G. A. VALE. 1970

Ducal Brittany, 1364–1399. By MICHAEL JONES. 1970

Thomas of Lancaster, 1307–1322. By J. R. MADDICOTT. 1971

Charles James Fox and the Disintegration of the Whig Party, 1782–1794.
By L. G. MITCHELL. 1971

The Nazi Party in Lower Saxony, 1921–1933. By JEREMY NOAKES. 1971

Papal Judges Delegate in the Province of Canterbury, 1198–1254. By JANE E. SAYERS. 1971.

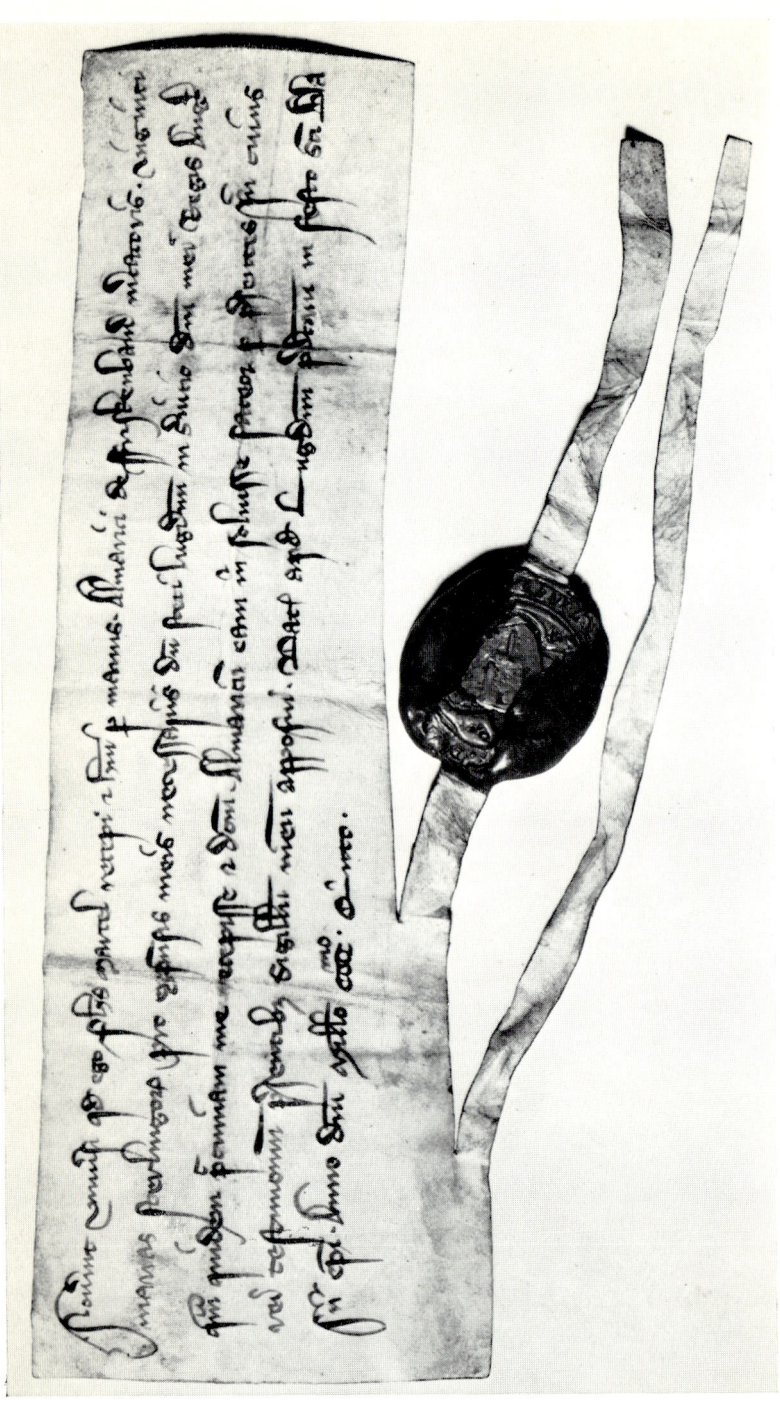

HANDWRITING AND SEAL OF THE FIRST *CUSTOS PROCESSUUM*

Receipt by Philip Martel to Amerigo dei Frescobaldi for twenty marks lent to him for his expenses in the king's service. Dated at Lyon, 3 February 1305/6. *Endorsed:* 'Sopra mastro Filippo Martelli di marche xx distribute per Londra.' *P.R.O. Exch. K.R. Ancient Deeds, 203*

English Diplomatic Administration
1259–1339

BY

G. P. CUTTINO

Professor of History
Emory University

SECOND EDITION
REVISED AND ENLARGED

OXFORD
AT THE CLARENDON PRESS
1971

Oxford University Press, Ely House, London W.1
GLASGOW NEW YORK TORONTO MELBOURNE WELLINGTON
CAPE TOWN SALISBURY IBADAN NAIROBI DAR ES SALAAM LUSAKA ADDIS ABABA
BOMBAY CALCUTTA MADRAS KARACHI LAHORE DACCA
KUALA LUMPUR SINGAPORE HONG KONG TOKYO

© OXFORD UNIVERSITY PRESS 1971

PRINTED IN GREAT BRITAIN
AT THE UNIVERSITY PRESS, OXFORD
BY VIVIAN RIDLER
PRINTER TO THE UNIVERSITY

PREFACE TO THE SECOND EDITION

THIS book appeared originally in 1940 as Volume XI in the Oxford Historical Series, edited by G. N. Clark, C. R. Cruttwell, and F. M. Powicke. In this edition I have made necessary corrections and have enlarged, in most instances substantially, every chapter except the second. I have also added as a fifth appendix the account of Bishop Langton's mission for Edward I in 1296–7, which I originally published in *Studies in British History*, edited by C. W. de Kiewiet (University of Iowa, 1941). The bibliography has been brought up to date.

G. P. C.

Emory University

PREFACE TO THE FIRST EDITION

THIS book is a study in the structure of English administration of diplomacy, based largely on a hitherto unexplored collection of manuscript materials. The main emphasis is placed on relations between England and France during the years 1259–1339, but much of what is said applies to the whole of the medieval period as well. It has not been my intention to write diplomatic history as such: I have tried rather to lay a basis for the vast amount of research that remains to be done in this field. I have already begun a detailed examination of the larger problems that naturally grow out of a study of this kind, particularly the legal aspects of Anglo-French relations during the period preceding the Hundred Years War. In one sense, then, the following chapters, although complete in themselves, should be regarded as an introduction to a more exhaustive work. They should also be of interest as a supplement to Professor Tout's account of medieval English administration.

It is a pleasure to acknowledge my debt to Professor V. H. Galbraith, now of the University of Edinburgh, and to Professor F. M. Powicke. I am deeply grateful for the kindness, inspiration, and guidance they have so unstintingly given while supervising the thesis on which this book is based. I wish also to express my thanks to Mr. Charles Johnson for many helpful suggestions and for reading the manuscript in its final form, to the Rhodes Trust, which has made this study possible, to the members of the staff of H.M. Public Record Office, and to a large number of friends and fellow students who have been willing both to read and to criticize.

G. P. C.

CONTENTS

HANDWRITING AND SEAL OF THE FIRST *Custos Processuum* — *frontispiece*

I. ENGLAND AND THE CONTINENT, 1259–1339 — 1

II. THE KEEPER OF PROCESSES — 29

III. THREE PROCESSES — 62
    (I) THE PROCESS OF MONTREUIL — 62
    (II) THE PROCESS OF PÉRIGUEUX — 87
    (III) THE PROCESS OF AGEN — 100

IV. CALENDARS AND REGISTERS — 112

V. AGENTS AND MECHANICS OF DIPLOMACY — 127
    (I) THE ENVOY — 127
    (II) THE COUNCIL AND PARLIAMENT — 144
    (III) THE CHANCERY — 151
    (IV) THE EXCHEQUER — 165
    (V) THE WARDROBE — 171

CONCLUSION — 187

APPENDICES — 192
    I. THE ACCOUNTS OF PHILIP MARTEL — 192
    II. THE ACCOUNTS OF ELIAS JONESTON — 194
    III. THE ACCOUNT OF ROGER STAUNFORD — 210
    IV. TABLES TO ILLUSTRATE CHAPTERS III AND V — 212
        1. English Claims at Montreuil — 212
        2–4. Pipe Roll Accounts of Envoys (3 parts) — 221
        5. Wardrobe Accounts of Envoys — 223
    V. THE ACCOUNT OF WALTER LANGTON — 224

BIBLIOGRAPHY — 251

INDEX — 261

ABBREVIATIONS

Anc. Cor.	Ancient Correspondence.
Anc. Pet.	Ancient Petitions.
C.C.R.	*Calendar of Close Rolls.*
C.C.W.	*Calendar of Chancery Warrants.*
Chan. Misc.	Chancery Miscellanea.
Chan. War.	Chancery Warrants.
C.Pap.R.	*Calendar of Papal Registers.*
C.P.R.	*Calendar of Patent Rolls.*
D.D.C.	Diplomatic Documents, Chancery.
Dip. Doc. Exch.	Diplomatic Documents, Exchequer.
D.N.B.	*Dictionary of National Biography.*
E.A.	Exchequer Accounts.
E.H.R.	*English Historical Review.*
E. (W. & H.)	Enrolled Accounts (Wardrobe and Household).
G.C.	*The Gascon Calendar of 1322* (Camden Third Series).
G.R.	*Gascon Register A (Series of 1318–1319).*
Hist. MSS. Com.	Royal Commission on Historical Manuscripts.
L.Q.G.	*Liber quotidianus contrarotulatoris garderobe.*
Misc. Bks. Exch. T.R.	Miscellaneous Books, Exchequer Treasury of Receipt.
MS. Add.	Additional Manuscripts (British Museum).
Parl. & Coun. Proc. Chan.	Parliamentary and Council Proceedings, Chancery.
Parl. & Coun. Proc. Exch.	Parliamentary and Council Proceedings, Exchequer.
Pipe	Pipe Rolls.
Rot. parl.	*Rotuli parliamentorum.*
Rot. parl. ined.	*Rotuli parliamentorum hactenus inediti* (Camden Third Series).
Rymer	Rymer's *Foedera.*
Ward. Debent.	Wardrobe Debentures.

(Whenever possible, chronicles are cited by names of the authors.)

I

ENGLAND AND THE CONTINENT
1259–1339

> ... quamquam pax inter illustrem regem Franciae et nos jamdudum prolocuta aliquamdiu cepit dilationem ... ipsam tamen pacem cum ipso rege effectualiter inivimus ... ad laudem Dei et ecclesiae Romanae commodum et honorem ...'
>
> HENRY III *to* ALEXANDER IV (1259)

PROFESSOR TOUT'S monumental reconstruction of medieval administrative history bears witness to the almost unbelievable extent to which the organization of the English government was perfected in the early period. But Tout's great study was necessarily limited to the domestic aspects of English history, although many pregnant remarks scattered through its pages suggest that the conduct of medieval foreign relations was scarcely the slipshod affair that it has hitherto been thought. The purpose of this inquiry, then, will be to discover how the medieval English government administered its diplomacy.

To do that, to recover the plans of the diplomatic machine, a large quantity of neglected manuscript materials will have to be utilized. Printed collections of documents are singularly lacking in information, and even the chancery rolls are of little help in picking out the story of the *custos processuum*, the officer with whom this study is concerned. Among the chroniclers only Adam Murimuth speaks of one of the keepers and he, who should have known better, spins a wild tale about the death of Martel, the first *custos*. The manuscripts, however, constitute a source rich in the details of administrative practice and in information about those larger problems to which the clarification of administrative procedure is but a necessary prelude.

Anglo-French legal entanglements are so intricate that historians have almost completely neglected them. A few cases in the Parlement de Paris, the great French law-court, have been but broadly sketched, and diplomatic conferences and commissions such as the processes of Montreuil and Périgueux, when mentioned, are dismissed in a sentence. The latter process, it is true, has fared somewhat better at the hands of M. Gavrilovitch and Mme Lubimenko, who have printed some of the proceedings, but their accounts are by no means complete. The legal aspects of Anglo-French relations have generally been passed over in favour of the more usual types of diplomatic intercourse, yet matters of homage, suits, and the settlement of mercantile and administrative grievances are the very foundations upon which the diplomacy of the two kingdoms rested.

But these manuscripts cannot be seen as an organic whole, and their relations one to the other cannot be understood, without knowledge of the purpose and method of their use. Until administrative organization has been clarified, any consideration of larger problems must necessarily be postponed. On the other hand, it will be possible and indeed desirable to touch briefly on the nature of those problems and their complexity and ramifications.

A great deal has been said about the results of the Norman conquest on England itself, but one fact is of cardinal importance for her foreign relations and needs to be particularly emphasized. By the connection established between England and the Continent a new element was introduced into medieval diplomacy. The novelty lay in the peculiar and paradoxical position of the kings who occupied the English throne. They were first of all vassals owing allegiance to the French crown for their enormous and lucrative continental holdings, but at the same time they were also absolute sovereigns of their island kingdom, and this sovereignty was grounded in the incontrovertible right of conquest. Here then were persons who exhibited in themselves a dual suzerain-personality, an oddity that soon caused as much trouble in history as a similar situation did in fiction. With the accession of Philip Augustus to the throne of France, French kings became obsessed with a burning passion to increase the power of the crown both politically and territorially: across the Channel the possession of sovereignty began to foster in English monarchs an extreme distaste for their feudal obligations on the Continent. Those parallel developments are the two most important factors in the history of foreign relations among western European countries for three centuries. Diplomacy was a seesaw between the two opposing forces, and a suitable crossbar to support the game was found in a treaty sealed at Paris in 1259.

It was in 1202, during one of the periodical rises of French fortunes, that King John's sobriquet, Lackland, became especially pertinent, for in this year he was formally deprived of his French possessions. Neither John nor his son, Henry III, was prepared to accept such a situation, but not until fifty years later did the opportunity to remedy it arise. At that time Louis IX had taken the cross and gone to the Holy Land; and, having become involved in most embarrassing difficulties with the infidels, he called upon his vassal for assistance. Henry saw his chance, and instead of complying with the French king's request, set about to erect offensive and defensive alliances that would strengthen his continental position and enable him successfully to prosecute his claims in France. The death of Blanche of Castile, regent of France, in 1252, Henry's alliance with Alfonso X of Castile, concluded in 1254,[1] and the threatened rupture with Germany over Charles of Anjou's espousal of the cause of Marguerite, countess of Flanders, all combined to force Louis to return from his crusade and to set in motion the preliminaries necessary to peace with the English king.

But meanwhile Henry himself was having troubles. His attempts to pacify Gascony had meant the expenditure of

[1] Rymer, i. 297, 310.

large sums, and when he returned to England his debts amounted to some 350,000 marks.[1] The alliance with Castile, moreover, was considered by the English to be of little use, and the double election of Richard of Cornwall and Alfonso X to the throne of Germany strained it to such an extent that its value in the event of a conflict with France became extremely doubtful. Finally, the conflict between king and barons, which seemed inevitable, appeared even more imminent after the Sicilian affair. So Henry was equally compelled to seek a *rapprochement*, and the two kings, through their accredited representatives, made peace at Paris in 1259.

By that treaty Louis IX gave to the king of England all the land that he held in fiefs or demesnes in the dioceses of Limoges, Cahors, and Périgueux, save for the homage of his brothers, should they possess any holdings in these territories. Fiefs enjoying the right of perpetual inalienability from the throne of France, however, were necessarily retained under the direct suzerainty of the king; and Louis agreed to indemnify the king of England correspondingly. Similarly, if Agenais fell to him after the demise of Jeanne, countess of Poitiers, who held it at the conclusion of the treaty, Louis promised Henry this territory; meanwhile it was agreed that the king of England should receive yearly a sum equivalent to the rent of the land. If Agenais fell to another, Henry was to receive the homage and the rent. The same stipulation was made for the lands in Quercy held by Alphonse de Poitiers, brother of St. Louis, through his wife, Jeanne de Poitiers, on condition that it could be established by inquiry that Richard Cœur de Lion had given them to Joan of England on her marriage to Raymond VI, count of Toulouse and grandfather of Jeanne de Poitiers. The king of France also allotted to the king of England after the death of the count of Poitiers all that the count held in Saintonge beyond the Charente river. If another lord inherited the land, the king of France undertook to procure

[1] Matthew Paris, v. 450, 521.

it by exchange or in some other manner and to give it to the English king, or to indemnify him with other lands selected by mutual agreement. Finally, Louis contracted to furnish Henry with a sum sufficient to maintain 500 knights for a period of two years. The understanding was that the money should be spent in the service of the Church or for the 'profit of the land of England', on the advice of persons chosen by the king of England and his barons.

Henry III, for his part, was to hold all the lands given him by the treaty and all the territory he possessed in France before the conclusion of the treaty, including the coastal islands, in liege homage as duke of Aquitaine and peer of France, performing the appropriate services after an inquiry had proved what the nature of these services was. Both Henry and his son renounced in favour of the king of France all their rights to Normandy, Anjou, Touraine, Poitou, and elsewhere in France, except the rights they reserved in Agenais and Quercy. The king of England undertook to secure the complete renunciation of similar claims held by his brother, Richard of Cornwall, and his sister, Eleanor, wife of the earl of Leicester. The vassals and cities of Aquitaine were required to take an oath, the *seurté*, to the king of France binding them to give neither counsel, subsidies, nor aid to Henry towards breaking the treaty. Should Henry make such an attempt, those who had taken the oath were bound to aid the king of France if the English king did not make amends within three months after summons of his overlord. The *seurté* was to be renewed every ten years at the request of the French king.

The two kings agreed reciprocally to pardon all damages suffered during the war or even when they were not engaged in open hostilities with each other, and both they and their sons bound themselves to maintain the peace.[1]

The first point that emerges from an examination of the

[1] The text of the treaty may be found in Rymer, i. 383. A manuscript copy exists in Dip. Doc. Exch. 1077. The originals are in the Archives Nationales at Paris. For the treaty and its execution see Gavrilovitch, *Étude sur le traité de Paris de 1259*.

treaty of 1259 is that a definite settlement of its terms would be possible only after lengthy inquiries were made into a mass of confused questions. The treaty did little more than to suggest some *point de départ* for the resolution of the difficulties inherent in it, yet it determined the nature of Anglo-French relations, and consequently of English foreign policy in general, for the next eighty years. The execution of its terms, and the negotiations that that involved, ushered in a phase of English diplomatic history unique in the medieval period, for it represents an almost continuous effort on the part of the Crown to solve a pressing foreign problem by peaceful negotiation. The effort continued almost without a break until Edward III realized what his three predecessors had been either unable or unwilling to see, discarded their methods, and plunged England into a century of war.

Little of the execution of the treaty had been accomplished at the death of Henry III. The claims of Richard of Cornwall and of the Montforts were settled to the satisfaction of the French king and on 4 December 1259, upon completion of the agreement, Henry publicly did liege homage to Louis IX.[1] The homage should have been renewed at each change of reign, but Henry excused himself to Philip III because of illness and died without having performed it.[2]

The financial stipulation for the support of 500 knights was one of utmost importance to Henry III. The extortions of the pope, the expenses of Richard of Cornwall in Germany, and squandering by the king himself made the need for money an urgent one.[3] Indeed, in Henry's mind one of the most cogent arguments for accepting the treaty was the support he could gain from it for his contest with the baronage. That the barons themselves had realized such a possibility is evident from the provision that the money thus acquired should be spent 'on the advice of persons chosen by the king of England *and his barons*'. Attempts by commissions to determine the amount the French king should

---

[1] Gavrilovitch, op. cit., pp. 28–34, 36, 49. [2] Rymer, i. 494, 495.
[3] Matthew Paris, v. 660, 661.

pay to quit himself of that obligation failed, but Louis advanced payments until a definite settlement was made in 1264. At that time the sum was set at 134,000 *livres tournois*, of which Henry had already received 76,000 *livres*;[1] the quittance of Queen Eleanor for the remaining 58,000 *livres* is dated in June of the same year.[2] Only 2,000 *livres* went for the service of the Church; the vast bulk was used in Henry's own interpretation of the phrase, 'for the profit of the land of England'.

By 1261 Louis's willingness to advance money to Henry had influenced the latter to accept the sum determined upon for Agenais, which Alphonse de Poitiers still held. The amount was fixed at £3,720. 8*s*. 6*d*. yearly, to be paid in two instalments at the Temple in Paris.[3] In the dioceses of Limoges, Cahors, and Périgueux, the only possessions into which he could enter immediately upon performing homage, Henry found himself faced with the *privilégiés*, the bishops of Limoges and Cahors, the count and county of Périgord, the bishop and city of Périgueux, and the city of Sarlat. The problem continued to exist under his three successors. The only definite settlement made during Henry's reign was the cession by the English king of Normandy, Anjou, Touraine, and Poitou. That clause legalized the conquests of Philip Augustus and Louis VIII over John Lackland and Henry III, and the kings of England were content to abide by this settlement.

For the sake of clarity, Anglo-French relations during the reign of Edward I can be divided into three periods.[4] The

[1] Rymer, i. 434.
[2] Gavrilovitch, op. cit., *pièce justificative* no. iv. The last mention of the question was a claim put forward by Edward III at the beginning of his reign. The French, with quittances in hand, had little difficulty in proving that the account had long since been settled, a fact which Edward recognized on 20 May 1331 (Rymer, ii. 819). [3] Ibid. i. 409.
[4] See Miss Salt's suggestive outline in her article, 'List of English Embassies to France, 1272–1307', *E.H.R.* xliv (1929), 263–78. She has appended a useful list of embassies, drawn from the list of exchequer accounts (*P.R.O. Lists and Indexes*, no. xxxv, pp. 188–95, 220–33), from the list of diplomatic documents (ibid., no. xlix), from the classes of Ancient Correspondence, the Liberate and the Treaty Rolls.

first, from 1272 to 1291, was concerned largely with the fulfilment of the treaty of Paris. When Alphonse de Poitiers died in 1271, Philip III seized his lands, wishing to resume the heritage he claimed over Agenais and Saintonge by virtue of a treaty between Louis IX and Raymond VII, count of Toulouse, in 1229. Death had prevented Henry III from doing more than to assert his claim, but Edward I, on his return from the Holy Land to England, passed through France to demand from Philip III the restitution of those lands stipulated by the treaty. The form in which he did homage alluded directly to that territory: 'Domine rex, facio vobis homagium inde pro omnibus terris, quas *debeo* tenere de vobis.'[1] Despite Edward's insistence, Philip managed to postpone settlement until 1279, when he definitely ceded Agenais by the treaty of Amiens.[2] It was not until the treaty of Paris of 1286 that Edward received Saintonge.[3] The inquiry concerning Quercy, handicapped by the increasing age of those who could serve as witnesses, dragged along until the same year. Edward renounced his rights there for a rent of 3,000 *livres tournois* on the lands for which he had promised to do liege homage as he had already done for the duchy of Guyenne.[3]

Neither king was capable of enforcing the clauses regarding the *seurté* and the *privilégiés*. The former had been executed neither in 1259 nor in 1269, and Edward's attempt to require it in 1275 was unsuccessful.[4] Of the *privilégiés*, only Raymond IV, viscount of Turenne, Pons de Gourdon, Gaillard, abbot of Figeac, and the count of Périgord were persuaded to transfer their allegiance to the English crown, and the count of Périgord later recanted. By the treaty of Amiens the two kings mutually renounced those two clauses, except for the oaths already taken. So the king of England

---

[1] *Flores historiarum*, iii. 31. Walsingham's statement (i. 11) is more definite: 'Post haec, Edwardus venit in Franciam, et a Philippo, Francorum Rege, magnifice susceptus est; fecitque homagium pro terris suis quas de eo tenebat, sub conditione restitutionis terrarum patri suo, in venditione Normanniae promissarum.'
[2] Rymer, i. 571.   [3] Ibid. 672.
[4] Ibid. 522, 531.

who theoretically received Limoges, Cahors, and Périgueux was, by the large number of privileged vassals in these dioceses, actually deprived of the greater part of this territory; nor was he reimbursed as the treaty of 1259 provided.

Edward's position as vassal of the French king interfered with his desire to make his rule really effective in his continental dominions and raised a multitude of difficulties connected with the right of his vassals to appeal to the Parlement de Paris. The treaty of 1259 had not determined the mode of procedure in such cases; this was done to a certain extent by two subsequent *arrêts* of the Parlement de Paris.[1] When the king of England should be cited in law in Gascony, Périgord, or in Limousin, an *arrêt* of 1269 provided that the case could be adjourned to the Parlement by letters addressed either to the king himself or to his lieutenant in the district where the case arose. In 1286 it was laid down that those who had made an appeal to the Parlement were put under the protection of the king of France, and that the seneschal of Gascony could not exercise jurisdiction over those who had appealed against one of his decisions. While an appeal was pending, the appellant was forbidden to resort to arms to defend himself against the English authorities. Such undermining of his feudal authority Edward attempted to counteract after Gaston de Béarn, Raymond, viscount of Fronsac, and Marguerite, countess of Limoges, had appealed against him to the king of France.[2] In 1283, as a special privilege valid only during his reign, Edward received assurance from Philip III that appeals brought to the Parlement against English officials in Guyenne would be referred to these officials for settlement during a delay of three months. If satisfaction were not given to the plaintiffs, the cases would then be judged by Parlement.[3] That privilege was not effective in alleviating difficulties, however. Complicated

[1] Gavrilovitch, op. cit., pp. 84, 85.

[2] These cases and others of the same nature are discussed by Gavrilovitch, op. cit., ch. iv. Those of Béarn and Limoges are summarized by Tout, *History of England (1216–1377)*, pp. 141–2.

[3] *Red Book of the Exchequer*, ed. Hall, iii. 1055.

further by Edward's inheritance of Ponthieu in 1279, the right of appeal to the Parlement de Paris remained a thorn in the English flesh until the outbreak of war in 1339.

During the second period, from 1293 to 1294, Edward attempted to keep the peace despite his awkward position as vassal and disputes between the Norman sailors on the one hand and the sailors of Bayonne and of southern England on the other. In May 1293 he dispatched Edmund of Lancaster and Henry Lacy to settle the maritime disputes, but their attempts proved abortive and Edward was cited before the Parlement de Paris.[1] He refused to attend the summons, protesting his good faith and declaring upon advice of his council that, since his court was independent, those who felt themselves injured had only to appeal to it in order to obtain justice.[2] But those overtures on the part of Edward, which were calculated to reconcile his duties as vassal with his royal dignity, were not accepted. In June 1294 he gave up the struggle and renounced the homage he had done to Philip the Fair.[3]

During the final period, from 1295 to 1307, the two kings were concerned with the re-establishment of peace and the execution of its terms. The preliminaries involved a discussion of the sentence of arbitration pronounced by Boniface VIII in his private capacity and the refusal of Philip IV to give up his alliance with England's enemies, the Scots. Boniface had awarded that all lands and claims in Gascony on either side should be placed in his hands, but Edward rejected his proposal and Philip persisted in keeping the territory. English envoys who went to the pope in 1300 to demand a definite award in writing had their request refused on the grounds that 'the French are full of great suspicion, and if the king of France knew that the pope was gracious to Edward I he would never have compromised with the

---

[1] *C.P.R.* (1292–1301), p. 15. Trivet (p. 328) and Hemingburgh (ii. 43) mention only Lancaster, while Rishanger (pp. 136–7) mentions only Lacy.
[2] Hemingburgh, ii. 43; Walsingham, i. 43–4.
[3] Rymer, i. 807; Hemingburgh, ii. 45; Walsingham, i. 47.

pope'.[1] Boniface was really in no position to compel either party, and the difficulty was resolved by other means: Edward's victory over the Scots and Philip's defeat by the Flemings finally brought the French to terms. By the peace that was concluded at Paris in 1303 the parties reverted to the *status quo ante bellum*.[2]

For the rest of Edward's reign the two major questions for settlement were the nature and implications of the homage required by the treaty, and the restoration of lands and assessment of damages and losses to both sides. When Edward II ascended the throne neither had been solved. Homage was probably never performed until January 1308, on the occasion of the marriage of Edward II, when he did homage as his father's successor.[3] For the solution of the latter problem the process of Montreuil, the first of three famous diplomatic conferences of its type,[4] was set up, but it soon adjourned with its work unfinished.

Henry III's foreign policy preceding the treaty of 1259 was influenced by his relations with Louis IX; likewise, Edward I's attitude towards continental problems was determined by his position as vassal of the French king. He pursued an unaggressive foreign policy himself and attempted to ensure peace on the Continent, realizing that he would inevitably be drawn into the struggles that might arise when all his energies were required for the conquest of Wales and the settlement of the Scottish succession.

His mediatorial services in the southern kingdoms were an integral part of that plan. He was anxious to consolidate his own position there, and he had no desire to see France

---

[1] See the report of the mission by the bishop of Winchester, printed by Black, 'Edward I and Gascony in 1300', *E.H.R.* xvii (1902), 522–7.

[2] In the same year it was finally determined that Edward should have the homage of the counties of Armagnac and Fezensac, another point left undecided by the treaty of 1259. Gavrilovitch, op. cit., pp. 82–3.

[3] Johnson, 'The Homage for Guienne in 1304', *E.H.R.* xxiii (1908), 728–9.

[4] A similar instance of the use of a conference or commission occurs in 1274 in connection with Anglo-Flemish relations: de Sturler, *Les Relations entre le Brabant et l'Angleterre au Moyen Âge*, pp. 124–5.

expand at the expense of Castile and Aragon. Yet it was essential that peace be preserved lest he find himself compelled as vassal of France to support by force of arms that very expansion he sought to prevent. His friendliness for the rulers of Aragon, Castile, and Sicily, however, and his efforts on their behalf, bore little fruit when their help was needed against France in 1294.

Before 1294 Edward made no attempt to take advantage of the hostility that existed in the various parts of the Empire to the French policy of expansion. He passed over the opportunity of securing a foothold in Provence and Savoy, and showed little resentment over his daughter's loss of the kingdom of Arles. The same policy was pursued in regard to the Netherlands. Flanders took the initiative in the commercial treaties that were arranged with England. Brabant furthered its marriage policy in order to augment the treasury of its duke; only the fortuitous death of Jean I gave Edward control of the duchy. Edward's role as arbitrator in the feuds of the Netherlands was matched by that of the king of France, and whatever territorial advantages he might have secured from Brabant and Holland as dowries for his daughters were offset by events like Philip IV's annexation of Ostrevant between 1286 and 1290. Likewise the count of Bar, oppressed by French expansion into Viviers, Beaulieu, Montfaucon, and Burgundy, was the initiator of the marital alliance with England in 1293 that proved of some assistance against France.

Edward I, therefore, unlike his grandson, cannot be accused of a long-conceived plot to build up a northern alliance against France. It was not until 1294 that he seized on the hitherto neglected opportunity, through his connections in Brabant and Holland, of erecting a coalition that would divert the attentions of France to her northern frontier and exhaust her there. The fields for diplomatic activity at that time were the Netherlands and Burgundy, with the German king, Adolf of Nassau, serving as a link between them. English diplomacy proved more productive in the

Empire than in the Netherlands: the branch of the wardrobe that had been set up to facilitate payment of subsidies to Edward's allies was removed, together with the Staple, from Dordrecht to Malines in August 1295,[1] and five months later Florent, count of Holland, concluded a treaty with the king of France.

After the treaty of 1303 Edward resumed his policy of caution exercised prior to 1294. The sacrifice of his allies in the treaty negotiations had dimmed the reputation built up by his activities as an arbitrator. Nor was he able to exert any appreciable influence over his late adherents: Bar fell completely under French influence and the English policy towards Flanders was dictated by France. Holland was lost when its count, Jean, died in 1299. As for his relations with princes of the Rhineland, Edward was merely engaged in paying them for their services during the war.[2]

Edward II inherited the same problems that had faced his father and was even less successful in dealing with them. Only the close personal relation to the French king, which had grown out of his marriage to Isabella of France, and a difficult domestic situation prevented the outbreak of hostilities that finally took place in the following reign. All the scenery was in place for the Hundred Years War; only the curtain needed to be rung up. The encroachment of French officials on English rights in France, which Edward I had in some measure been able to check, increased with such rapidity and violence that the barons actually feared the loss of Gascony.[3] Mutual recriminations grew so frequent that in 1310 Edward II took the initiative in proposing to the

---

[1] *Infra*, pp. 170–1; de Sturler, op. cit., p. 186.
[2] For Edward's foreign policy see Tout, op. cit., pp. 136–235, particularly chs. ix and x, and for special aspects of it, de Sturler, op. cit., Bock, *Englands Beziehungen zum Reich unter Adolf von Nassau*, and Kern, *Die Anfänge der französischen Ausdehnungspolitik bis zum Jahre 1308*. There is, however, no adequate printed treatment of the subject as such, and I am indebted for the substance of the above remarks to the unpublished Oxford B.Litt. thesis of Mr. H. Instein, 'Edward I as a Foreign Statesman' (1933).
[3] *Rot. parl.* i. 282.

king of France a conference between plenipotentiaries to revise the agreement of 1259 and all subsequent treaties in order to find some basis of *entente* between the two countries. The subsequent conference, the famous process of Périgueux, although lasting for only a few months in the following year, affords a clear picture of the state of Anglo-French relations at this time.¹

The claims of the two parties were never resolved because of the refusal of either to admit the rights of the other. There were too many difficulties to be met and overcome, too many points of litigation left in the shadow of the famous treaty that Louis IX had believed would establish peace between the two countries. In May 1313 Edward himself went to France in an attempt to remedy affairs with his father-in-law. The journey was not entirely without results. Philip the Fair accorded him complete remission of the penalties that his officers and those of Edward I had incurred in the exercise of their duties.² Some action was even taken to mitigate the abuses committed by the seneschals of Périgord, Saintonge, and Quercy, but just as the tension between the two crowns eased further complications set in.

Between 1314 and 1317 the English lodged complaint after complaint against the refusal of France to allow the English pound to be current in Aquitaine. In 1318 a new charge was made against the seneschal of Périgord, who refused to admit the remission of penalties conceded by Philip in 1313. Edward's attitude towards homage strained relations even further. Called upon in 1316, he adjourned the taking of homage until 1319. His excuse was the war with Scotland, and later he claimed that the summons of the king of France was irregular because it was made to him in England rather than in his French fief. Even in 1319 only simple and conditional homage was done, and this by procuration; Edward did not render it personally until the next year (1320). Following a conflict of jurisdiction over a bastide constructed by the lord of Montpezat at Saint-Sardos on what the French

¹ *Infra*, pp. 87–100.   ² Rymer, ii. 217, 220.

claimed to be their territory, Charles IV pronounced the confiscation of the duchy of Guyenne.[1]

The short war that followed was terminated by the treaty of 1325.[2] One of the principal clauses provided that Edward II would be obliged to do homage at Beauvais on 30 August. But Edward, using illness as a pretext, never crossed to the Continent again. His queen, Isabella of France, with the aid of a papal legate, finally persuaded Charles IV to accept the homage of her eldest son, who would be created duke of Guyenne for the occasion. That was done in September, and the young prince rendered homage to his uncle.[3] War broke out again, however, when Charles insisted on retaining Agenais as an indemnity. The peace of 1327 provided for a restoration of all conquests in consideration of an indemnity from Edward III, who had just succeeded his father.[4] The situation was once more carried back to the treaty of Paris of 1259, but in form only; the conquered lands were never restored to Edward III.

The attitude of Queen Isabella towards the French court and her part in shaping English policy during the latter part of the reign of her husband have already been clearly established.[5] During the minority of the young Edward III she was busy with the task of postponing the impending conflict with Philip of France. She dispatched many embassies to discuss all the old problems, particularly that of homage, and to offer marriage alliances,[6] while at the same time reprisals were being made against French merchants.[7]

When Philip of Valois ascended the throne he summoned Edward III to render homage at Amiens.[8] The ceremony took place on 6 June 1329, but the terms in which homage

---

[1] The details of this conflict have been worked out by Chaplais, *The War of Saint-Sardos*.

[2] Rymer, ii. 602.   [3] Ibid. 607, 608, 609.   [4] Ibid. 700, 707.

[5] Lowe, *Considerations which induced Edward III to assume the title King of France*.

[6] Rymer, ii. 766, 777, 785.

[7] Ibid. 751; C.C.R. (1327-30), pp. 175, 181-2, 313-14, 318, 353, 436, 443, 449, and *passim*.   [8] Rymer, ii. 765.

should be done were for a long time debated. Philip demanded liege homage, while Edward wished to do only simple homage. The distinction was important to both parties: the former bound a vassal personally to his lord and implied military service, whereas the latter merely showed recognition of a holding. The homage of 1329 was neither liege nor unconditional, for reservations were made concerning the lands that had been seized by Charles IV. Not until 30 March 1331, seventy-two years after the treaty that had stipulated it, did an English king agree to the precise terms of the homage and recognize it as liege.[1]

Meanwhile, in the Low Countries, where she was indebted for asylum preceding the seizure of the English throne, Isabella saw an opportunity to offset the resources of France and consequently bent her efforts to this end.[2] In pursuance of her policy she arranged the betrothal of her son to Philippa of Hainault, thus establishing a nucleus around which future alliances could be built.[3] It was by her counsel that Jean of Hainault was engaged to assist the English in their invasion of Scotland,[4] while the duke of Brabant, the counts of Looz, Chiny, and Gueldres, Henri de Bautersem, and others were approached on the subject of offensive and defensive alliances.[5] Commercial quarrels with Bruges, Ypres, and the allied cities were also adjusted, and ambassadors were sent to England at the request of the queen.[6] In Aquitaine she endeavoured to prevent the occurrence of any

[1] The whole question of homage is discussed briefly by Gavrilovitch, op. cit., pp. 52–3, and more fully by Déprez, *Les Préliminaires de la guerre de Cent Ans*, ch. iii.

[2] The relations between England and the Low Countries are discussed in detail by Lucas, *The Low Countries and the Hundred Years' War*, but the author has not examined the relevant documents in the Public Record Office.

[3] Rymer, ii. 718, 719; Froissart, ii (4ᵉ réédition), 190–1; *Istore et croniques de Flandres*, i. 334; Walsingham, i. 179–80.

[4] Froissart, ii (4ᵉ réédition), 110–11; Knighton, i. 445–6. He was paid for his aid with a subsidy from the clergy in parliament called at the behest of Isabella and Mortimer, with loans from the Bardi, and with money secured by pledging the crown jewels (*C.P.R.* (1327–30), pp. 168, 254, 395, 418; Rymer, ii. 713).

[5] Rymer, ii. 744, 749.

[6] Ibid. 700, 705, 742, 744, 746, 747.

incident that might lead to war with France, while at the same time she strengthened the bonds between England and the duchy by sending John, earl of Cornwall, to reform abuses there. It too was the focus of diplomatic attempts to secure retainers and alliances for the English crown.[1] The English likewise endeavoured to cajole Alfonso of Castile into an alliance by proposing a match between John of Eltham and the daughter of Marie of Biscay and by attempting to interest him in the question eternally raging over the position of the infidels in the Holy Land.[2]

After 1330, when Edward began to rule in his own right, the policy towards France was essentially the same as it had been during the regency. Busy at home with the reorganization of government and the war against Scotland, and occupied abroad with the formation of alliances, Edward used every means to establish and prolong negotiations with France until he should be prepared for war. The processes of Montreuil and Périgueux were reopened and feverishly pursued, and envoys constantly kept before Philip of Valois the proposal of a crusade that Edward had no intention whatsoever of undertaking.[3] Time was the important factor; as indicated by the solution of the homage question, English tactics were deliberately to contest every claim and point in litigation, yet finally to accede to the demands of France in order to prevent the outbreak of hostilities until the proper time.

The policy of Edward in the Low Countries and in the states along the Rhine, which resulted in the erection of an almost continuous eastern front from Switzerland to the North Sea, had as its basis two insistent needs: the necessity of counterbalancing the preponderant power of France, both in wealth and population, and of stalemating the French bias of the papal curia at Avignon, particularly that of Jacques Fournier, of the county of Foix, who in 1334 became Pope

[1] Ibid. 707, 750, 788, 789.
[2] Ibid. 736, 773, 790, 793.
[3] Déprez, op. cit., ch. iv.

Benedict XII.[1] It was essentially an effort to balance power by the same artifice that Henry III and Edward I had employed. Despite the obvious political differences between the fourteenth and the seventeenth centuries, the principle is quite analogous to that which was to rule Europe after the accession of William III to the throne of England. English relations with other countries followed the same general lines.

[1] Jenkins, *Papal Efforts for Peace under Benedict XII*, contains interesting material on this subject. M. Déprez's thesis, stated in op. cit., ch. iv, that Philip of Valois was duped by the pope to the benefit of the English, seems to be open to question. The bias of the papacy was most pointed in 1337-9, when the invasion of France seemed imminent. In July 1337 the Cardinals Peter and Bertrand were dispatched to prevent that. They were given considerable powers for the purpose: they could issue ecclesiastical censures against any clergymen or laymen who might oppose their mission, place lands under interdict, and deprive clerks of their benefices; they possessed the authority to enforce by public sentences whatever measures they might take to foster peace, and the power to relax penalties when due satisfaction was made; they were enabled to impose censures and penalties against the religious who might say or do anything against peace, and to grant a relaxation of a year or forty days' enjoined penance to penitents who heard sermons preached by or before them. All nobles and governors of cities, castles, and other places in France and England were ordered to assist them, and a mandate was issued forbidding all persons, lay or clerical, to invade either realm (*C.Pap.R.* ii. 537-8). At the same time those powers were issued Benedict was allowing Philip to see all papal communications addressed to England, Jülich, and to Lewis of Bavaria. In October Benedict required Edward to retract and abstain from all dealings with the heretic, Lewis, and refused Edward's request for licence to make an alliance with the emperor (ibid. 564, 565). In November Edward felt compelled to protest to the pope about a tenth given to Philip, ostensibly for use against Lewis, but evidently equally useful against Edward (ibid. 569-70; Rymer, ii. 1063). Later the pope informed Philip of the full schedule of diplomatic and military provisions drawn up between Edward and the emperor (*C.Pap.R.* ii. 565, 569). In 1338, when the Flemings allied themselves with England, the pope excommunicated them (*Chronique des quatre premiers Valois*, pp. 7-8). In November he threatened to inhibit the archbishops of Cologne and Besançon and the bishops in their sees from paying homage to Edward as vicar of the Empire and to enforce the inhibition with spiritual and temporal sentences (*C. Pap. R.* ii. 571). In 1339 Benedict planned to refuse the dispensation necessary for the marriage between Edward's son and the daughter of the duke of Brabant because he considered the marriage to be injurious to France (ibid. 575). Even after the outbreak of hostilities the pope ordered Edward to drop the imperial title and to raise the siege of Cambrai (ibid. 577). M. Déprez himself shows that the papacy looked askance at Edward's claim to the throne of France. He seems to have trusted too implicitly the material found in Baluze, on which see Mollat's warning in his *Étude critique sur les Vitae paparum Avenionensium d'Étienne Baluze.*

Briefly, Edward attempted either to form alliances, as with Alfonso of Castile, to ensure neutrality, or to prevent any aid being supplied to his enemies. The last two motives apply particularly to his dealings with the Italian cities and the kingdoms of Norway and Sicily.[1]

When all was ready, Edward lit the fuse by assuming the title to the throne of France.[2] His policy of action culminated in the Hundred Years War and stopped the normal development of the treaty of 1259 at the precise point when this development had almost reached its term.[3]

So much for the narrative of events. What interpretation is to be put upon them? Once the facts had been established, historians agreed, and still agree, on the immediate causes of the Hundred Years War: Edward III's claim to the throne of France; the traditional Franco-Scottish alliance; the influence of Robert d'Artois; *The Vow of the Heron*; the English interest in the Low Countries. It is in dealing with the underlying causes of war that differences of opinion have arisen.

When in 1930 T. F. Tout wrote his volume on the political history of England, his was the accepted interpretation of the primary causes of war:

> It was not the dynastic question that brought about the war, though, war being inevitable, Edward might well, as he himself said, use his claim as a buckler to protect himself from his enemies. The fundamental difference between the two nations lay in the impossible position of Edward in Gascony. He could not abandon his ancient patrimony, and Philip could not give up that policy of gradually absorbing the

---

[1] Rymer, ii. 917, 932, 946, 947, 949, 961, 1010, 1011.

[2] This ambition was not original with him. A letter of Edward II in 1317 contemplates a claim to the French throne at the time when Charles IV claimed his share of the kingdom upon the death of Louis X. Déprez, 'La Conférence d'Avignon (1344)', *Essays presented to Tout*, p. 306.

[3] Details of the diplomatic history of this reign have been worked out by Déprez and Lucas and summarized by Tout, op. cit., ch. xv, and by Cheyney, *Dawn of a New Era*, ch. v. A good background for the economic implications may be found in Pirenne's article, 'The Place of the Netherlands in the Economic History of Mediaeval Europe', *Economic Hist. Rev.* ii (1929); further material is available in *Collected Papers of Unwin*, ed. Tawney, in Unwin's *Finance and Trade under Edward III*, and in de Sturler, op. cit., ch. iv.

great fiefs which the French kings had carried on since the days of St. Louis. The support given to the Scots, the Anglo-imperial alliance, the growing national animosity of the two peoples, the rivalry of English and French merchants and sailors, all these and many similar causes were but secondary.[1]

A decade later, both Robert Fawtier and A. Coville were in substantial agreement with this point of view.[2] In other words, the feudal position of the duke of Aquitaine was made impossible by French *Ausdehnungspolitik*, which made use of the feudal contract to achieve what Fawtier has described in another book as *concentration concentrique*.[3]

More recently Dr. Templeman has suggested that the Gascon problem—which to him, too, is the central one—has been viewed through twentieth-century spectacles:

> The modern student can, if he chooses, say that what was at stake was whether these Gascon lands were to be included in the kingdom of France, or whether they were to remain under the rule of the English king. Yet it is very likely that such a statement of the case would have seemed almost meaningless to those who were actually busied in the dispute. . . . They would have said it was a quarrel about the adjustment of some peculiarly tangled jurisdictional and tenurial relationships in which the rights of both parties were deeply embedded. . . . [By the fourteenth century] such rights had become in fact what they had always threatened to become; nothing more than elaborate property rights regulated by feudal conventions.[4]

He finds no modern notion of sovereignty in the struggle, but rather 'an attitude which did not distinguish between the modern idea of sovereignty and the feudal notion of proprietary right because the need for that distinction was not yet generally apparent'.[5] Yet in stressing the 'medieval' point of view and in equating Edward III's position in Gascony

---

[1] Tout, op. cit., p. 337.
[2] Fawtier, *L'Europe occidentale de 1270 à 1328*; Coville, *L'Europe occidentale de 1328 à 1380*.
[3] Fawtier, *Les Capétiens et la France*.
[4] Templeman, 'Edward III and the Beginnings of the Hundred Years War', *Trans. Roy. Hist. Soc.*, 5th Ser., ii (1952), 78, 79.
[5] Ibid. 81.

with that of Balliol in Scotland, Templeman considers that Edward's observance of legal forms in his dealings with Scotland is suprising; and he thinks it curious that Philip IV and Charles IV returned Gascony after having confiscated it.[1] As for the outbreak of war, he has this to say: 'The reason why the crisis which came to a head in 1337 had a different outcome from those which had preceded it lies elsewhere. It lies in the fact that Edward III, Philip VI and Benedict XII were not men of the stature of Edward I, Philip IV and Boniface VIII.'[2]

In his magnificent interpretation of the reign of Henry III, Sir Maurice Powicke found 'no national feeling ... behind the continuous restlessness of these years [1217–59]', and felt that 'the statesmen of the thirteenth century had perforce to take short views and to live from year to year, if not from day to day', and had this observation to make about Anglo-French relations: 'Is it fanciful to reflect that the endless wrangles which followed the treaty of 1259 and which culminated in the Hundred Years War had the peculiar flavour of domestic disagreement? They were family quarrels within the framework of a wider feudalism and only gradually grew into national enmity.'[3]

In his last work, he wrote in the same vein about Edward I's dealings with his French overlord:

> Nor can it be said with justice—though it has often been said—that either Philip III or Philip the Fair was markedly hostile to Edward, still less that either king was moved by a deliberate intention to eject him from Aquitaine.... If it is true that the legists on whom Philip the Fair relied for guidance were inspired by an uncompromising and conscious 'ideology' in a policy of expansion at Edward's expense, they were not successful in persuading him to give unequivocal expression to it until 1293 nor in holding him to it for very long. Their principles and technique were in any case instruments of alert opportunism, not a series of vendettas.[4]

---

[1] Ibid. 81–4.
[2] Ibid. 88.
[3] Powicke, *King Henry III and the Lord Edward*, i. 161, 163, 240; cf. ii. 614.
[4] Powicke, *The Thirteenth Century*, p. 271.

And apropos of appeals to Parlement he added: 'He [Edward] was no stranger in Paris. He and his proctors were not faced by a hostile and self contained group of hard-faced lawyers. These legal contests, though they called for incessant vigilance, were waged, not among strangers in an alien land, but in a spacious fluctuating royal court, where friendly discussions behind the scenes were more important than the formal sessions of the *parlement*.'[1] In short, Powicke could find no villain in the piece, at least not as late as 1307.

The traditional interpretation has therefore been questioned on two main points, motives and policy, and the outbreak of war has been attributed to the weakness of a pope and two monarchs who permitted the situation to deteriorate rather than to a change in the times and consequently in points of view. What do other historians and the documents themselves have to say on these two points?

Dante placed Henry III in that part of Purgatory reserved for children and negligent rulers:

> Vedete il re della semplice vita
> seder là solo, Arrigo d'Inghilterra:
> questi ha ne' rami suoi migliore uscita.
>
> (*Purgatorio*, vii. 130–2)

It is now known that the treaty of Paris of 1259 was dependent upon the Sicilian business,[2] and that Henry III thought that by resuming the role of vassal he was securing a land whose wealth and potential wealth have only recently been established. Gascony helped to finance the Lord Edward's crusade;[3] Gascony supplied victuals and troops for the Welsh wars and bore the brunt of the cost of the Gascon war.[4] The bastides of Agenais alone brought in a rent of 1,500 *livres tournois* in 1272, and those of Périgord and Quercy, 1,458

---

[1] Powicke, *The Thirteenth Century*, p. 287.
[2] Ibid. 123.   [3] Ibid. 281–2.
[4] Trabut-Cussac, 'L'Administration anglaise en Gascogne sous Henry III et Édouard Ier de 1252 à 1307', *École Nationale des Chartes: Positions des thèses* (1949), pp. 153, 154. These facts and similar ones explain the continual deficit in the Gascon budget during the years 1252–1307 (ibid. 157).

livres tournois in 1304–5,¹ and the considerable number of them built after 1259 is in itself an indication of further economic development of the country.² By 1306–7 the rents, revenues, and dues received from the duchy amounted, in round figures, to £56,000, greater by some £456 than the total revenue of England during the same year.³ There is little wonder that Henry III was prepared to come to terms with Louis IX, yet in sealing the treaty of Paris this 'king of the simple life' blundered badly.⁴

Once feudal ties were re-established, French policy in Aquitaine was thoroughly consistent: 'Rex Francie habet exercicium ressorti et superioritatis in ducatu Aquitannie.'⁵ This was implemented by reserved cases (*cas royaux*) and appeals. Appeals constituted the most powerful weapon 'pour s'immiscer dans l'administration des grands fiefs', and royal officials who encouraged them were 'imbus, surtout depuis la mort de saint Louis, d'une véritable religion monarchique qui leur faisait considérer comme attentatoires à la majesté royale les privilèges, les juridictions seigneuriales, les franchises urbaines, tout ce qui s'opposait à leur fanatisme niveleur, et dont le roi, pourtant, s'accommodait bien mieux qu'eux'.⁶ The confiscations of the duchy by Philip IV and Charles IV were pressure moves to bring a recalcitrant vassal to obedience and to an affirmation of their suzerain rights over Aquitaine, but they gave royal counsellors the fallacious impression that confiscation could be repeatedly renewed, the better to strengthen their hold over Gascony.⁷

---

¹ Higounet, 'Bastides et frontières', *Le Moyen Âge*, liv (1948), 128–9.

² Trabut-Cussac, op. cit., p. 157. Trabut-Cussac, disagreeing with Higounet, thinks that the motive behind the extensive building of bastides was economic rather than military.

³ G.R., no. 11; Ramsey, *A History of the Revenues of the Kings of England, 1066–1399*, ii, Table III. Cf. Trabut-Cussac, 'Les Coutumes ou droits de douane perçus à Bordeaux sur les vins et les marchandises par l'administration anglaise de 1252 à 1307', *Annales du Midi*, lxii (1950), 135–50.

⁴ Trabut-Cussac, 'L'Administration . . .', p. 158, comes to this conclusion.

⁵ P. Chaplais, 'Gascon Appeals to England (1259–1453)', unpublished doctoral dissertation (University of London, 1950), pp. 11–12.

⁶ Perroy, *La Guerre de Cent Ans*, pp. 20, 21.   ⁷ Ibid., pp. 46–7.

'Les officiers du roi de France, toujours plus ardents que leur maître à envenimer les querelles, sénéchaux de Saintonge, de Poitou ou de Périgord, ne se faisaient pas faute de grignoter les droits ducaux au delà de cette frontière.'[1] The confiscation of Gascony in 1337 by Philip VI was the *casus belli*, and the war that followed was 'l'inéluctable aboutissement' of this policy.[2]

The French employed feudal means to attain non-feudal ends, and that these means were chosen is to be explained not only by the medieval respect for legal forms but also by the fact that war simply costs more than a lawsuit. That the ends were non-feudal and that they were recognized as being non-feudal seem to be beyond dispute. In the middle of the thirteenth century Jean de Blanot, in his *Tractatus de Actionibus*, 'maintained that a baron who rebels against the king commits the *crimen laesae majestatis*, the reason being that "rex in regno suo princeps est" '.[3] Guilelmus Durandus stated in his *Speculum Judiciale* that 'Rex Franciae est princeps in regno suo' and asserted that 'a sententia lata in curia Franciae non appellatur'.[4] 'The right to hear appeals was in itself one of the attributes of a sovereign lord.'[5] In about 1283 Philippe de Beaumanoir could say: 'Voirs est que li rois est sovrains par desor tous ... Et se ni a nul si grant desous li qui ne puist estre trais en se cort par defaute de droit ou par faus jugement.'[6] Charles IV told the ambassadors of Edward II in 1324: 'How can you have the audacity to offer on behalf of the duke of Guyenne to make amends for wrongs done to the king of France, his sovereign? The king, being emperor in his kingdom, has no other superior but God, and the law will not suffer a sovereign to be judged

---

[1] Perroy, *La Guerre de Cent Ans.*, pp. 42–3; D.D.C. 30/5/14, printed in my 'Historical Revision: The Causes of the Hundred Years War', *Speculum*, xxxi (1956), 476–7.

[2] Perroy, op. cit., pp. 49, 41.

[3] Quoted by Ullmann, 'The Development of the Medieval Idea of Sovereignty', *E.H.R.* lxiv (1949), p. 11.

[4] Quoted ibid. 10.

[5] Chaplais, op. cit., p. 3.

[6] Quoted ibid. 2.

by his subject.'[1] The application of the Salic law to the throne of France was nothing but a recognition of the pre-eminence of the kingdom and hence of the king.[2] 'It is surely not surprising', Professor Ullmann concludes, 'to find that the modern concept of sovereignty had its birthplace in France, even before Bodin in the sixteenth century.'[3] J. R. Strayer adds that

the officials of the French government, while they did not have a theory of sovereignty, did have a doctrine that was almost the equivalent. Within the boundaries of the kingdom, which they were trying to make definite, the king had 'superioritas et ressortum' and the right to take property for the common welfare. This doctrine was applied with great consistency to all lands held of the king. It created friction everywhere, with the bishop of Mende or the count of Foix as well as with the king of England. However, only the king of England and the count of Flanders could afford to express their indignation in a war.[4]

It was not long after 1259 that those responsible for English policy realized the blunder Henry III had made and began to recognize French tactics for what they were.[5] Every effort was bent towards undoing the effects of the treaty of Paris, and the arguments that were used to support this effort during the reign of Edward I certainly for the most part have to do with 'elaborate property rights regulated by feudal conventions'. About 1286 the English argued: 'Before 1259 Gascony was not a fief, but an allod;

---

[1] D.D.C. 32/3 m. 4, quoted by Chaplais, 'Règlement des conflits internationaux franco-anglais au XIVe siècle (1293-1377)', *Le Moyen Âge*, lvii (1951), 285.
[2] Perroy, op. cit., pp. 50-1.
[3] Ullmann, op. cit., p. 14. For other expressions of sovereignty in this period see the excellent article by Strayer, 'The Laicization of French and English Society in the Thirteenth Century', *Speculum*, xv (1940), 76-86.
[4] This is his own summary of facts established in Strayer and Taylor, *Studies in Early French Taxation*, pp. 1, 9, 41-2, 44-5, 56-7, 90, and in Strayer, 'Defense of the Realm and Royal Power in France', in *Studi in onore di Gino Luzzatto*, pp. 289-96.
[5] For the increasing importance of the council in this sphere, especially after 1332, see Willard and Morris, ed., *The English Government at Work, 1327-1336*, i. 42-51, and the article by H. S. Lucas in the same volume.

that is, a free land where the king of England held complete jurisdiction, mediate and immediate.' The French king was mistaken in claiming that the treaty had transformed Gascony into a fief because the treaty was a contract, and this contract, being unfulfilled, was void;[1] also, because there was no investiture, and as the *Libri Feudorum* (Lib. I, Tit. xxv) put it: 'Feudum sine investitura nullo modo constitui posse . . .'[2] In 1298 Edward I was prepared to agree to hold Aquitaine as a fief of the Holy See if he could be freed of dependence on the king of France.[3] And about 1306 there is a list of the 'principal and secret aims' of English diplomacy: 'to withdraw with impunity and honesty towards God and man' from the treaty of 1259; to restore Gascony to its pre-treaty status; to devise other means of achieving these ends should the king of France show any inclination to fulfil the terms of the treaty, 'quousque tempus optatum ad premissa videret iminere'; to postpone doing homage by asking damages in an amount so large that the income of France in three years would not suffice to pay it; to show all diligence in fulfilling the terms of the treaty of Paris of 1303; to keep control of the English Sea *de jure* and *de facto*; to get out of paying 600,000 *livres tournois*, the amount claimed by the French for losses at the hands of English and Bayonnese sailors.[4]

But the policies of Edward I and Edward II were ineffective.[5] Some new tack would have to be taken. After

---

[1] This is the argument advanced in D.D.C. 29/6/12, printed in *Speculum*, xxxi (1956), 473–6. Dr. Chaplais explains the importance of this point as follows: 'En effet, lors que deux rois concluent un traité, ils font un compromis; ils sont donc égaux en vertu de la règle "*Reges in compromittendo sunt pares*" et de son corollaire "*Par in parem non habet imperium*" ' (op. cit., p. 284).

[2] Chaplais, 'English Arguments concerning the Feudal Status of Aquitaine in the Fourteenth Century', *Bull. Inst. Hist. Res.* xxi (1948), 206–11. Gascony was certainly not an allod before 1259, and the *Libri Feudorum* was never recognized in France as having legal force; but the validity of these arguments is not the point in this connection. [3] Ibid. 205.

[4] D.D.C. 27/11, printed in my 'Another Memorandum Book of Elias Joneston', *E.H.R.* lxiii (1948), 94–103.

[5] See, for example, the memorial addressed to the chancellor in June 1334 (*infra*, p. 86 n. 4).

1330, when Edward III began to rule in his own right, clerks begin to advise that the methods of his father and grandfather be continued only 'quousque per dominum nostrum regem et ejus consiliarios corigantur vel fiant meliores'.[1] There is talk of 'la nacioun d'Engleterre' and there is talk of 'la sovereinete', and state papers begin to carry the classification 'Non ostendat alienis'.[2] There has been a change in policy, and this is the result of a change in point of view.[3] Dr. Chaplais concludes that 'the aim of the king of England, from the reign of Edward I onwards, was to achieve unchallenged sovereignty of the duchy of Guyenne', and calls attention to the system of judges of appeal established in the duchy as a step towards achieving this end.[4] The assumption of the title 'King of France' by Edward III was the ultimate legal step, and Perroy is of the opinion that Edward would have relinquished his claim in exchange for the sovereignty of Aquitaine.[5] Edward was still willing to do this after 1360,[6] and again during the conversations at Bruges, 1374-7, but Charles V was having no talk of sovereignty.[7]

The results of recent scholarship amount to this: The treaty of Paris of 1259, which recreated the feudal relationship that led eventually to war, was dictated by English commitments towards Sicily and by the desire to secure wealthy territory; and from the point of view of English interests, the treaty was a mistake. The confiscation of Gascony by Philip VI in 1337, which was the immediate cause of war, was the inevitable result of French attempts to exercise *superioritas et resortum* in Aquitaine. French policy was

[1] D.D.C. 30/3/25.
[2] D.D.C. 30/5/14; D.D.C. 30/2/21.
[3] Mr. N. G. Alford, in an unpublished M.A. thesis '*Homagium et servicium debitum* in Anglo-French Relations during the Middle Ages' (University of Iowa, 1941), has found the beginnings of this change in the reign of Edward II, particularly after 1317).
[4] Chaplais, 'Gascon Appeals ...', p. 6.   [5] Perroy, op. cit., p. 49.
[6] Chaplais, *Some Documents regarding the Fulfilment and Interpretation of the Treaty of Brétigny, 1361-1369* (Camden Miscellany, vol. xix).
[7] Perroy, *The Anglo-French Negotiations at Bruges, 1374-1377* (Camden Miscellany, vol. xix).

the reflection of a doctrine that is practically synonymous with the modern theory of sovereignty, and the nature of this doctrine was understood and expressed. English policy changed from an attempt to work within the terms of the treaty of 1259 and within the legal limits of the feudal relationship to a conscious effort to achieve unchallenged sovereignty over Gascony by assuming the title, King of France, and by going to war. This change of policy represents a change in basic attitudes.

Edward III, Philip VI, and Benedict XII may not have been men of the stature of Edward I, Philip IV, and Boniface VIII[1]—nor perhaps men of the calibre of Henry III, Louis IX, and Alexander IV—but they were products of their time, and times had changed. The cosmopolitanism and suzerainty of 1259 have become the nationalism and sovereignty of 1339.[2]

[1] *Supra*, p. 21.
[2] For the most recent account of the growth of the idea of sovereignty during this period see the excellent article by Cheyette, 'The Sovereign and the Pirates, 1332', *Speculum*, xlv (1970), 40–68.

II

THE KEEPER OF PROCESSES

'. . . ad salvo custodiendum omnes processus et memoranda jus dicti domini nostri et suorum contingencia . . . ad scrutandum quedam alia in diversorum ministrorum dicti regis custodia existencia . . . et ad informandum ipsos subrogatos super omnibus propositis et ordinatis in hujusmodi negociis . . .'
—*Instructions to* ELIAS JONESTON (1306)

WITH the enormous increase in diplomatic relations between England and the Continent growing out of the treaty of Paris of 1259, the English government was faced more and more with the necessity of developing some system adequate for the representation of its affairs in the courts of foreign nations. Increasingly significant, at least from the point of view of administration, foreign affairs began to approximate domestic questions in importance and proportion: diplomacy was beginning to assume its modern position as a major department of state. The now familiar figure of the resident consul or ambassador, of course, evolved only with the coming of the fifteenth century; that is, when English envoys were sent abroad, they went on a particular mission and remained for a relatively short period of time. Yet the traditional view that medieval diplomatic practice was a haphazard affair has little basis in fact. The existence of several departments of state, each concerned with some phase of foreign affairs, has confused the modern mind, imbued with ideas of bureaucracy and a clear demarcation of functions, into assuming that where multiplicity of control exists there can be no effective organization. Tout has said that

the practical mediaeval mind secured the happy mixture of good breeding and capacity . . . by putting a great nobleman at the head of a foreign embassy, while associating with him a bishop, who had, perhaps, begun life as a chancery clerk, to help out his intelligence, and a chancery clerk or two still on the make, to supply the necessary hard work and technical knowledge.[1]

Upon the solid foundation of the English clerk, indeed, was built an integral part of the medieval system for the administration of diplomacy. That system grew out of the peculiar circumstances of English foreign relations and flourished as long as these circumstances existed. The very fact that the period from 1259 to 1339 was largely a peaceful one indicates a reliance on the talents of the envoy, who of necessity had either to possess or to have access to knowledge of the most technical character. Comprehension of such matters as homage and the execution of treaties and the ability successfully to pursue suits of English vassals in the Parlement de Paris required an intimate acquaintance with relevant documents and the ability to make use of their contents. English officials, then, found themselves concerned with the organization of archives, and out of their efforts to cope with this problem arose something that may be called an embryonic Foreign Office.

The three great archives during this period were those of the chancery, the exchequer, and the wardrobe. The separation of chancery from the court was not recognized until the reign of Edward III, so that chancery records were not regarded as a fixture, as were those of the exchequer. The latter were occasionally examined by royal writ directing reference to be made *in situ*, but chancery rolls were usually dispatched bodily wherever they were needed. From the end of the thirteenth century those in current use were preserved in the vicinity of the Inns of Court, where the chancery masters and clerks lived.[2] Although the chancery was the ultimate authority for the issue of ordinary diplomatic communications that eventually found their way on to the close and patent rolls, the treasury of the exchequer was the main

[1] 'The English Civil Service in the 14th Century', in *Collected Papers of T. F. Tout*, iii. 203.
[2] Hall, *Studies in English Official Historical Documents*, pp. 19-20.

THE KEEPER OF PROCESSES

depository for this class of documents. The treasury was located in the Chapel of the Pyx at Westminster, and during the greater part of the fourteenth century also in an extension at the Tower. Treaties and papal bulls were reckoned among the traditional treasures of the realm and found their place beside them. Early in the history of the exchequer, however, there was a tendency towards specialization, whereby the custody of particular classes of records was entrusted to special officers, such as the exchequer marshal and the keeper of the chancery hanaper, or to other departments.[1] A large number of state documents, often originating in the chancery and exchequer, were for convenience of reference deposited in the wardrobe. There they were in the custody successively of the controller, the keeper, and the treasurer of that department.[2] The treasury of the wardrobe was situated under the Chapter House at Westminster, but after the famous burglary of 1303 it was transferred to the outer chamber next the Black Hall in the White Tower. Sometimes solemn instruments were drawn up in triplicate, so that the wardrobe, the treasury, and the chancery might each keep a copy.

The distribution of documents essential to the conduct of diplomatic negotiations among three departments of government was obviously inconvenient and unsatisfactory. Earlier conditions were even more chaotic; frequent entries on the close rolls reveal the habit of dispersing records, even to the extent of entrusting three or four documents to the care of one person.[3] The first instance of an attempt to remedy such

---

[1] Ibid. 23.

[2] Tout, *Chapters*, ii. 36 and n. 2. Cf. Kingsford, 'John de Benstede and his Missions for Edward I', in *Essays presented to R. L. Poole*, p. 334.

[3] e.g. 'Memorandum, that the chancellor delivered into the king's wardrobe at St. Albans, on the day of the Circumcision [1 January 1296], to Sir H. de Neuwerk, dean of York, who is going as the king's envoy to parts beyond the sea to treat for peace and truce between the king and the king of France, four rolls, to wit three relating to the truce between the king of France and the king of Aragon and the fourth relating to the truce between the late king and the king of France of that time; on condition that he shall cause answer to be made to him for them.' *C.C.R.* (1288-96), p. 505.

a state of affairs was the appointment of John of St. Denis, one of the king's clerks, as keeper of papal bulls from 1268 to 1288. Nothing is known of the organization of the office, however, and John was occupied with a great many other duties by virtue of his position as a member of the regular staff of chancery and as one who was entrusted with financial missions for the king. The one occasion on which he rendered service as keeper is represented by a list of bulls that appears to have been drawn up in order to justify Henry III's collection of a tenth of ecclesiastical property estimated according to the Norwich taxation of 1254.[1] The keepership of papal bulls represents a transitory experiment in the care of records and the memory of it may have lingered in the minds of English officials. At any rate, the frequency and complexity of foreign relations soon made it necessary to devise some method whereby important documents could be brought under one control and made available to envoys either before they set out on embassies or when they needed to consult them abroad. The council took the matter in hand by appointing an officer known in the records as the *Custos quorumdam processuum et memorandorum regis ducatum suum Aquitanie tangentium*.

The first to hold that office was Master Philip Martel, king's clerk and professor of civil law. In 1299, together with John Havering, he acted as a messenger from the king to the archbishop of Canterbury.[2] As is so often the case, there is no indication of the purpose of his mission other than 'to expound to him on the king's behalf concerning certain things that the king has much at heart'. It probably related to the increasing difficulties between the king and the primate arising from the pope's claim to the overlordship of Scotland. According to an entry in the wardrobe book for the year 29 Edward I, the clerk stayed with the king at Northampton and at Lincoln for three months (December 1300 to February 1301) on some business connected with Scot-

[1] Johnson, 'The Keeper of Papal Bulls', in *Essays presented to Tout*, pp. 135–6.
[2] *C.C.R.* (1296–1302), p. 301.

tish affairs.¹ In 1301 the king gave him ten oaks fit for timber with all their strippings from the forest south of Dene, an indication that he was already established in the royal favour.² In August of the following year he received respite for his debts and protection for the first of several missions to the court of Rome.³ The credence to Boniface, in which Martel is termed D.C.L., reveals that he went to hear the pope's pronouncement concerning the re-establishment of peace with France and to work for the expeditious conclusion of this matter.⁴ As a result of that mission he was instructed to prepare a report on relations with France for the information of the council. Martel's order involved giving advice on how the quarrels between the king's subjects and those of the king of France might be ended before Edward set out for the Continent, and outlining terms upon which peace should be made, paying due regard to the papal pronouncement and to the preservation of the ancient privileges and customs of Gascony.⁵ A subsequent journey to Rome in 1305 was probably concerned with the same general question, although the primary purpose was to carry to the pope a complaint from Edward against Archbishop Winchelsea.⁶ In October 1304 Martel had been directed to accompany Edward, prince of Wales, whom the king proposed to send to France to do fealty for the duchy of Guyenne, and to him

¹ App. i, no. 1. The payment of his expenses is listed among the *necessaria*. Later, in 1305, Martel was assigned to treat with the Scots (*Rot. parl.* i. 267).
² *C.C.R.* (1296–1302), p. 424.
³ Ibid., p. 596; *C.P.R.* (1301–7), pp. 54, 55, 60. He was accompanied by Henry Sampson and Master John de Sancto Claro.
⁴ *C.C.R.* (1296–1302), p. 600; Rymer, i. 943. The appointment is in *C.P.R.* (1301–7), p. 62.
⁵ D.D.C. 27/3/51, a copy of the time of Edward III.
⁶ *C.C.R.* (1302–7), p. 351; Rymer, i. 975. There are similar credences in *C.C.R.* (1302–7), p. 353, in *C.P.R.* (1301–7), pp. 384, 387, and in Rymer, i. 974, in the same year, in which Martel is described as a canon of Chichester. *C.Pap.R.* ii. 28 records the cassation of all proceedings taken by the clerk in a cause heard on appeal against the abbot of Bardney, and the revocation of a suit between Martel and the bishop of Lincoln to the apostolic see; the date is 1307, a year after the clerk's death.

fell the task of making excuses to the French king when the ceremony was postponed.[1]

The clerk received the first appointment involving his position as archivist on 28 January 1304. With Sir Robert Burghersh, constable of Dover Castle, he was to go to Calais a fortnight after Easter at the latest, to make an inquisition, in conjunction with deputies appointed by Philip of France, touching depredations committed by the men of Calais and of the Cinque Ports on one another.[2] In June further instructions directed him to go personally to the king of France to demand and receive full satisfaction for the losses inflicted on the English. The schedule attached to that appointment was a commission of oyer and terminer enabling him to settle the matters 'for the benefit of such as are willing to bring their actions before the commissioners'.[3] The lack of any power to force arbitration on claimants rendered the appointment ineffective, and a second was made in April 1306.[4] The letters issued on that occasion to Martel and Sir John Bakewell represent the part played by the English in setting up the process of Montreuil. With two others to be appointed by the French, they were assigned to inquire into losses incurred by merchants and others in both realms since the peace of 1303 or during former truces. Doubtful cases were to be referred to the two kings, Philip and Edward, as had been ordained before Pope Clement. A schedule attached to the appointment empowered the English deputies to go with the two from France to places concerned in the claims, to make inquiries in such places, and to compel full restitution

---

[1] D.D.C. 27/5/28; *supra*, p. 11. His expenses were to be paid out of the prince's wardrobe (*C.C.R.* (1302–7), p. 174).

[2] *C.P.R.* (1301–7), p. 208.

[3] Ibid. 237; cf. *C.C.R.* (1302–7), p. 196, and Rymer, i. 961. The mandate for letters of credence is in *C.C.W.* i. 225–6. Roger Sauvage replaced Burghersh, who was delegated to remain in England to dispatch the twenty ships that Edward I had promised the French king for use against Flanders. Martel's account with the wardrobe shows him to have been absent on the two missions from 7 April to 6 May and from 5 July to 25 October 1304 (App. i, no. 2).

[4] D.D.C. 27/5/12; *C.P.R.* (1301–7), p. 427.

THE KEEPER OF PROCESSES

to be made to French merchants, on condition that the French did the same.[1]

When the representatives met, however, certain difficulties arose that compelled the English to consult their king before continuing the negotiations. Since the proceedings at Montreuil had been set up by Clement V, Edward thought it advisable to lay the whole matter before the papal curia. Accordingly, he dispatched Martel to the court of Rome in July 1306 to request a new bull with certain amendments in the commission.[2] It was Martel's last diplomatic mission, for he died at Bordeaux on 21 September.[3] The bull he was sent to obtain was not issued until after his death: in letters patent of 19 May 1313 Henry, dean of St. Wulfram's, Abbeville, professes readiness to swear in two commissioners to renew the process of Montreuil on behalf of the king of England, by virtue of a bull of Clement V, dated at Avignon on 21 May 1309.[4]

On 4 October 1306 an order in council at the exchequer provided for the appointment of some person 'a garder et a complir les covenas des trewies et des pees faites et assinees entre le dit aiel [Edward I] et ses ancestres dune part, et les roys de France et ses ancestres dautre', and to act as proctor, envoy, and advocate at the papal curia.[5] On the same day the clerk of Philip Martel was named as his successor. In the little exchequer at Westminster, in the presence of the treasurer of the wardrobe, the chancellor, and the barons of the exchequer, Sir John Bakewell instructed Elias Joneston in the duties of the office.[6]

---

[1] There is an interesting letter from Martel, at Montreuil, to William Hamilton, the chancellor, dated 25 May 1306, relating to a claim by certain merchants of Berwick against certain men of Zeeland for robbery of their ship. The claim had been wrongly made at Montreuil, and Martel asked the chancellor to have it considered and adjusted by the council. Anc. Cor. xxv. 206.

[2] *C.P.R.* (1301–7), pp. 448, 453.

[3] The account was settled in the wardrobe by his brother and executor, John Martel, in March 1316. It shows Philip to have been abroad from 25 September 1305 to 10 April 1306, and from 13 July to 21 September 1306. App. i, no. 3.

[4] D.D.C. 27/8/28.   [5] D.D.C. 28/3/38, a copy of the time of Edward III.
[6] D.D.C. 27/11; cf. D.D.C. 28/1/22.

As clerk of Philip Martel and as keeper of documents himself, Joneston very early acquired an intimate knowledge of Gascon affairs. In 1310 he filed petitions to the king, in all probability containing suggestions regarding the opening of the process of Périgueux.[1] The petitions were referred to John Sandall, then treasurer of the exchequer, who was ordered to inspect them and to act upon them 'for the king's benefit and the promotion of his affairs in Gascony'. If Sandall thought it expedient, Joneston was to go to Gascony as adviser to the official representatives, John, bishop of Norwich, and John, earl of Richmond, and their colleagues. The king said he had been informed that unless Joneston, who had had charge of such affairs for a long while, went to Gascony, royal interests there might be injured and retarded.[2] Accordingly, Joneston crossed over to the Continent in the company of Roger Wadenho, Master Thomas Cobham, and Richard Plumstock, to play an important role in the subsequent negotiations.[3]

His years in the king's service were rewarded from time to time with benefices. In 1322 the king obtained for him the church of Waldershare in the diocese of Canterbury. Two years later he was presented to the churches of St. Nicholas, Guildford, in the diocese of Winchester, and St. Mary's, Cambridge, in the diocese of Ely.[4] In 1330 he exchanged the latter for the church of Bexwell in the diocese of Norwich.[5] But such evidences of royal favour were more than counterbalanced by the difficulty Joneston had in obtaining the settlement of his accounts.[6] In 1318 the treasurer

[1] *C.C.W.* i. 374.   [2] *C.C.R.* (1307–13), p. 293.
[3] Joneston is here described as having prosecuted the affairs of *surprise* (breaches of peace) and *interprise*. The expenses for the journey abroad were paid by the exchequer; those for the stay in Gascony by the regular accredited representatives (ibid. 289). Letters of protection are in *C.P.R.* (1307–13), p. 224.
[4] *C.P.R.* (1321–4), pp. 115, 363, 365. As vicar of St. Mary's, Joneston was ordained deacon by Hamo de Hethe, bishop of Rochester, in the parish church of Stone in that diocese on 1 June 1325 (Register of Hamo de Hethe, at Rochester, fol. 68*b*). I owe this reference to Mr. Charles Johnson.
[5] *C.P.R.* (1327–30), p. 540.
[6] Anc. Pet., file 167/8303, 8338, file 200/10000, file 203/10101, file 218/10886,

and barons of the exchequer were ordered to account with him for the wages and robes allotted to him in his office: two shillings a day when travelling abroad, one shilling a day while in England, and two pounds yearly for his robes. A similar order went to the keeper of the wardrobe in 1323.[1] Neither department seems to have taken any action, however, for after the accession of Edward III Elias petitioned to have his wages allowed at the exchequer or to have them charged on the constable of Bordeaux.[2] His reason for the latter request was that since his business particularly concerned Aquitaine the costs should be paid by the constable. In support of his argument he brought to the attention of the treasurer and barons of the exchequer an ordinance of 17 Edward II (Westminster 1324) to the effect that the exchequer was not held to account with clerks engaged in following processes in the Parlement de Paris, but only with 'solempnes messages'.[3] At the same time he petitioned the council for his wages, and letters were sent to the exchequer ordering the treasurer and barons to execute an old writ of 21 March 1316 directing payment of his salary.[4] After examining the writ of Edward II the barons replied that, although no account had been made with Joneston at the exchequer, he had received money regularly from the wardrobe.[5] In April 1333 another writ ordered John Travers, constable of Bordeaux, to pay the clerk's wages.[6] Within the next three years Joneston met with some success in his efforts, for his last petition, in 1336, mentions a previous accounting at the exchequer, and he had already made an account in

file 272/13600, file 290/14455, file 339/15999, as well as Anc. Cor. xxxv. 22, are petitions to the king and council, to the chancellor, and to Queen Isabella concerning this matter. Cf. *Rot. parl. ined.*, p. 56.

[1] *C.C.R.* (1318–23), pp. 39, 634. The council had determined the amount of his wages.
[2] D.D.C. 28/1/12; cf. Anc. Pet., file 289/14443.
[3] D.D.C. 28/1/13. Ibid. 28/1/14 contains reasons why his salary might be more conveniently charged on Guyenne, but the writing has almost entirely faded.
[4] D.D.C. 28/1/15.
[5] D.D.C. 28/1/16, 17.
[6] D.D.C. 28/2/57.

the exchequer at Bordeaux.¹ His final appeal, after more than thirty years of service, is a rather pitiful plea that he was in sore financial straits because he had been unable to enjoy the living from his church at Cambridge. A writ to the treasurer and barons in October 1336 evidently cleared up the whole matter, for there is no further mention of it in the records.² In answer to a petition presented at about the same time, the council allowed him leave to go to the court of Rome 'to pursue a grace' granted to him during the reign of Edward I.³ Most of his difficulties seem to have arisen from the reorganization of the accounting system that took place during the reigns of Edward II and Edward III.⁴

Towards the end of his career Joneston petitioned the chancellor to appoint someone to assume the duties of his office, which were becoming too onerous and dangerous for him; by this time he must have been almost sixty years of age.⁵ Accordingly, on 4 November 1332 he was ordered to

[1] D.D.C. 28/4/5 and 28/2/20. There is no record of the accounting at Bordeaux, but his first account covers a period from 8 July 1309 to 25 February 1332 (Pipe 6 Edw. III, m. 51).

[2] *C.C.R.* (1333–7), p. 615. The second account covers a period from 25 February 1332 to 2 October 1336 (Pipe 11 Edw. III, m. 39).

[3] 'Item, qe le dit Elis eit conge daler a la court de Rome appursuire une grace a lui grauntee en la dite court en temps lael nostre dit seignur, et qil eit lettres nostre dit seignur a tesmoigner la destourbaunce quaunt a la suite de la dite grace qil ad eu par enchaisoun del service nostre dit seignur et de soun dit piere, del an quint de soun regne tank ore, pur la dite grace renoveler ou chaunger en lieu meillour, et pur altres certoyns enchaisouns' (Anc. Pet., file 203/10101). Cf. Anc. Cor. xxxvii. 57, a letter to Joneston from Reginald, his chaplain, regarding the difficulties connected with his church. The grace mentioned here probably refers to a benefice granted to Joneston by virtue of the bull *Constitutus in presentia* of Clement V, dated 2 Ides January (12 January) 1306. The bull is an order to the bishop of Coventry to cause provision to be made to Elias Joneston, a poor clerk of his diocese, of a suitable benefice in the city or diocese of Coventry in the collation or provision of the archbishop of Dublin, if and when such should be vacant (Papal Bulls, 44/19). Bishop Langcon appointed Philip Martel to execute the bull on 20 March (idem) and Martel reported the execution of the commission on 17 April (ibid. 44/1).

[4] *Infra*, pp. 166–7.

[5] D.D.C. 28/2/20 and 28/4/7; cf. Anc. Cor. xxxvii. 100 and xxxviii. 83. The latter also asks that his records be put in safe keeping.

attend at the exchequer and in the presence of the treasurer and chamberlains to deliver by indenture to Master Roger Staunford the processes in his custody relating to France.[1]

There is some doubt, however, whether his successor actually assumed the office before 6 October 1336.[2] Another writ, dated 10 October 1333, directed Elias Joneston to deliver all processes and memoranda relating to Aquitaine to Master John Piers, clerk, 'in whose fidelity the king has confidence'.[3] The writ was probably never executed, because Piers and Andrew Ufford, to whom the custody of processes was offered, refused to accept the responsibility. They argued that the king would be forced to grant a disadvantageous peace to the Scots or to conclude a truce that would increase his subjection to France unless well-informed (*suffisaunz*) clerks were appointed to attend to the king's affairs. Processes in the court of France had become so rigorous that the seneschal of Gascony could no longer maintain the ancient franchises and customs of the duchy, and many nobles by force of necessity were on the point of submitting to the king of France. Representatives of that king were entering the cities and castles of Gascony to execute the *arrêts* and condemnations of the Parlement de Paris, and if refused entrance they resorted to arms and annexed the conquered territory to the kingdom of France.[4] Staunford's tenure of office lasted only from 6 October 1336 to 1 February 1339, since the need for further negotiations was stifled by the outbreak of war.[5] Edward III completely broke with the methods of his

[1] D.D.C. 28/2/54; cf. *C.C.R.* (1330–3), pp. 442, 511–12, and Anc. Cor. xxxii. 112. Joneston had apparently suggested Staunford as his successor (D.D.C. 28/8/21, 24). A memorandum of 6 October 1336 notes the delivery of documents by Joneston to Staunford in the chancery at London, in the presence of John Piers and of the treasurer and chamberlains (ibid. 28/10/7; cf. *E.A.* 333/11).

[2] Joneston's account ends on 2 October 1336 and Staunford's account begins on 6 October.

[3] *C.C.R.* (1333–7), p. 72. Anc. Pet., file 117/5850, is a petition from Joneston to the king and council asking that proctors be appointed in cases pending before the court of France. The reply, *in dorso*, appoints John Piers and orders Joneston to supply the relevant documents.

[4] D.D.C. 30/5/14.   [5] Pipe 12 Edw. III, m. 53, and E.A. 166/9.

three predecessors, for all traces of the office of keeper of processes disappear from the records on the eve of hostilities. Staunford died about the year 1345 at the church of St. Peter, Stamford, of which he was parson.[1]

Those, then, were the clerks who filled the office which existed roughly for thirty-five years. Organization centred around them as keepers of the documents. Elias Joneston himself was the clerk of Philip Martel, and it is reasonable to suppose that Martel had more than one clerk under him.[2] Joneston's accounts indicate that he had, at least from the year 1324, two clerks as his assistants, in addition to messengers for use on the Continent. The clerks had actual custody of the documents, and superintended the transportation of them by horses. It may be that they were also employed to transcribe charters, letters, and documents wanted by the keeper, business that suggests a close connection with the wardrobe. Joneston's accounts, running from 8 July 1309 to 2 October 1336, reveal that he actually accounted in the wardrobe from July 1311 to July 1313 and from July 1314 to July 1323. During that time he received £64. 6s. from the wardrobe, and held debentures amounting to £63. 12s. 2d., of which £28. 8s. was later paid to him in the exchequer.[3] In other years his receipts from the wardrobe were about half as great as those from the exchequer, £34. 18s. from the former and £60. 0s. 4d. from the latter. Other moneys, amounting to £43. 7s. 4d., came from various sources: the constable of Bordeaux and the receiver in Ponthieu; the archbishop of Canterbury and the bishop of Norwich; the wardrobes of the queen, the earl of Kent, and the earl of Chester; and from two private persons, John Vane and Peter Galeys. Expenses were more than half again as large as receipts, the total outlay being £398. 3s. 11d. Of that

---

[1] C.P.R. (1343–5), p. 374.

[2] His accounts record expenses 'pro passagio suo, hominum et equorum suorum'. App. i, nos. 2, 3.

[3] App. ii, nos. 2–5; Ward. Debent., file 481/125, file 483/251, 435, and file 484/118, 194, 276, 401, 593. These records show him to have been absent from England in April 1314, in June and July 1320, and in March and April 1323.

amount £348. 17s. went for his wages and £49. 6s. 11d. for *necessaria*. The necessary expenses included such items as boat-hire, portage, pontage, customs, transportation and transcription of documents, and the robes of his office.[1]

Staunford's account is very brief: it covers a period from 6 October 1336 to 1 February 1339. The only receipt was £5 from the exchequer. Of a total expenditure of £47. 17s., wages amounted to £42. 9s., robes to £5, and transportation of documents to 8s.[2]

Four deliveries, spread over a period from 1317 to 1333, between Elias Joneston, the exchequer, and various clerks, afford a clue to the extent and nature of archives in the custody of the keeper of processes. On 10 June 1317 Joneston delivered to the treasurer and chamberlains of the exchequer documents that fall into five large classes.[3] The first group consisted of pieces relating to the process begun at Montreuil and Bayonne by Master Philip Martel and Sir John Bakewell. Among them were papal bulls setting out the procedure the commissioners were to observe in taking their oaths, followed by the relevant appointments by the kings of England and France. It includes ordinances of the proctors regarding appellants and the respective claims of the French and English, pointing out the course of the investigation, and a public instrument relating its adjournment. A bull of Clement V and letters of the two kings concerning the resumption of the processes precede another public instrument containing a summary of proceedings at Montreuil for use at the subsequent process of Bayonne. There were similar public instruments recording the demands and

[1] App. ii, no. 1.
[2] App. iii.
[3] D.D.C. 27/14, partly printed by Palgrave, *Antient Kalendars and Inventories of the Exchequer*, iii. 116–22. Cf. D.D.C. 28/10/1, 4 and *G.R.*, nos. 2–4; the latter is a complete copy. The documents were returned to Joneston, some being redelivered by him on 10 February 1336, and others being delivered to Master Andrew Offord on 6 May 1336. There is a memorandum of an earlier delivery, on 4 October 1314, of certain documents received from Roger Sheffeld in the wardrobe to be delivered by Joneston to Richard Braughton and Henry of Canterbury, but the list is not given (D.D.C. 27/8/33 and 30/5/15).

replies of English envoys at Bayonne and a letter of adjournment of the Bayonne process. Finally, there were records of four processes on the completion of peaces with transcripts of the same, on seizures and excesses, and on the bastides of Libourne and Agenais. The second group consisted of eleven public instruments on the terms and execution of treaties and ordinances between France and England and included rolls and public instruments of Périgueux, as well as appeals of vassals to the court of France. The third class of documents related to Gascony, and most of these later found their way into a calendar.[1] Some concerned the internal government of the duchy, such as inquisitions and information about services, laws, and customs; others catalogued Anglo-French relations there, particularly the remission of penalties. The fourth group covered the same material for Aquitaine and added accounts of the *arrêts* and ordinances of the Parlement de Paris. The last group consisted of transcripts and indentures in the possession of various persons, including Joneston himself.

On 23 May 1329 at Westminster Joneston received various letters, instruments, and rolls pertaining to Aquitaine and other lands and islands of the king.[2] He was instructed

[1] *Infra*, pp. 121 ff.

[2] 'Memorandum quod xxiij die Maij anno regni regis Edwardi tercii post [conquestum tercio thesaurarius et camerarii scaccarii liberaverunt] apud Westmonasterium Elye de Joneston', clerico, processus, litteras, instrumenta, rotulos . . . Aquitaniam et alias terras ac insulas dicti regis tangencia, liberanda venerabili patri H. dei gracia [Lincolniensi episcopo, domini regis] cancellario, vel illi qui per consilium dicti regis fuerit nominatus apud Cantuariam vel Dovoriam. Et si [idem nominatus ea recipere] noluerit, ponenda ubi dictus cancellarius duxerit ordinandum, vel ad dictos thesaurarium et camerarios reportanda. In primis recepit omnes processus Monstrolli et Petragoris inter Anglie et Francie reges quondam et nuper inchoatos, contentos in quinque puchis extractis a nova cista de negociis Vasconie in Turri London' existente, de secunda particula calendarii inde facti, et eciam puchas predictas; videlicet, primam signatam per *L*, secundam per *M*, terciam per *N*, quartam per *O*, quintam per *P*. Item, sex libros et viginti et quatuor instrumenta pupplica; videlicet, tria de transcriptis pacum inter Anglie et Francie reges, et cetera de compromissis eorum et de graciis et de factis Judeorum et aliis factis diversis. Item, unam pucham de actis parliamentorum Francie in causis quondam et nuper inchoatis. Item, unum hanaperium continens commissiones patris domini nostri regis super resumpcione processuum super pacis conservacione et complemento

to deliver them to certain persons at Canterbury or Dover whom the council had named, and to return them to some place to be specified by the chancellor, or to the treasurer and chamberlains. He was given the processes begun at Montreuil and Périgueux 'contained in five pouches taken from the new box of Gascon negotiations existing in the Tower and included in the second part of the calendar made thereof'. Those documents came from the archives of the exchequer, and many of them were similar to the ones he had surrendered there in 1317. Besides individual pieces, which he carried in a leather sack, Joneston was actually given custody of Bishop Stapeldon's Gascon calendar.

Joneston made another transfer in January 1330, this time to Henry of Canterbury at Westminster in the presence of the chamberlains, in accordance with an order in council. In addition to transcripts of treaties between England and France, Henry received the form of homage done by Edward I and a citation and adjournment of homage by Edward II. Other miscellaneous items included a letter of Edward I on the marriage of his son to Isabella of France and the record of an interview between French ambassadors and Edward II.[1]

A draft receipt for certain documents to be handed over to John Piers in September 1333 shows that Joneston's

inter Anglie et Francie reges, et quasdam alias litteras diversas. Item, de priam particula coffinum ligneum signatum per castrum, cum septem litteris in eodem contentis. Item, unum kalendarium factum per dominum Walterum de Stapilton', nuper Exoniensem episcopum, thesaurarium, ad informacionem advocatorum et procuratorum assignatorum ad defensionem juris in [causis nuper] contra ipsum inchoatis et terram Vasconie et alias terras suas in partibus transmarinis existentes, ac insulas in mare Anglie tangentibus, ac ad informacionem senescalli Vasconie et constabularii Burdegale super bono regimine terre Vasconie predicte. Et tenetur idem Elias respondere dictis thesaurario et camerariis, vel nominato predicto, de omnibus per A. thesauraria predicta extractis et sibi per indenturam liberatis; postea recepit predictus Elias de Joneston' de prefato thesaurario et camerariis quondam saccum de corrio precii iij*s*. j*d*. ad imponendum memoranda predicta, de quo tenetur respondere. Item, liberantur eidem Elye super expensis suis versus Dovorriam xiij*s*. iiij*d*.' (D.D.C. 28/1/23). The documents were returned by Joneston to the treasurer and chamberlains at Westminster on 10 June 1336 (ibid. 30/5/15).

[1] D.D.C. 28/2/29.

archives extended even farther back than the treaty of 1259.[1] The receipt mentions three public documents on treaties with France, two entered into by Richard in 1191 and 1195 and one by John in 1200, which Joneston had received from Archbishop Melton, treasurer of the exchequer.[2] With them were eleven public instruments concerning the treaty of 1259 and various aspects of all subsequent treaties, and twenty-five similar instruments relating to the process of Périgueux.

Similarly, the documents kept by Roger Staunford covered an extensive variety of subjects, as is apparent from an indenture that specifies the books and manuscripts handed over to Staunford when he took office on 6 October 1336.

[1] 'Memorandum quod . . . die Septembris anno regni regis Edwardi tercii post conquestum vij⁰ apud . . . magister Johannes Piers recepit a magistro Elia de Joneston' virtute brevis regii cujus transcriptum presentibus est annexum processus, instrumenta, rotulos, litteras, cedulas, et memoranda infrascripta. In primis recepit tria instrumenta publica super tractatibus pacum inter Anglie et Francie reges indorsata; videlicet:—Primum instrumentum super pace regis Ricardi facta Messane. Secundum, super pace dicti regis Ricardi facta inter Gallion' et Vallem Rodolii. Tercium, super pace regis Johannis facta apud Galeto', que idem Elias recepit a domino W. de Melton', archiepiscopo Eboracensi et thesaurario scaccarii. Item, dominus Norwicensis habet:—unum instrumentum super pace Lodovici facta Parisius, sibi liberatum per dictum Eliam de mandato thesaurarii scaccarii. Item, idem magister Johannes recepit x instrumenta publica super pacibus subsequentibus; videlicet:—Primum, super pace Philippi, filii eiusdem Lodovici, facta Ambianis super reddicione terre Agennesii. Secundum, super reddicione terre predicte. Littera regis Edwardi de pace facta Ambianis. Tercium, super concessione trium milium librarum rendualium pro remissione calumpnie regis Anglie quo ad terram Caturcini. Quartum, super reservacione juris regis Anglie ne dicta remissio sibi prejudicet ante assisiam concessionis predicte. Quintum, super pronunciacione Bonifacii pape. Sextum, super confirmacione pacis facte apud Monstrollium. Septimum, super ratificacione ultime pacis Parisius facte. Octavum, super ratificacione confederacionis Parisius inite inter Anglie et Francie reges. Nonum, super declaracione modi confederacionis predicte. Decimum, super ratificacione et confirmacione ultime pacis Parisiensis predicte, facte per Anglie et Francie reges, factis apud Boloniam, et recitacione homagii per regem Anglie ibidem facti. Item, xxv instrumenta publica super processu pacis complementi per commissarios regum hincinde Petragoris inchoato; videlicet, xiij instrumenta publica scripta manu Arnaldi de Motis et x scripta manu Gaufridi de Bosco, et ij scripta manu Vitalis Beraudi. Item, iiij instrumenta publica de appellacionibus et submissionibus factis curie Francie per procuratores et ministros ducis Aquitanie in [pro]cessu de supprisiis et excessibus Petragoris inchoatis; videlicet, ij instrumenta scripta manu Gaufridi de Bosco, et alia [ij scripta] manu Bertrandi de Fonte.' D.D.C. 28/2/40.

[2] Rymer, i. 54, 66, 79.

THE KEEPER OF PROCESSES 45

The collection embraced five Gascon registers, pieces relating to the processes of Montreuil, Périgueux, and Agen, acts, petitions, delays, appeals, and cases in the Parlement de Paris, besides a prorogation of homage, a record of excesses committed in Périgord, a public instrument concerning Scotland, and a letter from the king of Castile renouncing his claim to Gascony.[1]

[1] 'In primis, v libros litteris alphabeti signatos coreo viridi coopertos de regimine ducatus Aquitanie; videlicet, primum signatum per *A* continentem cclvj folia, item alium signatum per *B* continentem cxlvj folia scripta, tercium signatum per *C* continentem ccliiij scripta xiij pargamena, quartum signatum littera *D* continentem cclxv folia scripta et tria pargameni [*sic*], quintum signatum per *E* continentem lxx folia scripta tantum, quando Rogero de Staunford' tradebantur in custodia. Item, vnum librum in coreo velluto ligato continentem iiij^{xx}x folia scripta. . . . Item, j pucham de actis parliamentorum regis Francie continentem xiij rotulos signatos per *O* litteram, primum xxvij peciarum, secundum xvj peciarum, tercium xiij peciarum, quartum x peciarum, quintum ix peciarum, sextum ix peciarum, septimum viij peciarum, nonum (*sic*) vij peciarum, decimum trium peciarum, undecimum ij peciarum, duodecimum ij peciarum, terciodecimum j pecie. Item, j pucham vij instrumenta pupplica scripta manu magistri G. de Bosco, super processu pacum Petragoris inchoato. Item, aliam pucham continentem xj instrumenta pupplica sub manu A. de Motis, de processu super pacis complemento Petragoris inchoato. Item, duo instrumenta puplica scripta manu W. Beraudi. Item, unum instrumentum puplicum Andree de Tange super reddicione terre Scocie. Item, duo instrumenta pupplica super peticionibus episcopi Exoniensis factis regi Francie super pacum complemento. Item, unum instrumentum puplicum super delacione facta appellacioni per magistrum Austencium Jordani facte. Item, unum instrumentum pupplicum recusacionis. Item, unum instrumentum puplicum super appellacione. Item, duo instrumenta pupplica super jure dicti regis in castro Montis Pesati et appellatio interjecta ad curiam Francie a proclamacione armorum. Item, duo instrumenta puplica de factis magistris R. Eriom et R. de Gloucestre et tractatibus habitis. Item, xxij rotulos de excessibus et inobedienciis Petragoris contra ministros regis Anglie propositis et quatuor cedulas annexas quorum unus rotulus continens viginti quatuor pecias, alius xvij pecias, tercius xv pecias, quartus xij pecias, quintus xj pecias, sextus viij pecias, duo quilibet vij pecias, unus v peciarum, tres iiij peciarum, quatuor quilibet trium peciarum, sex quilibet duarum peciarum. Item, unum rotulum viij peciarum de novo processu Agenn'. Item, unum rotulum ix peciarum continentem materiam duarum guerrarum tempore patris. Item, unum cophinum ligneum cum quinque litteris sigillatis sigillo regis Castelle de quietaclamacione terre Vasconie et unam litteram nunciorum dicti regis Castelle super facto predicto. Item, unum rotulum viij peciarum de peticionibus regis Anglie et responsionibus ad easdem factis Pictavie. Item, unam litteram Karoli, regis Francie et Nauuarre regis, de prorogacione homagii. Item, unam litteram cum ix sigillis super prorogacione homagii regi Francie faciendi. Item, duas puchas, quarum una continet viij rotulos parvos super processu diversarum bastidarum Agennesii

Fortunately, two memorandum books of Elias Joneston are preserved in the Public Record Office, which throw much light on the range of activities of the *custos processuum* and the use he made of the archives in his possession. The first is a manuscript of six folios containing documents belonging to the years 1306–18.[1] It begins with a petition from Joneston to the chancellor, asking that he use his influence to obtain the appointment of others who would relieve the clerk of his duties. The first petition includes a record of Joneston's appointment to the keepership, which makes it possible to suggest a date for the composition of the book. It is clear, in the first place, that the book was written in the reign of Edward II, for the appointment occurred in the reign '*patris domini nostri regis*'. There is also mention of a petition presented by Joneston 'in penultimo parliamento', that was answered 'respondebitur coram rege et magno consilio'. Now the only petition Joneston is recorded to have made in parliament took place in the assembly held at Westminster in August 1312. That petition was answered, 'Quant les autres clercs qe sont ordenez dentremettre des busoignes de Gascoigne vendront, le roi serra auisez par eux de queux seruise et peniblete les ditz Elys et Roger [de Wadenho] li ont seruy et leur ferra due reguordon solom lour desser et solom lour demande.'[2] Finally, Joneston remarks that 'ad dictam peticionem in *ultimo* parliamento nichil erat responsum'; this would mean the Hilary parliament of 1315. Since the petition can be identified with those two parliaments, it follows that the document must have been written some time between February and December 1315; that is, before the Hilary parliament of 1316.

Unlike the second memorandum book, the first appears to be essentially a report by Joneston to the council on his activities, perhaps drawn up in support of his petition. It is

et transcriptum testamenti comitis Pictavie et alia pucha continet xv rotuloset cedulas de processu comitis Marchie' (D.D.C. 28/10/5). Ibid. 28/10/6 is a partial copy. For the documents on Montreuil listed in the indenture see *infra*, p. 85 n. 1.

[1] D.D.C. 27/11, printed in *Speculum*, xvii (1942), 74–85.
[2] *Rot. parl. ined.*, p. 56.

incomplete, for the original plan as outlined at the beginning was to include ten items: A. Form used by Martel and Joneston in examining processes and memoranda. B. Principal results to be sought in negotiations. C. Acts and arrangements approved by Masters W. de Sardene and R. de Braunton as being a suitable way of proceeding to achieve those results. D. Ordinances of Gascon advocates at the Parlement de Paris disapproved of by Martel, Sardene, and Braunton. E. Secret reasons for observing the form of a process to bring about the aforesaid results; these are either to be deliberately revealed to the king of France and his council at the proper moment or to be unexpectedly sprung on French diplomats in the course of conversations. F. Arguments used by Martel to the king of France at Verneuil to induce him to consent to the form of such a process. G. General state of the process of Montreuil as it concerns the king, his subjects, and their possession of the superiority and admiralty of the English Sea. H. State of specific cases in the process. I. Dilatory exceptions in the matter of homage, proposed by Martel, the bishop of Worcester, and others at Verneuil. K. Materials for a peremptory exception that Martel never had the occasion to use.

Of these, only the first three items (A–C) remain. In place of the other seven (D–K) is appended a list of four supplications to the king of France, all bearing the date 1318. They were delivered to members of the council at the exchequer by Austence Jourdain, one of the king's proctors in France, and afterwards sent to Guillaume du Breuil, a famous French advocate employed by the English, no doubt to be used in defending cases before the Parlement de Paris. The supplications, which apparently bear no relation to the remainder of the book, must have been added by Joneston after completion of the main part of the memorandum. The petition was not effective in relieving the clerk of his office, and he probably used his book, adding those four pieces, in the course of his duties after 1315. At any rate, their presence suggests a connection between the *custos* and those interminable proceedings before the Parlement. The first of the supplications is a request that the king of France restrain his seneschal in Périgord from usurping English rights. The second and third ask postponement of the execution of an *arrêt* that had been made against Edward II on behalf of the men of Saint-Sardos and others because of the death of one Pierre Vigier. The last seeks a delay until the next Parlement of a case between the community of Bordeaux and certain French merchants. Letters of the king of France in reply to the requests are given in full.

Joneston's second memorandum is also a book of six folios.[1] The majority of the entries concern records relating to the process of Montreuil and are contained in a long section in which are listed certain documents delivered by the clerk to the exchequer in 1317.[2] There follow two writs dealing with the custody of archives, one addressed to Thomas Cobham and Richard Plumstock on 5 August 1312 ordering them to take over the documents in Joneston's custody, and the other issued on 20 December 1315 to Joneston himself, directing him to deliver his records into the exchequer. There is a report on the petition for compilation of the Gascon calendar,[3] and a copy of the form used by Edward I in charging ambassadors to France and other continental countries. Two interesting entries for 1304 are written in French. The first concerns the homage to be done by Edward I or his son, according to the treaty of Paris of 1303. Edward proposes to send the prince of Wales to perform that act at Amiens on Michaelmas next, 1304. He demands, however, that his lands be restored in accordance with the terms of peace, and that he be quit of military aid as duke of Guyenne. Twenty ships are promised to Philip IV for use against Flanders, while the Flemish are to be expelled from England in return for the banishment of the Scots from France. Finally, Edward will require the *seurté* to be taken by the nobles and cities of Gascony and will dis-

[1] D.D.C. 27/14, printed in *E.H.R.* lxiii (1948), 90–103.
[2] *Supra*, pp. 41, 42.   [3] *Infra*, pp. 118–9.

cuss with Philip the question of prisoners of war. The second is a message from Edward to Philip, explaining that the prince could not render homage while England's enemies, the Scots, still remained in France. Taken together the two entries add valuable details to what is known of Edward II's supposed visit to France in 1304 and leave little doubt that homage was never performed at this time.[1]

This second book seems to have been compiled by Joneston for his own use, as a sort of catalogue or index to his archives. There are no clues to the date of composition, but it was probably written shortly after 1317, the date of the first entry, in time to be of service in discussions growing out of the process of Périgueux. Some of the documents may well have formed the bases for certain sections missing from the first memorandum book. The portions of that book relating to the process of Montreuil (G-H) could have been compiled from the pieces mentioned in the first part of this book, while the two entries written in French could have been used in framing the dilatory exceptions in the matter of homage (I).

The first memorandum book also contains the instructions that were given to Joneston when he took over the office in 1306. He was directed

> safely to keep all processes and memoranda touching the right of our lord the king and his subjects, the custody of which he has had since the death of his master; and to search for others that belonged to him [Martel] at the time of his death in Bordeaux, and to carry all the premises to the exchequer to be delivered to those whom the said lord the king will have caused to be appointed in the place of his master; and to examine whatever other documents exist in the custody of various ministers of the said king, and to do all these things in which he was charged by his said master, and to inform those appointed concerning all things proposed and ordered by his said master in those affairs, from the time when the said Elias served him in them.

The duties of office had not changed essentially when Roger Staunford succeeded to them. He was instructed 'to cause

[1] *Supra*, p. 11.

them (the documents) to be kept safely, to be shown by him when required to the commissioners, envoys, and proctors of the king for counsels and treaties in these affairs, for their information'.[1] The specified job of the *custos processuum*, then, was to keep the documents, to examine them for the information of envoys, and to make them available for diplomats when wanted.

The first of those duties has already been considered. The form used by Martel and his successor in examining documents demonstrates the thoroughness of their work.[2] As a basis for their recommendations they first searched the registers of feudal recognitions, the charters of rights and privileges of the king's Gascon subjects, the petitions and plaints regarding the breach of these rights, the chancellor's rolls, and all other documents bearing on the former liberty of Gascony. That enabled them to say for what services, dues, and other feudal duties the king was liable in his capacity as lord of Gascony, and under what circumstances a confiscation of the duchy would be legally justified. Proceeding from the particular to the general, apeces and ordinances between France and England prior to 1294 were then considered, followed by the matter of the quarrel between the two kings and their subjects, and the form of the process begun by the king of France in the same period. Next came all subsequent truces and compromises, including the arbitration of Boniface VIII, its execution, and the peace of Montreuil. They studied the ordinances of the advocates of Gascony regarding the regimen of the duchy of Aquitaine, and investigated all processes in the court of France relating to the English. Finally, Martel and Joneston went back to negotiations concerning Gascony preceding the treaty of 1259, and the laws of Richard I and his predecessors relating to the keeping of peace on the English Sea.

From such an examination came a mass of detailed advice for the use of envoys on almost every possible contingency that might arise in the course of negotiations.[3] Should the

[1] *C.C.R.* (1330-3), pp. 511-12. [2] D.D.C. 27/11, A. [3] Ibid. 27/11, B-C.

THE KEEPER OF PROCESSES

king deem it necessary, it must be made possible for him to renounce the original treaty of Paris 'with impunity and honesty towards God and man'. If, on the other hand, it appeared that the king of France had been diligent in fulfilling the terms of that treaty, methods must be evolved by which negotiations could be continued until the time was ripe for more drastic action. Envoys must be prepared to exhibit a sincere desire to implement the terms of agreements in order to forestall unfavourable action by the French, yet at the same time to work for the restoration of Gascony and Aquitaine to their former liberties. Damages for injuries done by French officials should be collected, but the king and his subjects had to be protected against claims made by the French at Montreuil. Preservation of sovereignty and the right of admiralty on the Narrow Seas was essential. With those points in mind, the *custos* drew up ordinances to instruct English diplomats in the line of procedure to be observed in making their representations: Call attention to the care with which the king has observed the papal arbitration; Be careful not to concede the slightest legal acknowledgement to the occupation of any part of Gascony by the French; Devise means to postpone cases regarding the demesnes of the king in the duchy until he has been informed about its ancient rights, liberties, and customs; Cite reasons by which the king can escape from continuing in his vassalage to the French throne; Try to obtain a change of precedence in English cases before the Parlement de Paris.

In framing such instructions Martel and his successor worked on the principles that the king was bound by oath to preserve the liberties of Gascony and that he must protect himself from the attempts of his French overlord to subvert his demesnial rights there. The list of instructions could be elaborated even further; it indicates that the keeper of processes almost literally put the words of argument into the mouths of English diplomatic representatives. Perhaps that is one explanation, at least during this period, for the paucity of instructions contained in the credences and appointments found on the various rolls of chancery.

The *custos* made documents available to envoys either by actually surrendering or by transporting them to the Continent when they were required. Joneston's accounts show that on four occasions in 1309, 1310, and 1311 he was dispatched by the council with his archives to the English proctors, commissioners, and advocates at the Parlement de Paris.[1] At various times during the years 1324–6 he accompanied the bishops of Norwich and Winchester, the queen, and the earl of Chester to keep the processes and memoranda they required.[2] In 1329 he was summoned to accompany Edward III on his journey to do homage at Amiens, and carried with him the necessary documents. In 1330 he was sent again to the Parlement de Paris,[3] and in the same year furnished the complete dossiers, one official and one secret, taken abroad by Henry of Canterbury for use in the negotiations regarding homage.[4] Later in the year Joneston again took the documents to the advocates in Paris.[5] Several deliveries were made between 1331 and 1334. In December 1331 Joneston drew up a memorandum of documents carried abroad to John Stratford, the chancellor, by John Shordich. Stratford was busy with negotiations in France and required information on petitions addressed to the king of France for the remission of penalties.[6] On 24 April 1332 the bishop of Winchester and others received a mandate to

---

[1] App. ii, no. 1: once in 1309, from 7 September to 9 October; twice in 1310, from 20 to 29 April and from 29 September to 31 October; once in 1311, from 1 January to 25 March.

[2] App. ii, no. i: from 13 to 29 September 1324; from 8 December 1324 to 23 January 1325; from 14 March to 10 April 1325; from 29 September 1325 to 1 February 1326.

[3] Ibid.; cf. D.D.C. 30/5/15. Joneston was in France from 26 May to 12 June 1329 and from 26 February to 18 March 1330.

[4] Déprez, *Les Préliminaires de la guerre de Cent Ans*, p. 52 and n. 2. Cf. *C.P.R.* (1327–30), p. 482; *C.C.R.* (1330–3), p. 129; *supra*, p. 43.

[5] App. ii, no. 1: from 26 February to 18 March. Joneston undertook other journeys in 1313, 1314, 1323, and 1331 for the purpose of delivering letters.

[6] D.D.C. 28/2/9.

continue the process of Périgueux and to procure from Joneston the relevant memoranda. They were delivered to Henry of Canterbury in the same month.[1] Another delivery relating to Périgueux and to the resumption of the process of Montreuil was probably made to Simon Stanes in 1334.[2] At the same time Joneston was sending copies of processes to Paris. In July and October 1332 he dispatched processes to English advocates at the Parlement with a request for their counsel as to the best course to be pursued in order to regain Agenais and other lands occupied by the king of France. Some of them were taken by Henry of Canterbury, while others were sent by the bishops of Norwich and Worcester.[3] Joneston himself went abroad several times during the years 1332–5.[4] Two more instances of deliveries occurred during Joneston's tenure. In March 1333 he was ordered to produce the processes pending in the court of France and elsewhere, before the king's advocates and counsellors who were about to assemble in the Parlement de Paris.[5] Finally, in September 1333 John Piers was to receive documents bearing on the relations between England and France, but his appointment as envoy was later vacated by surrender.[6]

It is clear that in the exercise of his duties the keeper of processes was intimately concerned with the execution of foreign policy; such, indeed, was the very *raison d'être* of the office. But preoccupation with what might be termed 'the mechanics of diplomacy' did not preclude participation in more important business. His position inevitably meant that he would be called upon to assume prominence in the actual determination of policy. Having established such a department with its centralized archives, it is only logical that the

---

[1] Ibid. 28/2/27, 29; cf. ibid. 28/8/10.
[2] Ibid. 28/3/49, draft instructions. Cf. Déprez, op. cit., p. 102, and Mirot and Déprez, *Les Ambassades anglaises pendant la guerre de Cent Ans*, p. 562.
[3] App. ii, no. 1.
[4] Idem: from 19 to 23 May 1332, from 19 April to 24 June 1333, from 6 October 1333 to 6 March 1334 (without his documents), from 4 April to 5 September 1334, and from 24 January to 2 April 1335.
[5] D.D.C. 28/2/56. [6] Ibid. 28/2/40; *C.P.R.* (1330–4), pp. 466, 467.

council should depend on the incumbent for a great deal of technical advice and that it should even look to him for suggestions. Thus when Philip Martel was summoned to attend parliament at Westminster in September 1305, he was there to attend the king and his council in a professional capacity.[1] He was among the twenty men who, in conjunction with ten representatives of the various estates of Scotland, drew up the great ordinance for the affairs of Scotland. Maitland spoke of him in that connection as a master of chancery and as a member of Edward I's council.[2] There is, however, no evidence that Martel was a chancery clerk, nor is there any proof that he was a sworn councillor. The distinction between councillor and counsellor must be strictly observed in this instance: Martel was more likely only one of many upon whom the king *qua* king called for advice. He had already been summoned with others of the king's clerks to appear before John Langton, the chancellor, at London on 18 March 1302 to give counsel on the king's affairs, and he was present in the parliaments of 1301 and 1302.[3]

Few documents remain from the time of Martel's tenure, and those which are left are almost hopelessly mutilated, but that he was able to advise on a variety of questions can perhaps be deduced from a badly damaged memorial relating to the right of English admiralty prepared by him.[4] Martel was probably a much more important person than either of his two successors. In a letter to the pope in July 1306 he is described as 'dilectum clericum et *secretarium* nostrum', an indication that he was at least a confidant of the king.[5] He also had his place among the officials who

---

[1] *C.C.W.* i. 251; *C.C.R.* (1302–7), p. 340.
[2] *Memoranda de parliamento*, pp. xlv, cviii.
[3] Palgrave, *Parliamentary Writs*, i. 91, 110, 113.   [4] D.D.C. 29/9/3.
[5] Prynne, *The History of John, Henry III, and Edward I*, p. 1095. At this time *secretarius* usually means confidant (Dibben, 'Secretaries in the 13th and 14th Centuries', *E.H.R.* xxv (1910), 430–44). The following undated letter furnishes yet another instance: 'Roy a mestre Phelipe Martel, saluz. Pur aucunes choses qe nous vous auroms obliez de dire, lesqeles nous avoms molt a cuer, vous mandoms qe vous recorgez a nous, veues ces lettres, si qe vous soiez a nous a Peccham icest meisme

administered the archbishopric of Canterbury. In 1294, when the see was vacant, Martel served on a commission to visit the prior and convent of Ewenny, in Llandaff diocese, and to correct and reform what was necessary there. He took a prominent part in the episcopal election at Chichester in 1305.[1]

Documentary evidence about his successor is more extensive. Elias Joneston's relations with the council were so frequent that Professor Baldwin has found in him an early *clericus de consilio*.[2] It is hardly likely, however, that he served the council in that capacity, especially since there is no evidence to substantiate such a point of view. Joneston's path often crossed that of the council, but only by virtue of his position as *custos*. In 1308–9 he drew up a memorandum urging that the process of Montreuil be resumed, advising *expediens est percavere* regarding the questions involved in the process lest the king lose all his rights in Gascony, and he even suggested lines along which negotiations might be pursued.[3] No clearer example is needed to demonstrate that this clerk was alive to the dangers to England inherent in the French policy of eating away English power through judicial conflicts. Whether his opinion was solicited is doubtful, but the council acted by providing for the renewal of the process. Drawing on the material his predecessor had collected from an examination of registers in the treasury, Joneston in 1315 submitted articles for the consideration of

---

mescredy matyn. Et ce ne lessz en nule manere. Peccham, xj septembre' (Anc. Cor. xxxvii. 147).

[1] Churchill, *Canterbury Administration*, i. 562 n. 1, ii. 121. Canterbury was a valuable training-school for government officials because of its own vast administrative organization and the large amount of business it transacted at the papal court. Prominent men in foreign affairs like William de Sardene, Gilbert Middleton, and Adam Murimuth served as officials of the court of Canterbury. Middleton was also auditor of causes. Walter Thorp, Middleton, and John Offord were Deans of the Arches (ibid. ii. 237–42). Mr. Charles Johnson suggests that Philip Martel may also have been Dean of the Arches.

[2] Baldwin, *The King's Council*, p. 363.

[3] D.D.C. 29/6/11, 12. The latter is a clearer copy, but the two should be consulted together. See also *infra*, p. 84.

the dean of York and his colleagues on peremptory exceptions that might be proposed to the processes in the court of France.¹ Again, in 1317–18 he outlined the relations between England and France with a view to avoiding penalties for neglect to do homage. Those considerations, with three letters of Philip of France attached, suggested that the council instruct envoys in certain matters of law and custom in the French court and invest them with sufficient power to act.² J. F. Baldwin prints a document that furnishes another indication of Joneston's close connection with the council. It records articles dealing with processes in the court of France, in this instance the work of the bishop of Winchester, given to him to be submitted to the council as from the king.³ The last memorandum that he tendered during the reign of Edward II concerned the difficulties with France and the remedies to be applied regarding the outrage at Saint-Sardos. Other processes were discussed, as well as the nature of the tenure and homage by which the king of England held his French possessions.⁴

At the accession of Edward III it seemed that the new king and his council were to continue to appreciate the efforts of the *custos*. In 1329 Joneston was ordered to study the whole question of Guyenne and to propose whatever remedies he judged necessary.⁵ In the next year he was present in the council at Osney, furnishing for its use documents relating to treaties with Flanders and to the quarrel between Flanders and France.⁶ In April 1332 he submitted

---

¹ D.D.C. 29/9/2. This is a repetition of the suggestions made in Joneston's first memorandum book (*supra*, pp. 46 ff.).

² D.D.C. 29/8/19. Cf. Parl. & Coun. Proc. Chan. 5/14 and ibid., Exch. 2/11, papers in which Joneston requests that the prelates and nobles assigned to consult on petitions touching Gascony advise the king to appoint clerks of the council 'a survoer ses busoignes'.

³ Baldwin, op. cit., p. 471.

⁴ D.D.C. 29/9/24.

⁵ Déprez, *Les Préliminaires*, p. 49 note.

⁶ 'In primis, recepit j rotulum j pecie continentem transcriptum littere confederacionis facte inter regem Anglie et comitem Flandrie. Item, j rotulum j pecie, cum vij cedulis eidem rotulo consutis, continentem copiam littere confederacionis inter

both a verbal and a written report to the bishops of Winchester and Worcester on a plan for avoiding interference by the court of France in Gascon affairs.[1] Three years later he made several proposals that Southampton and other cities of England and Gascony should appoint proctors to carry on processes in the court of France and in the papal curia.[2] But at the same time he urged that an effort be made to withdraw certain cases from the Parlement de Paris. If that could be done, the cases were to be turned over for settlement to diplomatic commissions composed of representatives from England and France. In suggesting such a course the clerk was apparently thinking of the negotiations at Montreuil and Périgueux. Yet the methods of Edward I and his son were becoming impossible to continue. Joneston does not seem to have realized that, for in the same year he petitioned for the appointment of English proctors to carry on the litigation in the Parlement de Paris in place of proctors from France and Gascony, who, as he pointed out, feared death or exile too much to act effectively.[3] He saw the weakness in the individuals but did not grasp that judicial bickering was insufficient to stem the tide of French aggression. In wording a second petition for the resumption of the process of Montreuil he seems to cast a wistful eye over the methods of Edward I and to wonder just what course his grandson planned to follow.[4] The old clerk was

regem Anglie et comitem Flandrie. Item, j rotulum v peciarum continentem articulos quos comes Flandrie misit regi Francie reddendo homagium suum. Item, j rotulum j pecie continentem gravamina illata comiti Flandrie per regem Francie, pro quibus reddidit sibi homagium suum. Item, j rotulum j pecie continentem formam tractatus habiti super confederacione inter regem Anglie et comitem Flandrie. Item, viij cedulas tangentes treugas sive suferencias inter Anglie et Francie reges, et confederacionem inter regem Anglie et comitem Flandrie. Item, vij cedulas tangentes confederacionem predictam.' D.D.C. 28/10/3 (7 July 1330).

[1] Ibid. 28/8/20.   [2] Ibid. 30/3/14 and 28/3/28, 30.
[3] Ibid. 28/3/41.
[4] 'Item, quod duo ex commissariis anglicis dicti domini nostri nuper assignatis exequantur mandata regia sepius eis directa pro processibus apud Monstrellum et Petragor' super hujusmodi convencionem pacis et treugarum ad dictos fines quondam inchoatis ad similes fines resumendis, et quod duo advocati et duo procuratores et unus notarius de Anglia tam ex parte domini nostri regis quam communitatis

beginning to live in the past; his last appearance was at Lynn in June 1337, where he performed his final task of forbidding any acts of hostility against the French.[1] He addressed the monition to the mayor and others in the common hall of the town. Acting on behalf of the bishop of St. David's and Sir William Trussel, who had been appointed commissioners to carry into effect the existing treaties between England and France, Joneston particularly warned shipmasters, arguing that maritime disturbances had been the principal cause of English misfortunes in Gascony and Scotland.

The activities of his successor, Staunford, in an advisory capacity seem to have been negligible. His account mentions a charge for carrying documents to various *tractatus* at York and Nottingham in 1336–7. In the next year Staunford, with his documents, followed the archbishop of Canterbury from London to Northampton and Stamford, returned to London, and then travelled to Dover and back.[2]

Besides the personal relationship between the council and the *custos*, the two were connected indirectly through certain clerks. In 1309 Master Thomas Cobham, king's clerk, received an order to examine the articles of agreement, truces, and peaces made between Edward I and the king of France. Joneston, who actually delivered the writ, furnished the specified documents. Cobham was to certify the king's council by letters as to the state of the premises, especially those which he knew required immediate attention, in addition to any dubious points he might discover through his examination.[3] Two years later he was appointed to make a second inquiry, reporting both his own findings and the information with which Joneston could furnish him.[4] Together with Master Richard Plumstock, Cobham made still

subditorum ejusdem dictis commissariis assistant, et commissiones et alie littere necessarie eis fiant cum effectu.' D.D.C. 30/3/25.

[1] D.D.C. 32/17, a roll of three membranes also containing a discussion of points connected with the processes of Montreuil and Périgueux. Cf. ibid. 28/9/3.
[2] App. iii. [3] *C.C.R.* (1307–13), p. 240.
[4] Ibid. 348; cf. *C.P.R.* (1307–13), p. 338.

THE KEEPER OF PROCESSES

another study of the documents in August 1312, this time to draw up a report for the approaching parliament.¹ In October 1314 Joneston was directed to deliver certain documents that he had received from the wardrobe 'to the clerks and knights about to treat on these matters at Westminster on the morrow after All Souls'.² He made two more deliveries in March 1333 and June 1335, to Master Austence Jourdain, Master Gérard de Puy, Master John Piers, and others to enable them to report on French affairs in subsequent parliaments.³ The same practice continued after the appointment of Roger Staunford to the keepership. In October 1336 a writ of *certiorari* was sent to Masters John Piers and Thomas Sampson through Staunford and Henry of Canterbury. The latter explained that the king wished the counsel of the former on the best way to defend his rights in processes pending in the court of France.⁴ The last record of a similar demand, although there must have been many more, is dated in November 1337, when a request was made for counsel on French affairs.⁵

Such is the story of the keepership of processes, a story remarkable and commonplace: remarkable because from the vantage-point of the twentieth century it is surprising to look back six hundred years and find medieval man grappling with one of the problems of government in so modern a fashion; commonplace none the less, for the fourteenth-century English official took such things as a matter of course. They were fast becoming as ordinary a part of his life as his religion. In problems of the soul he said his prayers, paid his money, did penance, and thereby expected salvation, or at least a short term in purgatory, with much the same certainty as the modern man who pushes a button on the

---

[1] D.D.C. 27/14/d. Cobham had first acted in this capacity in 1305 (*C.C.R.* (1302–7), p. 340); Plumstock, in 1311 (*C.C.R.* (1307–13), p. 351).

[2] D.D.C. 30/5/15.

[3] Ibid. 28/2/37; Déprez, op. cit., p. 111 note.

[4] *C.C.R.* (1333–7), p. 711; Rymer, ii. 947. Joneston had delivered processes to Piers at parliament in London in March 1336 (App. ii, no. 1).

[5] Lescot, app. v; Déprez, op. cit., p. 179 nn. 4, 5.

wall and expects the electric light to burn. Likewise, in problems of government he referred questions to the proper person or department and expected them to be dealt with. By the fourteenth century there were plenty of proper persons and departments: English administration was literally honeycombed with specialists. For the most part they were people of little personal importance and were consequently immune to the vicissitudes of politics. They were clerks who spent the best part of their lives filling up folios of parchment, rummaging through archives, journeying abroad, and standing ready with vital information and technical advice before the council-tables of state. Theirs was a hard life and a busy one, and they were paid more frequently in promises than in cash. Often their names lie buried among the very manuscripts they wrote, but they are always there—hundreds of them—working quietly yet efficiently behind the scenes. If the English yeoman was the backbone of his country, the official cleric was certainly its brains.

To such a group belonged Martel, Joneston, and Staunford. Called by the king's council to fill a particular gap in administration, they admirably served this purpose. All of them were experts in law and procedure both at home and abroad, specialists in foreign affairs, first-rate archivists, and excellent advisers in questions falling within their purview. The office they held lay at the very heart of the diplomacy contingent upon the execution of the treaty of Paris of 1259. From the extraordinarily complete archives of that diplomatic clearing-house came instructions in material and procedure for English envoys and technical advice and suggestions for the council in the determination of policy. After all, is it strange that the English government, possessing as it did a chancery and an exchequer with a long and successful history behind them, should conceive the idea of another department to deal with business of increasing magnitude? The *custos processuum* represents but another step in specialization of functions, the force that underlies the whole of administrative development. Placed against the background of the general reorganization of administration that took place in the early fourteenth century, it admirably illustrates how efficient men of the Middle Ages could be and points again to the continuity of what Tout has called 'the English civil service'.

III

THREE PROCESSES

'Quid enim prodest anglicis litigare contra regem Francie in regno suo et totum consilium suum ac contra vos qui estis conjudices nostri? Et certe nichil!'
                               PHILIP MARTEL *in a speech to* CLEMENT V (1306).

(1) THE PROCESS OF MONTREUIL

MONTREUIL-SUR-MER was a little town in the department of Pas-de-Calais, situated at the point where the river Canche flows into the sea. The passage of time has left fifteen kilometres of land between it and the coast, but much about the place is still as it was six centuries ago. There is the citadel, surrounded by medieval towers and walls, whose impregnability was strengthened by the military genius of Vauban. One of its towers, called today La Tour de la Reine, was the prison of Bertha of Holland, whom the indolent, egotistic Philip I repudiated for Bertrade de Montfort. Within those walls was enacted in 1306 one of the strangest episodes in Anglo-French diplomatic relations, for in May and June of this year Edward I and Philip IV strove to settle by an arbitration commission certain long-standing difficulties between them. Montreuil, however, had enjoyed a respectable existence for a long time before the meeting of the commissioners gave its name currency in historical records. The Gothic church of Saint-Saulve was two centuries old when the representatives met, and the Hôtel-Dieu had seen a hundred years of life. The town secured its communal charter in 1188 and was probably just as proud of its relics of Sainte Austreberthe. A merchant of Montreuil had brought them from Pavilly, in Normandy, long before the Conquest and founded an abbey under this vocable near his home. At the time—and this must have influenced the choice of the representatives—the place was a thriving port centrally located for traffic passing through the Channel.

The process to which the town was to give its name had its genesis in the treaty of Paris of 1303, sealed after Boniface VIII had arbitrated in his private capacity between Philip and Edward. One of the most important provisions of the treaty was that some assessment and settlement of damages and losses incurred by the subjects of both parties should be made. Most of the losses had to do with plundering of Channel trade, and negotiations for the settlement of piracy claims go back even to 1293. In that year Edward sent to France the bishop of London, Sir Roger Brabazon, and Master William Greenfield, who was later to serve as chancellor, as commissioners to investigate maritime hostilities together with representatives of Philip.[1] In 1297 the matter was taken up again, and there are records of conversations that took place between the two kings at this time.[2] The first is entitled 'Le premier respons fet au roi d'Engleterre par le roi de France'. Edward's brother and the earl of Lincoln had offered in his behalf to inquire into and make amends for 'damages done by mariners of one side and the other', and desired a truce in order that this proposal might be carried out. The king of France expressed his willingness to negotiate, but asked first that confiscated goods be restored. To such a request Edward replied, in 'Le respons fet as messages le roi de France', that he could make no statement without taking advice. That he promised to do as quickly as he was able, and meanwhile undertook to prevent his subjects from pillaging French ships. The reply, 'Le respons fet au roi de France par levesque de Londres', was delivered orally to Philip by Richard of Gravesend. Not only had Edward consulted his council, but he had also heard complaints of his own merchants against the French.[3]

[1] *Lettres des cours de France et d'Angleterre*, ed. Champollion-Figeac, i. 404.
[2] Ibid. 424–9.
[3] These amounted to £77,065 damage suffered by the men of Bayonne, England, and Ireland at the hands of the Normans. The complete list is printed 392–400.

He was prepared to settle the claims of both parties in any one of three ways: those who had suffered losses might come before him 'to show their plaints' and receive satisfaction in his court; plaints might be arbitrated by two commissioners from each country; or the whole question might be submitted to the pope and settled according to a decision to be taken by the College of Cardinals. Negotiations were still pending in 1298, when Sir Geoffroi de Joinville and Masters John Lovel and Thomas de Legore were appointed to consult with three French envoys on the matter.[1] Further commissions were issued for the same purpose in 1301 and 1302.[2]

The business of making the necessary arrangements was very slow, and the king's merchants continued to ask redress.[3] Something was being accomplished, however, for the next piece of correspondence bears directly on the subject of the process. It is a bull of Clement V notifying Philip the Fair that the prior of the Friars Preachers and the guardian of the Friars Minor at Paris were empowered to receive the oaths of two commissioners to be appointed by the French king.[4] Letters in pursuance were addressed to the prior and guardian at the same time. The English commissioners, Philip Martel, the first *custos*, and Sir John Bakewell,[5] received their appointments on 5 April 1306 and took their oaths in London.[6] The French nominees, Etienne de Bourret,[7]

---

[1] Rymer, i. 900.   [2] Ibid. 936, 940.

[3] On 16 October 1305 the clerk of the mayor of Bayonne laid a claim for £5,905 against the French before the king at Westminster. *Lettres des cours*, ii. 14.

[4] There are two copies of this bull, *Ex parte tua*; one in G.R., no. 67, dated 13 November 1305, and the other in D.D.C. 31/19, m. 1, dated 13 February 1306. The names of the English representatives are given, although the only existing record of their appointment is dated in the following April.

[5] Bakewell is the spelling preferred by Tout (*Place of Edward II*, pp. 221, 301, 306). Sir John was an alderman of London, seneschal of Ponthieu from 1299 to 1305, and baron of the exchequer in 1307–8. Foss (*Judges*, ii. 225) spells the name Bankwell, from Bankers, at Lee, co. Kent, and records that the knight was also appointed justice to perambulate the forest and later served as justice itinerant.

[6] D.D.C. 27/5/12.

[7] Bourret, *dép*. Tarn-et-Garonne.

sub-dean of Poitiers, and Sir Jean de Ver,[1] were given letters on 8 May.[2] The four formed a bipartite commission that was instructed to inquire into damages and losses, to satisfy any plaintiffs whose claims should be unquestionably clear, and to refer any doubtful cases to the two kings for final settlement.

It should be made clear at the outset just what a process is and in what relation it stands to other methods of obtaining redress of grievances. Short of actual piracy the normal way to secure damages was by means of letters of request and letters of marque. The issue of them was not regulated by statute until the reign of Henry V, but they were in use in the reign of Henry III and possibly even earlier. By a comprehensive act passed in 1414 to prevent breaches of truce, an official called a conservator was appointed to inquire into such matters. The act states that he was to proceed 'as the admirals of the kings of England before this time reasonably, after the old custom and law on the main sea used, have done or used'.[3] Thus the admiral of the fleet was the person upon whom the responsibility for keeping truces and punishing violators fell.[4] If violations occurred, the aggrieved person could have recourse to letters of request, which demanded satisfaction or restitution within a reasonable period of time. Several letters of request of increasing severity of tone might be issued before more forceful means were resorted to. Should they fail, letters of marque were granted, and these allowed the aggrieved to attack and seize

---

[1] Ver, *dép.* Oise.

[2] D.D.C. 29/5/12. Commissions of the Parlement de Paris always consisted of one cleric and one lay member when the cause was civil or a mixture of civil and criminal; strictly criminal cases called for two lay members (Aubert, *Histoire du parlement de Paris*, ii. 92).

[3] Holdsworth, *History of English Law*, ii. 473. The provision for the appointment of a conservator was, of course, merely the legal recognition of a long-standing practice.

[4] Yet until the middle of the fourteenth century the only power admirals exercised was a disciplinary and administrative jurisdiction over seamen and others on board their fleets, and even in these matters their jurisdiction was not exclusive. *Select Pleas in the Court of Admiralty*, ed. Marsden (Selden Soc.), i. xli.

the property of the aggressor without being liable to condemnation for robbery or piracy.[1] The process, on the other hand, is simply an action at law. The process of Montreuil was a series of legal cases involving maritime losses brought for hearing and settlement before what amounted to an international commission. The nearest modern analogy—and there is not too great a difference between the two—would be proceedings before the Permanent Court of Arbitration at The Hague.

The first document remaining from the actual record of proceedings at Montreuil is a mutilated page entitled *Articuli ad formam querelarum faciendam*. Those 'articles to set forth the form of suits' were probably drawn up by the commissioners for the guidance of plaintiffs in presenting their claims; at any rate, they furnish a precise list of the information wanted. The names of ships and ships' masters were to be given, as well as names of those owning the cargoes carried. If a cargo consisted of wools or leather, apparently the plaintiff had only to state the amounts collected. If, on the other hand, other merchandise was involved, then it was necessary to have letters sealed with the common seal of the place where the merchandise was loaded. He must also mention the time when the ship left port. Several facts were to be furnished regarding the actual depredation: the place, and whether it was in sight of others by whom the depredation could be proved; whether the ship was plundered and carried away with the goods in it and, if so, where the ship reached shore; whether it was despoiled off the coast in sight of men on land or of ships at anchor off shore. If the merchandise was removed from one boat into another, sailors who were on board at the time had to testify to this fact. Witnesses were likewise to be produced if the cargo had been seized in port. The remaining information concerned the imprisonment of sailors and the conversion of seized goods into cash. In regard

[1] By the time of Henry IV letters of request were issued under the privy seal, letters of marque under the great seal. *Black Book of the Admiralty*, ed. Twiss, i. 389–94.

to the former, plaintiffs were to advise the commission of the duration of imprisonment, by whom it was effected, and the means of delivery; that is, 'whether by justice or through mercy'. As to conversion, they must tell 'whether any other merchants of England were in port by whom the seizure of goods can be proved, and whether through a public announcement of them rumour is common in England'.

A significant note is added at the end of these articles. With such information before them the commissioners were not to proceed according to French or English law, but by 'a certain sincere equity' agreed upon among themselves they were to establish 'the course of a summary process'.[1] The course of that summary process embraces four categories of material: general petitions, claims against the French, claims against the English, and replications.

There appear to have been only two general petitions, and both were submitted by persons who describe themselves as 'proctors of the commonalties of subjects of the king of England in his kingdom and in other lands under his jurisdiction'. The first is an extravagant demand for compensation for damages inflicted by the Scots after the truce of 1297 and the peace of 1303.[2] The English argued that, since the Scots were allies of the French, the French were financially liable for losses of the English. Accordingly they demanded that French proctors be summoned to answer English proctors for such claims. Their losses due to breaches of truce were estimated at £900,000; in addition, a sum 'au treble et plus' of this amount was asked for losses in Scotland by 'persones de Seinte Eglise et pur countes, barouns, et altres nobles' of England, and a third sum for expenses of English nobles in maintaining and protecting castles, cities, and lands held in Scotland 'of the gift of the said king of England'.

[1] D.D.C. 27/5/25. A copy of the articles is printed in *Rot. parl.* i. 277 under the date 1308, in connection with one of the many attempts to reconstitute the process. That part of the *Rotuli*, however, is based on the Hale MS., and it is quite probable that the document belongs to the year 1306. Certainly it corresponds very closely to the procedure described below.

[2] D.D.C. 31/20, a roll of three membranes, printed in *Lettres des cours*, ii. 19–23.

They advanced similar claims for 'murdres, homicides, arsouns, robberies' committed by Scots living in France during the years 1303–6. These amounted to £600,000! There is no record of any action having been taken on this first petition, and it seems probable that the commissioners themselves were unable to accept the reasoning of English proctors. Certainly the reparations asked were so tremendous that they would not have been paid even had the English secured a judgement in their favour. The French could have argued, too, that the commission had no power to listen to any but strictly English and French claims.

The second general petition, a part of the memorable *Fasciculus de superioritate maris* which fired the minds of Selden, Coke, and Prynne, was aimed at the piratical acts of Reyner Grimaud, admiral of the French fleet.[1] The argument it presents rests on the premise that by law, statute, and ordinance the kings of England had been in peaceable possession of sovereignty of the sea of England for time out of mind. The exercise of that sovereignty, so the petition runs, was delegated to the admiral of the fleet, together with full cognizance, justice, and other appurtenances. Grimaud seized English ships in violation of the terms of the treaty and, worst of all, claimed sovereignty of the English Sea. It was against such a claim that the proctors protested, not only in the name of England but also of 'la marine de Genue, Cataloigne, Espaigne, Alemaigne, Seland, Hoyland, Frise, Dennemarch, & Norway et de plusours aultres lieux del Empire'. Action on the petition was apparently taken when individual claims against Grimaud were heard. It seems likely, however, that the questions of admiral jurisdiction and sovereignty remained moot points, for the French commissioners could hardly have accepted the view that sovereignty of the sea belonged to England and not to France.[2]

---

[1] D.D.C. 32/19/1, printed by Coke (*Fourth Part of the Institutes*, pp. 142–4) and discussed by Selden (*Mare clausum*, cap. xxvii, xxviii). Grimaud (Grimaus or Grimaldi) was a Genoese in command of sixteen Genoese galleys then in the service of the king of France.

[2] Coke and others used this petition to illustrate the antiquity of the Court of

English claims against the French are set forth in two badly damaged documents. One is a fragment of a roll dealing with damages asked by people of Sandwich.[1] The other, which repeats two items from the Sandwich roll, is a register of sixteen folios containing summaries of cases heard by the commission.[2] The former merely lists damages, but the latter records the progress of almost every case; together they concern claims amounting to £1,882. 16*s*. put forward by forty persons who had shipped cargoes worth £3,250. 3*s*. 5*d*. in twenty-eight different vessels. There is, however, no reason to suppose that these were the only plaints heard, for mention is made in the documents of other cases of which no record has survived.

The record of cases preserved in the register affords valuable clues to the form of procedure. At the top of each folio—one side is usually given over to a single claim—are written the names of plaintiff and defendant, e.g. *Ricardus Bush: contra Reynerum Grimaus*. The *libellus*, or statement of the claim, follows, always in the same form; e.g. 'This shows Richard Bush, of London, to the auditors deputed by the king of France and the king of England to redress damages done to the people of one land and the other . . .' The name of the ship is given, together with its route and the contents and value of its cargo. The plaintiff cites the name or names of the despoilers, the place and time of depredation, and the port into which the cargo was taken and sold. Occasionally he includes information regarding the amount of damage to the ship itself and the imprisonment or death of the people on board. He then asks a certain sum for damages, and the *libellus* concludes with the formula,

---

Admiralty. The earliest occurrence of the term 'admiral' is in 1295, but the Court of Admiralty was not set up until the battle of Sluys (1340) had affirmed the English king's claim to sovereignty of the sea. Before that date cases that were later to come *coram admirallo* were dealt with in the common-law courts, in chancery, and by the council. *Select Pleas in Admiralty*, i. xv, xxxv.

[1] D.D.C. 29/5/18.
[2] Ibid. 27/7. A précis of part of the register may be found in Fulton's *Sovereignty of the Sea*, pp. 744–9.

'To which things aforesaid in whole or in part the said Richard offers to swear, according to what belongs to him and what he can prove it to be worth.'[1]

The defendant might then propose a *contestatio negativa* or an *exceptio dilatoria* or both.[2] The former was a flat denial of the charges made in the *libellus*. In almost every instance it is accompanied by a statement that the accused could not have committed the crime because at the time of its occurrence 'il navoit onkes este en ces paiis' or was 'au chimin envenant a Calois', or 'a sekke terre', or at any other spot but the one in question. The *contestatio* usually ends with a plea that the defendant be quit of the charges or at least that he be allowed to make a further statement of his case. Thus, in replying to the charge of Richard Bush (no. 1 in the table), Grimaud states,

And he is ready, should the court be at all doubtful—which it should not be—to prove a thing so notorious that everybody is aware of it; and says that in such a notorious matter you ought to require proof against him and not put him in any difficulty of plaint.

The *exceptio dilatoria*, as the term implies, was a statement calculated to delay the course of proceedings. It can best be explained by citing an example. Johan Pedroge's dilatory exception to the accusation of Thomas Cros (nos. 7, 10, 12, 24 in the table) was: 'the said Johan says that he is not held to answer. For the said demand makes no mention of him, and Henri de Geneve and Michel de Navarre, whom the demand concerns, are out of the kingdom and in such a place that they cannot now be reached.' In other words, if Johan's exception were admitted, Thomas's case would have to be stayed until Henri and Michel could be found and brought to justice. The *exceptio*, then, was a legal loophole through which the defendant could crawl to comparative safety. To such defences the plaintiff proposed a *repplicatio*.

---

[1] The first table in Appendix IV gives the precise information furnished in each case. Folios. 4, 14–16 are unfortunately illegible.

[2] For procedure in proposing exceptions see du Breuil, *Stilus curie parlamenti*, ed. Aubert, cap. xiii.

That might be a contradiction of the defendant's reply or an offer to submit further proof to substantiate the accusation. Usually, however, the proctor for the plaintiff found himself temporarily worsted by the defendant's exceptions and had to postpone his case 'tant quil eut conseil de son maistre pur le mieuz aviser de la verite'.

One defence is worth noting in detail, since it is the only real argument in the entire register. Odard de Maubusshon and Johan Pedroge are replying to the accusation of having plundered the ship *Michel de Arwe* (no. 16 in the table). They admit having committed the deed, but not in the manner in which the plaintiffs had described. The king of England, they assert, had ordered that no comfort be given to enemies of the king of France, yet when the vessel was taken 'without force or distress', in it 'lettres feurent trouvees ... qe aloient a ceux de Bruges dargent qils devoient resceivre en la dite vile'. Accordingly, the ship was seized and those on board were taken to Calais and thrown into prison 'as enemies of king and kingdom'. All the prisoners, however, save one Johan de Masworth, contrived to escape, and this fact convinced the French of their guilt: 'and according to custom of all those in your land and especially in the entire kingdom of France, any person who is taken for a crime and breaks prison is held to be convicted of the deed.' Particularly did they not consider themselves liable for the lost cargo, for their king 'had the cargo taken in the ship as forfeit to himself'. The unfortunate Masworth, who was still languishing in prison, clamoured for his release and for the return of some wool he had lost. The French replied that if he had not broken prison it was because he had been chained too securely to have been able to escape with his companions. The advocate continues,

and according to the custom in use in the entire kingdom of France, when several persons are in prison on criminal charges and some of these persons escape, if those who remain do not do all in their power to retain them and do not inform the guard of the prison, they are as equally convicted and attainted of the deed for which they are in prison as those who escape; for this reason he says that his [de Masworth's] goods are forfeited to the king and his body to the mercy of the lord.

Having dealt with the accusation, the defendants concluded by reminding the court that its commission did not give it power to deal with cases in which the plaintiffs had been trafficking with enemies of France in violation of the terms of truce agreed upon by Edward I and Philip IV.

The claims of the French against the English are similar to those filed by the English, except for the fact that they are not entered in a register and accordingly furnish none of the answers of the defendants. They remain in some seventy separate documents, which were sorted alphabetically by the names of plaintiffs.[1] Most of them bear endorsements of the names of plaintiff and defendant, of the towns in which each resided, and of the amount of damages asked.[2] The total sum of claims comes to about £19,537. 6s. 10d.[3]

The fourth class of documents belonging to the process is composed of replications that are detached from the particular cases to which they are related and have been recorded together on separate leaves. The first of these is the *reppli-*

---

[1] D.D.C. 27/6/6–76.

[2] The number of defendants in each English town is as follows: Winchelsea, co. Sussex, 19; Dartmouth, co. Devon, Littlehampton, co. Sussex, London, Romney, co. Kent, and Sandwich, co. Kent, each 4; Harwich, co. Essex, Rye, co. Sussex, Boston, co. Lincoln, and Weymouth, co. Dorset, each 3; Dunwich, co. Suffolk, Hythe, co. Kent, and Yarmouth, co. Norfolk, each 2; King's Lynn, co. Norfolk, Newcastle, co. Northumberland, Orwell (Edrewelle, Erdrewelle), co. Suffolk, Poole, co. Dorset, Portland, co. Dorset, Shoreham, co. Sussex, Southampton, Teignmouth, co. Devon, and the Cinque Ports (mentioned as such), each 1.

[3] This figure is incomplete, lacking three documents (D.D.C. 27/6/6, 25, 70) that are indecipherable. Three other documents bear records of French claims. The first is a claim for £88. 8s. against Pieres de la Vyne and others of Portsmouth for wines belonging to the men of La Rochelle seized on board the ship *Seinte Marie de Castre Enordiales* (ibid. 27/5/27). The second asks £197. 10s. for wool belonging to Piere le Monnier seized by the king of England at Winchester, Bristol, and Southampton (ibid. 27/6/1). The third is an imperfect roll, almost all of which is illegible, that contains various claims (ibid. 29/5/23). The form of documents relating to cases suggests that claims were first written on individual slips of parchment, then enrolled, and perhaps finally entered in a register. The absence of a register of French claims is due to the fact that the commission adjourned before many French claims were heard.

catio of English claimants to the defence of Odard de Maubusshon.[1] It sets out the arguments of six groups of plaintiffs and makes a summary appeal for their validity. The defence of Odard in most of the cases was that he acted under orders of the admiral in seizing the ships and had surrendered the cargoes to the king of France. The English were unwilling to allow him to shift responsibility, for they claimed that he took their goods 'to his own profit and has thereby been enriched, so by law he ought to answer; and reason, use, and custom of the country are not contrary to our demand'. In one instance the defendant asks that all claims of certain plaintiffs be disallowed because in one an accusation was made against him at a time when he was not captain of Calais. The English countered that they would consult their clients about the accusation in question, but that the mistake in this demand should not be allowed to jeopardize the validity of their other claims. In another instance the defendant insisted that the plaintiff present 'son garant des biens qe il li demande en la manere qil est contenu en sa peticion'. In other words, the claim for damages had not been supported by the necessary warrant or proof of ownership.[2] The plaintiff requested that the judges set a day 'qe ne soit trop longs et gref du dit Willeame' on which he could present his *garant*, which had to be obtained from the authorities of the town where the merchandise was loaded.[3] The other document in this class is a fragment of the reply of English proctors to the defence of Reyner Grimaud.[4] It contains little but a contradiction of the defendant's statement and an offer to prove the plaintiffs' allegations. It ends with a phrase characteristic of such replies: 'And they make protestation

---

[1] Ibid. 29/5/19, a roll of two membranes.

[2] *Supra*, p. 66.

[3] This matter was probably considered by the auditors as a dilatory exception; cf. du Breuil, op. cit., cap. xii.

[4] D.D.C. 27/6/5. There is also a book of four leaves, now stained almost beyond legibility, that contains various documents relating to acts of piracy by the Normans, the Bayonnese, and men of the Cinque Ports, one of which is the replication of the men of the Cinque Ports to charges against them (ibid. 27/15).

that if the defendants propose or have proposed facts (*fais*) in their defence, such facts be neither received nor held of any value and that no process be founded on them.'

So much for the nature of the cases themselves; two further points need to be made. Both plaintiffs and defendants were entitled to be represented by proctors, but there is no evidence that the latter ever took advantage of this right. One of the procurations has been preserved: Roger Baroun of Flitcham, a burgess of Lynn, appoints William, clerk of Philip Martel, as his proctor in all cases 'qe joe ai ou purrai avoir countre totes persones et vers toutz, taunt pur moi qe countre moi, pri devant touts juges et touts justices et especiaument devant les auditours deputez depar les rois de Fraunce et Dengleterre'. The letters are dated on 18 May 1306 and were sealed not only with Roger's personal seal but also with 'le commun seal de la ville de Lynn'.[1] The commission had the power to issue writs of summons. The surviving example is a writ from the French commissioners to the bailiff of Calais, ordering him to bring certain defendants before them at Montreuil.[2]

The procedure, then, may be summarized thus: the plaintiff issues letters of procuration to his representative;

[1] D.D.C. 27/6/2.

[2] 'Maistre Estenes de Bourret, souden de Poiters, clers nostre seignur le roi, et Johans de Verre, chevaliers de celui seignur, deputez depar celui seignur vis les prises et les forfaitz qe les gentz du roiagme de France ont fait aus gentz du roiagme Dengleterre durans les treuves et puis la paiz confermee entre les deux rois, au bailli du Caleys ou a son lieutenant, salutz. Comes nous vous aions autresfoiz mande qe vous adjornessez pardevant nous a Monsteroll' as certains jours Haime Pyn, Henri Ofgrendik', Symon Davin, Guy Sodin, Petre Hues, et les heirs de Gile Prime et Petre Petier a respondre a Jeme le Reve, de London', et autres marchans de Douver, liquele ne sont venu nenvoie a la dite jornee; enquores vous mandoums et comandoms depar le roi qe vos adjornez les dites persones pardevant nous a Monsterol' sus la meer a cestui samadi devant la seint Johan Baptiste a respondre au dit Jeme sur plusours malefacions et prises qil li ount faites devant les treves et puis la pees sicome li dist, et lour faites saveir qe sil ne vinent a la dite jornee ou envoient sufficiant procureur pur eus defendre, nous irons avant contre eus sicome reisons serra. Et vous mandoms qe vous metez en vostre main depar nous touz lour biens quelquil soient en tiele manire qe vous nous en sachiez desores enavant a respondre. Et ce qe vous averez fait, nous rescrivez par vous lettres pendans. Done le mardi dapres la seint Barnabe (14 June) lan m ccc et six.' D.D.C. 27/6/4.

the proctor states the claims of his client before the commission (*libellus*); the auditors issue a writ of summons to the defendant; the defendant appears before the court and submits his defence (*contestatio negativa* and *exceptio dilatoria*); the proctor for the plaintiff replies to the statement of the defendant (*repplicatio*). It seems likely that there was also a special time in the proceedings accorded for the production of testimony and the reception of evidence from witnesses. The commission may even have appointed certain days for hearing particular cases.

The process appeared to be working out successfully at first. In April 1306 Clement V sent a demand to Edward I for the release of goods belonging to certain merchants of Amiens and Corbie (*dép.* Somme), which the French claimed to have been seized after the issue of the papal ordinance establishing the process of Montreuil.[1] Edward replied on 5 June that there was no truth in the allegation; and he was able to report that the process was in progress. His own representatives, he stated, 'puis continuelment a cele busoigne ount este et oncore sount entendaunz, issint qe en cele ordenaunce faite devant vous il i ad eu nule defaute en nous nen nul de noz'.[2] Clement acknowledged his letter by a bull, dated at Bordeaux on 30 June, in which he urged an early settlement of the claims of the two countries,[3] but two weeks before this bull was issued the troubles at Montreuil had come to a head.

On 15 June the four commissioners met in the house of Jean, called 'de Buetin', at about the hour of vespers and made a deposition regarding their differences before a notary public.[4] The French stated that they wished to proceed in

---

[1] Papal Bulls, 44/14.   [2] D.D.C. 31/19, m. 3.
[3] Papal Bulls, 44/20, enrolled on D.D.C. 31/19, m. 4.
[4] There are two copies of the instrument, existing in D.D.C. 29/5/13 and 31/19, mm. 5–6. The second is supposedly an enrolment of the first, but it is actually much abbreviated, although it alone of the two furnishes a list of the witnesses to the deposition. The major part omitted in the second version deals with a claim by Peter de Saint-Paul, a merchant of Bayonne, against Johan Pedroge. The English commissioners complained that no justice had yet been done to Peter, although Johan

the business according to the form assigned to them by their king, just as it was contained in the petitions, responses, and defences of both parties.

But [as the deposition continues] it was necessary for the sake of common convenience and that the subjects of the king of France might be relieved from costs, vexations, and expenses—and this was always the intention of the lord king of France and of those commissioners deputed by the same lord king—that they betake themselves to the coasts of Normandy, Poitou, and Brittany especially to admit the plaint and demand of plaintiffs of the kingdom of France and of others asserting themselves to have been exceedingly damaged by the English and other subjects of the kingdom of England, and to transfer through the commissioners of each realm the petitions and plaints of the said plaintiffs to those places.

After that, they were prepared to proceed to England and to receive plaints there, promising to proceed 'just as right and reason demand'.

To such a proposal the English replied:

We have come together here by common consent of all our people. Many plaintiffs of the kingdom of England have come to complain about your people, and we have already begun to take steps by receiving and even hearing answers of others from the kingdom of France against the petitions of many English people. Truly we believed and hoped that at Montreuil we should admit the petitions of all plaintiffs of the kingdom of France, especially since certain days have already been determined upon for English plaintiffs to come here and prosecute their suits themselves or through their legally constituted proctors. We have already waited a long time to carry out the business as it ought to be done according to law and reason. Since it seems to us that you wish and intend to proceed contrary to our intention and the manner fixed

had confessed to the crime in a written statement. The witnesses to the document were: Deinis d'Aumale, bailiff of Amiens, and Jean de Rumell, mayor of Montreuil; Masters Jean, called 'Comterel', Jean Bousserit, Vincent de Careron, Jean and Guillaume d'Evessent, all clerks of Montreuil; John de Scoihe, a priest of Norwich; Masters Nicholas de Garçon, of Amiens, and Elias Joneston, Edmund of Wellesworth, William of Sherborne, clerks from the dioceses of Coventry, Canterbury, and Salisbury respectively. All those persons, except perhaps the bailiff and the mayor, probably assisted in the process.

and agreed upon among us and the form committed to us, we should by no means dare to proceed in such a way without having consulted our lord. Before we continue we must consult the lord king of England just as you have consulted or have been able to consult the lord king of France by letter or through messengers.

To allow time for the English commissioners to see their king, it was agreed to leave the process *in statu quo* until the quinzaine of the feast of the Blessed Remigius (15 October) next following. At that time they were to reconvene in some appointed place. If, after having seen their king, the English should want to meet again earlier or to postpone the meeting until a later date, they consented to signify their intentions to the bailiff of Amiens, who in turn was to notify the French commissioners.

So the commissioners parted. On his way back to England Martel stopped for an interview with the king of France at Croix-St-Leufroy, 'to demonstrate', as he put it, 'my diligence and that of my said colleague in the office of inquiry to which we have been nominated and elected, lest any default be imputed to our lord or to us'. The record of that mission, particularly interesting because it is set down in the form of a dialogue, is only fragmentary.[1] Nevertheless it reveals the fundamental difficulty that had hampered the success of the process. First, however, the old question of the merchants of Corbie is settled.[2] When the document begins, Philip Martel has already seen the king of France and is now offering to answer the various 'articles' proposed by the French earlier in the day. The record proceeds:

To which it was replied in this manner: 'Lord Philip, there is not enough time at present. Come back immediately after dinner so that we shall then be able to address the council of our lord, for all those of the council will then return.'

At which hour the said Philip returned to the aforesaid place, and in the presence of the chancellor and the aforesaid knight answered in this manner the first article concerning the goods of merchants of Corbie

---

[1] D.D.C. 29/5/24.   [2] *Supra*, p. 75.

and elsewhere that were arrested in England: 'I say that the completion of the execution of the aforesaid bull ought not to be hindered because of the contents in the said article. Nor can a breach of any ordinance be attributed to my lord, for these goods were seized with legal right long before the said ordinance was made in the presence of the said pope. The form of law required according to English laws and customs in matters of this sort has been observed in every respect, just as you will see by inspection of the relevant letters if you have them shown.'

The letters having been shown and read, the said chancellor answered the aforesaid merchants in this manner: 'By the letters you show it is apparent that your goods have been arrested on account of the debt of the lord our king long before the ordinance made before the lord pope. Therefore apply to the clerks of accounts to obtain restitution thereupon to the extent of the estimation of the aforesaid debt, and afterwards, as you have suggested, to those hereupon deputed by the said kings in order to have satisfaction for the damages incurred by you at the hands of the people of the lord king of England in valuation of the aforesaid goods.' And with those words the plaint of the said merchants before the king of France and his council came to an end.

After settlement of the case of the merchants of Corbie Martel and the French council discussed the demand that probably had most to do with bringing the process to a bad end. Philip the Fair insisted that the commission first devote its attention to considering the primary possession of English demesnes in France and conflicts of administration in these territories. He expected it to review the entire feudal relationship from the treaty of Paris of 1259 onwards. Edward's intentions ran to no such lengths. He wished the commission to consider damages inflicted on both parties since the publication of truce between the two countries and afterwards to set up another body to hear complaints for losses preceding the late war. Martel explained it thus:

And that for the good of peace of each realm it ought to be begun thus, I shall point out to you the reasons why my lord is moved to observe the said order in respect to the completion of the aforesaid peace. First . . . he is moved by the fact that the recent war had its beginning in the lack of law about such damages. More losses and dangers will arise, but not out of the demesnes of the aforesaid kings.

Further, in re-forming peace between them the said kings have completely remitted all rancours, injuries, misdeeds, and hatreds that arose by reason of their demesnes, and they will arrive at such an understanding that war between them probably need not be feared unless it arise out of deeds of their peoples—which God forbid! Very frequently my lord has been bound by oath to certain of his people of the duchy of Aquitaine who have suffered damages of this sort that he will support them in such matters according to their ancient laws and liberties. Those things my same said lord cannot pass over, nor can he in any way defer acknowledgement of them to the prejudice of his people without breaking his oath or offending the law. Such is not the case with losses and injuries done to him in his demesnes. And you ought to be able to say the same thing about your lord.

The counter-proposals of the English were described by the French chancellor as being preposterous, and Martel and his colleague, Sir John Bakewell, set out to report to their lord. Bakewell was taken ill at London, however, and Martel went on alone to see the king. After listening to his story Edward decided that the matter had better be explained to the pope, so the clerk was sent personally to present the matter to Clement V in July 1306. Elias Joneston, who accompanied him on his mission, has left a full report of the speech in which Martel related the failure of the process.[1]

The English commissioners damned the French on four separate counts. The first was that the French were unwilling to award damages that had been clearly proved by written confession of certain defendants. Instead they insisted on hearing all claims of both parties before allowing any sentences to be executed.

The second reason is best expressed in Martel's own words to the French:

We perceive that the lord king of France has himself or through his councillors undertaken the defence of those about whom the people of England complain. And you who are deputed together with us and who ought to represent no one person but who ought to do justice and

[1] D.D.C. 29/5/14-15.

equity hereupon—you adhere to a group of your people by helping them with counsel and defending them against us so that they shall not be able personally to answer for their own deeds and to have truth done, by permitting them to answer captiously through advocates and legally to retract confessions at will in circumstances not allowed by law. And you were ordered by your lord king that you so aid and counsel them lest they incur any loss. That seems to be against the ordinance of the lord pope and against our oaths. Of what use is it for Englishmen to go to law against the king of France in his kingdom, against his whole council, and against you who are our co-judges? Certainly none! Further, for that reason we and the king of England and his council ought to act likewise against your plaintiffs. God forbid, for such a situation would have no solution!

The third reason had to do with the French proposal to proceed first to Normandy, Brittany, Poitou, and afterwards to England and Ireland to receive claims. The excuse they gave was that the people in those regions had been so impoverished by the English that they could not come to Montreuil to plea. Martel told the pope:

We answered that according to law it ought not to be done, by the fact that *actor forum rei sequi teneatur*, and because the majority of the prosecutors of the realm of France have been domiciled in Calais and places in the vicinity. Further, such a method would be difficult, tedious, costly, and useless because we should take up many days and years without any result. For despite our wandering from house to house or from city to city and despite the fact that many are paupers, they would still have to come to England themselves or send proctors to present and prosecute their petitions there since those of England cannot come to them. And so this wandering would be in vain.

The last complaint was that French defendants had used in their defences the excuse of absence.[1] By that trick they endeavoured to exclude all the plaints of Englishmen, or at least so to cut away the bases of their petitions that no proof could be forthcoming. That was alleged to be 'against the way of proceeding first begun and agreed upon among us'.

[1] *Supra*, p. 70. To-day 'excuse of absence' would be called 'alibi'.

From such an indictment Martel went on to request a new bull with amendments in the commission that he thought would obviate the difficulties to which the process had been subjected. He asked for seven changes: after having taken oaths in two or three places of each kingdom, the auditors should consent personally to conduct a judicial inquiry, the same to be agreed to by the two kings; the auditors should commit for settlement those matters to which for one reason or another they could not personally attend to trustworthy and honest men to be chosen by them, but they themselves were to retain the final decisions;[1] cases should be heard and decided by proper fine, and defendants should be compelled personally to answer for their own deeds without quibbling of the advocates; awards based on clearly proved cases should be executed within a period of four to six months; names of the commissioners should not be mentioned in the bull in order that a change in personnel might not necessitate a fresh rescript; the auditors should compel witnesses who for some reason withdrew from the proceedings to assert the truth of their testimony; rescripts in pursuance should be sent to the prior of the Friars Preachers and the guardian of the Friars Minor in regard to their receiving the oaths of the commissioners.

After the mission to the pope the thread of negotiations is lost until October 1306. In the meanwhile Martel had died before the new bull could be issued.[2] On 15 October Sir John Bakewell appeared in Paris in fulfilment of the agreement reached by the commissioners at Montreuil on 15 June.[3] He wandered from place to place seeking the French representatives: to the chapter of the Friars Minor in the presence of the guardian, to the prior of the Friars Preachers, to the palace in the presence of the chancellor, to the house of Sir Jean de Ver at the Porte-St.-Martin, and even to Notre Dame, but all search was vain. So Sir John

---

[1] Commissioners from the Parlement de Paris were not allowed to delegate their authority. Du Breuil, op. cit., cap. xxvii, § 7.
[2] *Supra*, p. 35.
[3] *Supra*, p. 77.

made a public deposition before one John Hervey in which he described his peregrination and painstakingly listed the names of those who could vouch for his appearance at each separate place.[1] Having completed his part of the bargain, and no doubt by that time a very exasperated man, he apparently returned to England immediately.

Bakewell's amusingly ignominious journey marks the end of the first stage of the process and provides a convenient break in the narrative of its history. What significance is to be attached to the activities of the commission, and what implications does the process have? The use of arbitration as such is not unusual. It was frequently employed in all ages where ordinary justice was defective and by the thirteenth century it was especially common. The Greeks used it in commercial cases, although strangers among them customarily came before judges of their own nations. Since plundering of ships was the principal complaint in cases that gave rise to arbitration, the practice occurs only occasionally in Roman maritime history, for in its palmy days the Empire was practically free from piracy.[2] But what is extraordinary about Montreuil is the use to which arbitration was put and the form that it took. Not only were the subjects considered by the commission legal cases, they were also diplomatic questions that had been mentioned in a treaty of peace, the most solemn form of diplomatic instrument. Further, it is odd that the kings of England and France should have entrusted the matter to representatives chosen from the interested parties instead of turning it over to some disinterested third party like the pope.

The procedure of the commission also calls for comment. Rules for arbitration were generally borrowed from Roman and canon law, but sometimes they are modified in points of detail by local customs. In the instance of Montreuil procedure in the Parlement de Paris was undoubtedly the in-

[1] D.D.C. 29/5/16, enrolled on D.D.C. 31/19, mm. 6–7.
[2] On these points see Pardessus, *Us et coutumes de la mer*, and Tardif, *La Procédure civile et criminelle aux xiiie et xive siècles*, particularly pt. 1, ch. ii.

fluence at work, and its procedure also was derived from those two great legal systems. For example, the word *auditour*, which is the term most frequently employed by litigants in addressing the four arbitrators, was used in the thirteenth century and at the beginning of the fourteenth to describe the referendary, a particular kind of commissioner sent out by the Parlement. Parlementary commissioners were either judges, persons instructed *ad inquirendum et definiendum*, or referendaries, persons instructed *ad inquirendum et referendum*.[1] Moreover, judging from the actions of the French representatives throughout the process, they seem to have considered themselves mere referendaries of the Parlement; and it is significant in this connection to note that the cases actually came before this court after the proceedings at Montreuil had failed. Again, the form of procedure followed by the arbitrators corresponds very closely to that laid down by the Parlement for its commissioners.[2] Even so, Edward's appointees probably agreed to such a way of doing things without much persuasion on the part of the French. Every Englishman who had judicial dealings with the Church or with continental countries must have been acquainted with Roman and canon law. That was particularly true of Martel, ex-official in the court of Canterbury and *custos processuum*, and Bakewell, sometime royal justice and seneschal of Ponthieu. Yet it seems that the French commissioners had the upper hand, especially since the auditors had been told to disregard English and French law and to work out an independent procedure.[3] From another point of view the procedure is even more interesting, for it anticipates that used by the English Court of Admiralty.[4] The suggestion naturally arises that this court drew upon

[1] Guilhiermoz, *Enquêtes et procès*, p. 27; see ibid., pp. 27–66, for a discussion of commissions and the relation of procedure in the Parlement to Roman and canon law. Practically every point of law in the process of Montreuil has its parallel in the law of Parlement.
[2] Cf. du Breuil, op. cit., cap. xxvii–xxvii *quater*, and Aubert, op. cit. ii, ch. 3.
[3] *Supra*, p. 67.
[4] Cf. *Select Pleas in the Court of Admiralty*, i, ii.

the great continental legal systems for much of its form; but this is part of another question which hardly falls within the scope of diplomatic administration.

Taken as a whole, the process throws considerable light on the attitude and capability of those who formulated English foreign policy at the time. One of the most curious points about it is that Martel never mentioned to the pope the discussions that had taken place at Croix-Saint-Leufroy. All the complaints of the clerk had to do with the failure of the French to observe the letter and spirit of a procedure agreed upon before the commission began to sit; none of them referred to the basic difficulty that undermined the process. But there is little doubt that Martel was given precise instructions as to what he should say to the pope. The explanation seems to lie in the fundamental weakness exhibited by Edward I in his dealings with France. He lacked the power to penetrate the screen of tactics thrown up by his enemies as a cover for their real aims. In all likelihood Philip IV never intended the business of Montreuil to succeed, for by drawing it into his own court he could take another step towards destroying the authority of his vassal. Edward was too bent on observing forms—Bakewell's trip to Paris in October 1306 is sufficient proof of this—and ever anxious to act so that 'il i ad eu nule defaute en nous nen nul de noz'.

It is unnecessary to linger very long over the details of the subsequent history of the process. After 1306 it ceases to be an actuality and becomes instead a convenient lever in diplomacy. Some attention was given to it during the years 1307–11, and Edward II's journey to France in May 1313 was the signal for a revival of interest in its reconstitution. The same thing occurred when Edward III went to France to perform homage in 1326 and 1329. During the period 1333–9 it often served as the red herring that the astute young English king dangled under the nose of Philip of Valois.[1] Several instructions and writs to reopen the

[1] Déprez, *Les Préliminaires de la guerre de Cent Ans*, pp. 53, 92, 95, 97, 102.

process were actually issued in those years, but nothing came of them.¹

The counsellors of Edward III scarcely knew what course to plot in the face of continued French aggression through the medium of the Parlement de Paris and the acts of French administrative officials. In their eyes the only remedy, and the least objectionable alternative, was to return to the policy of Edward I, who, to them, had known in his time how to get himself out of embarrassing situations with some facility.

¹ D.D.C. 28/2/41, 28/3/5, 46, 49, 30/3/23, 27, 28, 30/1/17, and 30/4/3. The last is a long certificate of Master John Piers as to commissions and letters necessary for resuming the process. Most of the documents are also concerned with the reconstitution of the process of Périgueux, which had suffered the same fate as that of Montreuil. The last inventory of documents relating to Montreuil (6 October 1336) shows the following records to have been in use: 'Item, iiij bullas, unam directam priori fratrum Predicatorum et gardiano Minorum Parisius et aliam directam decano Abbatisville et duas directas regi Anglie clausas. Item, duo instrumenta pupplica, unum integrum factum apud Monstrollium in recessu auditorum continens diversas causas recedendi et formam resumpcionis processus ibidem inchoati, unum aliud corosum vermibus in medio et in lateribus factum Parisius super protestacione domini Johannis de Baugquell' post mortem magistri Philippi Martel. Item, unum rotulum quinque peciarum cum duabus cedulis continens [*sic*] tenores citacionum super diversis excessibus per ducem et subditos in mari et in terra. Item, unum rotulum duarum peciarum continentem primam sufferrenciam captam et primam prorogacionem facientem mencionem de secunda et tercia. Item, quatuor commissiones et unam litteram executoriam, unam directam domino Johanni de Baugquell' ad inchoandum processum Monstrollii cum littera executoria ejusdem, aliam directam J., episcopo Norwicensi, et J. de Brittania ad resumendum dictum processum Monstrollii, terciam directam magistris Thome de Cobham et Gilbertum [*sic*] de Midelton' ad resumendum processus predictos. Item, j rotulum ix peciarum continentem peticiones gencium regni Anglie apud Monstrollium propositas. Item, unum rotulum iiij peciarum continens [*sic*] responsiones domini Reyneri de Grimbaus factas ad peticiones gencium regni Anglie apud Monstrollium propositas et specialiter Martini de Raceborgh' et Johannis de Hetheye. Item, unum rotulum ij peciarum continentem repplicaciones gencium regni Anglie factas ad responsiones domini Reyneri predicti. Item, j rotulum ix peciarum et j cedulam continentes requestas gencium Anglie et responsionis [*sic*] Johannis Peidrok' ad easdem. Item, unum rotulum v peciarum continentem responsiones domini Odardi de Maubushom apud Monstrollium ad peticiones gencium regni Anglie. Item, unum rotulum ij peciarum continentem replicaciones contra Johannem de Peidrok'. Item, j rotulum x peciarum continentem peticiones gencium regni Francie contra gentes regni Francie [*sic*] apud Monstrollium propositas. Item, lxxv cedulas de peticionibus Gallicorum contra gentes regni Anglie. Item, iiii rotulos et dimidium continentes nomina dampna passorum querelas eorum coram regum commissariis apud Monstrollium' (D.D.C. 28/10/5; cf. ibid. 28/10/6, a partial copy).

All of them seemed to be puzzled by the diplomatic practices of his grandson. Thus as early as 1308–9 Elias Joneston was already warning the council not to allow the delay in continuing the process of Montreuil to be extended 'ad aliqua negocia prejudicialia ipsi domino nostro'.[1] In 1334 he urged in such words as these that the process be renewed: 'Item, si placeat dicto domino nostro et suo consilio hujusmodi negocia cordi habere et super articulis arduis, periculis et dubiis iminentibus in eisdem consulere et remedia ordinare cum diligencia qua decet in tam arduis, prout tempore dicti avi sui erat observatum.'[2] Some five years later Alexander Bicknor doubted whether the process could be resumed, for after having examined the relevant documents he concluded that 'common cognizance could only be extended to damages suffered on land and sea before the beginning of war'. Joneston, who continued to advise that the commission be re-established, countered with an opinion that cognizance could be extended to include all damages that took place while truces and peaces were in force. His argument was based on the fact that 'duplex erat cognicio: prima, videlicet, consuetudinaria et secunda conventionalis et arbitralis nominata'.[3]

And so it went on: the frequent petitions and advice are but variations on the same theme.[4] In all the thirty-odd documents dealing with the course of the process after 1306 there are but two exceptions. Some anonymous person at the beginning of Edward III's reign advised the king to

[1] D.D.C 29/6/11 *dorso*, part of a long memorandum of the state of Anglo-French relations at the time.
[2] Ibid. 30/3/25; ibid. 30/3/13, 24, 26 are other copies.
[3] Ibid. 30/7/12.
[4] For example, the following passage from a memorial addressed to the chancellor in about June 1334: 'Item, quod impossibile seu difficile erit omnibus advocatis Anglie et Vasconie dictum dominum nostrum regem et suos in curia Francie conservare a guerre et exheredacionis periculis vel a maiori subjeccione erga coronam Francie quam eorum antecessores esse consueverint nisi placeat paternitati vestre reverende quod littere necessarie ad defensionem juris dicti domini nostri in premissis fiant, prout quidam ex cancellariis patris et avi ipsius domini nostri fieri fecerunt.' Ibid. 28/3/25.

consider the matter to be closed, lest the French be aroused to obtain by war what they had failed to get through negotiation. He even feared that the papal curia would support any fresh demands the French might make.[1] Before the outbreak of the Hundred Years War Alexander Bicknor made another representation to the effect that the king had probably forfeited the right to resume the processes of Montreuil and Périgueux because the conditions of the original agreement had not been fulfilled, because the commissions of the deputies were defective, and because the king had allowed such matters to come within the purview of the Parlement de Paris.[2] That is the last mention of the process, for the beginning of hostilities put an end to such discussions, as indeed it did to all diplomatic negotiations emanating from the treaty of Paris of 1259.

(ii) THE PROCESS OF PÉRIGUEUX

The process of Montreuil was an attempt to deal almost exclusively with claims for maritime losses incurred during open hostilities. The process of Périgueux was an attempt to deal with matters far more fundamental: the fulfilment of what remained to be carried out of the terms of the various treaties from 1259 to 1303; some settlement of disputes arising from seizures, occupations, breaches of peace, and conflicts of jurisdiction along the disputed northern borders of the duchy of Guyenne.[3]

The state of Gascony, both internally and externally, was a major problem in the reign of Edward II, another unfortunate legacy left to him by his father.[4] Constantly beset by

[1] Ibid. 29/10/4.
[2] Ibid. 28/5/20.
[3] This process deserves to be treated in a separate monograph. In 1322 there were in the English archives 67 documents dealing with the process (*G.C.*, nos. 666–732). Thirty of these survive, in addition to an imperfect journal (23 leaves) kept by the English commissioners and covering a period from 3 November 1310 to 25 August 1311 (D.D.C. 27/9). Except for details of English and French proposals and counter-proposals, I have had to restrict myself to a general account for reasons of space.   [4] Tout, *Place of the Reign of Edward II*, pp. 191–202.

troubles along the Scottish border and by baronial dissension at home, it is little short of remarkable that Edward II was able to devote so much time and energy to the affairs of the duchy. Almost every expedient was tried before finally in 1323 at Pontefract Edward issued his own ordinances for the reform of Gascony.[1] But important as they are, the internal affairs of the duchy are peripheral to the story of the process of Périgueux and cannot be dealt with here.[2]

What was crucial and what impelled Edward to initiate negotiations culminating in the process is nowhere better revealed than in a lengthy document entitled 'Informacio facta per magistrum Arnaldum de Codico, judicem Petragoricinii, Anno Domini 1310 de occupatis in Petragoricinio, Lemovicenio, et Caturcinio per dominum regem Francie et alios in prejudicium domini regis Anglie.'[3] A few excerpts chosen at random from this document bear eloquent testimony to the state of affairs in the duchy:

> *Occupied in Périgord.* The lord king of France has usurped these places in Périgord: the castle and castellany of Mussidan; the place of Sourzac, in the parish and appurtenances of which has been constructed a new bastide called Villefranche-de-St-Louis [today, St-Louis-en-L'Isle]; the parishes of Montagnac, St-Julien-de-Bourdeilles, St-Front-d'Alemps, La Trevisa, Sauvetat, Déville, Pont-St-Mamet, Galmanes, and other parishes of the castle and castellany of Mussidan; and also outside that castellany, the hospital of St-Antoine and a place called Le Pizou, to the prejudice of the lord king of England and duke of Aquitaine; all and each of which may or may not be of the fief or *arrière-fief* of the said count of Périgord thus privileged. The said lord king of England and duke of Aquitaine had and held after the time of the said peace openly and publicly, peacefully and quietly and also for thirty years at least all resort and superiority and levied or caused to be levied in the aforesaid places common tax continually in each and every place aforesaid and still does so, except that the lord king of France or his people at least recently impeded the said lord king of England and

---

[1] Rymer, ii. 505–6.
[2] Edward's commissioners at Périgueux were also charged with collecting information for the reform of the duchy. Some idea of their activities in this connection may be got from *G.C.*, nos. 2040–59.   [3] *G.R.*, no. 54.

duke of Aquitaine and his people in the levy of the said common tax in the place of Sourzac, and also there and elsewhere with regard to all the jurats of the bastide called St-Louis since the time when the said bastide was begun at least, and the said lord king of France or his people for more than twenty years and for at least thirty seized the resort, obedience, and superiority of all and singular aforesaid. . . .

Item the lord king of France after the time of the said peace acquired and appropriated to himself in Périgord the said bastide of St-Louis, and the demesne and justice of Lisle, the castle and castellany of Bourdeilles, the place of Aubeterre, the moiety of the town of Sarlat [today, Sarlat-la-Canéda] through pariage, notwithstanding that he had sold that moiety to the consuls of the said place and abbey, and the bastide of Domme.

All these things especially are notorious, because they are self-evident and cannot be concealed by any tergiversation.

This report of Arnaud de Codico appears to have come to the attention of Philip IV.[1] Some time in 1310 he issued commissions to Robert II de Fouilloy, bishop of Amiens, and Robert VI, count of Boulogne, to review the charges. They were also to deal with the fulfilment of treaties and 'to inquire concerning the settling of breaches of peace whensoever committed against him in parts of the duchy for a year before the war and afterwards'.[2] Edward's letters, dated 2 August 1310 at Northampton, appointed John Salmon, bishop of Norwich, Jean de Bretagne, earl Richmond, and Guy Ferre and William Inge, knights.[3] They were given 'power and special mandate to seek and receive in our name the assignments of lands that ought to be assigned to us and restitutions of usurpations and seizures held to our prejudice; and to issue quittances for receipts'. They were also to make restitution of usurpations by the English 'and to do all those things that together are to be done between lord Philip, king of France, and his people and us and ours'.

[1] Gavrilovitch, *Étude sur le traité de Paris de 1259*, p. 97.
[2] *G.C.*, nos. 47–8.
[3] *Rôles gascons*, iv, no. 429; Rymer, ii. 113. Nineteen other letters (*Rôles gascons*, iv, nos. 393–411) were issued under the same date, but most of these were returned and never used (cf. *G.C.*, nos. 215–29).

Before the commissioners actually met, months were consumed in collecting materials, such as copies and then originals of the pertinent treaties,[1] and written evidence taken in the duchy, and in arguments concerning procedure. As to procedure, what was at stake is clear from a letter written by Edward to Philip on 12 December 1310, when Edward was at Berwick-on-Tweed.[2] It is worth quoting at length:

We have received letters from the bishop of Norwich and the earl of Richmond and our other envoys who were sent to you and then to Aquitaine saying that you answered them in a friendly fashion and kindly and that you are prepared to fulfil and complete what touches the fulfilment of previous treaties; but that it is not your intention to proceed concerning usurpations and breaches of peace committed before the war between you and Edward our father by those deputed by you and us together, but *racione superius vestri dominii*, by your deputies alone. And notwithstanding the fact that it is and has been our intention to have these settled by the two groups of deputies together, we wish and intend to discuss this difference of intention with the earls of Lincoln [Henry de Lacy] and Pembroke [Aymer of Valence] and Sir Otton de Grandson, who were present at negotiations during the time of our father. This we are unable to do because of their absence and because of the situation in Scotland. We ask that this matter be postponed until our meeting, which we hope to have as soon as the war permits. We are ready to proceed with the fulfilment of treaties. We apologize for not having sent solemn envoys to you this time, but time and distance do not permit.

A copy of this letter was sent to Norwich and his colleagues with instructions to proceed carefully after 'having had sound and mature counsel of skilled and worthy men of our council in the said duchy' and not to use the commissions regarding usurpations and breaches of peace unless compelled by urgent necessity.[3] At the same time, Edward issued fresh commissions to his representatives.[4] They had been streng-

---

[1] Lubimenko, *Jean de Bretagne, comte de Richmond*, p. 82 n. 4.
[2] *Rôles gascons*, iv, no. 435.   [3] Ibid., nos. 436, 437.
[4] Ibid., no. 430; Rymer, ii. 121.

thened by the addition of a staff of experts including Masters Thomas Cobham, Richard Plumstock, Elias Joneston, and Roger Wadenho; and Henry of Canterbury was to follow.[1]

The problem was to persuade Philip to agree to a joint commission. While negotiations were continued to achieve this end, preparations began for a suit before the Parlement de Paris.[2] The French proposed 'certain articles ... touching the status of the king in the duchy', and these were sent to England with a request for advice. On 18 April 1311 the bishops and other prelates and clergy, assembled at London, together with Masters Thomas Cobham, Walter Thorp, Gilbert Middleton, and others skilled in law, were ordered to examine the articles and to advise the king's council in London how best to instruct Salmon and his colleagues.[3]

Salmon got his answer on 7 May, and again the letter is worth quoting in detail:

> The articles proposed against us in the duchy of Guyenne by the people of the king of France, which you sent to us for advice and counsel, we have delivered to the good people of our council who ought to know best about such a matter to examine and to advise us of the best counsel and defence for us in the things aforesaid; and they, after much deliberating and treating about the said articles and other memoranda that we had turned over to them, have answered us that they cannot fully counsel since they are ignorant of the facts of what your needs are and of the customs of the country. But they have told us that the best counsel at present is to ask the king of France to postpone consideration of the aforesaid articles until our meeting. Consequently, we have ordered to be sent on a mission to the king of France certain people of our council, clerks and knights who are fully informed of the counsel we have had previously on the things aforesaid. You are to send competent people to inform and advise them so that they be at Paris on the octaves of the Nativity of St. John the Baptist [2 July].

[1] *Rôles gascons*, iv, nos. 443, 449, 478.

[2] D.D.C. 27/9. Cf. *G.C.*, no. 1190: 'Littera locum tenentis in ducatu Aquitanie, sine sigillo, directa domino duci super avisamento consilii de recusando commissarios regis Francie in processu de suppriisiis et excessibus, et de appellando et submittendo totum factum cognicioni regis Francie.'

[3] *C.P.R.* (1307-13), p. 338; *Rôles gascons*, iv, no. 492.

You sent us a transcript of a commission obtained by Master Bernard Pelet from the king of France that seems to our council to be very prejudicial to us. We are amazed and annoyed, because you had strict orders not to reveal any commission that might give the people of the king of France the impression that you were empowered to discuss *auncienes choses passees*, but only those since the last treaty of Paris. If you suspect any possibility of danger to us in the duchy *par voies maliciouses*, set about surreptitiously to put in order our castles, cities, boroughs, towns, and other fortresses and inform us immediately of what you have done.

Send letters by the bearer of these to our envoys before they come to Paris advising whether they should go to the king of France or not, for we think that affairs may be in such a state that it could be more dangerous to send the mission than not to do so.

We have heard that there is to be a general council in Avignon at Michaelmas. Put aside what you are doing and be there to counsel our other envoys, since the state of Gascony is bound to be discussed.[1]

Meanwhile, on 8 March 1311 Philip had agreed to a joint commission. The bishop of Amiens, the count of Boulogne, Ives de Laudunaco, and Hugues Cullier were empowered 'at the request of the men of the king of England' to fulfil all that remained to be done in reference to the treaties and to see to it that all that remained to be given to the French was granted by the English.[2] On the subject of usurpations and breaches of peace Philip was adamant; they were matters for Parlement. Clearly he had come only halfway. Thus the scope of the entire process was accordingly narrowed.

On 27 April 1311 the commissioners met in the House of the Friars Minor in Périgueux. Besides the three[3] French and four English representatives, there were present Jean d'Arrabloy, French seneschal in Périgord and Cahorsin, Master Jean Chauvet, proctor of the French king in the seneschalsy, Jacques de Saint-Lupin, canon of Amiens, Master

---

[1] *Rôles gascons*, iv, no. 494.

[2] Gavrilovitch, op. cit., pp. 124–8.

[3] Hugues Cullier had died sometime between 8 March and 27 April 1311 (MS. Julius E. i, fo. 304r).

Jean de Martel, chaplain of the church of Amiens, Guillaume de Cazes, doctor of laws, Masters Arnaud de Codico and Guillaume Conques, 'persons skilled in law', and many others who were 'especially asked for and summoned in these matters'.[1] It is perhaps significant that Périgueux was the capital of the seneschalsy whose seneschal reviewed all appeals from the domains of the duke of Aquitaine that eventually reached the Parlement de Paris.[2]

Once credentials had been exchanged, the English proposed to begin immediately with discussions about the fulfilment of treaties, but the French countered that proceedings concerning seizures ought to come first. To this the English replied that basing discussions of seizures on terms of the various treaties, transcripts of which they had brought with them, was more logical and expeditious. Accordingly the transcripts were read—a time-consuming process suggestive of some modern international meetings, and equally dull.[3]

On 2 May 1311 the English commissioners made their proposals: 'Articuli propositi per gentes domini regis Anglie de hiis que juxta formam pacum sibi sunt facienda.'[4] These were based on the treaties of 1259, 1279, 1286, and 1303, and on the arbitration of Boniface VIII pronounced in 1298. They were: (1) full possession of all seigneurial fiefs, allodia, jurisdictions, and other rights in the three cities and dioceses of Limoges, Cahors, and Périgueux, and especially the fealty of Brantôme; (2) the entire temporality and fealty, fiefs, and demesnes in Saintonge beyond the Charente river that had come into the hands of the king of France after the death of the count of Poitou; (3) 180 *livres* of annual rents alienated by the count in Saintonge after the first treaty;[5] (4) vassalage of the bastide of Parcoul, in Dordogne; (5)

---

[1] Gavrilovitch, op. cit., pp. 124–8.   [2] Ibid. 85.
[3] Ibid., 126–7.
[4] See *G.C.*, no. 666 for citations. There is also a copy in *Archives Nationales* J655/24.
[5] 50 *liv.* in St-Sornin, 40 *liv.* in Pont-l'Abbé d'Arnoult, 30 *liv.* in Corme-Royal, 20 *liv.* in Port-d'Envaux, 20 *liv.* in the priory of St-Eutrope de Saintes, 20 *liv.* for a chaplaincy in the castle of Saintes.

314. 18*s*. 4*d*. *livres tournois* of rents that remained to be paid from the 3,000 *livres* promised by the king of France to the duke of Guyenne; (6) a part of Agenais not yet handed over to the king of England,¹ and the rents seized by the French from that part assigned to England in 1259 but not surrendered until 1279; (7) 21,000 *livres tournois* for arrears assigned to the English king according to the treaty of Paris of 1286. In addition, the English complained of abuses committed by the seneschal of Périgord and Quercy—twelve instances are cited—who was trying to hand the duchy over to France by favouring appeals carried to the court of France, by protecting the appellants, who in turn committed a multitude of abuses, and by banishing upon unjust pretexts the inhabitants of the duchy.

Five days later (7 May) the French responded to the English articles: 'Responsiones ad requestas gencium Anglie facte per gentes regis Francie.'² The answers correspond to the articles as numbered above. (1) By what treaty or clauses of a treaty are these things asked for? Which of these things asked for did the king of France have and hold at the time of the treaty, and precisely what does the king of England and duke of Aquitaine claim to hold? As to Brantôme, no answer can be given until the bishop of Périgueux, the abbot and convent, and the lord of Bourdeilles, 'who are said to have lordship and jurisdiction in the said town, and which they hold from the lord king', can be summoned and heard. (2–4) They are ignorant of the things and places sought, and no answer can be given until an inquisition has been made on the spot. (5) The king's court has retained cognizance of

---

¹ The fief *de Camineriis* and the following parishes in the diocese of Périgueux: Eymet, St-Pastour, St-Nazaire, St-Macaire, Gardelle, Queyzaguet, Razac-d'Eymet, Montguyard, Fraisse, Cause, Ste-Marthe; the following parishes in the diocese of Agen: St-Jean-de-Duras, St-Pardoux-Isaac, St-Étienne, Boisset, St-Sernin, Roumagne, St-Hilaire, Moustier, *de Fissaco*, St-Germain; the following parishes in the diocese of Agen around Tournon-d'Agenais: Valprionde, St-Agnan, Belvèze, Olmières, Varlicou, Sept Arbres, Moncessou, St-Amans-du-Pech, *de Sancta Marsa*, Montagudet, Marmon, St-Rémy, Castanède.

² See *G.C.*, no. 667 for citations.

this matter, and no answer can be given until it has decreed. (6) Inquests were made by order of the king's court concerning these places, but Hugues Cullier had them, and he is dead. Therefore they cannot answer. As to the rents, they wish to know the treaty and the clause of the treaty by which they are demanded. (7) These matters, too, are pending in the king's court, especially in the Chambre des Comptes and Parlement, so that no answer can be given.

The English responded in turn to these responses: 'Replicaciones super requestis gencium Anglie ad responsiones gencium Francie.'[1] They based their claim to the three cities and dioceses on the first and third treaties, those of 1259 and 1286, citing the phrase 'Ceo est a savoir'[2] in the one and the clause 'Nos vero ... omnia alia in feodis'[3] in the other. As to Brantôme, they have nothing to do with the bishop, the abbot, and the lord, since their business is not with them but with the king of France and his deputies. Claiming ignorance of places mentioned does not constitute grounds for delaying discussions, since the names of the places could be got from a study of the treaties. Nor would they be put off by an inquest in Agenais, since by terms of the treaty the places claimed were expressly to be restored to the king of England. The treaty of 1259 is again cited to buttress the monetary claims. The other objections are untenable under terms of the instructions given to the commissioners.

On 23 May the French again responded: 'Triplicacio gencium domini regis Francie proposita contra replicaciones gencium domini regis Anglie ad responsiones dictarum

---

[1] See *G.C.*, no. 668 for citations.

[2] Presumably the 'c'est a dire' in the following: 'Que nos donons au devandit Roi de Angleterre, e à ses heirs, e à ses successors, toute la droiture, que nos aviens, e teniens en ces trois evesches, a es' cites, c'est a dire, de Limoges, de Cadors, e de Perragort, en fiez, e en demaines ...' Rymer, i. 389.

[3] 'Nos igitur ... volumus & concedimus ... omnia alia, in feodis & domaniis, allodiis, juridictionibus, hobedientiis, & aliis quibuscumque consistentia, quae sunt in dictis tribus civibus & dioc' & specialiter obedientia de Brancolmio, deliberentur dicto Regi Angliae ...' Rymer, i. 672.

gencium regis Francie ad articulos pacum.'[1] There is little that is new in these counter-reponses. They express their willingness to abide by terms of the treaties, but they refuse to change any of their positions regarding the articles proposed by the English. In connection with the article concerning the three cities and dioceses and Brantôme two fresh points are made. Fifty years or more have elapsed since the treaty of 1259, so that it is difficult to be certain who held what then and who holds what now. As to Brantôme, both canon and civil law require that the bishop, the abbot, and the lord be heard before any final determination of the issue can be made. To all the other articles, 'respondent ut supra'.

The final round in the sparring over the English articles took place on 26 May: 'Quadriplicacio gencium regis Anglie super requestis gencium Anglie, et finalis responsio gencium Francie ad requestas supradictas.'[2] Conciliatory before, the English now emphasize the evasion of obligations by the king of France. It is for him to hand over all the holdings in the three cities and dioceses, delivering clearly and openly 'fiefs as fiefs' and 'demesnes as demesnes' and retaining those privileges that were accorded to him in the first treaty. It is for him, not for the English king, to name those holdings that belong to him. To the objection raised to citing the treaty of 1259, the English remind the French commissioners that they also cited clauses from the treaty of 1286, to which the present king of France was a party and by which he granted the lands now requested. They conclude:

> Moreover, to all other things opposed or proposed by the said lords, the bishop of Amiens and his colleagues, the said lords John bishop of Norwich, the earl of Richmond, etc., say that the aforesaid objections or proposals ultimately ought not nor cannot reasonably impede or postpone the granting of their requests or the fulfilment of treaties, saving reasons otherwise alleged by grace of counter-proposals, nor exonerate in any reasonable way the lord king of France, nor excuse the said lords, the bishop of Amiens and his colleagues, especially since in those matters in which they say that they wish to be informed by

[1] See *G.C.*, no. 669 for citations. [2] See *G.C.*, no. 670 for citations.

others or to consult others, they should long since have consulted and been informed. Nevertheless, out of superabundance, the said lords, the bishop of Norwich and the earl of Richmond, although unwilling, will wait for three weeks that they may know what finally is to be done in the premises by the said lords, the bishop of Amiens and his colleagues. . . . Nor, so far as it is in their power, do they consent or do they wish to consent on any point to an ordinance of the court of the king of France.

Thus ended the first round of interchanges at Périgueux. It was now the turn of the French to present their articles: 'Requeste gencium regis Francie.'[1] These were presumably the same as those proposed on 6 February 1311[2] and sent to England for advice of the council.[3] They were: (1) reparations amounting to 926,000 *livres tournois* for damages suffered before the last Gascon war and during the rebellion of Bordeaux, for depredations committed against the abbey of La Réole, and for the garrisons of the châteaux of Bordeaux and Langon made prisoners by adherents of the duke; (2) 100,000 *livres tournois*, to be demanded at the proper time and place, for the goods of Jews, confiscated in Agenais by the king of England; (3) restoration of the part of Agenais returned to the duke and of other places surrendered as part of Agenais when in reality they belonged to Quercy;[4] (4) all the islands adjacent to Normandy, Saintonge, and Poitou; (5) recognition of their rights over the church of Bordeaux and all its dependencies, and over other parishes, abbeys, bishops and chapters and their dependencies, and rights to a group of bastides in Agenais, to the entire county of Périgord, and to the acquisitions of Philip IV and his predecessors.[5] The treaties of 1279 and 1286 and the arbitration of Boniface were cited in support of these claims.

[1] See *G.C.*, no. 673 for citations.
[2] D.D.C. 27/5.
[3] *Supra*, p. 91.
[4] Castelsagrat and Montjoi 'et plura alia loca'.
[5] Bishops and chapters of Agen, Périgueux, Bazas, Saintes, Bayonne, Dax, Cahors; monasteries of Moissac, Cluny, Sarlat, St-Martial de Limoges, La Sauve-Majeure, St-Sauveur and St-Romain de Blaye, La Chaise-Dieu, St-Sornin de Toulouse, Figeac; priories of La Réole and La Daurade de Toulouse; the diaconate of Issigeac.

Probably several days later the English answered: 'Responsiones ad requestas gencium Francie per gentes Anglie.'[1] Again, the answers correspond to the French articles as numbered above. (1) They are not prepared to admit matters contained in the arbitration of Boniface, but only those contained in the treaties. The treaties mentioned only the restitution of lands and revenues. No amount for damages was fixed, and in any event, damages applied to both sides and should be settled mutually. Nevertheless, 'they are prepared to do what they ought about the aforesaid, provided the form of the treaty is adhered to'. (2) They make no comment, for nothing is asked for at present. (3) By terms of the treaty, the whole of Agenais was granted to the king of England. Castelsagrat and Montjoi were handed over in part-payment of 3,000 *livres* promised in the treaty. (4) The treaty makes no mention of islands. (5) None of the churches, parishes, abbeys, bishops, and chapters are mentioned in the treaties, nor do they fall within the three cities and dioceses. As to acquisitions, what are they and when were they acquired?

The French rebuttal was presented on 16 June: 'Replicaciones gencium regis Francie super requestis earum.'[2] They reaffirmed their intention to demand only those things that were included in the terms of the treaties and their unwillingness to violate any articles of the treaties; but they softened none of their demands. Additional evidence from the arbitration of Boniface is cited in support of the demand for compensation. The treaty of 1259 is quoted again in connection with Agenais, with the lands granted in error there, and with the islands. On this last point, for example,

> they say that these can especially be demanded by virtue of the first treaty, since the king of England surrendered to the king of France all right whatsoever that he ever had in the land of Normandy and in the whole duchy in the land of Poitou or elsewhere and in the islands, if he or his ancestors indeed ever had any, especially since the islands are part of the duchy of Normandy, for they are part of the bishopric of Coutances. Therefore by reason of the said treaty they can demand

---

[1] See *G.C.*, no. 674 for citations.   [2] See *G.C.*, no. 675 for citations.

them, and they do so demand. And they say the same about the islands of Saintonge, since Saintonge is commonly included in Poitou.

In dealing with the last point (5) made by the English, they cite a provision in the treaty of 1303 whereby the king of France was obligated to return only those lands that the duke of Aquitaine held before the war, and they maintain that the places mentioned were not held by the duke. And so for all the other points made by the English: additional citations of treaty articles, but no change in position.

The last interchange took place on 19 June: 'Replicaciones facte per gentes regis Anglie ad responsiones gencium domini regis Francie super requestis ipsarum gencium domini regis Francie, et triplicaciones gencium regis Anglie ad replicaciones predictas.'[1] This is a lengthy document, but there is little new to be found in it except additional citations from treaties. The phrase 'dicunt dicti episcopus et comes ut alias dixerunt in responsionibus suis' recurs again and again. The basic position of the English representations was that no concessions could be made that were not specifically mentioned in treaties. The treaty of 1259 was coming to resemble Holy Writ: chapter and verse could be found in it to support almost any argument. The really significant portion of the document is the summation, for it clearly indicates the reasons for the failure of the process:

> In truth, since we John, bishop of Norwich and the earl of Richmond, Guy Ferre and William Inge, knights, have asked, in the name of our lord the king of England, that certain things be handed over and delivered to him and to us for him by you, lords Robert, bishop of Amiens, and Robert, count of Boulogne, and your colleagues in the name of the king of France, which things asked and required remain to be surrendered and delivered according to the forms of treaties and conventions formerly entered into between the said lords, the kings of France and Englandand their ancestors, as is clearly apparent by the terms of the said treaties; and you . . . have delivered nothing to our lord the king of England or to us in his behalf either in fact or indeed

[1] See *G.C.*, no. 676 for citations. There is also a copy in *Archives Nationales*, J654/22 bis.

by word, we are led to believe, and not unjustly, that you intend neither to do nor to say anything, just as we and any diligent persons who analyse your responses can clearly intuit, since your said responses, by reason of the fact that they are irrelevant and insufficient, are such as cannot nor ought not to stand in the way of deliveries and restitutions of the said things asked by us.

Item, since you . . . have asked . . . that many things be restored and handed over to the same lord king of France or to you for him, which requests . . . cannot nor ought not to be made by virtue of the aforesaid treaties, as is clearly apparent by inspection of the articles containing your petitions and by inspection of our answers to them.

And we . . . given what has transpired thus far, truly believe that you . . . intend to do and say nothing that will in effect pertain to the fulfilment of treaties, and so we truly believe that our remaining here is utterly useless, since our remaining here any longer will not lead to the fulfilment of treaties. And because we intend and wish to certify to the aforesaid lords the kings of France and England everything that has taken place up to now, we urge you . . . likewise to certify everything . . . to the said lord king of France.

Three days later William Inge left for Paris to complain about the proceedings to the king of France.[1] On 15 December 1311 Edward ordered the bishop of Norwich and a host of other specialists to be present 'with other prelates and magnates of our council' at Westminster on 17 January 1312 for special *colloquium et tractatum* concerning the process of Périgueux. At the same time the constable of Bordeaux and others were instructed to collect the relevant documents and send them to the meeting.[2] What took place at that meeting is not recorded. The process of Périgueux became a lever in diplomacy, and the long and tedious tale of the numerous attempts at renewal and of final abandonment need not be told here.

(III) THE PROCESS OF AGEN

The process of Agen had its genesis in the homage of 1329.[3] Philip VI was willing to make concessions if Edward III

---

[1] D.D.C. 27/5. [2] *Rôles gascons*, iv, nos. 586–9. [3] *Supra*, pp. 15–16.

would recognize that he held his French possessions in liege homage as a peer of France. That he did on 30 March 1331. In April, Edward, disguised as a merchant, made a hurried and secret trip to France, and the two kings met at Pont-Sainte-Maxence.[1] The outcome of the interview and the subsequent negotiations was the establishment of a joint commission for restitution of lands in Agenais.[2]

It seems likely that Edward III was persuaded to urge the establishment of a process by certain of his clerical advisers. There exist copies of three petitions to the king of France that are obviously the work of such persons.[3] The first urges the king of France to resume amicable negotiations for mutual restitution of lands in Gascony. The second bears the caption, 'Peticio ad differendum tempus recompensacionis faciende et resumpcionem omnium processuum prejudicialem [sic] domino nostro regi', and the third the title, 'Peticio ad similem graciam habendam a tempore date littere gracie supradicte'. The numerous clerks who always surrounded the king and served as his technical experts had long memories where diplomacy and legal forms were concerned. They might well have recalled the establishment in 1274 of a commission in connection with Anglo-Flemish relations.[4] They might think back, too, to the processes of Montreuil and Périgueux. Further, many of them had experience as English proctors at the Parlement de Paris, which employed commissions as a normal part of its procedure.[5] Every one of them would be familiar with canon law, and one of its principles, which was laid down in the ninth century and extended by Gregory VII to civil processes, was *Spoliatus ante omnia restituendus*.

---

[1] Murimuth, p. 63; Déprez, *Les Préliminaires de la guerre de Cent Ans*, pp. 73, 76.

[2] For the complicated history of claims to Agenais see the introduction in my *Le Livre d'Agenais*.

[3] D.D.C. 28/2/10, tentatively dated December 1331, but undoubtedly belonging to the period before March 1331.

[4] De Sturler, *Les Relations politiques et les échanges commerciaux entre le duché de Brabant et l'Angleterre au Moyen Âge*, pp. 124–5.

[5] De Breuil, op. cit., caps. xxvii—xxvii *quater*.

At any rate, on 5 July 1331 John Travers and John Hildesle received letters 'de quibusdam prisis, occupacionibus, et detencionibus post treugam nuper inter reges Francie et Anglie captam examinandis, et in statum pristinum reducendis'.[1] Both men were particularly well qualified to serve as commissioners, for both were trained in law, and Hildesle was especially conversant with diplomatic affairs and with the question of homage. Sir John Travers was of a Lancashire family and had been returned as a member for this county to the parliament that met at Carlisle in 1307. Under Edward II he had frequently served as commissioner of array, assessor of aids, and custodian of the lands forfeited by Thomas of Lancaster and his adherents.[2] As king's clerk he had held the office of treasurer's remembrancer at the exchequer in 1323–4 and followed this by a term as constable of Bordeaux, the chief financial minister of Gascony.[3] On 2 March 1329 he became a justice of Common Pleas and later acted as a justice in Eyre for the Channel Islands, but on 10 June 1331 surrendered this post because of 'not having leisure to act'.[4] On 29 June of the same year he again received appointment as constable of Bordeaux,[5] the position he was holding at the time of his activities in the process of Agen. He died before 3 July 1339, for at this time certain houses in the parish of St. Andrew, Holborn, which belonged to him and which came into the king's hands for debts due at the time of his death, were granted to two chancery clerks at two marks a year, until they should be redeemed by payment of the full account.[6] Master John Hildesle, parson of

[1] Gascon Rolls 43, m. 12. On 6 July the treasurer, barons, and chamberlains of the exchequer were ordered to pay the expenses of the two travelling to Gascony, and to ordain for the wages of Hildesle, which were to be paid by Travers as constable according to the treasurer's certificate (*C.C.R.* (1330–3), pp. 251–2).
[2] Foss, *The Judges of England*, iii. 532.
[3] Tout, *Place of the Reign of Edward II in English History*, pp. 311, 351.
[4] Foss, loc. cit.; *C.P.R.* (1330–4), p. 146.
[5] Tout, *Chapters in the Administrative History of Mediaeval England*, vi. 68.
[6] *C.P.R.* (1338–40), p. 308; cf. *C.C.R.* (1343–6), p. 136. Tout has wrongly listed him as again holding the office of constable from 17 July to 22 September 1343 (*Chapters*, vi. 69).

the church of Thynden and canon of Chichester, from 1316 onwards was continually employed on diplomatic missions.¹ His knowledge of Gascon affairs was profound, for it was under his guidance that the great Gascon register of 1318–19 was compiled.² In 1323 he was one of the twelve 'clerks of the first bench' in chancery.³ Seven years later he served as proctor for the king at the Parlement de Paris and took under his surveillance those points that arose concerning homage.⁴ He was raised to the bench of the exchequer on 18 December 1332 and remained in this office until he became chancellor of the exchequer some two years later. In the latter post he is several times found in attendance at the king's council and at parliament, where he tried petitions.⁵

Two better men, then, could hardly have been found for the legal and diplomatic business involved in the process of Agen. The French representatives on the commission were equally well qualified. One was Master Bertrand Boniface, canon of Paris and professor of civil and canon law; the other was Sir Pierre Raymond de Rabastens, seneschal of Poitou.⁶ The duties of the four commissioners are succinctly stated in a renewal of the original letters of appointment to Travers and Hildesle in February 1332:

> Nous, voillantz que droit soit fait en quant que a nous atteint, vous, & chescun de vous, pronoms, elisoms, & deputoms, par cestes presentes noz lettres, d'oier, ovesque, les deputez le dit Roi de France, ou par vous meismes, si avant come a nous appartient, les pleintes de touz ceuz qi pleindre se voudrent de surprises, purprises, & occupacions, faites contre les dites accordes, & a faire restitucion & complissement de droitur sur meisme les choses.⁷

Most of their work seems to have been done before 1333; and this date may be taken as a convenient dividing line in the history of the process. After 1333 the personnel of the

---

¹ Foss, op. cit., iii. 443.
² *Infra*, pp. –119 ff.
³ Davies, *The Baronial Opposition to Edward II*, app. no. 74.
⁴ *C.P.R.* (1330–4), pp. 22, 38.
⁵ Foss, loc. cit.; *C.C.R.* (1333–7), p. 468.
⁶ D.D.C. 32/8, m. 1; Déprez, op. cit., p. 78 n. 6. ⁷ Rymer, ii. 832.

English commissioners was constantly changing and few, if any, sessions were held.[1]

Manuscripts preserved in the Public Record Office that relate to the process of Agen number about thirty. Of those, about half have to do with letters and records of commission, that is, with appointments to serve on the commission; and they are the least interesting of the lot. The remaining documents are about equally divided between actual rolls of proceedings and a closely related group of proposals and memoranda, petitions and complaints, that point the course of the process. Unfortunately, almost a third of the total number are now almost completely illegible owing to damage and stain.

The most illuminating are two portions of a roll of proceedings of the commissioners.[2] Together the two make up almost five membranes of a roll, and there is good reason to believe that, lacking only three membranes, it is the same record that the English government itself possessed in 1336. In that year Roger Staunford had in his possession 'unum rotulum viij peciarum de novo processu Agenni'.[3] The two fragments in question cover a period from 3 January to 11 April 1332. During that time the commission sat in the

[1] Bertrand Ferrand replaced Hildesle in March 1333, John of Oxford and Arnold Payne were added to the panel, while Travers was retained (Gascon Rolls 45, m. 8). On 26 March 1334 commissions to resume the process were issued to William Airmyn, bishop of Norwich, Henry Gower, bishop of St. Davids, William Trussel, John Shordich, Thomas Astley, John Ufford, John Travers, John of Oxford, William Clinton, and Bartholomew Burghersh (Rymer, ii. 880; D.D.C. 28/3/46); and on 5 November 1334 Simon Stanes and Austence Jourdain were appointed in place of Travers and Payne (D.D.C. 30/3/15). The *nuncii* accounts show that Hildesle was abroad from 5 July 1331 to 7 June 1332, Airmyn from 30 September 1333 to 8 January 1334, Shordich from 7 April to 6 July 1334, Clinton in October and November 1334, and Stanes from 24 December 1334 to 1 May 1336 (Mirot and Déprez, 'Les Ambassades anglaises pendant la guerre de Cent Ans', *Bibliothèque de l'École des chartes*, lix (1898), nos. 24, 41, 51, 53, as corrected by Larson, 'English Embassies during the Hundred Years' War', *E.H.R.* lv (1940), 423–31).

[2] D.D.C. 32/8, 30/2/11, printed in *Speculum*, xix (1944), 171–8.

[3] D.D.C. 28/10/5. There is also a document whose caption is 'Articuli extracti de processu nuper Agennum [inchoato]', which is now for the most part illegible (ibid., 30/2/29).

house of the Friars Preachers at Agen,[1] except for a period from 21 January to 3 February, when they moved to nearby Villeneuve-sur-Lot and Penne-d'Agenais[2] and another period from 11 to 28 February, when they were at Laroque-Timbaut.[3] During that time a great many individual cases were apparently disposed of. Unfortunately, the surviving manuscripts do not bear any record of them or of what the particular questions at issue were or of the way in which decisions were reached. Presumably the commissioners recorded such cases on separate leaves, for the roll refers to *cause singulares* and *sicut in earum processibus clarius continetur*, but these have been lost. Only a few scattered remarks reveal the commission at work.

English and French proctors present their credentials, and the commission swears in a substitute named by the English proctor. When the commission goes to Villeneuve-sur-Lot, letters are issued to the baillis of Villeneuve, Monflanquin, Villeréal, and Tournon d'Agenais.[4] They must publish the news in order that plaintiffs may come and present their claims. The commissioners travel about for the convenience of those who have complaints to make, and they go to Laroque-Timbaut because the inhabitants of Puymirol[5] 'ad locum predictum Agenn' tunc venire nequiverunt vel non audeant'. They can summon witnesses, take evidence, and hear special pleas. But all these actions might be expected of any court of law. What is important is to know how the commission proceeded in the matter of restoring lands.

At the outset it seems clear that the commission divided the cases that came before it into two categories, which may be called 'individual' and 'communal'. Into the former fell pleas by individuals within a community against individuals

[1] Agen, *dép*. Lot-et-Garonne.
[2] Villeneuve-sur-Lot, *dép*. Lot-et-Garonne; Penne-d'Agenais, *dép*. Lot-et-Garonne, *arr*. Villeneuve-sur-Lot.
[3] Laroque-Timbaut, *dép*. Lot-et-Garonne, *arr*. Agen.
[4] Monflanquin, Villeréal, Tournon d'Agenais, *dép*. Lot-et-Garonne, *arr*. Villeneuve-sur-Lot.
[5] Puymirol, *dép*. Lot-et-Garonne, *arr*. Agen.

in another community. For example, *A*, a citizen of Villeneuve-sur-Lot, asserts that he is a subject of the king of France and that certain of his possessions were seized by *B*, who is a subject of the king of England and resides in Penne-d'Agenais. Such cases the commission apparently heard and determined, although the records of their decisions have disappeared. Into the second category fell cases involving whole communities, and of these there are several mentioned specifically in the two fragments of the roll that have survived. The French towns of Saint-Aignan[1], Villeneuve-sur-Lot, Pujols,[2] and Tournon-d'Agenais separately in three suits plead for restitution of certain lands seized by the English town of Penne-d'Agenais, and Penne sues each of these in turn.

Those in charge of the process early laid down the principles upon which such cases were to be heard: 'ordinavimus ad obviandum maliciis et diffugiis parcium coram nobis litigancium.' The plaintiff had first to prove the legality of his petition. That he could do by having it sworn to by four reputable witnesses. When the judges were satisfied on that point they assigned a day to the defendant 'ad proponendum et probandum factum contrarium'. If the defendant neglected to appear at the appointed time, either in person or by proctor, the commissioners took the profits and emoluments of the possessions at issue into the hands of the court. Such action, however, did not preclude the defendant's pleading his cause at a later date. Accordingly the commissioners proceeded to sequestrate all property in each of the communal cases that came before them. Such action did not imply a decision, however, for after an objection on the part of the English proctor, the court clarified its policy in this matter. By ordering sequestrations the commission did not intend, it stated, to determine at the time whether proofs and claims that had been advanced were sufficient to allow or deny

---

[1] St-Aignan, *dép.* Lot-et-Garonne, *arr.* Villeneuve-sur-Lot, *c.* Penne-d'Agenais.

[2] Pujols, *dép.* Lot-et-Garonne, *arr.* and *c.* Villeneuve-sur-Lot.

restitution or even to establish whether the property at issue had actually been seized. Nor did it intend to prejudice the right of either king by any decisions it had made or might make. Actually decisions in communal cases were suspended until general commissions should arrive from England and France to enable the court to act in cases of land seized since the year 1324. Meanwhile the judges restored sequestrated property to those from whom it had been taken, with the understanding that this should not prejudice any claim outstanding against it.

And here the record comes to an abrupt and tantalizing end. The commission apparently adjourned, but not before making a joint recommendation to the kings of England and France on the subject of the process.[1] The joint report is an illuminating document, for it provides for the first time a detailed statement of the basis on which the four commissioners wished to proceed. Of even greater interest is the fact that they took pains to analyse in great detail the advantages and disadvantages inherent in the *cedula* they proposed.

The memorandum begins by expressing a pious hope for an amicable adjustment of the points at issue:

It would be both agreeable and gratifying to God and all the world should it please their lords the kings of France and England that their subjects, or the successors of their subjects, who in time of war or disturbances have lost revenues and immovable goods in the duchy of Aquitaine or elsewhere, with the exception of the eleven exiles[2] and

---

[1] 'Transcriptum indenture facte inter commissarios Anglie et Francie regum in ipsorum recessu a partibus Vasconie super forma commissionum faciendarum in negociis eis commissis, quequidem indentura signatur sigillis commissariorum predictorum et liberata fuit magistro Roberto de Stratford exhibenda clericis assignandis ad examinandum processum predictum.' D.D.C. 30/3/17; cf. ibid. 30/1/3 and 30/3/16, copies of the same.

[2] This refers to the War of St-Sardos. The English officials who destroyed the bastide of Montpezat and massacred the French who were found there were summoned to answer for their actions before Parlement at Toulouse. When they failed to appear, an *arrêt* of banishment was pronounced against them. See *supra*, p. 14; Gavrilovitch, *Étude sur le traité de 1259*, pp. 109–10; Chaplais, *The War of Saint-Sardos*, pp. xii–xiii.

such lands as were confiscated and acquired by those kings by special sentences in individual crimes committed at other times than during war, be restored to the rights and status they had at the time Charles count of Valois left Paris to seize the duchy for the lord king Charles in 1324; and that such subjects make recognitions, do homage, or swear oaths for those things they recover, according to the requirements of the circumstances to whichever king at present holds as purprestures those things to be restored; and that such subjects be compelled thenceforth to observe the settlement.

The detailed commentary in the memorandum is obviously the work of the English representatives, for the distinction is often made between *subditi regis Francie* and *subditi nostri*. Nevertheless, it reveals the give-and-take that must have characterized the sessions of the commission and it illustrates admirably what fundamental questions the mere wording of letters of commission involved.

Videtur cedula onerosa, so the document runs, for seven reasons. (1) In the first place, the eleven exiles are excepted from the scheme of restoration; consequently, all French subjects will retain their lands, but not all English subjects. (2) The clause excepting lands confiscated by special sentences is objectionable, for it is not clear to the commissioners what lands are meant. (3) English subjects will actually pay homage and swear oaths of Frenchmen. (4) It is not clear whether or not after restoration has been made the French will wish to ask arrears, (5) and whether at some future time they will wish to punish those who supported the king of England. (6) The words *res occupate* (purprestures) are ill chosen, for the French claim that the things they took before the truces were lawfully possessed by them. (7) Finally, the English are worried lest this last point prejudice the petition their king intends to make to the French king regarding such lands.

Ex parte alia videtur illa cedula bona for an equal number of reasons. (1) By it the English have technical grounds for a *dilacio*, (2) and in the interim they can ascertain more fully the will of their king and duke. (3) Further, English subjects will, after all, recover what they have lost by war or in times preceding and following truces, and they certainly cannot hope to do so unless the French are likewise permitted to recover their losses. (4) An obvious advantage lies in the provision that all who possess anything in English towns will hold from the king of England, for the French understanding is that their subjects should recover everything seized by the English and hold it of the king of France—*quod est valde durum*. That, of course, meant that there would be some people in Bordeaux and other English towns who would hold immediately of the king of France. (5) The king of England will be relieved on many scores, for the *cedula* overcomes objections inherent in a previous accord reached between the two kings. That agreement provided that, whereas French subjects might recover losses sustained at any time, the English could recover losses sustained only since the time of truce. Accordingly, some English subjects would go begging and the king would have to provide compensation for them out of his own pocket. (6) Naturally if the natives (*nostrates*) recover their lands, they will make better subjects of the king of England. (7) It is clear, finally, that unless the king consents to these suggestions as a basis for settlement, English subjects must attempt to recover their lands through their own actions, and the outcome of such attempts is doubtful.

After casting the merits and demerits of their scheme the commissioners drew their general conclusions, and these constituted a favourable recommendation of their proposals. The question of the eleven exiles, it would seem, was not a great drawback, for the French had assured them that it was the intention of their king to treat all persons equally. Likewise they did not see much force in the exception concerning lands confiscated by special sentences, because their colleagues had agreed to restore all lands regardless of the time or nature of the confiscations. The provision relating to the doing of homage was not very desirable, but it would be even less desirable for the king of France to have homage for the lands he had seized and continued to hold. The question of arrears, on the other hand, applied to both sides equally; and while there might be considerable difficulty in determining such matters, the commissioners were of the opinion that arrears should be allowed. On two points, however, they urged special action. Some guarantee was necessary to ensure that those who had supported the king of England should not be punished in the future for events that had already transpired. The words *res capte* might be substituted for *res occupate* to satisfy the French objection on the verbal technicality. Such a change would not prejudice the king of England's proposed petition, for there were other grounds on which the petition might be founded.

Apparently, then, the judges adjourned their task because of technical defects in their letters of commission. If those could be remedied, there was a possibility that some amicable settlement of Anglo-French claims might be reached. And, as a matter of fact, the suggestions of the commissioners were acted upon. In 1333 a draft memorial was presented to the English council asking for the appointment of new commissioners. It took care to urge that letters should be drawn up in such a way that they would contain no defects that the French might exploit in order to bring cognizance of cases to the Parlement de Paris. The author of the memorial was aware of French tactics: he demanded that English commissioners bring their appeals to their own king instead of to the French court.[1] Somewhat later another person made a suggestion intended to prod the French king into action, threatening to seek the intervention of the pope unless Philip kept his promise to appoint new commissioners.[2] Actually, both Edward and Philip made new appointments in 1334, and the letters they issued were based upon the recommendations that had been made by the original commission.[3]

The new commissioners met only to violate the famous admonition of Fulbert of Chartres against 'gnawing the bone of contention with the tooth of temerarious cavilling'. It was

[1] D.D.C. 28/2/21.   [2] Ibid. 28/3/18.   [3] Ibid. 30/3/15.

THE PROCESS OF AGEN

the beginning of the end. On 29 September 1334 they met in the house of the Carmelites at Langon.[1] The French quibbled again over the terms of the letters of commission. There was disagreement over whether restitutions should be made only in Agenais or throughout the duchy. The English flatly refused to surrender the castles of Blanquefort and Veyrines.[2] In October the seneschal of Gascony told Edward that a French representative had gone to Paris to obtain letters from the king of France that would authorize the French commissioners to seize the county of Ponthieu until the English restored the two castles. He wrote also of the French proposal to submit doubtful cases under seal to Paris for determination by Parlement.[3] A screed addressed to the English chancellor added further accusations. French officials were threatening Gascon nobles with disinheritance, exile, and death in order to induce them to transfer their allegiance to the king of France. The French seneschal in Agenais had appealed to Parlement to confirm the original condemnation made by Charles IV. To such weighty warnings was attached a plea that clerks with sufficient wages be appointed to examine the situation.[4] Other allegations came from the commissioners themselves. The English complained that their French colleagues were attempting to extort oaths of fealty to the king of France.[5] And on that note the process comes to an end. The opportunity for peaceful settlement of the difficulties between the two kings had passed. Other attempts were to be made, it is true, but these were half-hearted proffers made at the very moment when Edward III was setting about to erect in the north a vast coalition against Philip VI. The process of Agen was a failure, as were the processes of Montreuil and Périgueux before it, because feudal and national claims were incompatible.

[1] Langon, *dép*. Gironde.
[2] D.D.C. 30/3/8; ibid. 30/3/7, a fragmentary copy. Cf. Gascon Rolls 46, m. 2. Blanquefort and Veyrines, *dép*. Gironde, *arr*. Bordeaux.
[3] D.D.C. 30/3/10–12; cf. ibid. 30/3/9, 28/3/23. Philip actually was transferring cases to Parlement (*Archives historiques du département de la Gironde*, vii. 166).
[4] D.D.C. 28/3/24; cf. ibid. 30/4/7. [5] Ibid. 32/13, 28/8/38.

IV

CALENDARS AND REGISTERS

'... dominus Edwardus, rex Anglie illustris, sollerterque con siderans quot dispendia quotque dilacionum periculosarum fastidia, defectus et carencie litterarum, processuum, et memorandorum in negociis vel causis suis et subditorum suorum ad instructionem necessariorum vel utilium, eo quod ubilibet reposita ex difficili reperiebantur, causas hujusmodi et negocia prosequentibus frequencius intulerunt ... quibusdam clericis suis ... injunxit quod distinctis titulis certum facerent kalendare ...'

Preface to the Gascon calendar (1322)

THE reasons that lay behind the creation of the office of *custos processuum* led at the same time to the compilation of a series of great manuscript books of diplomatic documents.[1] The practical impossibility of dealing with a large number of originals, combined with the necessity of remedying the rather sad condition of the main depositories, demanded that records in constant use should be accessible in summary form. As a general rule, originals were thought too precious to be let outside the confines of the treasury; by far the majority of documents in the archives of the keeper of processes were transcripts. The books that proved effective in

---

[1] For the student of administrative history the fourteenth century offers a series of notebooks and registers of which a profitable survey could be made. See Maitland's article on 'The History of the Register of Original Writs' (*Collected Papers of F. W. Maitland*, ii. 110–73), Bock's paper, 'Some New Documents illustrating the Early Years of the Hundred Years War (1353–1356)' (*Bulletin of the John Rylands Library*, xv (1931), 60–99), the manuscript of Thomas Hoccleve on the common forms of the privy seal (*Catalogue of Additions to the MSS. in the British Museum in 1854–1875*, ii. 3, edited as 'The Formulary of Thomas Hoccleve' by Mrs. Elna Jean Bentley (Ph.D. dissertation, Emory University, 1965); H. C. Schulz, 'Thomas Hoccleve, Scribe', in *Speculum* xii (1937), 71–81), the *Liber epistolaris Ricardi de Bury*, ed. Denholm-Young, and the privy seal registers mentioned by Perroy (*Diplomatic Correspondence of Richard II*, pp. xvii–xxvii).

overcoming those difficulties were Liber A and Liber B, products of the reign of Edward I, and the Gascon register and Gascon calendar and Bishop Stapeldon's calendar, made during the reign of Edward II.

Liber A is a manuscript of 457 folios, of which 115 are blank and two are missing; its companion is a smaller volume of 371 folios, of which 115 are blank.[1] Unlike the two later books, these are *registra munimentorum*, and consequently contain more than a mere inventory of documents then existing in the various archives of the state; all the materials found in them are complete transcripts of originals. The contents cover a wide range of subjects relating both to internal affairs and to foreign relations. Under the latter head fall transcripts of papal bulls and treaties, letters, and other diplomatic documents of the reigns of Henry III and Edward I concerning relations with Brabant, Norway, Navarre, Aragon, Castile, France, Savoy, and Sicily, as well as matter relating to the English possessions in France.[2]

A table of contents at the beginning of each book indicates the groups of documents that follow. Various signs and figures mark the principal divisions, while letters refer to the chests, hampers, coffers, and other receptacles in which the originals of the documents transcribed in the volumes were deposited. Someone in the seventeenth century numbered the folios to facilitate reference. Most of the entries are accompanied by brief summaries written in the margin apparently after the actual transcription had been done, and papal bulls are noted *canabi* or *serici*, that is, whether letters of justice or letters of grace. There are many fine majuscule letters into which the scribes drew amusing faces, perhaps those of their fellow clerks. They were done at the transcribers' leisure, for many blanks are left for these initial capitals.

The large number of blank folios were placed between the various major divisions to allow space for additions at

[1] Misc. Bks. Exch. T.R., vols. 274, 275.
[2] See the lists printed in Giuseppi, *Guide to MSS. preserved in the Public Record Office*, i. 211–12.

some future time.¹ Liber A is actually incomplete. The missing sections are 'Titulus Scocie in cofro T, Quidam rotulus de processu placitorum inter quasdam partes Baione', and 'Item, libri compoti garderobe de anno xix°, videlicet, libri contrarotulatoris'. Among the items in the coffer marked T were evidences found in ancient chronicles existing in monasteries of England and Scotland proving the right of the king of England to the lordship of Scotland.² Other entries included a treaty between Henry II and the king of Scotland, and documents bearing on homage and the Scottish arbitration of Edward I.

The handwriting in the two volumes indicates that they were the work of several different persons over a period of several years. Many of the marginal summaries are written in a script curiously like that found in contemporary notarial instruments, and this suggests that the clerks who performed the task were notaries from the chancery and the wardrobe. On the other hand, the lack of specific names in the recorded payments for the transcription raises a question whether the transcribers were of sufficient importance to be notaries.

Work on the registers probably began shortly after September 1282. At that time three clerks submitted an inventory of certain documents seen in the treasury at Edinburgh.³ The reported collection included various papal bulls and diplomatic documents touching England, Norway, and Flanders, particularly as to their relations with Scotland.

---

[1] Sir Goronwy Edwards, however, thinks that these blank folios indicate the method used in compiling the volumes. According to his theory, quaternions were distributed to various clerks, each of whom filled as much of his quaternion as his material required. As different clerks wrote different sections, fresh quaternions were used to begin each new class of records, and accordingly a great amount of parchment remained blank.

[2] '... ex quo liquido apparet quod reges Anglie ab antiquo habuerunt et habere debent subjectionem, homagium, fidelitatem, et superius dominium regni Scocie.' These exist today among the Scottish Documents Exch. 100/112, 139, 140, 152–62, 164–71, and 3/46. Many of them were printed by Palgrave, *Documents and Records illustrating the History of Scotland*, i. 56–134.

[3] Rymer, i. 615. By a recent act of parliament these documents were returned to their original depository in Scotland.

CALENDARS AND REGISTERS 115

Assuming that the documents in coffer *T* were to have been the last transcribed into Liber A, the date of its completion would be about 1292, the date of the settlement of the Scottish arbitration. Liber B appears to be the later of the two registers. The fact that it is better organized and written and that most of the blanks left for initial capitals are in the second volume substantiates that conclusion.

The greater part of actual transcription was done in the wardrobe, possibly under supervision of the controller. Entries in wardrobe books of 1290, 1297, and 1300 reveal that a collection of bulls and documents relating to the marriage of the Maid of Norway and to the confederation with the count of Flanders were in the archives of the department.[1] The following payments by the wardrobe in 1300 and 1305 refer to the expenses of transcribing Liber B:

Domino Henrico de Sandwico, capellano domini Johannis de Drokenesford, pro denariis per ipsum solutis pro stipendiis quorundam clericorum transcribencium quasdam compromissiones factas in curia Romana per nuncios regis Anglie et regis Francie, per manus, Johannis Poveray, apud Westmonasterium, mense Maii, 5s. Eidem pro pergameno empto ad dictas compromissiones inscribendas, 1s. 2d. Summa, 6s. 2d.[2]

Domino Roberto de Cotingham, moranti apud Westmonasterium per preceptum regis ad faciendum transcribere omnas bullas et previlegia a summis pontificibus temporibus retroactis regi concessa, ac in alia scripta diversa tangencia confederaciones factas inter Anglie et Francie reges, et alia scripta in thesauraria regis apud Turrim London' inventa, pro expensis suis et quorumdam clericorum de cancellaria morantium ibidem in comitiva ejusdem Roberti pro dictis bullis et scriptis transcribendis et examinandis, a xxiij die Novembris usque xvij diem Decembris, utroque computato, per xxv dies, per quas morabatur circa idem negocium, ut in pane, vino, cervisa, cane, pisce, salsa, busca, et aliis ad expensas predictas necessariis, 9 *li.* 17s. 10d. Eidem, pro denariis per ipsum solutis sex clericis de cancellaria transcribentibus et examinantibus bullas et scripta predicta pro stipendiis suis infra dictum tempus, 37s.[3]

---

[1] Chan. Misc. 4/5, fos. 10, 11*d*; ibid. 4/6, fo. 5; *L.Q.G.*, p. 59.
[2] *L.Q.G.*, p. 67.   [3] E.A. 369/11, fo. 34.

After completion of the work the transcripts in the registers were checked against the original documents for accuracy. That is the only satisfactory explanation for a series of names found among the marginalia of each book; for example, *examinatur per J. de Haverhulle*. Other names, difficult to identify, are those of Draghton, Jernemue, Havonte, Bosse, Tumbe, J. de Derb', Robertus de Colle, and Stowe.[1] In inserting their names the clerks were following the customary chancery and wardrobe practice of placing on writs and debentures the names of the responsible clerks.[2]

The treaty of 1259 raised more questions than it settled. The working out of its intricate terms had a profound effect on archival history. The Gascon Rolls begin in the reign of Henry III and continue until the fall of Bordeaux; the *trésors des chartes* at Bordeaux and at other centres in Gascony date from the administrative reform of the duchy by Edward I. A distinction must be made between records preserved in Gascony and those preserved by what would now be called the Home Government. The former were the products of local administration and were probably more numerous than their counterparts in Westminster and in the Tower. There was already a 'keeper of the rolls' in Gascony by 1284,[3] and the Gascon ordinances of Edward I must have resulted in a considerable bulk of records. The constable of Bordeaux, for example, was to 'have another faithful and suitable clerk for whom he is willing to answer who shall be continually in the same castle [of L'Ombrière] to write papers and rolls pertaining to the office of the aforesaid constabulary'. Again, 'it is ordered that in addition there be in all bailliages a

---

[1] Of these, Robert Cole appears in *C.C.R.* (1279–88), p. 386; a Hugh, an Adam, and a John Gernemuth (Jeremuta) ibid. (1272–9), p. 111, ibid. (1279–88), p. 548, ibid. (1288–96), pp. 124, 272, *C.P.R.* (1272–81), p. 272, and ibid. (1281–92), pp. 178, 352; while both a Walter and a John Stowe are in *C.C.R.* (1279–88), p. 544, ibid. (1288–96), p. 447, and in *C.P.R.* (1292–1301), p. 339. John of Derby was a chancery clerk employed in the wardrobe (MS. Add. 7966 A, fol. 47).

[2] Maxwell-Lyte, *The Great Seal of England*, p. 266.

[3] *G.C.*, no. 194.

scribe of bailliages, a public notary'. Then, there were records of assizes, judges of appeals, auditors of causes, the constable's controller, receivers, collectors of customs, and baillis; in short, the same sorts of documents now to be found in the Public Record Office.[1] These were augmented, at least on one occasion, 23 May 1291, by transcripts of thirty-two letters relating to the duchy furnished to the seneschal, John Havering, by John Droxford, controller of the wardrobe in London.[2] But what the Gascon archives really contained can only be guessed at, because so far as the duchy of Aquitaine is concerned, the Gascon War of 1294–7 had as cataclysmic an effect on local archives as did the French Revolution.

The English constable at Bordeaux at the time, Robert Leisseth, faced with the possible loss of the city, sent the records first to a house of the Friars Preachers in Bordeaux and then to England for safe keeping. These were 'transcripts of ancient registers of feudal recognitions and of charters and a great many other documents', presumably housed in the castle of L'Ombrière at Bordeaux, by which the king's council in Gascony 'was accustomed to inform itself concerning lands and ancient laws, liberties, and conditions of the country'.[3] But the crew of the ship in which they were being transported, because they had not been paid their wages, dumped the whole lot in the house of the White Friars on Oléron and went their way. Soon afterwards—shortly after 22 March 1294—the French took the island, plundered the friary, and captured the records.[4] Apparently only one of the records was ever recovered, and this was 'a book with a black cover, containing part of the fees and dues of the lord king and duke in that duchy of Aquitaine,

---

[1] *G.R.*, no. 35.
[2] *G.C.*, nos. 1209–43.
[3] D.D.C. 27/14, fo. 3ᵛ, printed in *Speculum*, xvii (1942), pp. 81–2. It had apparently been the custom to issue important documents in duplicate, one copy being sent to England and the other kept in the treasury at Bordeaux (*G.R.*, no. 153).
[4] Galbraith, 'The Tower as an Exchequer Record Office in the Reign of Edward II', *Essays in Medieval History presented to T. F. Tout*, p. 234.

in which book are contained 118 written folios and 5 blank folios'.[1] This was bought from an esquire of Oléron about 1302–3 by Pierre Aimeri, constable of Bordeaux, for 15 *livres tournois*.[2] In 1310, on the eve of the process of Périgueux, John Salmon, bishop of Norwich, and Jean de Bretagne, earl Richmond, made an extended inquiry into the state of Gascony. One of their commissions was 'to set up a public archive',[3] and the mangled report submitted to them listing the 139 documents found in the castle of Bordeaux bears eloquent testimony to the appalling state of the archives.[4]

In July 1315 Master Guillaume de Cazes, on behalf of the king's council in Gascony, presented a petition to the council at Westminster.[5] It stated that, owing to the loss of the documents, the Gascon council had been unable to argue with the French over seizures and breaches of peace, and that by the English commissioners at the process of Périgueux, 'sine dictorum originalium transcriptis sufficiens declaracio ad conservacionem juris ... fieri non potest'. Accordingly, he asked that transcripts be made and sent to the castle at Bordeaux. The records wanted were those 'in the treasury of our said lord in England, in the custody of his treasurer or of the keeper of his wardrobe', those brought back from France by Richard Burton, and those brought back by the bishop of Norwich from Gascony and surrendered in the wardrobe, as shown by a memorandum made to William Maldon, a notary public.

The petition was referred to Elias Joneston, whose expertise made him the most knowledgeable clerk in such matters. His report outlines the contents of the memorandum to Maldon, which fell into ten groups: letters and commissions of acquittance from the chancery rolls from 1259; acquittances from Cahorsin; expenses of knights for two

---

[1] E.A. 160/1, m. 3.
[2] *Les Archives historiques du département de la Gironde*, tome lv, p. 5.
[3] G.C., no. 217. [4] G.R., no. 42.
[5] D.D.C. 27/14, fo. 3ᵛ, printed in *Speculum*, xvii (1942), 81–2.

years; homages of Armagnac, Fezensac, Fézensaguet, 'which can be found in a large sack in the Tower of London and in the coffers of the wardrobe there'; homage of the viscount of Auvillar and Lectoure; all the documents contained in the same sack relating to Saintonge and Agenais, especially those involving the count, Alphonse de Poitiers, and the bastides; privileges granted by the kings and dukes to communities, churches, and others, to be gathered from grants and confirmation of these privileges and the replies of the council in parliament to petitions on these matters; a list of churches founded by the kings and dukes; cases to come before the duke; and feudal recognitions, copies of charters, and debts, the last to be taken from a collation of the ancient rolls of accounts of the duchy of Aquitaine.

On 29 November 1318 by a writ under privy seal dated at York, John Hildesle received instructions to compile registers of documents pertaining to the duchy of Aquitaine, and his wages were set at 4*s*. per day. Elias Joneston was associated with Hildesle. Other clerks who assisted were William le Eyr, Roger Nottingham, Thomas Chester, John Newark, John Dunwich, and John Darlington.[1] Most of the Gascon documents were kept at this time in the wardrobe treasury in the Tower, and there in all probability the work of transcribing was carried out. The wardrobe treasury was the outer chamber (today part of the Sword Room) next the Black Hall (now the Weapon Room) in the White Tower. It was secured by two large and two small locks on the outer doors and contained at least forty-five locked coffers in which the muniments were stored. On 17 November 1318 the forty-nine keys to these locks had been surrendered by Roger Northburgh, the outgoing keeper, to Roger Waltham, the new keeper, at the exchequer in a bag bearing the seals of Henry of Canterbury and Elias Joneston. Waltham delivered them to Walter Stapeldon, treasurer of the exchequer, on the following 7 December, 'pro scrutinio de quibusdam

---

[1] Issue Rolls, 186, mm. 4, 5, 11; K.R. Memoranda Rolls 92, Michaelmas *Recorda*, m. 5d; printed in *E.H.R.* liv (1939), 298–9.

rebus Londonii faciendo'.¹ Other documents were borrowed as needed from the archives of the exchequer.²

The scribes worked from originals and transcripts, which were stored in roughly the same order as they had been in the reign of Edward I. It may be assumed that a sheaf of documents was handed to each of the fifteen clerks, who then proceeded to fill his quaternion. The transcription was then checked by an examiner, who made a notation on the document before returning it to its coffer.³ Curiously enough, no notice appears to have been taken of the fact that more than half of the documents in the first volume compiled had already been copied into Liber B. This was available in the Exchequer Treasury of Receipt.

The work seems to have been completed by 6 March 1319, the date of full payment made to the scribes by merchants of the Bardi Society.⁴ The total recorded cost is £33. 18*s*. 7*d*. In a little more than three months the clerks had copied a total of 991 folios and 16 *pargamena*, which were eventually bound up in five registers covered in green leather: Registers A (256 folios), B (146 folios), C (254 folios and 13 *pargamena*), D (265 folios and 3 *pargamena*), and E (70 folios).⁵ The 144 quaternions were handed over to William Montague, the newly appointed seneschal, who took them with him when he left for Bordeaux in March 1319.⁶ They were not to remain there long. The transcripts were so full of errors that on 24 November 1319 an order went out directing that they be returned to London for rechecking against the originals.⁷ Shortly afterwards Hildesle left for

---

¹ Galbraith, op. cit., pp. 231–47.

² K.R. Memoranda Rolls 92, Michaelmas *Recorda*, m. 5d, printed in *E.H.R.* liv (1939), 299.

³ e.g. D.D.C. 25/2/2, which is one membrane of a roll, is endorsed 'Examinatur hoc instrumentum cum vii cedulis ad prosecucionem J[ohannis] de Hildesle' (= G.R. 59–62).

⁴ Issue Rolls 186, m. 11, printed in *E.H.R.* liv (1939), 299.

⁵ D.D.C. 28/10/5, printed *supra*, p. 44 n. 1.

⁶ *C.P.R.* (1317–21), pp. 311, 312, 314.

⁷ Gascon Rolls 33 (13–14 Edward II), m. 3, under the rubric *De transcriptis liberandis magistro Johanni de Hildesle*. I owe this reference to Dr. Pierre Chaplais.

CALENDARS AND REGISTERS

Gascony to collect the quaternions.[1] They were returned to London and deposited in the wardrobe, where they were bound into five volumes covered with green leather. The work of revision, if actually undertaken, was never completed, and the manuscripts were never sent back to Gascony. They are last mentioned in 1336,[2] and the only surviving one is British Museum Cottonian MS. Julius E. i.[3] It contains 346 documents covering almost every aspect of Gascon history from 1027 to 1318.

The Gascon petition of 1315 and the sorting of documents by Hildesle and his colleagues possibly attracted the attention of Walter Stapeldon, who became treasurer of the exchequer in February 1320. At any rate, Stapeldon soon decided on a similar compilation of a more comprehensive character for use by the home government. On 6 August 1320, by warrant under the privy seal, Master Henry of Canterbury was ordered

to make a calendar divided into titles of all processes, letters, instruments, and rolls touching the duchy of Aquitaine in the treasury and wardrobe, in order to have a fuller memory thereof in the future, as shall seem good to him, and according to what has been previously said to him by the king's council, and to cause the matter to be done by those whom he shall see fit to take for this purpose, and to put in due form

---

[1] His letters of protection are dated 22 November (*C.P.R.* (1317–21), p. 401), and he received an advance of 20 marks towards his expenses on 29 November (Issue Rolls 189, m. 3).   [2] *Supra*, p. 45 n. 1.

[3] My edition of this, *Gascon, Register A (Series of 1318–19)*, for the British Academy, is in press. A second series of registers, copies of the first, numbered A, B, C, D, was compiled in 1354–5 and sent to Bordeaux. Some time after 1468 these volumes were transferred to the Chambre des comptes in Paris. Only one, Liber B, has survived. This found its way, shortly after 1600, into the library of the dukes of Brunswick, where it was catalogued as Wolfenbüttel MS. 2311. Bémont edited it in 1914, but identified it incorrectly (*Recueil d'actes relatifs à l'administration des rois d'Angleterre en Guyenne au XIIIe siècle; Recogniciones feodorum in Aquitania*). Between 1455 and 1468 a third series of registers was compiled for local use at Bordeaux. These were copies of those of 1354–5, to which two more, E and F, were added. These have completely disappeared. See Trabut-Cussac, 'Les Cartulaires gascons d'Édouard II, d'Édouard III et de Charles VII', *Bibliothèque de l'École des Chartes*, cxi (1953), 65–106, and my 'The Archives of Gascony under English Rule', *The American Archivist*, 25 (1962), 315–21.

the undecided processes pending and continued until the next parliament of France, for the information of the king's advocates, and to cause to be transcribed what he shall deem necessary before the quinzaine of Michaelmas [13 October].¹

A mandate in pursuance to the treasurer and chamberlains of the exchequer ordered them to allow Henry free access to the archives and to pay his wages.

Apparently nothing was done about the matter for a long while, for the clerks in charge of the processes in the court of France excused the delay in exercising their functions by blaming Henry of Canterbury. He, strangely enough, excused himself on the grounds that he was unwilling to undertake the job alone.² Soon afterwards Master John Bush, a wardrobe notary, and Master Jordan Morant were commanded to help him. Bush, however, was unable to assist and in June 1321 Master Richard Burton was appointed in his place.³ Neither Burton nor Morant did much, for Elias Joneston and Roger Sheffeld, experts in such matters, replaced them in July 1321, a month before Stapeldon left office.⁴ The instructions were somewhat extended by this last writ. In addition to making a calendar of the specified documents they were 'to have the said documents stored separately, so that they can easily be found, and when necessary to have transcripts made of such instruments'. The exchequer and the wardrobe were to share the expense of compilation. Even then, it was not until the whip-hand and reforming zeal of the bishop of Exeter, who came back into office in May 1322, had been loosed that the task was completed. The finished calendar in duplicate was delivered into the treasury by Stapeldon on 21 May 1322 and by him given to Robert Baldock, keeper of the privy seal, on 5 December, no doubt for custody in the wardrobe.⁵ The duplicate of it

¹ *C.C.R.* (1318–23), p. 319; cf. Anc. Cor. xxxii. 77, dated 5 October at Sheen.
² D.D.C. 27/12/24, printed in my 'Henry of Canterbury', *E.H.R.* lvii (1942), 310.
³ *C.C.W.* i. 521.   ⁴ *C.P.R.* (1321–4), p. 5.
⁵ Palgrave, *Antient Kalendars and Inventories of the Exchequer*, iii. 437; Tout, *Place of Edward II*, pp. 170–2. Exch. L.T.R. Memoranda Roll 92, m. 18ᵛ: 'De

was later sent to Bordeaux and was still in the archives of the constable in 1435.[1] This copy has presumably disappeared.

The calendar is a volume of 100 folios, done on parchment in fine court hand.[2] The handwriting suggests that it was largely the work of Elias Joneston, although the task was too great for him to complete alone in such a short time. The preface, which curiously enough omits any mention of Stapeldon, contains interesting comments by the compilers. It begins with a miniature discourse on kingship, stating that the duty of a prince was not only to work for the well-being of his subjects, making them rich and happy, but also by his foresight to guard them against any possible vexation and injury. Therefore Edward, realizing the dangers, delays, and inconveniences caused his people by the inaccessibility of documents scattered throughout the treasury and wardrobe, set his clerks to the task of making the calendar. They make no effort to conceal how unwelcome was the thankless task that they felt ill prepared to undertake; God alone, *ex quo omnis est sapiencia*, had given them the knowledge indispensable to such a work. They beg indulgence, therefore, for any possible gaps, imperfections in method, and errors of classification.

After collecting and examining the documents, Henry of Canterbury and his colleagues divided them into five sections, the first two dealing with Anglo-French conventions and the remaining three with Guyenne. The first section

quibusdam libris tangentibus ducatum Aquitanie: Memorandum quod xxj die Maii hoc anno [1322] W[alterus] Exoniensis episcopus, thesaurius, liberavit hic duos libros compositos per magistrum Henricum de Cantuaria qui intitulantur sic, "Kalendare seu reportorium munimentorum et memorandorum ducatus Aquitanie tangencium", compositum anno gracie 1321, et liberantur camerariis de scaccario ad custodiendum etc. Postea quinto die Decembris anno xvj°, unus dictorum librorum liberatur magistro Roberto de Baldok.'

[1] Exch. L.T.R. Foreign Accounts 70, 75.

[2] *Kalendare litterarum, processuum, et memorandorum ducatus Aquitanie* (Misc. Bks. Exch. T.R., vol. 187), edited by me as *The Gascon Calendar of 1322*. M. Déprez published the preface, index, and three of the relevant writs in 'Le Trésor des chartes de Guyenne', *Mélanges Bémont*, pp. 234–42.

contains papal bulls relating to Aquitaine and to marriages; letters of the king of Castile and his proctors touching Aquitaine; letters of the kings of France and their envoys on various peaces and truces; similar letters of the king of England and his envoys, and of the French ambassadors, treating also of marriage contracts; a notarial instrument on the compromise of the two kings made through the mediation of Boniface VIII; and letters of the kings relating to Aquitaine.

The second section consists of private letters addressed to Edward I by the queen of France, his brother, Edmund, and Hugh de Ver during the negotiations at Paris on the subject of the surrender of Gascony to the king of France, and Edward's replies to them; divers schedules, memoranda, and letters of the queen of France and Edmund on the same subject; rolls and memoranda touching the Gascon war, and preparations made before and after it; records bearing on various embassies sent to France, England, and the papal curia; rolls, schedules, and memoranda concerning the revision and completion of truces and alliances, including reasons to justify the king of England in declaring war, reasons why the Scots should not be included in the peace, memoranda of Henry's visit to France and an act of Blanche, daughter of the French king, public instruments of peace between the two kings and a copy of letters of grace conceded by Philip, and various aspects of the processess of Montreuil and Périgueux.

The third section is composed of letters regarding the island of Oléron, Bordeaux, Bazas, Bergerac, Bayonne, various parts of Landes, Béarn and its count, Armagnac, Fezensac, Bigorre, Agenais, Saintonge, and Périgord, along with obligations, quittances, and letters to and from various persons in Aquitaine.

The fourth section concerns the process on the bastide of Agen between the king of England and the executors of Alphonse de Poitiers; and processes between the king and the count of La Marche, the men of Auvillar, the viscount of Fronsac, Marie, lady of Aubeterre, over Castillon, Bernard de Ravignan, Raymond de Castenet, the bishop and chapter of Puy over Bigorre, W. Eschamat, Gausbert Fumel, the abbot and convent of Sauve-Majeure, Gombald de Tiran, Raymond de la Cour, the prior of La Réole, the dean of Bordeaux over the priory of Belvès, the abbot and convent of Grandselve, the archbishop of Bordeaux over *londrage*, and Jourdain de l'Isle over a duel.

The final section contains rolls, schedules, and memoranda relating to the seneschal of Saintonge, Gaston de Béarn, and to Bordeaux, Périgueux and its environs, Bayonne and environs, Landes, and Bigorre; various processes, acts, memoranda, and instruments having to do with Aquitaine; Gascon petitions and answers; indentures of similar instruments surrendered by the wardrobe to envoys and later restored; inquiries made in Gascony in 1310; accounts and revenues of the duchy; and several registers and cartularies containing material relating to the duchy.

The compilers divided each of the five sections into chapters and placed an index at the beginning of the book whereby its contents could be easily ascertained. It was an eminently practical work designed to facilitate the use of diplomatic documents; blank pages were left so that the contents could be kept up to date. The enrolled documents, originals or copies, were placed in coffers, baskets, and sacks which were marked by signs corresponding to those in the margin of the calendar. Such an index to the archives must have seen considerable service; no doubt it was a great boon to Elias Joneston, who had custody of it from 1329 to 1336.[1] Transcripts were also made from it on three occasions immediately following its completion. Certain documents relating to Béarn, France, and Scotland were needed in negotiations, and the list of copies to be taken was drawn up from the pages of the calendar.[2]

The Gascon calendar apparently suggested to Bishop Stapeldon the idea of a similar work comprising general

[1] *Supra,* p. 42 n. 2. [2] D.D.C. 29/9/11, 29/10/6, 22/9/128.

documents. The compilers definitely state in the preface that the second calendar was done at the treasurer's instigation. On 28 July 1321, while the Gascon calendar was still in progress, Henry of Canterbury, Elias Joneston, and Roger Sheffeld were ordered to make 'a calendar of all letters, processes, instruments, and memoranda in the treasury and wardrobe affecting the realm and the king's lands in Ireland, Wales, and Scotland, after the completion of the beforementioned calendar of documents touching the duchy of Aquitaine'.[1] Canterbury, however, took no active part in the work; Joneston and Sheffeld, assisted by three exchequer clerks, carried out the actual compilation.[2]

The calendar, completed late in 1323, represents Stapeldon's efforts to organize the treasury as a record office. In the preface he states how unsatisfactory the state of the archives had become, because of the practice of moving or transferring royal muniments from person to person and from place to place. Consequently, the calendar is only concerned in a secondary fashion with diplomatic documents and is the least important of the several compilations in this respect.[3] The method, however, was precisely that used in compiling the Gascon calendar. Of the twenty-seven divisions, only thirteen concern diplomacy: (3) papal bulls; (10) quittances relating to foreign pensions and loans; (11) homages, safe conducts, inquests, enrolments, etc.; (18–27) letters and memoranda relating to Holland, Bar, Brabant, Sicily, Ponthieu, Castile, Aragon, and Burgundy. Stapeldon's calendar, then, served as a supplement to the Gascon calendar and as a means of bringing Liber A and Liber B up to date.

[1] *C.P.R.* (1321–4), p. 7. [2] Galbraith, op. cit., p. 236.
[3] The complete calendar is printed by Palgrave, op. cit. i. 1–155.

V

AGENTS AND MECHANICS OF DIPLOMACY

The medieval English foreign office consisted roughly of two main branches or divisions. The first was a quasi-permanent organization, an office extraordinary, which, although intimately connected with the great departments of state, actually existed as a separate organ of administration. Its keeper, to draw a rough analogy, was a sort of permanent under-secretary of state for foreign affairs. The scope of his activities, however, was necessarily limited. With all his multifarious duties he could scarcely be concerned with every phase of the everyday conduct of diplomacy: it was enough that he should keep his archives and use them for the benefit both of those who formulated and of those who executed English foreign policy. Had his office been otherwise, had it embraced everything concerned with diplomacy, it would, indeed, scarcely have been medieval. There remains, then, the second division, which has to do with the envoy and the mechanics of ordinary diplomatic representation. It also concerns the roles played by the council, the chancery, the exchequer, and the wardrobe in foreign affairs, particularly in relation to the activities of the English diplomat.

(1) THE ENVOY

What were some of the usages of diplomacy during the medieval period and what, in the medieval mind, was an envoy? Several treatises, based on papal decretals, were written about *legati* of the thirteenth century, referring mainly to the papal legate rather than to the secular diplomat. In his *Speculum legatorum*, however, Guilelmus Durandus offers a definition of both types. He writes, 'Legatus est seu dici potest, quicumque ab alio missus est . . . siue a principe, vel a papa ad alios . . . siue ab aliqua ciuitate, vel prouincia ad principem vel ad alium. . . . Sed et nuncii, quos apud nos hostes mittunt, legati dicuntur, quorum legatorum causa sancta res est.'[1] He qualifies his definition by two further statements: 'Potestas legati dependet ex virtute literarum. Litera legationis debet continere principalem causam commissionis legati.'[2] The term, *legatus* or ambassador, then, implied two essentials: a person properly accredited according to an established formula; and a person empowered to represent his employer, not merely to express his point of view and to execute his wishes, but to personify his dignity. The phrase 'to personify his dignity' is an important one. As Rawdon Brown has pointed out, the consideration of one court for another was shown by the ceremonial with which envoys were received, 'and the minute accounts of these receptions with which the diplomatic archives abound, are not the effusions of gratified vanity, but rather the narratives of facts of political significance'.[3] The ambassador represented the most solemn type of diplomatic agent, and in the fifteenth century the right to an embassy had come to be accorded in Rome only to rulers of independent states, unless the pope chose to make an exception. Further, it was generally admitted that private individuals could not employ ambassadors, but merely *nuncii* or *procuratores*.[4]

[1] Hrabar, ed., *De legatis et legationibus tractatus varii*, p. 32. [2] Ibid. 34.
[3] *Calendar of State Papers, Venetian*, i. li. For example, Edward III's cool reception of the messengers of Philip reveals the attitude of the English court towards France (Froissart, ii. 228), and the grace with which the doge of Venice replied to the agent of the English crown reflects a certain desire for amicable relations with England (*Cal. State Papers, Venetian*, i. 8–9), as do the festivities that marked the arrival of the English envoys in the Low Countries (Jean le Bel, i. 78, 121; Froissart, ii. 189–90, 351, 376, 378).
[4] Behrens, 'Treatises on the Ambassador Written in the Fifteenth and Early Sixteenth Centuries', *E.H.R.* li (1936), 619. Cf. Queller, *The Office of Ambassador in*

Actually, the word 'ambassador' seldom occurs in English records,[1] and even *legatus* is rare, save in reference to the papal legate. The usual terms are *nuncius, nuncius specialis*, or simply *fidelis noster*, and the second of these is customarily employed in connection with *procurator*. What the distinction was between the *legatus* and the *nuncius* in the thirteenth and fourteenth centuries is not clear. In all probability the *nuncius specialis* was identical with the *legatus* or ambassador, while the difference between the *nuncius* and the *legatus* was possibly the same as that drawn in the fifteenth century. At that time the *nuncius* 'might be either the envoy of a private individual who as such had no right to an ambassador, or else of a person or a body which had such a right, but did not when employing him choose to exercise it. In this case he was simply the bearer of a message or a letter.'[2] Froissart gives a good illustration of a *nuncius* at work. The chronicler is relating the story of how the bishop of Lincoln defied the French king:

> And the bishop of Lincoln entered the chamber of the king, greeted him and bowed before him, all the other lords following. He delivered his letters to the king of France, who received them and broke the small seal that was around them. The letters were written on parchment and fixed with a great seal that hung from them. The king looked at them for a short time and then handed them to one of his clerks to be read. ... When Philip heard the letters read he turned to the bishop and began to smile, telling him that he had transacted well the business for which he was sent.[3]

the Middle Ages, p. 70: 'A very great amount of evidence exists, however, to indicate that this development was extremely rudimentary and that it did not consistently prevail anywhere, even at the papal curia, before the sixteenth century. Ambassadors were sent and received by the very widest variety of persons and corporate bodies and for all sorts of important and relatively trivial affairs.'

[1] The only instance I have noted appears in the account of Master Richard Plumstock, sent to Avignon in 1315–16. The phrase is, 'ad tractandum cum *coambaxatoribus* meis super negociis domini regis exponendis ad curiam'. E.A. 309/20.

[2] Behrens, op. cit., p. 622.

[3] Froissart, ii. 425–7. The practice of having a clerk to read diplomatic communications was also followed in England (ibid., 4e réédition, ii. 230–1).

If the fifteenth-century distinction is applicable to an earlier period, it is interesting to infer that the monarch of the thirteenth and fourteenth centuries had at his command the same subtlety employed by the modern state when it distinguishes between 'sending a note' and 'making a diplomatic representation'.

The *procurator* was originally a legal representative, and for the most part retained this characteristic. In France he was the official of the Parlement de Paris most conversant with its intricate procedure. To gain such an office a person had to be registered on the roll of Parlement, to be twenty years of age, worthy and capable, and to swear an oath.[1] The proctor-general of the Parlement bears a certain resemblance to the type of *procurator* found in diplomacy. His principal function was constantly to defend the rights of king and crown, and to watch over the integrity of the royal domain. He intervened in administration, in questions of commerce or industry, instruction or diplomacy. It was his task to communicate to the Parlement the treaties concluded by the king and to discuss their terms.[2] The diplomatic *procurator* combined the functions of the proctor and, to a more limited extent, those of the proctor-general: he was originally employed to transact legal business; only later did he assume diplomatic functions. Even then he was an agent rather than a representative. In the fifteenth century it could be said that 'the proctor spoke in his own name on behalf of his master, but the nuncius spoke in his master's name and was like a magpie or a musical instrument: "loquitur enim per se sed non a se" '.[3] That is probably the reason why credentials of envoys engaged in framing treaties contained both the terms *nuncius* and *procurator*; in such matters the agent had also to be the representative.[4]

[1] Aubert, *Histoire du parlement de Paris*, i. 219.
[2] Ibid. i. 156; ii. 183.   [3] Behrens, op. cit., p. 622.
[4] *Infra*, p. 155. Similar to the *procurator* was the *commissarius*. Queller makes a clear distinction between *nuncius* and *procurator*: 'Unlike the simple *nuncius*, the procurator could act and speak in his own person on behalf of his principal. Since he could negotiate and conclude wihout reference to the principal, the use of the

THE ENVOY

In addition to the main groups of envoys there were numerous persons whose duty it was merely to carry written messages to be delivered and read by others. Such simple errand-runners or messengers were called *cokini* (inferior servants or messengers), *valleti* and *garciones* (grooms or servant-boys), *sumetarii* (persons in charge of sumpter-horses), *cartarii* (persons in charge of carts), *sartores* (tailors), and *falconarii* (falconers).[1] Messengers had another important duty: they were assigned as escorts to foreign envoys in England. In this role they served to enforce the royal safe conduct granted to such persons and to counteract any attempts at espionage. Edward I was especially wary of foreigners and used his own messengers and couriers to accompany both messengers bearing letters and envoys.[2]

The purpose of the majority of embassies was diplomatic; that is, to draw up treaties and truces, to seek alliances, or to arrange the final settlement of terms of agreements already established. Some, however, were concerned with commercial affairs, such as the purchase of destriers in Spain and Sicily,[3] or with the redress of mercantile grievances,[4] or such business as is illustrated by the interesting series of documents printed by Rymer relating to the extradition of Thomas Gournay and others through the efforts of Giles d'Espagne.[5] The duration of an embassy naturally depended on the character of the business to be transacted, the obstinacy or agreeableness of the parties concerned, the length of the journey, and the personal ability of the envoy. To an appreciable extent it was circumscribed by the rank of the diplomat: the higher the rank of an ambassador, the more

procurator was indicated when it was desired to allow some flexibility to a trusted negotiator. For most ceremonial purposes, on the other hand, the symbolic representation of the *nuncius* was more suitable' (op. cit., p. 59).

[1] All these types can be found in E.A. 308/1, 4.
[2] Hill, *The King's Messengers 1199–1737*, pp. 95–6. For the year 1299–1300 Miss Hill has counted 359 journeys, 340 of which were domestic and 19 foreign (ibid., p. 87).
[3] Rymer, ii. 830, 862, 917.
[4] Ibid. 1011 *et passim*.
[5] Ibid. 819–21, 839, 840, 843, 850.

slowly did he travel, for the ostentation of the latter had to be in keeping with the dignity of the former.[1]

The more important English embassies were colourful affairs, expressly so in order to impress prospective allies with the wealth and might of the kingdom of England. The chronicles abound in descriptions of them. The journey of that 'gentil prelat', Henry Burghersh, bishop of Lincoln, to the Low Countries was perhaps the most famous during the years prior to the outbreak of Anglo-French hostilities in 1339. His retinue probably included minstrels,[2] and there were ten *chevaliers banerès* and forty other young bachelors who attended the feast given in London by the king to the whole company before its departure 'beyond the sea, at great expense'.[3] When the company arrived at Valenciennes, each of the barons occupied a separate hostel and dressed himself in fine clothes to meet the count of Hainault.[4] If Froissart can be believed, each lord carried 100,000 florins with which to keep his court.[5] At any rate, the journey to Valenciennes was a slow and expensive one. The people of that city marvelled at the great estate maintained by the envoys, although it must have been a strange sight to see the English knights and squires wearing a piece of white cloth over one eye in fulfilment of a vow to the demoiselles of their country never to see with both eyes until they had performed some feat of arms in the realm of France. When

[1] For example, when Henry of Lancaster, Bartholomew Burghersh, and William Montague were going abroad in 1329, thirty others accompanied them, among whom, in the retinue of Lancaster, were four knights, six clerks, and four *valleti* (Rymer, ii. 772). Forty ships were required to transport the bishop of Lincoln and his colleagues back to England in 1337 (ibid. 974), and when the bishop went abroad in 1338, fifty-seven people accompanied him (ibid. 1027). In the same year the earl of Northampton took seventy-four people with him on a mission (ibid. 997, 1039), while William de la Zouch, the king's clerk, took only five people in his company to make a hasty provision for the king's journey abroad (ibid. 762).

[2] Hist. MSS. Com., *11th Report*, iii. 216.
[3] Jean le Bel, i. 124.
[4] Froissart, ii. 347. 'Quant chil ambassadour furent venu à Valenchiennes, il se logièrent sus le marchié à leur aise en trois hostels, au Chine, à le Bourse, et à l'ostel à la Clef' (4ᵉ réédition, 354).
[5] Ibid. ii. 374.

the company arrived in Flanders many costly dinners were given in order to recommend Edward III and the English cause to the Flemish, and the venerable and wealthy Simon le Courtissien entertained lavishly in return.[1]

But the position of an envoy was not always a happy one. A safe conduct from the country to which he travelled was necessary, and a monarch's desire to protect his own interests might well restrict the activities of the envoy who could not discover some means of circumvention. One of those rare instances in which the chancery rolls throw light on the details of diplomatic practice will serve to illustrate the point. The king is sending to Ralph Basset, constable of Dover, instructions for the reception of the archbishop of Vienne and the bishop of Orange, papal envoys:

the constable is to say to them himself, as of his office, in fitting manner: 'Lords, you have come by the king's conduct, please shew it.' And when it is shewn, he is to charge the points well, saying: 'Lords, by custom it pertains to the office of constable, at the entry into the land of any stranger carrying power, especially in times of disturbance, to charge those thus entering to shew and signify to the king before all things the cause of their coming and what they bring; but it seems to me that you have done so wisely and advisedly, as appears by words of the conduct, wherefore I abstain from doing so. But, in addition, lords, as pertains to my office and is accustomed, I forbid you, on the king's behalf, from carrying or doing anything in this land that shall or may be prejudicial to or against the king, his crown, land, or any man of his land, under the peril that appertains; and that you do not henceforth receive or use any order that shall or may come to you that shall or may be prejudicial or contrary to them, as is aforesaid, under the same peril.[2]

The envoy often ran the risk of actual physical danger. Joneston, it will be remembered, spoke of his duties as being *ardua et periculosa*.[3] Even letters of safe conduct did not always afford effective protection. When Sir Nicolin de Flisco, a citizen of Genoa in the employ of Edward III,

---

[1] Ibid. 374, 377–8; 4ᵉ réédition, 376.
[2] C.C.R. (1323–7), pp. 563–4; Rymer, ii. 628.   [3] *Supra*, p. 38.

went to the pope to urge the English monarch's claims to the throne of France, he was abducted by the contrivance of the pope's own steward. The steward, it is true, afterwards committed suicide, and the pope hastened to punish the accomplices.[1] What might often happen is revealed by a letter from Benedict XII to Sir Robert de Pomayo, castellan of Beaucaire. In it the pope professes to be much disturbed over the fate of Sir Robert Litelburs, an English knight sent on a mission to the papal curia. Litelburs, in company with Robert Swinfen, clerk, and Giles of Brabant, was returning to England with letters from the pope to the king. While passing through the diocese of Valence he was seized and robbed of his horses, his money, and the papal letters, and carried off to the castle of Beaucaire and kept there. The pope ordered the whole company to be freed immediately, lest Robert incur the sentence imposed on those who seized and detained persons travelling to and from the apostolic see.[2] Such instances, of course, were much more frequent after the outbreak of war; during hostilities a person took his life in his own hands if he undertook a mission through the enemy's country. For that reason clerics bulk large in the ranks of envoys; in addition to their administrative experience they were comparatively safe under the protection of the Church.

Four large groups composed the personnel of the medieval English foreign service. The first was made up of the higher nobility and the higher clergy, men who were intimately associated with the domestic affairs of the realm. The second group consisted of those who, while being lesser nobles, commoners, or clerks, nevertheless held responsible administrative positions in the government. The third group was a large and heterogeneous one. Among its members were citizens and merchants of London and the counties, some of whom were members of parliament. Many served as justices or attorneys, while others were minor clerks. A few were foreigners, particularly the merchants of Italian

---

[1] *Gesta Edwardi de Carnarvon*, p. 139. [2] *C.Pap.R.* ii. 574.

cities. The fourth was a group of specialists and can be left for later consideration. The years 1327–39 provide an excellent period from which to take a cross-section of those groups. They are the years of almost constant effort on the part of the crown in the field of diplomacy,[1] yet they are so typically medieval that any generalizations that can be made about personnel will apply, with few exceptions, to the period as a whole.

Among the nobles who served the king was William Montague, later earl of Salisbury. Employed on diplomatic missions almost from the beginning of Edward III's reign, he was foremost among those courtier lords who had worked for the emancipation of the king from the control of the regency. He participated in the arrest of Mortimer in 1330,[2] and afterwards received enormous grants from his enemy's forfeited lands. A close companion of the king, he accompanied him to France on a hurried and secret visit in 1331.[3] The year before Edward began to rule in his own right, Montague received a release from all his debts to the crown.[4] After 1330 he attained considerable influence in the government and was able to place his clerk, Thomas Garton, in the office of controller and later keeper of the king's wardrobe, and to cause the promotion of his brother, Simon, to the bishopric of Worcester.

Hugh Audley, afterwards earl of Gloucester, had been a Lancastrian. A brother-in-law of Hugh Despenser and the husband of Margaret of Clare, countess of Cornwall, he had taken an active part in the quarrel with Mortimer.[5] After 1330 his debt to the crown was cancelled, and pardons were granted for trespasses against the peace, robberies, larcenies, and homicides he had committed. He served as justice of oyer and terminer, and was hereditary sheriff of Rutland.[6]

---

[1] *Supra*, pp. 18–19. [2] Murimuth, p. 62; Avesbury, p. 285.
[3] Murimuth, p. 63; *Chronicon Anglie*, p. 3. [4] *C.P.R.* (1327–30), p. 373.
[5] *Annales Paulini*, p. 343; *Gesta Edwardi de Carnarvon*, p. 99.
[6] *C.C.R.* (1327–30), pp. 528–9, 592; ibid. (1330–3), 608; *C.P.R.* (1334–8), pp. 217, 528, 551–2. For further information on these earls see Tout, *Chapters*. iii 36–9. Montague is in the *D.N.B.*

William, baron Ros of Hamlake, evidently supported the party of Isabella, for he was made keeper of Yorkshire before Edward's accession, and was empowered to take over the castle of Pontefract.¹ The fact that he did not serve as an envoy after 1330 bears out such a surmise. In the first year of the reign he received grants of a yearly farm from Lincoln and York, and a release from his debts to the crown.² Additional grants and licences were later made to him, including two licences for alienation in mortmain to a chantry and convent.³ He served as justice of oyer and terminer, as keeper of Northamptonshire, and as attorney for one William de Barentino. Later he was appointed to inquire into the state of Lincolnshire, to arrest suspected persons in Yorkshire, and in 1337 to lay before the men of Lincoln the decisions of the council at Westminster and the king's intention regarding the safety of the realm.⁴

Of the ecclesiastics, William Airmyn, bishop of Norwich, was a member of the court party. Beginning as an official in chancery, he became keeper of its rolls, treasurer of the exchequer, keeper of the great seal, and keeper of the privy seal. He was clerk of parliament, and there is strong evidence that he was author of the famous *Modus tenendi parliamentum*. Most of his career as a soldier and civil servant was served under Edward II, but he vigorously supported the young king and was given temporary charge of the great seal on 30 November 1326, before the contest for the throne had been decided.

The most colourful figure of this group and the man who stood nearest Edward in personal affection and favour was Richard Bury, bishop of Durham. He was leader of the group that liberated the young king from the control of Mortimer and Isabella. Perhaps the most famous bibliophile of his age, he was able, through his numerous offices, to collect a famous library of rare manuscripts. During his

---

¹ *C.C.R.* (1327–30), p. 69.   ² Ibid., 64; *C.P.R.* (1327–30), p. 171.
³ *C.P.R.* (1330–4), pp. 150, 177, 275; ibid. (1334–8), 122, 467.
⁴ Ibid. (1330–4), 60, 295, 454; ibid. (1334–8), 208, 367, 503.

missions abroad he met and became a friend of Petrarch. A member of the household of Edward II and tutor to the young Prince Edward, he held at one time or another the posts of constable of Bordeaux, receiver of the chamber, keeper of the privy seal, cofferer and keeper of the wardrobe, treasurer, and finally chancellor.

John Thoresby, who was to become a great administrative figure after 1339, was bishop of St. David's, then of Worcester, and finally archbishop of York. He was the notarial expert who drafted many of the treaties negotiated in the Low Countries on the eve of the Hundred Years War. Beginning as the king's notary and clerk of the chancery, he was keeper of the rolls of chancery, deputy keeper and keeper of the privy seal, keeper of the great seal, and finally chancellor.[1]

Bartholomew Lord Burghersh belongs in the second bracket. He was the brother of the famous Henry, bishop of Lincoln, and a staunch supporter of the court party, and had taken an active part in the intrigue against Edward II.[2] He inherited his father's offices of constable of Dover Castle and warden of the Cinque Ports and, with but slight intermission, held both positions until his death in 1355. That Burghersh filled those posts almost continuously is evidence of the confidence the king had in his ability, for they were offices that involved the command of the chief channel of commerce between England and the Continent during a time when relations with France were especially hostile. He also served as admiral of the fleet from the mouth of the Thames westward, as warden of the Tower, and as chamberlain. A brave soldier, an invaluable diplomatic agent, an able administrator, he was finally appointed one of the

---

[1] Sketches of these bishops may be found in the *D.N.B.* See also Tout, op. cit. iii: for Airmyn, pp. 43–4; for Bury, pp. 25–8, 36; for Thoresby, pp. 43, 85–6, 158–9, 206–7; and Mr. Denholm-Young's excellent paper, 'Richard de Bury (1287–1345)', *Transactions of the Royal Historical Society*, Fourth Series, xx (1937), 135–68. For Airmyn and the *Modus*, see Galbraith, 'The *Modus tenendi parliamentum*', pp. 81–99, and my 'A Reconsideration of the *Modus tenendi parliamentum*', pp. 33–6.

[2] See *D.N.B.* and Tout, op. cit. iii. 23 and iv. 115, 126–8.

guardians of the realm, but died before he could serve in this office.

Sir Reginald Cobham was also an active member of the court party, and became a confidant of the king during the years 1337–40.[1] Jean le Bel described him as a person 'held in high esteem and reputed for his valour'.[2] He was one of the bannerets who held no administrative position, but as an influential personal favourite of the king gained extensive royal grants.[3]

Sir William Herle and Sir Oliver Ingham were justices. Herle was chief justice of Common Pleas and held this position almost continuously until 1337.[4] Most of his career was spent as a serjeant-at-law during the reign of Edward II, although he was a member of Edward III's council until his death in 1347. Ingham, justice of Chester, was a partisan of Mortimer.[5] He served as justice in a session at the Guildhall in which London protagonists of Thomas of Lancaster were tried, but was himself arrested in 1330.[6] Later, however, he was restored to favour and as seneschal of Gascony often undertook diplomatic missions.[7]

The position of the merchant-banker in governmental affairs is admirably illustrated by the activities of William de la Pole, of Kingston-on-Hull.[8] A merchant-prince comparable to the famous Frenchman, Jacques Cœur, de la Pole was one of Edward's most extensive creditors, holding the financial posts of mayor of the Antwerp staple and secondary baron of the exchequer. Edward's acute appreciation of certain aspects of diplomatic affairs is apparent from his choice of this commoner[9] and merchant for missions to Bruges, Ghent, Ypres, and Flanders, the foreign territories where de la Pole's influence would count most effectively.

---

[1] Tout, op. cit. iii. 89–90, 120. [2] Jean le Bel, i. 2–3.
[3] *C.P.R.* (1334–8), pp. 117, 346, 401. [4] See *D.N.B.* and Tout, op. cit. iii. 9.
[5] Ibid., especially iii. 13, 34 n. 1, 37.
[6] *Annales Londonienses*, p. 243; Burton, ii. 360. [7] Rymer, ii. 893.
[8] See *D.N.B.* and Tout, op. cit. iii. 91 and n. 5, 99, 103–5; iv. 85–90.
[9] *Return of the Members of Parliament*, i. 80, 97, 105, 108, 112, 120, 125.

Sir Geoffrey Scrope was another of the judges to be selected for service abroad.[1] He was, in fact, so attracted to diplomatic affairs on the Continent that he resigned his position as chief justice *coram rege* to become an envoy. He was one of the leading members of the court party and a bitter enemy of the Stratfords.

The third group was by far the largest, and was composed of people about whom biographical material is very scanty. The range of their activities was extensive. John Causton was a sheriff of London, king's ulnager, and collector of customs.[2] Robert Keleseye was a citizen of London and a chancery clerk. He also served as justice of oyer and terminer and held several benefices.[3] Thomas Brayton, parson of Campsall church, was queen's attorney and king's clerk.[4] Laurence Fastolf, canon of Lincoln and London, raised loans for the king.[5] Edmund Grymesby was parson of the church of Preston Bisset, king's clerk, custodian of the rolls for the chancery of Ireland, and purchasing agent for the king.[6] Antonio di Passano, of Genoa, and Andrea de' Portinari, of Florence, were two of the foreigners who occasionally served as envoys.[7]

These persons represent only a selection from a much longer list, yet this small group is indicative of the general nature of the whole. From 1327 to 1339 there were some 125 envoys sent abroad, and this rough estimate does not take into account the vast number of clerks and other persons who made up the retinues of the larger embassies.

[1] See *D.N.B.* and Tout, op. cit. iii. 9, 88, 115, 123, 276.
[2] *Annales Londonienses*, pp. 248, 250; *C.C.R.* (1327–30), pp. 70, 85–6, and ibid. (1330–3), 94, 382–3; *C.P.R.* (1327–30), p. 20; *Return of the Members of Parliament*, i. 90, 96, 99, 102, 112, App. i. x.
[3] Tout, op. cit. ii. 280 n. 3; *Annales Londonienses*, pp. 248, 250; *C.C.R.* (1327–30), pp. 167–8, and ibid. (1330–3), 290, 313, 420; *C.P.R.* (1327–30), p. 133, and ibid. (1330–4), 58, 87, 372, 510.
[4] Tout, op. cit. iii. 153 and vi. 13–15; *C.P.R.* (1334–8), pp. 40, 186, 217, 223, 546.   [5] Tout, op. cit. iv. 88 n. 6; *C.P.R.* (1334–8), p. 260.
[6] *C.C.R.* (1327–30), p. 168, and ibid. (1330–3), 416, 600, 605; *C.P.R.* (1330–4), pp. 413, 470, and ibid. (1334–8), 7, 39, 128, 313.
[7] Tout, op. cit. ii. 315; iv. 393 n. 1; v. 7 n. 2, 258 n. 6; *C.P.R.* (1330–4), p. 330.

As might be expected from a study of other branches of administration, the first outstanding fact about the foreign service is the continuity of its personnel. The great political changes of 1326–7 and 1330 had very few repercussions in the diplomatic sphere. The adherents of Lancaster and of Mortimer, the members of the court party, all were mingled indiscriminately with those who had served under Edward II; administrator accompanied politician. Nor was continuity limited to the whole. As chancery clerk under Edward II, a person might serve in a minor capacity on a large embassy; as chancellor under Edward III, the same clerk might head an embassy. Classes and groups of envoys were inextricably mixed and, using the normal advancement that took place in the great departments of state, the monarch had a foreign service with a definite scheme of promotion. The wisdom of such a practice is obvious. It provided a personnel that was at once well trained in the mechanics of diplomacy, conversant with its etiquette, and cognizant of the *affaires du moment* in both the foreign and domestic situation.

The mixture of noble and cleric, too, was not without a purpose. The very fact that some prominent earl was employed on a mission could make the embassy an impressive one, one to be heard with respect by foreign courts. It was not necessary that he be skilled in the technical side of diplomacy: the administrative cleric, with his staff of efficient clerks, could attend to such matters. The former represented the theatrical, the latter the practical side of diplomacy; both were essential. The very flexibility of the system had much to commend it. Burghersh, as admiral of the fleet, was an ideal choice for embassies dealing with maritime problems, while such a financial and wool specialist as de la Pole was indispensable for matters concerning commerce. Likewise, Italian merchants, whose business took them through all the countries with which England had relations, could conveniently attend to the smaller and less important questions. They may be compared with tha-

section of the modern consular service composed of nationals of one country employed by the government of another to act as its resident commercial and legal agents. The combination, then, of skill and showmanship, of plan and convenience, contrived an admirable instrument for diplomatic representation, and one that was quite satisfactory until changing international conditions produced new needs.

Those changing international conditions are connected with the transition of leading European states from a condition of political decentralization to one of comparative unity. At their heads were rulers anxious to consolidate their lands and to gain personal prestige by territorial aggrandizement. The resultant increase in international rivalries laid upon governments the necessity of acquiring more extensive and precise information about the actions and intentions of other governments. From the middle of the fifteenth century, therefore, envoys sent out *ad hoc* began to be superseded by resident ambassadors.[1] It is generally accepted that such a practice originated in the Italian states in their relations with each other, and was eventually adopted by other European countries. It must not be assumed, however, that the English resident ambassador, at least, suddenly sprang full-grown from the brain of necessity in the fifteenth century: the roots of the office are much deeper. Although their names are often unknown, there were semi-permanent English representatives at the courts both of France and of Rome from a very early period. The presence of those in France probably dates from the beginning of the litigation following the treaty of Paris of 1259, of those in Rome from a time when royal requests for papal privileges and concessions came to be more than occasional demands.

The technical nature of the business to be transacted at the two courts made the presence of such representatives essential. To become embroiled in a suit before the

---

[1] In 1231 Frederick II appointed Sicilian consuls for Tunis (Henricus Abbas and Peter Capuanus), and this is the first instance of a western monarchy's maintaining permanent representatives overseas. Kantorowicz, *Frederick the Second*, p. 288.

Parlement de Paris was to become lost in a labyrinth of legal technicalities. The plaintiff had first to propose, then to adduce—'ad fundendum intencionem suam'—conventions by letters sealed at the Châtelet. To these the defendant opposed replies 'ad finem quod suum factum [the fact alleged by the plaintiff], tanquam nullum et invalidum, recipi non deberet'. Then began the litigation—'lite, super predictis, coram dicto ballivo, inter dictas partes, legitime contestata'—accompanied by an oath—'jurato hinc inde de veritate dicenda'. Each party produced his witnesses—'testibus hinc inde productis, examinatis, et eciam publicatis' —and put his conclusions—'concluso in dicta causa'. The judge then notified the litigants of the date set for the hearing of the case—'et certa die dictis partibus assignata ad audiendum jus'—and at the appointed time delivered his verdict— 'per suum judicium pronunciavit quod defensor sufficienter probaverat intencionem suam, et adjudicavit eidem suam predictam intencionem'. Appeal from the verdict was to the Parlement. This, of course, represents only the skeleton of procedure. Before the litigation began, the defendant might propose either dilatory exceptions to retard the full debate, or peremptory exceptions to dispense with argument by rendering the plaintiff's case rejectable from the beginning. Countless other rules and customs had to be known and followed to the letter in order to forestall a premature or an adverse decision.[1]

A similar situation existed at the papal curia. The papal bull, or analogous document, was the means by which a petitioner's demands were either given the consent of the pope or committed to trial. The *narratio* of the bull, the part setting forth the facts of the case, was based on the *supplicatio*, a formal document in which the petitioner made his requests. The execution of the latter, therefore, had to be done in an elaborate phraseology in order to prevent accidental or deliberate misinterpretation. Nor was the process by which the bull was drawn up, sealed, and enrolled a

[1] Aubert, op. cit. ii, *passim*.

simple one. Its every step through the papal chancery and apostolic chamber had to be carefully watched: officials had to be solicited, bullied, paid the correct fees; the plans of interested and opposing parties had to be discovered and, if necessary, frustrated.[1] To perform these functions a person needed an intimate knowledge of the machinery of the Parlement and of the curia. No uninstructed foreigner, no casual envoy, could possibly hope to cope with such problems.

The men to whom such tasks fell came from the fourth group in the personnel of the English foreign service. They were highly trained specialists like Martel, Joneston, and Staunford. John Bakewell, Richard Braughton, Henry of Canterbury, Thomas Cobham, John Piers, Richard Plumstock, Roger Sheffield, Simon Stanes, and Andrew Ufford were all probably members of the group, and the list could undoubtedly be enlarged.[2] Almost all of them were trained in some branch of law, and the majority must have been acquainted with Roman law,[3] for knowledge of this subject was certainly prerequisite to any dealings with the Parlement de Paris. Bakewell had served as justice for common pleas in Cambridge as early as 1298.[4] Cobham was a doctor of civil law and a professor of sacred theology, and represented the king before the Parlement in 1312.[5] He had also served

[1] Behrens, 'Origins of the Office of English Resident Ambassador in Rome', *E.H.R.* xlix (1934), 642.

[2] These persons should not be confused with regular advocates of the Parlement de Paris like du Breuil, de Sens, Jourdain, and de Cazes, who were often retained by English kings to plead their cases (see Aubert, op. cit. i, ch. vii). Those advocates were either Frenchmen or Gascons and were paid regular fees for their services (e.g. *infra*, p. 170). That such a practice had its disadvantages is evident from a petition of Elias Joneston: 'In primis, commissarii, advocati, et procuratores anglici petuntur assignari per dominum nostrum regem pro eo quod gallici et vascones propter mortis et exheredacionis timorem ac propter alia pericula et dampna procedere non audent . . .' (D.D.C. 28/3/41; *supra*, p. 57).

[3] This seems to be implied in such writs as that addressed to Cobham in 1311, ordering him 'and others skilled in law' to examine certain articles advanced by subjects of the king of France in Aquitaine, touching the state of the king in the duchy. *C.P.R.* (1307–13), p. 338.

[4] *C.C.R.* (1296–1302), p. 291; cf. *supra*, p. 64 n. 5.   [5] *C.C.R.* (1307–13), p. 488.

in the papal curia under Edward I.[1] Both Piers and Plumstock were professors of civil law; both had served as proctors in France, the former in 1333, the latter in 1314.[2] That the others were equally skilled can be inferred from their close relations with the *custos processuum*.[3]

From such a group came the king's proctor at Rome, whose business it was to bring the royal wishes before the pope and to take the proper steps to ensure their fulfilment. The proctors in Paris performed a similar service in regard to cases before the Parlement. In the course of time both came to discharge functions other than those that originally explained their presence in the two courts. To the apostolic see came representatives of every state in Christendom, and enterprising agents often found opportunities to meet and talk with statesmen of all countries. The papal curia was the medieval League of Nations—and equally ineffective. Yet it is not difficult to imagine that much of the groundwork of diplomacy was done at Rome or in the palace at Avignon. Being on the scene, these proctors were potential instruments for discharging diplomatic business not important enough to require the dispatch of a special embassy. Likewise, they were able to instruct the envoy in intricate procedure, and to furnish political information. In the end, they became the first permanent diplomatic representatives.[4]

(ii) THE COUNCIL AND PARLIAMENT

The precise scope of the council's powers and activities in foreign affairs has already been suggested by the relations of the *custos* with this body.[5] It was inevitable that the subject of foreign relations should be one with which the council was constantly preoccupied. In addition to its importance, the subject was of such a nature that it could

[1] E.A. 309/12.
[2] *C.P.R.* (1330–4), p. 466; ibid. (1313–17), p. 203; cf. *supra*, p. 129 n. 1.
[3] *Supra*, ch. II.
[4] Queller, op. cit., pp. 75–8, disagrees with this view, but he has not read D.D.C. or Dip. Doc. Exch.   [5] *Supra*, pp. 53 ff.

hardly be treated in a routine manner. Formulation of the broad lines of foreign policy rested with the monarch, and in this the council acted in an advisory capacity. The administrative details connected with the execution of policy, on the other hand, were relegated almost entirely to that permanent section of it composed of ministerial officers from the chancery, the exchequer, and the wardrobe.

The medieval council, however, attended to a vast amount of business that today is distributed among the several departments of state, and such matters formed only one item among many. Accordingly, the creation of the office of *custos processuum*, viewed from another angle, represents one solution of the ever-increasing problem of dealing with a great deal of business quickly and effectively. To the *custos* the council delegated the thankless job of diplomatic hack. He studied the documents and drew up suggested lines of action and instructions for envoys. The infrequency with which foreign affairs are mentioned in the surviving proceedings of the council would suggest that the majority of such questions were settled merely by giving oral approval or disapproval to what the *custos* had to say.[1] Indeed, some of Joneston's petitions seem to indicate that the council was not exercising enough initiative in these matters. Such a systematization of diplomacy, however, could not obviate the necessity of its dealing directly with some of the more important problems. During the reign of Edward I Scottish affairs might often fall into that category;[2] in the following reign, such knotty negotiations as those between England and France with regard to Béarn.[3] Under Edward III the

---

[1] For instance, machinery could be set in motion by such a note as the following, which was obviously not dependent upon written details: 'Item, de littera domini regis mittenda domino regi Francie, de negociis burgensium Sancti Audomari ad respondendum pro domino Edwardo de novo auxilio' (Parl. & Coun. Proc. Chan. 66/6). Or again, a letter under the *targe* (privy seal) to be sent to the constable of Bordeaux about French affairs (ibid. 6/24). In matters of foreign affairs, as well as in others, the council could issue warrants for the great seal on its own authority (Maxwell-Lyte, *The Great Seal*, p. 181).

[2] D.D.C. 30/4/15, negotiations at Montreuil concerning Scotland.

[3] Ibid. 29/9/11.

question of the form, citation, and adjournment of the king's homage to the French throne was the peg on which a whole series of negotiations was hung.[1] Larger *tractatus* or *colloquia* were called by the king from time to time to consider foreign problems. Writs summoned the more important magnates and prelates to deliberate on affairs relating to Gascony and Aquitaine or to advise *super negociis nostris transmarinis*.[2] Yet those instances are exceptional: ordinarily the *custos* provided the facts, the council the final decisions.

Mercantile and Gascon affairs, two subjects closely related to diplomacy, were always included among the agenda of the council. The former usually concerned inquiries made regarding depredations committed by French ships on English merchants, but sometimes consisted of advice, given at the king's request, on the advisability of shipping wool to Flanders for settlement of financial obligations growing out of alliances.[3] The series of documents relating to the latter is a long one. There are several memoranda and one report of a committee of the council outlining measures to be taken in regard to Gascon problems.[4] In addition to these, the council often had to consider articles sent from the corresponding body in Gascony. The custom was to record the observations of the council between the paragraphs of such documents. Settlement of some questions would be referred to the seneschal of Gascony, who was to act with the advice of the king's council in the province. Others might be dealt with immediately, and these were marked *placet regi*, while more difficult points would be tagged *informetur rex*, to be referred to the king.[5]

The control of foreign affairs, then, ultimately rested with the council, or with the king and council. The question must

[1] D.D.C. 28/2/30. This and the two preceding references are transcripts of documents on these subjects.
[2] Instances of such meetings occur in 1295, 1296, 1299, 1311, 1313, 1317, and 1324. Palgrave, *Parliamentary Writs*, i. 30, 47, 78; ii, part 1, 43, 91, 171, 325, 663.
[3] Parl. & Coun. Proc. Chan. 66/13, 18; 7/9, 10.
[4] Ibid. 6/24; Parl. & Coun. Proc. Exch. 2/5, 10, 12.
[5] Baldwin, *The King's Council*, pp. 377–8.

now be asked: To what extent was that control shared by parliament, whether it be an 'afforced' council or a more representative assembly? It is hardly the purpose of this study to indulge in the subtleties employed to distinguish between parliament and parley, but some light can be thrown on the range of questions considered by those bodies that were somewhat broader in composition than the administrative council usually concerned with diplomacy. There were six parliaments before 1339 in which foreign affairs received some attention—those of 1279, 1305, 1316, 1325, 1331, and 1332.

The Easter parliament of 1279, to which no commons were summoned, can be dismissed with little discussion. Its records merely mention that truces have already been concluded between the king and the count of Holland, and an order is sent out instructing merchants who have lost goods to present their claims in parliament.[1]

The records of the Lenten parliament of 1305 contain the following note: 'Memorandum quod pro negociis pro quibus Dominus de Cuk venit ad Regem de partibus transmarinis assignantur Episcopus Dunelmensis, Episcopus Cestrensis, Comes Lincolnie, Adomarus de Valencia, Johannes de Drokenesford & Johannes de Bensted &c.'[2] That, as Maitland has fully explained, represents the appointment of a committee of the council to deal with the final settlement of financial claims growing out of the alliances Edward I had made after 1294.[3] Two members of the committee, Droxford and Benstead, as keeper and controller of the wardrobe,[4] would also be members of the administrative council, and it is likely that '&c.' refers to similar persons.

Among the memoranda of the Hilary parliament of 1316 is the record of a series of negotiations held with envoys of Robert, count of Flanders. The matters under discussion were dissensions between English and Flemish merchants,

---

[1] *Rot. parl. ined.*, p. 5.   [2] *Rot. parl.* i. 176.
[3] *Memoranda de parliamento*, pp. 339–42.   [4] Tout, op. cit. vi. 26, 28.

and 'Robertus Comes Flandrie Nuncios suos subscriptos in Angliam misit super hiis tractaturos; Qui una cum Consilio Domini Regis in Parliamento suo anno regni sui quinto apud Westmonasterium summonito . . .'[1] There follows a complete account of the form the conference took at Westminster and in the continuation of the meetings held at York.[2] The final conference and the treaty resulting from it are given in detail: 'Inter quos quidem Nuncios & Consilium Domini Regis in Parliamento suo apud Westmonasterium, anno &c. octavo, Tractatum fuit in forma subscripta . . .'[3]

The Midsummer parliament that met at Westminster in 1325 was the first of three specifically called for the consideration of foreign affairs.[4] It was a special session on Gascony to which the commons were not summoned. The records of the proceedings are fragmentary. There is a speech, apparently from the king, asking for advice. It is evident that some authoritative statement, some explanation of the capitulation of La Réole that would exculpate the king's immediate friends who had been blamed for the disaster, was presented and entered on the parliament roll, but this roll has not survived. The other document records the advice given in reply to the king's request. It is not clear who gave the advice, except that they must have been persons concerned with the administration of Gascony and particularly with the defence of La Réole in 1324.

The king summoned the Michaelmas parliament of 1331, as the bishop of Winchester put it in his opening speech, 'pur les busoignes touchantes la Duchee de Guyenne, & les Terres du Roi par dela la mier, sur pees ou autre issue a faire des dissensions eus entre les Rois d'Engleterre & de France, par encheson de mesmes les Terres . . .'.[5] Speaking for the king, the chancellor demanded the counsel and advice of the archbishop of Canterbury and all the other prelates, earls, barons, '& autres Grantz du Roialme'. The question was whether the difficulties with France should be

---

[1] *Rot. parl.* i. 356.   [2] Ibid. 357–8.   [3] Ibid. 358–9.
[4] *Rot. parl. ined.*, pp. 94–8.   [5] *Rot. parl.* ii. 60.

solved by negotiations for a treaty and marital alliance or by a declaration of war. The magnates chose the former course and suggested envoys, and both proposals received immediate royal assent.

The last instance is that of the Lenten parliament of 1332. The king of France had decided to go on a crusade in March 1334 and solicited Edward's company, 'entendant par tant a faire meiloure exploite sur les enemis Dieu'. He had sent letters and messengers to England for that purpose, '& ce feust l'encheson pur qoi le Parlement feust somons . . .'.[1] The king asked the advice of the prelates, earls, barons,'& de touz les autres Grantz en pleyn Parlement'. The opinion was that the date set by the king of France was too early, and that of 2 February 1335 was proposed in its place. The date was not to be binding, however: 'si est acorde & assentu par touz en pleyn Parlement, qe si avis soit a nostre Seignur le Roi par son bon Conseil, & qil soit purveu d'y aler & en stat, et q'il le pust bonement faire & par Trete od le Roi de France, homme puisse esloigner ou encourter le temps qome le preigne.'[2] That advice, it should be noted, was tendered not only by the magnates, but also by 'touz les autres somons a mesme le Parlement', a phrase that would include the commons.

In two instances, then, in 1305 and 1316, parliament was clearly not concerned with the foreign affairs that were being considered; a committee of the council or the council itself was conducting the negotiations. In 1316 the discussions were continued after the close of parliament and into the sessions of the following one. The logical assumption is that in those two instances the only reason for the mention of such business at all in the parliamentary records is the fact that the council was present in parliament. Envoys coming to England would have in any circumstances to treat with the council or with a section of it. As the council was in parliament at those particular times, it was merely a matter of convenience to carry on negotiations there. The special

[1] Ibid. 64.   [2] Ibid. 65.

session of 1325 was unusual. Since further records are lacking, it can only be hazarded that those who gave advice in answer to the royal request were probably members of the English council who were acquainted with the situation, or members of the Gascon council.

The parliaments of 1331 and 1332 were definitely concerned with diplomacy. In the first instance, apparently only the prelates and magnates acted as advisers; in the second, it is clear that the commons also participated. In 1332, however, the real decision was left to the discretion of the council, even if it should choose to nullify the advice given by parliament. The space such matters occupy in the records would suggest that, even though they constituted the primary reason for summoning parliament, they were settled in very little time and that they represented a very small proportion of the amount of business done. On the other hand, the assumption is not altogether a safe one: questions causing the stormiest debates may be recorded only in the form of the final decision that was made on them. That such was perhaps the case is illustrated by another group of documents. Elias Joneston made a series of deliveries, in 1312, 1314, 1333, 1335, to enable certain persons to draw up reports for subsequent parliaments.[1] Similarly, in 1337–8 a request was made to the treasurer and chamberlains of the exchequer to hand over certain documents or transcripts relating to the processes in France to John Piers and Andrew Ufford for examination in time for the next parliament.[2] Yet if those reports were ever made, they were not recorded on the rolls of proceedings. The same is true of the Easter parliament that met at York in 1319. The writs of summons expressly state that its members were 'to treat and advise on certain arduous affairs and particularly on those concerning the duchy of Aquitaine', but no mention is made in the records of such discussions.[3]

---

[1] *Supra*, pp. 53 ff.
[2] D.D.C. 28/4/29. The date is approximate.
[3] Palgrave, op. cit. ii, part 1, 215.

All these instances, however, must be placed against the whole of parliamentary history during this period. Interpreted even in the most favourable fashion, they pale into insignificance beside the vast amount of other business transacted. The instances of 1331 and 1332 must be seen merely as indications of a development that was to take place later. It was still a far cry from the time, in 1365, when it could be said that treaties were ratified in parliament.[1] Foreign affairs remained for a long while *negocia regis*, and as such were almost exclusively within the purview of the council.[2]

(III) THE CHANCERY

The general trend in the history of the chancery is manifest at an early date in the role this office played in diplomacy. A separation from immediate contact with the king was a condition of its independence: but the first result of this was the rise of the more personal and intimate seals of the king. Gradually the great seal came less and less to express the personal wishes of the monarch, and the importance of chancery diminished in favour of the offices containing those instruments that intervened between it and the crown. In the end, the administrative aspect of chancery became virtually non-existent: only the activities of the chancellor as a judicial officer were left to represent it, and these activities were the last evolved and the least dependent on the great seal itself.[3]

---

[1] *Rot. parl. ined.*, p. 276. Lucas, 'The Machinery of Diplomatic Intercourse', p. 330, records that the treaty of peace and marriage made with Robert of Scotland at Edinburgh in 1327 was confirmed at Northampton on 4 May 1328 *per ipsum regem et totum consilium*. This confirmation is printed in Rymer, ii. 740–1 from the original in the Public Archives of Scotland. It is not found on the parliamentary rolls.

[2] Cf. Chrimes, *English Constitutional Ideas in the Fifteenth Century*, p. 118: 'We can detect, henceforth [1409], an apparent facility with which the kings invoked the necessity of consulting the estates of the realm in the course of their diplomacy— especially at moments when it seemed desirable to show reluctance or make difficulties in granting unpalatable concessions to other rulers.'

[3] Wilkinson, *The Chancery under Edward III*, pp. 52–3.

Whatever predominance it had enjoyed in foreign affairs, by the end of the thirteenth century the chancery had become little more than a secretariat in these matters. It has been said that in its secretarial capacity it had an absolute control over the composition and preservation of the domestic and foreign state papers.[1] Yet the chancellor, like any other administrative official, was completely subject to royal control, whether exercised directly, in the person of a deputy, in conjunction with the council, or through the intermediary of the personal seals.[2] The only documents relating to foreign affairs under the jurisdiction of chancery were the close, the patent, and the various groups of treaty rolls: the vast series of Diplomatic Documents is a very recent and artificial compilation. Originals, as it has already been pointed out, were kept in the treasury of the exchequer.[3] Furthermore, the great majority of foreign letters emanating from chancery were highly formalized. On receipt of a warrant for issue, the chancery clerk had but to copy from a formula book, inserting the proper names. The department, in short, handled only the most ordinary diplomatic work; its regular business was much too large to allow it to meet the fresh demands occasioned by the increase in foreign relations during this period. The importance of the chancellor in diplomacy was not manifested through the department, of which he was head, but through and by virtue of the council, of which he was a member. Through the members of its staff, however, the chancery did exert an indirect influence in the sphere of foreign relations. In the first place, it still served as a training-school for diplomats, offering a group of skilled clerks from which envoys could be selected. In the second place, through the loan of its clerks it gave assistance to the understaffed wardrobe, which had come to be the diplomatic department *par excellence*.

J. F. Baldwin has pointed out that among the clerks of chancery 'especially were those "more discreet" and "more

---

[1] Hall, *Studies in English Official Historical Documents*, p. 57.
[2] Wilkinson, op. cit., p. 19.   [3] *Supra*, pp. 30, 31.

secret" than the others, who were entrusted with confidential correspondence or were employed as messengers or as proctors or agents in dealing with foreign courts'.[1] Some of these, such as Masters William Weston, John Shordich, John Walewayn, and Andrew Offord, were even retained as members of the king's council. Offord, for example, a brother of John Offord, chancellor and later archbishop of Canterbury, was a doctor of civil law and king's clerk. He had already served on several royal commissions when, in 1346, he was retained as a councillor with wages of 100 marks a year when 'beyond the seas', and 50 marks a year when in England, in addition to the customary allowance of two robes yearly. Immediately he was appointed to treat with Philip of Valois, 'styled king of France'.[2] Occasionally there were persons, like Walter Skirlaw and Richard Ronhale, who took little or no share in the routine work of chancery, but were widely employed in foreign negotiations.[3] Of the greater clerks of the department under Edward III, eleven served in some position on diplomatic missions.[4]

The chancery provided additional assistance to the wardrobe when the staff of the latter was inadequate to take care of its work in times of pressure. That was particularly true during wartime, but even under ordinary circumstances help was necessary when the yearly account had to be compiled or when an extraordinarily large number of privy-seal letters or of diplomatic documents had to be drafted

---

[1] Baldwin, op. cit., p. 79.   [2] Ibid. 81–2.
[3] Tout, op. cit. iii. 400 and note, 446 and note.
[4] These were Master John Branketre, a notary (*C.P.R.* (1354–8), pp. 168, 183; ibid. (1364–7), 53; Rymer, iii. 420, 444, 494; *C.Pap.R.* (Petit ons), i. 341); Thomas Brayton (Rymer, ii. 872, 875; Mirot and Déprez, *Les Ambassades anglaises pendant la guerre de Cent Ans*, p. 557); Robert Chigwell (*C.C.R.* (1337–9), p. 464); Edmund Grimsby (Mirot and Déprez, op. cit., p. 559); Robert Keleseye (Rymer, ii. 862, 875); John Langetoft (*C.P.R.* (1334–8), p. 564); Simon Multon, D.C.L. (ibid. (1370–4), 462; Rymer, iii. 1024, 1026); Andrew Offord, D.C.L. (*C.P.R.* (1345–8), pp. 12, 478; ibid. (1348–50), 24; *C.C.R.* (1343–6), p. 662; ibid. (1346–9), 55, 67); John Thoresby (Rymer, ii. 695); Robert Wickford, D.C.L. (Rymer, iii. 853); John Wodehouse (*C.C.R.* (1327–30), p. 504; Rymer, ii. 1039). Cf. Wilkinson, op. cit., pp. 154, 155, 158, 159, 161, 167, 169, 173, 175, 208.

or copied. The compilation of Liber A and Liber B, for instance, was done with the aid of chancery clerks.[1] In March 1297 Robert Cottingham paid fourteen chancery clerks the sum of 33*s*. as sixteen days' wages for writing 'quedam brevia secreta et quasdam ordinaciones factas apud Clarendon'.[2] Thirteen more were employed in March 1301 to write letters under the privy seal directed to Robert Burghersh, to the barons of the Cinque Ports, and to the 'custodians of the passage' in all the ports of England.[3] Jacob of Kingston, Hugh of Bradelby, Robert of Wardcope, and Adam Airmyn received 6*d*. each for similar services in May 1321.[4] Somewhat later twenty-one clerks drew £3. 5*s*. 6*d*. for writing more letters.[5]

But the normal function of the chancery was to issue and enrol ordinary diplomatic documents. What they were, the order of their issue, and their diplomatic can best be ascertained through the study of a continuous series of them. The negotiations with France in 1303 and those in 1324–5, which resulted in treaties, together afford an almost complete collection of such documents; any links that are missing can be supplied from similar groups. The examination of the two series will reveal a diplomatic of diplomacy that applies to most of the medieval period.

The first document essential to an envoy about to set out on a foreign mission was that which gave him power to treat. Such a letter was always issued *ad unam causam*; that is, it allowed its holder to negotiate with only one end in view. The representatives who went to France in 1303, for example, went to arrange both a peace and an alliance, and separate letters were required for each purpose. The reason

[1] *Supra*, p. 115; cf. Tout, op. cit. ii. 70 and note.
[2] MS. Add. 7965, fo. 16*d*; cf. Chan. Misc. 4/6, fo. 5, where some of the clerks are named: William of Rasen, Ives of Durham, John of Ireland, and John of Derby.
[3] MS. Add. 7966A, fo. 39. The wages were 6*s*. 6*d*.
[4] MS. Add. 9951, fo. 5*d*.
[5] MS. Stowe 553, fos. 25, 26*d*. One of the clerks was John of Killerby. Some of the letters were 'pro cariagio, navigio, congregacione mercatorum ac pro receptis mittendis per viij dies vicissim in parliamento tento apud Eboracum'.

for such a multiplication of credentials was quite practical. The ambassador first produced his weakest procuration, keeping the others in reserve until he had reached a limit in negotiating. By gradually revealing his powers in order of their strength and effect he could often wring concessions from the other party with a minimum of commitments on his own part. The document takes the form of letters patent, with the addition of certain significant clauses. The first is the usual clause of address. The second is the clause of constitution: A, B, and C are made, ordained, and constituted the true and legitimate representatives of the king. The third is the clause of limitation, establishing the minimum quorum. If A, B, and C are unable to agree in every phase of the deliberations, A and B, A and C, or B and C can act with binding force. The same clause also states the purpose of the treating and the parties with whom the negotiations are to be pursued. The fourth is the clause of guarantee, in which the king promises for himself and his heirs to recognize and to uphold whatever action may be taken by A, B, and C, or by a quorum of them. The fifth is the usual clause of signification by letters patent. Dating is by place, day, and regnal year. The form and its variants are shown by the following clauses from letters giving power to treat for peace (in the left-hand column),[1] and others giving power to treat for alliance (in the right-hand column):[2]

Address

Edwardus, &c., universis presentes litteras inspecturis salutem.	Edwardus, &c.

Constitution

. . . facimus et constituimus veros et legitimos procuratores et nuncios speciales . . .	Noverit universitas vestra quod nos, de fidelitate et circumspectione . . . plenam fiduciam optinentes, ipsos nostros, &c.

---

[1] D.D.C. 29/5/3/1.
[2] Rymer, i. 950; cf. D.D.C. 29/5/3/2 and Treaty Rolls, 8, m. 175.

Limitation

Dantes eisdem et duobus ipsorum, si omnes insimul non concurrant, plenam et liberam potestatem ac speciale mandatum tractandi, nomine nostro et pro nobis et heredibus nostris, cum...

Dantes, &c.

Guarantee

Promittentes insuper pro nobis et heredibus nostris et ratum et firmum habere et habituros quicquid per dictos procuratores et nuncios nostros, tres vel duos ipsorum in forma superius expressa ... super quibus approbandis ... servandis, faciendis, et complendis nos et heredes nostros et bona nostra omnia obligamus.

... habituri perpetuo, pro nobis, &c. ... tres, aut duos ipsorum tractatum, initum, firmatum, assecuratum, roboratum, ac factum fuerit in premissis et, ad ea omnia fideliter observanda, nos haeredes nostros, & omnia bona nostra specialiter obligamus.

Signification

Et hoc omnibus quorum interest vel interesse potest ... significamus per has litteras nostras patentes.

In cuius rei, &c.

Date

Datum apud ... die ... anno regni ...

Datum apud ... die ... anno domini ... regni vero nostri ...

Supplementary to the procuration was the letter of credence and, if the former was held, the latter was not always necessary. Letters of credence occur most often in connection with an embassy whose business required no long series of negotiations. They were particularly used when an envoy had nothing more to do than deliver an oral or written message (the message itself was called the credence). The very nature of such a document demanded that it take the form of letters close. Consequently, the wording varies with the situation, but there are always four clauses. The

THE CHANCERY

address is either to one person or to a group of persons. The clause of notification records the fact that such-and-such people have been appointed envoys, and the clause of supplication asks credence for them. Dating is usually only by place and day. Occasionally a message is conveyed in the wording of the second clause. Two credences, of 1304 and 1324,[1] illustrate the customary form and some of the variations in wording:

Address

Magnifico principi, domino & consanguineo suo carissimo, domino Philippo, &c., Edwardus, &c., salutem & prosperos ad vota successus.

... salutem, & sincerae dilectionis affectum.

Notification

Mittimus ad vestram praesentiam dilectos & fideles nostros ... nostros nuncios speciales, ad quaedam vobis, nostro nomine, exponenda.

Cum injunxerimus dilectis & fidelibus nostris ... quaedam negotia, nos specialiter contingentia, vobis ex parte nostra seriosius exponenda.

Supplication

Vestram excellentiam regiam deprecantes, quatinus eisdem nunciis nostris in hiis, quae vobis ex parte nostra expresserint viva voce, velitis fidem credulam adhibere, & nobis inde significare vestrae beneplacita voluntatis.

Vos, affectuosis precibus, requirimus & rogamus, quatenus eisdem ... & eorum cuilibet, in hiis, quae vobis ex parte nostra exposuerint vel exposuerit viva voce, fidem indubiam praebere velitis.

Date

Datum apud ... die ...

Datum, &c.

Having letters of procuration and credence, the envoy next received letters of protection, of attorney, and occasionally of safe conduct. While many of the first two types were issued on authority of writs or bills of privy seal, the chancery

[1] Rymer, i. 966; ii. 549.

apparently could issue them on its own authority as *brevia de cursu*.¹ In such cases they were granted upon direct application of the envoy, who had only to attach his seal, in order that the resulting letters might be warranted *per testimonium X*. For example, the earl of Richmond, going abroad in 1324, applied directly to the chancery as follows:

> Isti sunt profecturi ad partes transmarinas in comitiva comitis Richemundie: Bertrannus de Mountbouch', Ricardus de Pereres, milites; Magister Willielmus Pollard, persona ecclesie de Whassynburgh.
> Et dictus comes petit quod Gerardus de Cusancia, clericus, et Ricardus de Crek', clericus, possint esse generales attornati sui.²

Letters were issued 'by testimony of the earl'.³ Letters of protection took a person, his men, lands, and goods into the special protection of the king while he was absent from the kingdom. Clauses of *volumus* allowed exemption from pleas and plaints except in certain definite classes of suits. Letters of attorney are self-explanatory.⁴ Both classes were specifically limited in time, although they could be renewed *in absentia*. In form they are letters patent and, since they were by no means limited to the uses of diplomacy, it is unnecessary to give examples here.⁵ Letters of safe conduct, on the other hand, were used primarily for diplomatic purposes. The majority of them were issued to foreign representatives coming to England, but occasionally also to English diplomats going abroad. Although in form they are letters patent, the clauses are the same as those of letters of credence, except for the insertion of a clause of signification before the

---

¹ Maxwell-Lyte, op. cit., pp. 85, 210-11. Envoys occasionally received such privileges as respite of homage, of debt, and of knight service (*C.C.R.* (1327-30), pp. 107, 206, 223, 362, 389, 421, 544; *C.P.R.* (1327-30), p. 131).

² Chan. War., file 1737/7. There is a hole for filing and a place where the seal was appended.   ³ *C.P.R.* (1324/7), p. 56.

⁴ Queller, op. cit., p. 115, does not understand that letters of attorney were concerned exclusively with ordering an individual's private and personal affairs in England while he was abroad.

⁵ For examples see Hall, *A Formula Book of English Official Historical Documents*, part 1, 70-1.

date. An example from the year 1302 shows their general nature:[1]

Address

Rex omnibus amicis & fidelibus suis ad quos, &c., salutem.

Notification

Cum mittamus... exhibitorem praesentium, ad partes transmarinas, pro quibusdam negotiis [with certain specified parties] expediendis ibidem.

Supplication

Vos amicos rogamus, vobis fidelibus mandantes, quatenus eundem ... nostri contemplatione recommendatum habentes, eidem aut familiae suae, in personis, aut rebus eorum, in eundo ad partes praedictas, ibidem morando, & inde redeundo non inferatis, seu quantum in vobis est, inferri permittatis injuriam, molestiam, dampnum, impedimentum aliquod, vel gravamen; set eis potius salvum & securum conductum habere faciatis amore nostri, quotiens ab eodem ... super hoc, ex parte nostra, fueritis requisiti.

Signification

In cuius, &c., usque ad ... proximo futurum duraturas.

Date

Datum apud ... die ...

Occasionally an envoy would be issued 'blanks'. These were either totally blank pieces of parchment to which the seal was appended or letters in which merely the name of the person to be appointed, say as proctor in Rome, was left blank. Obviously these allowed the envoy an astonishing degree of latitude and discretion.[2]

Armed with these documents, the envoy was ready to proceed abroad. Sometimes passage would be provided for him. In 1303, for example, Robert Burghersh, constable of Dover and warden of the Cinque Ports, had to provide a speedy and safe passage for the king's special envoys to France, 'as the king understands that certain malefactors

---

[1] Rymer, i. 938. [2] Queller, op. cit., pp. 130-6.

sailing the sea commit very many evils and damages upon persons passing from side to side'.[1]

Once on the scene, the ambassador kept in touch with the king through the medium of reports.[2] In 1325 the bishop of Winchester made such a report on behalf of himself and his two colleagues, the bishop of Norwich and the earl of Richmond. It provides a remarkable insight into what actually took place during negotiations. The envoys began by proposing an alliance. The objected to the unwarranted *empeschement* by the French on English territory and demanded a restoration of such lands as had been seized. In order favourably to influence the outcome of the treating, excuses were made for the king's consistent failure to perform homage, and redress was promised for grievances arising from the action of English officials without royal command. The French countered with talk of the affair of Saint-Sardos, of broken treaties, of the harbouring of banished persons, and of imprisonment of French messengers. The sparring continued. The English went on to tell how the French king had been confirmed in his action regarding homage by the doctors and the great clerks of the University of Paris. The report concluded with an account of the king of France's proposed invasion of Aquitaine and of the wholesale and willing submission that would result; finally, of what was being said in the French council, and of the prospects for an agreement.[3]

The treaty was the final document with which the envoy was concerned. Unlike the charter, it was the record of a future transaction, in that it anticipated a ratification by the high contracting parties or their representatives. The procedure, then, was essentially modern in character: accredited envoys, after lengthy negotiations, drew up and sealed an agreement that, to be valid, had to be confirmed by the

[1] *C.C.R.* (1302–7), p. 81. Other instances occur in Rymer, ii. 786, 787, 793, 843, 850, 974, 1029, 1045. The courtesy was sometimes extended to diplomats and royal visitors from other countries (ibid. ii. 733, 920, 922, 927, 1033).

[2] These, of course, had nothing to do with chancery, but they are worth mentioning in order to complete the picture. [3] Dip. Doc. Exch. 1535.

respective parties. There are two forms of the treaty. The first is Anglo-Saxon in its barbaric splendour, beginning with a pious proem. The date follows, giving day, place, and year of grace. The third clause is one of procuration, reciting the powers of the envoys. The fourth is the clause of narration, which sets forth the terms of the agreement. The final clause is the customary one of signification. That may be called the impersonal or chirographic form, and was done in Latin; it was replaced by a form more suggestive of letters patent, usually written in French. In the latter and more personal form the address is general. The second clause is that of notification, which states that the respective envoys, being fully empowered, have agreed on terms. The clauses of narration, of procuration (with the relevant letters quoted in full), of signification, and of date follow. The two styles may be compared in the following treaties, of 1269[1] and of 1325:[2]

Proem

In nomine Sancte et Individue Trinitatis, Patris, et Filii, et Spiritus Sancti Amen.

Address

A touz ceus, &c., saluz.

Date

Die... apud... anno gracie.

Notification

Nous... messages et procureurs du roy... nostre trescher et tres redoute seigneur... en son non et pour lui avons accorde pour bien de paiz... aianz plein povoir a ce des diz roys nos seigneurs selon ce quil est contenu es lettres ouuertes seelees de leurs seaus, desquelles lettres la teneur est contenue ci dessouz.

---

[1] Dip. Doc. Exch. 1272; cf. Misc. Bks. Exch. T.R., vol. 274 (Liber A), fol. 442, and Rymer, i. 480.   [2] Dip. Doc. Exch. 56; cf. Rymer, ii. 602.

Procuration

Hec perpetue pacis et finalis concordie fuit inita compositio per . . . plenam habentes potestatem tractandi, componendi, et diffiniendi super . . . per litteras ipsius regis . . . patentes, inter ipsos reges, heredes, seu quoscunque successores suos, perenniter observanda, nec ulla temporum mutatione dissolvenda; ita, videlicet

(Terms of treaty)

Narration

(Terms of treaty)

Procuration

(Letters quoted in full)

Signification

In cuius rei testimonium factum est hoc scriptum in modo cirographi, cujus una pars, sigillata sigillo predictorum . . . residet penes regem Anglie; et alia pars, sigillata sigillo predicti regis Anglie, residet penes regem . . . supradictum.

En tesmoing desquelles choses nous conseilliers, messages, et procureurs dessusdiz avons mis noz seaus en ces lettres.

Date

Donne a . . . jour . . . lan de grace . . .

The forms for ratification and promulgation of treaties were essentially the same, both being letters patent. In addition to the usual clauses of address, signification, and date were clauses of notification, inclusion, and ratification. The form and contents are easily ascertainable from the following specimen:[1]

Address

Edward, &c., a touz ceux, &c., saluz.

[1] Dip. Doc. Exch. 1581.

Notification

Sachez qe nous avoms veu et regarde les lettres overtes de noz messages et procureours et des conseillers et procureours du . . . souz escritz en la fourme qe sensuite.

Inclusion

(Full text of treaty document.)

Ratification

Nous totes les choses desusescrites et chescune de celes agreoms, ratifioms, et approvons.

Signification

En tesmoignance, &c.

Date

Done a . . . jour . . . lan de grace . . . et de nostre regne . . .

The precise stages in treaty procedure have been worked out in detail for the treaty of Paris of 1259. There were four main stages:

(1) *Pax inita*. After the preliminary contacts had been made [as a result of considerable pressure from the pope], both kings appointed some trustworthy negotiators to whom they gave letters of proxy (*littere procuratorie*) with full power (*plena potestas*) to enter upon peace talks (*pacem inire*) with the other side and take the appropriate oaths (*pacem firmare*). In addition, the envoys were given letters of credence (Lat. *littere de credencia*; Fr. *lettres de creance*), asking the recipient to believe the message conveyed by them, and instructions (Lat. *credencia, oneracio*, &c.; Fr. *creance, charge*, &c.) according to which negotiations were to be carried out. Once these documents had been exchanged, arrangements were made for the two delegations to meet, and negotiations (*tractatus*) began, which eventually resulted in the drafting of articles of peace (*articuli pacis, composicio pacis, forma pacis*, &c.).

(2) *Pax firmata*. Soon after the agreement had been reached, a solemn meeting took place where the envoys on both sides took the oath on their principal's soul that he would observe the articles of peace (*juramentum in animam regis*).

(3) *Ratificacio*. Their mission accomplished, the negotiators returned home to report the progress made to their respective masters. It only

remained for the latter to ratify the agreement and exchange between them formal letters, authenticated with their seal, by which they promised to observe the articles of peace.

(4) *Publicacio.* After it had been ratified, the treaty was published so that the peoples of both countries concerned could know its terms and abide by them.[1]

There was no apparent rule followed in the enrolment of the various types of letters. They are found almost indiscriminately on the close, on the patent, and on the treaty rolls, although in practice letters of procuration and treaties were usually entered on the French, Gascon, Scottish, Almain, or Roman rolls. Some of the more secret diplomatic correspondence was never enrolled at all in chancery, for some letters went to the wardrobe for enrolment as if they had been issued under the privy seal.[2] So far as it is known, the official who was probably responsible for writing, passing under the great seal, and enrolling diplomatic documents was the prothonotary, but the early history of this officer is by no means clear.[3]

Instruments for foreign consumption were usually written in a different fashion from those to be used in England. In letters patent reference was sometimes made to the great seal in the clause of signification. 'Palace of Westminster' often replaced 'Westminster', and dating was given according to the year of grace as well as the regnal year.[4] The most significant difference, however, was in the use of the cursus. The cursus was a style of writing based on the difference between accent and quantity. It became fixed in the papal chancery after 1118 and, carried by the papal notary, soon spread to other European chanceries. Besides discouraging falsification of documents, it gave a tone of magnificence.

---

[1] Chaplais, 'The Making of the Treaty of Paris (1259) and the Royal Style', pp. 237–8. The remainder of this article deals in detail with the complications of this treaty.

[2] Maxwell-Lyte, *Historical Notes on the Use of the Great Seal*, pp. 364–5.

[3] Ibid., pp. 274–5, 380; Denholm-Young, 'The Cursus in England', *Oxford Essays presented to H. E. Salter*, pp. 86–7.

[4] Maxwell-Lyte, op. cit., p. 237.

As diplomatic instruments were probably read aloud, such a method of expressing the ordinary in an extraordinary fashion made for a grandiloquent and flattering oration. It was the medieval etiquette of diplomacy Its use in the English chancery was partly due to the influence of foreign notaries.[1] It is probable that the six *prenotarii* of the late thirteenth century were acquainted with the art of dictamen, and that some of these are to be identified with those chancery clerks who were always notaries. At any rate, the English chancery used the cursus from about 1250 to 1450: the Roman rolls show constant employment of rhythm, as do even the royal letters of Henry III.[2]

(IV) THE EXCHEQUER

The traditional view of the exchequer did not ascribe to it any diplomatic functions other than those of a fiscal nature or those that casually grew out of the clerical assistance it sometimes furnished to other departments. Baldwin, however, argued that the exchequer shared with the council the direction of foreign affairs. His conclusion was based mainly on the fact that 'among the numerous archives [of diplomatic documents] . . . there are a great many passages which describe the action of the king's council in association with the barons of the exchequer . . .', supported by the knowledge that the exchequer was the principal custodian of treaties and other diplomatic documents which were deposited in the treasury.[3] Tout very rightly criticized such a conclusion as a misinterpretation of evidence. His remarks so adequately sum up the exchequer's role in diplomacy that they are worth repeating:

> It was, however, primarily and essentially a 'segregated' revenue department, and its 'secretarial', nay, even its judicial aspects, were quite subordinate to its prime function. . . . Though the exchequer

[1] For a discussion of notaries, see *infra*, pp. 184–6.
[2] Denholm-Young, op. cit., pp. 86–90.
[3] Baldwin, op. cit., pp. 215–16.

was strengthened by certain councillors on particular occasions, and the council held its meetings on exchequer premises (just as at a later time it transacted a great deal of diplomatic business in the Star Chamber), there was in the reign of Edward I clear differentiation between the council and the exchequer. The fact that a great variety of documents, including some 'diplomatic documents', was stored in the exchequer for safe-custody and reference does not show that the exchequer had control over foreign relations. A mandate to the exchequer to consider the relations of English and Flemish merchants suggests simply that it was a matter not of diplomacy, but of finance.[1]

Indeed, it is probable that the exchequer did not even deal with diplomatic accounts until the reforming ordinances of the reign of Edward II. The series of Exchequer Accounts begins with 36 Henry III, yet the accounts of *nuncii*, save for two exceptions in 22–3 Edward I and 13 Edward II, do not begin to appear regularly on the Pipe Rolls until 16 Edward II. In many cases it is certain and in a majority of the remaining instances it is more than probable that until about 1322 most of the accounts were household accounts. That does not mean, of course, that the exchequer made no payments to envoys before that time, but it does suggest strongly that most of the accounting was done through the wardrobe. The Westminster Ordinance of 1324 attempted to correct the practice by ordering all envoys of high rank and other persons sent on important diplomatic missions to account directly to the exchequer. They were to receive a lump sum, or a sum based on some estimate of their daily expenses, for which they were personally accountable to the exchequer within three months of their return.[2] The former issuing of wardrobe prests to such persons had caused inordinate delay in the settlement of accounts, since they could not be compelled to account with the wardrobe.

The extent to which the ordinance was executed was not considerable. Part payments before the beginning of an embassy were not always made, and some payments were

---

[1] *Collected Papers*, i. 193.
[2] Tout, *Place of Edward II*, p. 179; *Chapters*, ii. 265.

not necessarily made through the exchequer at all. Instances can be found of money's being supplied out of the temporalities of vacant sees, out of debts to the king, and most often out of the pockets of Italian merchants.[1] Summaries of the Pipe Roll accounts of envoys reveal the same thing, as is shown in the tables printed in the Appendix.[2] Furthermore, the Westminster Ordinance was suitable only for times of peace. The years immediately preceding the Hundred Years War saw a recrudescence of the diplomatic and military wardrobe, in the use of which Edward III was reverting to the wardrobe traditions of his grandfather. At the same time the privy seal was beginning to impinge on the fiscal activities of both departments. The Walton Ordinances of 1338 provided that no chancery writ ordering payment from the exchequer was to be valid unless warranted by the privy seal. Payments were also to be made on the direct authority of the privy seal to the exchequer. These stipulations included persons engaged on 'solemn' diplomatic deputations, with the requirement that they should receive no wages or allowances for expenses incurred without such a written and certified warranty.[3]

In the end, the activity of the wardrobe in such spheres, as Tout has so well expressed it, 'dried up before the hostility of parliaments, the stubborn prejudices of the exchequer, the growing complexity of the machine of state, and the increasing tendency to distinguish between the king's private and public capacities'.[4] When that took place, the system of accounting with envoys became a more or less stabilized procedure administered by the exchequer.

The king or the king's council, when the former was absent and, as the medieval phrase put it, *ad partes transmarinas*, in charging an ambassador with a diplomatic mission, sent to the treasurer and barons of the exchequer a letter of

---

[1] *C.C.R.* (1337–9), p. 307; ibid. (1327–30), 230, 434; Rymer, ii. 764, 792, 915; *C.P.R.* (1327–30), pp. 140, 450, 513, 523.

[2] These figures (Appendix IV, Tables 2–4) should be compared with those given below in connection with the wardrobe (Table 5).

[3] Tout, *Chapters*, iii. 70–3, 149.   [4] *Place of Edward II*, p. 161.

privy seal. These officials made a first payment for expenses, costs of the journey, and other items. The remaining payments were spaced over a period of time, even often paid to the envoy through the medium of bankers whose societies had already become acquainted with bills of exchange.

On his return the envoy remitted to the exchequer of account an exact bill for his expenditures: *particula* or *particule compoti*.[1] He mentioned very exactly the money he had received from the exchequer and from other sources, indicating the term of payment, the day, and the sum, which was checked against the sums inscribed on the Issue Rolls. In a like manner he indicated his wages, the days of his departure and return, never omitting to mention whether the first and last days were taken into account. Besides his wages, he noted the expenses of the journey, going and returning, for himself, his servants, horses, men-at-arms, and others, the cost of duties or market tolls, customs of ports, equipment of ships, pontage, and pilotage. When the journey on the Continent was a long one, the ambassador recorded exactly the days and places of sojourn. He also mentioned whether he reported on his return to the king or to the king's council, and where the meeting took place.

By comparing the amounts of the sums expended it could be estimated whether the ambassador, having rendered his account, received more than the necessary amount or, on the other hand, whether the treasurer was indebted to him *in supplementum*.[2] To each account of an envoy was attached a schedule on parchment, called *memorandum* in the parlance of the exchequer, on which was indicated the current term (i.e. Michaelmas or Easter), the regnal year, the amount paid out, the day and even the object of the embassy.

The clerk of the exchequer then added at the bottom of the document the notation *unde respondebitur* to show that

---

[1] These were enrolled in an abbreviated form on the Pipe Rolls: cf. E.A. 309/28 and Pipe 4 Edw. III, m. 46; E.A. 309/30 and Pipe 8 Edw. III, m. 41; E.A. 309/31 and Pipe Edw. II, m. 28, for examples.

[2] The latter was usually the case: see the tables in Appendix IV.

the ambassador was held for the presentation of an exact account. On the return of the envoy, the schedule was re-examined and compared with the account rendered. The duration of the embassy was then entered on the memorandum. The account of the ambassador was forthwith revised, and two auditors, one from the barons and the other from the clerks, heard it at the exchequer of account. The chamberlains at the exchequer of receipt were then instructed to pay what was owed. They filed the mandate, and consequent payments and assignments were noted on it. After the enrolment was made, the account and the memorandum, sometimes even the letters of the king ordering payment, were placed in a sack or pouch of soft skin for preservation. On the sack was inscribed the name of the ambassador, together with the nature and duration of the embassy and the regnal year. On authority of the original writ to the treasurer and barons the chamberlain satisfied the claims of the envoy. He was paid in one of four ways: in cash; by allowance, yearly payments against future debts to the crown; by grant of custody of lands; or by assignment, an order to pay directed by writ or by writ and tally to some official such as a collector of customs.[1]

The accounts themselves reveal a great many interesting items. Wages, for instance, varied from a shilling to ten marks *per diem*; the usual amounts were half a mark, ten shillings, a mark, or five marks, varying with the rank of the person. More was allowed when the envoy was travelling on the Continent than when he was travelling in England. Two entries show what expenditures were sometimes necessary at the papal curia. The account of the bishop of Hereford in 1320 records a payment of a thousand marks (£666. 13*s*. 4*d*.) to pope, cardinals, and notaries for a bull, and to a messenger to fetch it.[2] John Stratford's account, running from 1322 to 1325, covers several journeys to the courts of Rome and of

---

[1] Mirot and Déprez, op. cit., pp. 552–4; Larson, 'The Payment of Fourteenth-century English Envoys', *E.H.R.* liv (1939), 403–14.

[2] Pipe 18 Edw. II, m. 20.

France. Among its items is, 'Et dato per consilium nunciorum Waltero, clerico Andree Sapiti, qui laborat in negociis predictis et in eisdem multa scripsit, pro labore suo, in vi florenis Florentie, percipienti ut supra xxs.'[1] The bishop of Exeter's account of a journey to France in 1325 includes the salaries paid to the king's advocates at the Parlement de Paris. The payment, amounting to £36. 14s. 11½d., was authorized by writ of privy seal; its recipients were Masters Eudes de Sens, Guillaume du Breuil, Regon' Lyoart, and Jean de Atteyo.[2]

The accounts of Robert Segre deserve special attention, for they are correlative with that of Bishop Langton[3] and throw light on the financial side of Edward I's diplomatic activities in the Low Countries. His first account was made in conjunction with Lewis of Savoy, and extends from 22 July to 10 October 1294. The only receipts recorded are £22,000 from the treasury by a royal writ of liberate. The king of the Romans received £20,000 through his proctors, in part payment of a larger sum promised by Edward. Florent, count of Holland, received £1,800, of which he transmitted £1,000 to the archbishop of Cologne and £500 to the dean of Cologne and Hartrad of Merenbergh. Payments of £5 to a notary of the dean of Cologne and of £33. 0s. 7½d. to *nuncii* brought the total of money expended to secure alliances to £21,838. 0s. 7½d. Other terms were Segre's personal expenses, £20. 4s. 4d., and £69. 12s. 7d. for the transportation of money. The latter included the rent of houses in which to store it in Holland, Zeeland, and Brabant, and for the repair of a tower in Dordrecht used for the safe custody of the funds. The total expenditure was £21,927. 17s. 6½d.[4]

The second account extends from 18 November 1294 to 13 November 1296. In addition to £25,126. 13s. 4d.

[1] E.A. 309/27, m. 3.
[2] E.A. 309/31; cf. Pipe 17 Edw. II, m. 28. Jean de Atteyo is perhaps Jean d'Ay (Delachenal, *Histoire des avocats au parlement de Paris*, p. 338), but Lyoart is not listed by Delachenal.
[3] *Infra*, pp. 173-88.
[4] Pipe 27 Edw. I, m. 31.

received at Westminster, other funds were supplied from wool and loans. Customs on wool of merchants of Yarmouth, London, and Southampton received in Holland and Brabant brought £3,069. 6s. 2½d., and the sale of the king's wool added £195. Loans, largely from the Italian merchants Bardi and Riccardi, amounting to £2,833. 14s. 3½d., brought the total receipt to £31,224. 13s. 10d. Of that, £28,365. 13s. 4d. was spent in buying allies. Adolf, king of the Romans, was paid £20,000, the dean of Cologne and the lord of Merenbergh £500. The archbishop of Cologne received £4,300, his brother £100, and his nephew £60. Other payments were £600 to Lof of Cleves and £2,466. 13s. 4d. to Henri, count of Bar. Miscellaneous expenditures included £1,038. 7s. 11d. for transportation of the money from London through Yarmouth to Dordrecht and thence to Malines. A payment of £1,253. 18s. was made to the great wardrobe. Segre's wages and those of his company amounted to £126. 4s.; *nuncii* received £87. 2s. 4d. The total outlay was £30,862. 5s. 7d.[1] As M. de Sturler has so well remarked, the accounts are valuable for the indications they give of the intimate connection between the Staple and diplomacy.[2] Segre followed that organization when it was removed from Dordrecht to Malines, and transacted through it the financial operations connected with wool that his accounts mention.

(v) THE WARDROBE

The prominence of the wardrobe in diplomacy was to a considerable extent due to its flexibility. As a department exercising the functions of a mobile exchequer, it was

---

[1] Pipe 27 Edw. I, m. 31 *et dorso*, the enrolled version of E.A. 308/18. There is a discrepancy of £216. 9s. 11d. in the receipts and of £89. 17s. in the expenses between the two; I have used the figures on the Pipe Roll.

[2] *Les Relations entre le Brabant et l'Angleterre au Moyen Âge*, pp. 180, 183-8, 197-8, 204-6, 207. The first account, however, is not analysed, and the second only partially; exact figures are not given. There is an error in his reference to the membrane of the Pipe Roll.

admirably suited to distribute funds used for diplomatic purposes; as one exercising the functions of a chancery, it was peculiarly fitted, through the presence in it of the privy seal, to deal with the more secret and extraordinary foreign correspondence. In time of war, or the preliminary arrangements for war, its position as a department for foreign affairs was particularly noticeable. It received and distributed the greatest proportion of the national revenue and became the body most nearly corresponding to the foreign office and to the diplomatic service. But its activities in peacetime were no less important. The re-entry of England into close and involved relations with France had changed the whole face of diplomacy, making it a subject that could not be handled in the old routine or formalized fashion. Some less crystallized organization was needed to supplement older departments, and it was this function that the wardrobe served.

On the financial side of diplomacy its activities were threefold. Until about 1322, as it has been suggested, the accounts of the more 'solemn' envoys were handled through the wardrobe. The payment of the less important envoy, the messenger, was almost entirely in its hands. During the reigns of Edward I and Edward III the department, or a section of it, actually transferred its operations to the Continent, the better to cope with the task of paying prospective allies.

The general nature of the accounts of 'solemn' envoys is apparent from the figures printed in the Appendix.[1] They are very similar to the *particule compoti* that were rendered in the exchequer. They contain, however, many more details concerning expenditures and, since they were usually arranged in chronological order with the place and date of payment noted, they are particularly valuable as indications of routes that envoys followed in their travels. In drawing up his statement the envoy followed the general scheme later employed in accounting with the exchequer. On his return his bill was checked in the wardrobe under the supervision of

[1] Appendix IV, Table 5.

the cofferer. If the wardrobe made any payments before the departure of the ambassador, the amounts were entered in the *jornalia*, or day-books, of the department and later transferred into the larger account-books under various headings, usually under *necessaria, prestita*, or *unde respondebitur*, in the order named.[1] Accordingly, any such payments recorded on the envoy's bill could be checked against the entries in the department books. Apparently no royal writ ordering account was necessary: the only instance occurs in 1316, when a letter under the privy seal was sent to the keeper, ordering him to account with the bishop of Ely for a mission to Ireland, and to allow him £2 *per diem*.[2] Once the envoy's bill was viewed by the cofferer, his personal clerk, or the two clerks of the accounting-table, he might be paid in either of two ways. Payment was often made directly in cash, and in this event the person sometimes gave a receipt. The bill was then sent by the wardrobe to the exchequer to be filed as a voucher. Otherwise, the ambassador would receive a bill or debenture. They were little slips of parchment bearing the name of the examining clerk and the seals of the keeper or the cofferer or of both. The holder presented them at the exchequer, where they were usually settled in instalments with each sum and date of payment noted on the slip. When the bill was finally paid, it was marked *persolvitur*, taken up, and filed at the exchequer. There are no instances where receipts exceeded expenditures, so the envoy was never faced with the necessity of making a cash payment to the wardrobe.

One or two examples will serve to indicate the variety of detail the accounts contain. There is an account, composed of nine membranes, that records the mission of Hugh de Ver to the court of Rome in 1297, 'en les busoignes le rey Dengleterre'.[3] Hugh finally left Canterbury on 16 March, after he had been called back from France by the king.

---

[1] In many cases these entries form the only surviving record of some embassies, and a complete list would make a formidable register of envoys.
[2] E.A. 309/19, m. 2.   [3] E.A. 308/20.

He sent his valet, Richard de Ruilly, with other esquires, thirteen boys, and twenty horses along to Paris 'pur luy attendre et eiser les chevaus'. They crossed the Channel at a cost of £11. 13s. 1d. and arrived in Paris ten days later. There the company was met by others who came from Gascony: a knight, two chaplains, a clerk, five gentlemen, six 'hommes de mestier', seven sumpters and boys who ate in the hall, five 'garscons a gages', along with ten horses. The retinue awaited their lord from 26 March to 3 April, at a cost of £20. 10s. 11½d.

Hugh de Ver's journey to Paris by way of Wissant with a knight and two esquires amounted to £4. 17s. 6d. In calculating these sums the relative values of sterling, *petits tournois*, and of *tournois gros* are noted. On his arrival de Ver gave a banquet for those who had assembled with him 'pur parler des busoignes le rey'. The menu and cost is very carefully recorded in *petits tournois*:[1] bread, 4 *liv.* 1s. 3d.; wine, 4 *liv.* 15s. 9d.; fruit, 13s. 1½d.; potage, 3s. 9d.; eight pound of almonds, 5s.; 200 herring, 15s. 7½d.; other saltwater fish, 5 *liv.* 12s. 6d.; fresh-water fish, 9 *liv.* 16s. 3d.; sauce, 12s. 2d.; salt, oil, flour, and powder for pastries, 6s. 9d.; fuel for cooking, 11s. 10d. Miscellaneous expenses included feed and stables for fifty-one horses, 6 *liv.* 18s. 2d.; flares for lighting, 7½d.; fur, 18s. 7d.; wages for nineteen boys and a page, 14s. 10½d.

The embassy left Paris on 4 April and arrived at Lyon ten days later, having travelled through Bar-sur-Seine and down the Rhône valley. On 17 April it was at Chambéry, in Savoy, preparing to cross the Mont-Cenis Pass into Italy. From Chambéry to Susa, at the foot of the pass on the Italian side, the journey took almost a week. From Susa a leisurely progress took the company to Rome by 26 May, through Turin, Pavia, Piacenza, Parma, Lucca, Florence, Siena, Viterbo, and Sutri. The return journey began on 9 July. A brief stop, from 23 July to 5 August, was made at Lucca.

---

[1] Based on the account, roughly 1s. sterling = 4s. 8d. *petits tournois* = 3¾d. *tournois gros*.

Travelling back by the same route, the embassy reached Wissant on 7 November, having spent a total of £608. 9s. 3½d.

The most unusual and the most interesting for details are the accounts of G. Langele, who in 1292 went on a mission to the khan of Persia.[1] The journey began at Genoa, where the first provisions were bought. They consisted of covers, skins, and furs, the price of which varied with the person for whom they were intended: grey squirrel of fine quality for Langele, smaller furs for others, and wool for the remaining members of the company, as well as cloaks of various styles. At Brindisi the embassy's scutifer purchased furs of white wolf and leopard, along with a supertunic of grey squirrel for Langele. Other items for travel included cross-bows, thin silk and taffeta, tents of cotton enforced with buckram, pavilions of ox skin, cloth of vermilion, green, and yellow, bearing the arms of Langele, fustian and cloth of Ypres and Flanders, saddles covered with red and yellow cloth, goatskins for wine, sacks for bread, leather pockets for money, phials, pots, crockery, copper, and many other items. In Constantinople heavy gloves were bought, to be used on the return journey when winter was approaching. Cold weather and scarcity of supplies caused the company to sleep together, two in a bed, for a week in Constantinople.

The embassy was composed of twenty people. Besides Langele, there was a chaplain, Stephen, and a clerk, John. Nicholas of Chartres was scutifer responsible for the expenditure of funds. Four men-at-arms, Manfred, Gerard, Hubert, and Richard, a barber who also served as a physician, three falconers, a cook, and seven servants completed the number. On the outward journey Nicholas of Chartres carried two gerfalcons ringed with silver as a present to the khan. They were fed daily on beef. On the return, the company brought a leopard, nourished on live mutton, evidently as a gift from the khan to Edward I. The group travelled as far as Tabriz,

---

[1] E.A. 308/13–15. They have been published by Desimoni, 'I conti dell'ambasciata al chan di Persia nel MCCXCII', *Atti della Società Ligure di Storia Patria*, xiii (1879), 537–694.

south-east of the Caucasus, only to find the khan absent from his capital. Nicholas of Chartres left the company and, together with another member, spent almost a month, from 15 April to 7 May, wandering over Asia Minor looking for him.

The return journey, which followed roughly the same route as the outward journey, began on 22 September from Marand, somewhat west of Tabriz. Travelling overland through Khoi, Arjish, Melasgird, Erzerum, and Baiburt, the embassy arrived at Trebizond on 13 October. Leaving there a week later, it reached Constantinople on 9 November. The voyage from Constantinople to Otranto took thirteen days, from 26 to 29 November. Following the eastern coastline of Italy as far as Barletta, the company then set out westward through Troja, Montesarchio, and Acerra to Naples, arriving there on 14 December. From Naples the route led through Capua, Mignano, Ceprano, Anagni to Rome. There they spent Christmas and met the celebrated Riccardi, merchants of Lucca. The journey was resumed three days after Christmas; through Viterbo, Montefiascone, and Aquapendente they arrived in Siena for New Year's Day (1293). Thence they crossed through S. Casciano and Pistoja to Lucca and followed the coast by way of Avenza and Rapallo to Genoa, completing their travels on 11 January. The account ends on 23 January with the company still in Genoa. An estimate cannot accurately be made of the expenses of the outward journey, because of the fragmentary condition of the manuscript. The cost of the return journey, however, reckoned in florins, *perperi*, *aspri*, and in *lire genovine*, was £3,363. 2s. 8⅖d.[1]

---

[1] Desimoni, op. cit., pp. 647–55. The reduction into sterling is based on the following ratio: 1 florin = 1½ *perperi* (or 36 *carati*) = 18 *aspri* = 14 *soldi* 5 *danari* = £1. 16s. sterling. Expenditures were:

	£	s.	d.
At Trebizond and Tabriz (*aspri* 7722)	722	4	1⅕
At Constantinople (*perperi* 289 *carati* 22)	347	18	9⅗
In Southern Italy (*fiorini* 351 6d.)	631	17	9⅗
In Central Italy (*fiorini* 138 1d.)	248	8	3⅗
At Genoa and environs (*fiorini* 702 3s. 1d. and *lire genovine* 506 7s. 9d.)	1412	13	8⅖

THE WARDROBE 177

The figures for the expenses of the ordinary messengers are not very great, for there were large numbers of such people and they were paid very little. Using the years for which figures are available, the total under Henry III is £2,318. 11s. 7½d.; under Edward I, £1,847. 14s. 1½d.; under Edward II, £1,113. 8s. 10d.; and under Edward III, £942. 0s. 10½d.[1] The total of the four figures amounts to £6,221. 15s. 5½d. The figures include sums paid to messengers carrying letters in England as well as abroad. The results to be gathered from a separation of the two categories would not be significant enough to warrant the necessary time and effort. The important fact is the downward trend of the totals. That is possibly due to the fact that under Henry III some of the accounts of 'solemn' envoys are to be found mixed with those of common *nuncii*; the number of these decreases through the following reigns being included under other headings. It can also be explained by the increase in the number of embassies themselves, since they would usually have their own messengers and include expenditures for them in their own accounts.

The role that the wardrobe played in securing and paying prospective allies is illustrated in the account of Walter Langton, bishop of Coventry and Lichfield.[2] Langton went abroad while he was treasurer, and his post was filled by John Droxford, controller of the wardrobe. His account, which was made in the wardrobe, affords clear evidence of the

---

[1] These sums are based on figures found both in the wardrobe books and in wardrobe accounts on the Pipe Rolls under the title *nuncii*. The years covered are 42–5 Hen. III, 49 Hen. III–2 Edw. I, 2–26 Edw. I, 28–34 Edw. I, 1–2 Edw. II, 6 Edw. II, 8 Edw. II–2 Edw. III, 2–14 Edw. III. There is a record of £26. 9s. 6d. spent for similar purposes by the queen's wardrobe in 37 Henry III (E.A. 308/1). Some *nuncii* in the roll for the Welsh war, 10 & 11 Edw. II, went abroad; the figures for them amount to £7. 17s. (E.A. 308/5). There is a discrepancy between two sources for 15–17 Edw. II: MS. Stowe 553 gives £157. 9s. 4d., E. (W. & H.) 2, m. 20, £176. 1s. 11d.; I have used the latter.

[2] E.A. 308/19, printed *infra* as Appendix V. Cf. de Sturler, op. cit., pp. 149 n. 37a, 151 n. 52, 159 n. 91, 181 n. 29, 205; and *supra*, pp. 170–1. For a detailed discussion of the diplomatic activities of the wardrobe during the various times when it was actually moved to the Continent see Tout, *Chapters*, ii. 61–6, 107, 115–18, 142; iii. 87, 91, 96, 115, 120; iv. 102–7.

importance of this department in foreign affairs. Working directly through his embassy, which was the largest and most significant until the time of Edward III's activities in the Low Countries, it controlled the mainspring of diplomacy and engineered the chain of alliances against France that stretched almost from the Alps to the North Sea.

Receipts amounted to £34,726. 17s. 3d. The most important sources were wardrobe prests, which accounted for £18,146. 8s. 7½d., and funds from the exchequer, which accounted for £10,000. Italian merchants, mainly the Frescobaldi, furnished £4,961. 9s., while the receiver of the count of Flanders supplied £1,000. Other sources were not so significant: £385. 2s. 11½d., due to advantages from exchange rates, £200 from a burgess of Ghent, £30 from wool customs at Sandwich, and £3. 16s. 8d. gained by the sale of wine.

The expenses, which amounted in all to £42,457. 14s. 10¾d. and thus created an adverse balance of £7,730. 17s. 7¾d., may be grouped under the titles *confederationes*, *vadia*, *necessaria*, and *dona*. The first of these represents payments for alliances and is the largest of the four items, being £36,872. 4s. 4d. Guy of Flanders got the bulk of that amount, £26,800. The nobles of Burgundy, the term used in the account to describe the district of Franche-Comté, received £8,250, Blanche of Navarre, £1,566. 14s. 4d., Jean, duke of Brabant, and Jean, lord of Cuyk, £237. 10s. Jean of Bar was paid a large sum, only £18 of which can be ascertained because of the fragmentary condition of the manuscript.[1] There are few details about the alliances

---

[1] These payments to allies should be compared with those recorded in fos. 155d–156d, 158 of MS. Add. 7965, the wardrobe account for 1296–7. They were £36,526. 2s. 8d. to Guy of Flanders, £15,295. 9s. to the magnates of Burgundy, £1,032 to Jean and Henri of Bar, £500 to Jean of Holland, and £424. 12s. 10½d. to Jean of Brabant and others; total £53,778. 4s. 6½d. Thirty-six barrels of money were transported from Westminster via Sandwich to Ghent by Robert Segre, Ralph Manton, and William Eston in June 1297 (ibid., fos. 18d, 24d–25). The cash was intended for the counts of Flanders and Bar. William Dogmersfield had charge of the king's jewels which, after being transported from Bruges to Brussels, Malines, Louvain, and Antwerp during the months of August and September 1297, were

contracted, apart from the mere figures. One entry records that Guy of Flanders had received £8,500 from the exchequer in February 1296, before the embassy left England. Another suggests that the agreements regarding sums to be expended to various allies were written in England and carried abroad for delivery. That implies a series of negotiations carefully planned in advance. Of the military aid to be furnished, the account mentions only that Jean of Bar agreed to supply fifty men-at-arms.

The second title of expenses, the wages, comes to £2,161. 15s. 2¼d. Langton's household expenses were £1,388. 9s. 5½d.[1] Payments to messengers, again incomplete, amounted to £699. 6s. ¾d.; sailors received £73. 13s. 8d. and clerks, 6s. These items disclose that the ships used to transport the company were called *La Rose de Sandwich* and *La Floyne de Sandwich*. The third title includes certain necessary and miscellaneous expenditures making a total of £3,224. 4s. 7d. The largest entries are payments for victuals, £1,511. 4s. 10½d. Other sums were for wine, £800, miniver, £460. 3s. 9d., loans on the sale of wool, £368. 7s. 4d., canvas, £78. 16s. ½d., and for sacks, baskets, carts, and parchment, £5. 12s. 7d. The expenditures for victuals, largely beef and bacon, and those for wine and canvas were in preparation for the arrival of Edward I, who crossed to the Low Countries in 1297.[2] The last title, gifts, is the smallest of all, being only £199. 10s. 9½d. Of that, £138. 15s. was tagged *obsides Vasconie*, and represents a series of payments to hostages in the hands of Philip IV and to persons who had escaped from prison in France and were making their way towards England. The remainder,

---

stored in the wardrobe at Ghent and later pledged to secure funds for the payment of allies (ibid., fo. 18).

[1] MS. Add. 7965, fo. 35, is a record of Langton's expenses from 25 December 1296 to 19 November 1297, including those of clerks, valets, and merchants remaining in his company; the total is £983. 8s. 1½d.

[2] MS. Add. 7965, fos. 45–7, contains two interesting entries relating to such provisions. Robert Segre spent £3,619. 5s. 10½d. on stores provided in Flanders and Brabant; Elias Russel's account for wine amounted to £4,858. 10s.

£60. 15s. 9½d., was spent in various small sums for a number of different things.

It is very difficult to trace the movements of the embassy except in a very general way. The account, rendered at Clifton in July 1298 by William Eston, covers a period from 23 July 1296 to 20 November 1297. It is not arranged chronologically, for the company did not travel together in one group. Langton himself visited France, Bourbonnais, Cambrésis, Flanders, and Brabant, but some members went as far afield as Gascony, Savoy, Rome, Burgundy, and Germany. Letters of protection were issued to Langton in January 1296, and in June Richard Dymmere and John de Hotoft were nominated to act as his attorneys during his absence.[1] Some attempt was made even at this late date to settle Anglo-French difficulties in a peaceful way. Papal envoys, the cardinal bishops of Albano and Palestrina, had been urgently offering their services as mediators since March 1295.[2] Accordingly, Langton was empowered to arrange truces between Philip IV, on the one hand, and the king of the Romans and Edward I, on the other. Instructions were issued to Edmund of Lancaster, who had already gone abroad, to take counsel with the envoys and cardinals, and Adolf of Nassau, the duke of Brabant, and the count of Bar were urged to send representatives to participate in the proposed conferences. At the same time, however, Langton was given powers to arrange alliances and conventions with Renaud of Gueldres, Florent of Holland, and the count of Cleves.[3] He went first to Paris, arriving there not long after 1 June. On 18 July the cardinals wrote to Archbishop Winchelsea from Paris, requesting that they be allowed to consecrate Langton in the bishopric to which he had been elected. They had already received power to ordain him.[4] It is fairly certain from the account that Langton remained in Paris until the end of July. During that time the pope was

---

[1] *C.P.R.* (1292–1301), pp. 179, 193.   [2] *C.Pap.R.* i. 562–3.
[3] Rymer, i. 834, 835, 837, 838, 840.
[4] Hist. MSS. Com., *Various Collections*, i. 262; cf. *5th Report*, app., p. 446.

in constant communication with his legates and had even written to Philip IV and King Adolf, urging them to adopt the papal suggestions.[1] But Langton, apparently despairing of any fruitful negotiation, journeyed south to Bourbonnais, probably to gain first-hand information regarding the situation in Gascony and to secure the services of the lords of the Pyrenees, such as the bishop of Comminges. On his return to Paris in October, however, a proposal was made to hold a conference of all the disagreeing parties at Cambrai in the presence of the cardinals.

The treasurer was then recalled to England to report to the king and to be present at Bury St. Edmunds 'to ordain concerning a subsidy'.[2] A French sergeant escorted the ambassador from Luzarches to Wissant. The meeting at Bury was momentous. In February Boniface VIII had issued his famous Bull, *Clericis laicos*, in which it was laid down that no lay authority could exact supplies from the clergy without the express authority of the apostolic see. On the basis of that decretal Archbishop Winchelsea refused to allow the king any grant from the clerical estate. The consequent lack of money for war probably influenced Edward to continue his diplomatic efforts. At any rate, on 18 November Langton received fresh letters of protection and was sent to the conference at Cambrai. Letters of credence in his favour were directed to the king of the Romans, and he was empowered to treat with the magnates of Burgundy.[3] The continued efforts to secure peace had by this time attracted the attention of chroniclers, and Langtoft told in his quaint verse how the treasurer and his colleagues were making another attempt at negotiations and expressed the pious hope, 'Condure les face Deüs et ben remener!'[4] Langton remained at Cambrai from 15 to 28 December and then travelled to Wissant, reaching the port on 1 January 1297. He was back in England by 10 January, for letters

---

[1] *C.Pap.R.* i. 567–8. [2] *C.C.R.* (1288–96), p. 513.
[3] *C.P.R.* (1292–1301), p. 210; Rymer, i. 848, 849.
[4] Langtoft, ii. 274; cf. *Flores historiarum*, iii. 290–1.

were issued at this time to him and his colleagues, empowering them to contract a loan of £7,500 for the king's use.[1] There he remained until the end of February.[2] The second period of negotiations had been a failure as far as peace with France was concerned, but Jean of Brabant had been secured as an ally in return for a promise of 40,000 *livres tournois noirs*.[3]

One final effort for peace was still to be made, but a serious attempt to secure allies was henceforth to be the main preoccupation of the embassy. Boniface VIII had receded from his position in *Clericis laicos* through a new bull, *Romana mater*, and money from the clergy was at last forthcoming. At the same time, French encouragement to the Scots was proceeding apace, and this gave Edward further reason for raising arms against Philip. Letters of credence were addressed to Amédée of Savoy, the counts of Holland, Bar, Flanders, Hainault, and the dukes of Brabant and Lorraine, the archbishop and dean of Cologne, and the bishops of Liège and Utrecht. With these and with many others Langton was able to confirm or seek alliances. He was also given procuration to settle disputes among the princes of the Low Countries and the Rhineland: Jean of Brabant, the archbishop of Cologne, and the counts of Flanders, Hainault, and Holland.

The last stage of the embassy was the longest and most important. The ambassadors were empowered to pledge the tin in Cornwall and Devon that Edmund of Lancaster had granted to the king and to contract loans from merchants and cities to pay the king's diplomatic obligations. An ordinance was drawn up by the king and council regarding the wool to be bought and sent abroad for use by Langton and his colleagues.[4] This was the period when the greater part of the system of alliances was erected and when most of

---

[1] *C.P.R.* (1292–1301), p. 226.
[2] Letters of credence and protection were issued to him on 6 and 12 February (*C.P.R.* (1292–1301), p. 234; Rymer, i. 857, 858, 859, 860).
[3] *C.P.R.* (1292–1301), p. 232.   [4] *C.P.R.* (1292–1301), pp. 292, 299, 302.

the payments recorded for this purpose in the account were made. The activities of the embassy centred mainly in Flanders and Brabant; Langton was busy in Bruges, Antwerp, Brussels, Lille, Courtrai, and Ghent. The information furnished by the account ends with him at Bruges on 1 August, but the company did not return to England until October and November. Edward I himself arrived in Flanders late in August, and it is probable that the treasurer spent some time with the king at Ghent, giving him details of the state of alliances and bringing the business of the embassy to a close.[1]

The activities of the wardrobe as a diplomatic chancery are more difficult to determine. From the end of the thirteenth century to the middle of the fourteenth the department made enrolments of letters that it issued, but almost all of the documents that have survived are in the nature of warrants for the great seal. Nevertheless, there are certain indications that the wardrobe must have exercised functions of considerable importance as a secretariat for foreign affairs. The records, however, leave much to be desired, and it must be said at the outset that any conclusions on this question are necessarily based on deductions from rather meagre evidence.

There are several entries in wardrobe books that reveal that the department handled a great many diplomatic documents. In 1290 a payment of three shillings was made to Thomas Langton, 'pro uno forcerio de corio ferro ligato novo, empto ad imponendum bullas et litteras garderobe'. Arnold Bon received a similar payment for a sack in which to impound various letters touching the marriage of Scotland. Six more boxes were needed for other letters.[2] In 1296 the exchequer allowed John Droxford funds 'ad scripta tangencia ducem Brabantie et alios imponenda'.[3] A payment four years later suggests that privy seal letters were being sent to the

---

[1] Langton probably returned to England by way of Louvain, Malines, Lierre, Hoogstraeten, Bréda, Geertruidenberg, and Dordrecht. MS. Dodsworth 76, fo. 16.
[2] Chan. Misc. 4/5, fos. 10, 11*d*, 15*d*.
[3] Issue Rolls, Exch. of Rec., 90, m. 1.

pope, if *curiam* can be interpreted as referring to the papal curia: 'pro . . . una pucchia cum bullis et aliis diversis litteris contrarotulatoris missis ad curiam per eundem involvendis . . .'[1] Certainly the wardrobe was responsible for the transmission of other letters to Rome. In 1301 John of Winchester drew 5s. 7d. for a coffer 'pro quibusdam litteris patentibus sigillis magnatum Anglie signandis et mittendis ad summum pontificem infraponendis, et pro iij lb. de cotone empto pro dictis sigillis salvo custodiendis'.[2]

Entries relating to the composition and transcription of diplomatic documents afford further indications. In 1286 R. de l'Isle was paid a shilling for writing three 'great letters' in the chancery, apparently required for use by the wardrobe.[3] In March 1297 John of Derby, a chancery clerk employed in the wardrobe, earned three shillings for five days' work in writing several 'secret writs'.[4] There are payments amounting to £64. 9s. 2d. in that year and in 1300 for the transcription of bulls and other memoranda.[5] Other transcriptions were made of various quittances of the count of Holland[6] and of all the rolls and pells relating to Gascon payments in the years 22–7 Edward I.[7] Another interesting entry relates to the treaty sealed at Paris in 1303. Through an envoy the wardrobe paid 4s. 4d. for the parchment, wax, and silk cords used in writing and sealing that instrument.[8]

The presence of notaries in the wardrobe is perhaps the strongest evidence of its secretarial activities in matters of diplomacy. Notaries were skilled in foreign fashions and well versed in the art of dictamen. The king frequently retained several papal notaries and paid them annual pensions. Master Berard of Naples, for instance, served from 1284 to

[1] *L.Q.G.*, p. 59.
[2] MS. Add. 7966A, fo. 39d; cf. Round, 'The Barons' Letter to the Pope', *The Ancestor*, nos. vi. 185, vii. 248 (1903), viii. 100 (1904).
[3] Chan. Misc. 4/3, fo. 12.   [4] Ibid. 4/6, fo. 5.
[5] MS. Add. 7965, fo. 18; MS. Add. 35291, fo. 37.   [6] *L.Q.G.*, p. 69.
[7] Issue Rolls, Exch. of Rec., 102, m. 2, an allowance to Droxford for this purpose.
[8] E.A. 309/4.

1288 at an annual fee of eighty marks, and Master Angelo from 1284 to 1291 at twenty marks.[1] They are often found as envoys or as recipients of payments made by envoys.[2] Those in the wardrobe were usually royal notaries, and it is possible to trace the activities of two of them in some detail. In August 1304 Master William Maldon, working with Master William Dorturer, received £6. 13s. 4d. for writing thirty-five public instruments concerning the collection of a papal tenth in England, Wales, Scotland, and Ireland.[3] From 23 March to 5 June 1312 he was busy transcribing other letters and bulls relating to the same subject. For that he was paid £7. 6s., or 2s. *per diem*.[4] A debenture records a payment of £13. 11s. 3d. to him from 20 to 30 November 1315. It included an allowance for horses, but the specific services for which he was rewarded are not mentioned.[5] He received £11. 6s. 8d. for a period from 30 November to 23 December 1319, during which time he transcribed for Edward II's intended journey abroad peaces and confederations made between the kings of England and France.[6] Master Andrew de Tange was employed during the same time. From 21 December 1300 to 27 February 1301 and from 28 April 1302 to 16 March 1306 he worked at writing public instruments 'super homagiis et fidelitatibus Scottorum', for which he drew £87.[7] Similar business from 25 November 1316 to 7 July 1318 brought him an additional £50. 13s. 4d.[8] There are many other entries, in which

---

[1] Liberate Rolls, Chan., 60, m. 2; 61, mm. 1, 2, 3, 5, 8; 64, m. 2; Issue Rolls. Exch. of Rec., 50, mm. 1, 2; 52, m. 2; 64, m. 3.

[2] A payment of five pounds to Gerard, notary of the archdeacon of Cologne, pro labore suo circa negocia domini regis' (1294–5) (Pipe 27 Edw. I, m. 31); £1. 19s. 9½d. for salaries of notaries and £5. 5s. for the expenses of one going as a messenger to the king of the Romans (1300–1) (E.A. 308/27); repayment of £47. 5s. 3d. to the Frescobaldi for funds advanced to notaries for writing and registering bulls (1306) (E.A. 369/11, fo. 34); 1,000 marks for similar services (Pipe 18 Edw. II, m. 20).

[3] MS. Add. 8835, fo. 15d.   [4] MS. Nero C. viii, fo. 58d.
[5] Ward. Debent., file 482/250.   [6] MS. Add. 17362, fo. 13.
[7] MS. Add. 7966A, fo. 37; E.A. 369/11, fo. 48.
[8] Ward. Debent., file 483/590.

names are not always given, of the occasional employment of notaries. Some were transcribing or composing various instruments on the reformation of treaties between England and France, as in 1300,[1] others writing 'instrumenta . . . et memoranda et alia regem et regnum suum tangencia', as in 1307–8;[2] almost all the work was concerned with some form of diplomatic document.[3]

On the basis of these and similar instances in the accounts it is difficult to escape the conclusion that a great deal of foreign correspondence came out of the wardrobe, and that important diplomatic documents owed a great deal of their form to the wardrobe clerks even when ultimately sealed in chancery. That the privy seal must have seen considerable use in such matters while it was in the custody of the controller of the wardrobe can perhaps be inferred from its importance after becoming a separate department. Already by 1338 most of the letters carried abroad by *nuncii* were letters of privy seal.[4] By the reign of Richard II the main diplomatic work was in the hands of the privy seal and the signet offices. Not only did the privy seal office issue numerous letters dealing with foreign affairs, but it was the normal place for using, keeping, and to a certain extent for receiving diplomatic documents.[5] It is reasonable to assume that such a diplomatic tradition must have existed in some degree before the separation of the seal. Certainly its very nature, and the nature of the department of which it originally formed a part, made it an instrument ideally suited for such work.

---

[1] *L.Q.G.*, p. 67. [2] Pipe 16 Edw. II, m. 50.
[3] MS. Add. 7965, fos. 15*d*, 16*d*; MS. Nero C. viii, fo. 55*d*; Misc. Bks. Exch. T.R., vol. 203, fos. 179, 350; cf. ibid., fos. 183, 193, and Tout, op. cit. ii. 70 n. 2.
[4] Misc. Bks. Exch. T.R., vol. 203, fos. 218–40.
[5] Perroy, *The Diplomatic Correspondence of Richard II*, introduction.

CONCLUSION

ENGLISH relations with France from the treaty of Paris of 1259 to the outbreak of the Hundred Years War form a curious phase in medieval diplomatic history. They are characterized by a reliance on the normal channels of negotiations rather than by a resort to military efforts. The treaty of 1259 ushered in a new era in diplomacy, creating a continuous series of attempts to solve its tortuous problems and colouring the whole of English general foreign policy.

The character of that period was such that it became one of utmost importance in the development of English administration. No longer can it be thought that treaties were made and forgotten, that each step in diplomacy was an entity in itself, having no connection with what had gone before. But if the work of embassies was to prove effective, if litigation in the Parlement de Paris and conferences such as the processes of Montreuil and Périgueux were to be pursued with any intelligence, some organization was needed to supplement the departments of state then existing. Diplomacy became a matter for archivists who were equipped with the means and training to follow and to advise upon the most technical questions. Documents were scattered among the repositories of chancery, exchequer, and wardrobe, and these departments were concerned with a great many other matters than those of diplomacy.

The office that the council created to correct such conditions was that of the *custos processuum*. Under the head of three successive clerks, Philip Martel, Elias Joneston, and Roger Staunford, the organization functioned continuously from 1306 to 1339. The reason for its being discontinued lies in the complete change wrought by Edward III when he decided to dispense with diplomacy and to resort to war. The *custos processuum* represented nothing less than a permanent secretariat for French affairs. He had his group of clerks and equipment and made his accounts first to the wardrobe and later to the exchequer. His archives were extensive, and it was part of his job to make them available to English envoys both at home and abroad. The course of litigation in the Parlement de Paris was particularly under his surveillance, and he performed the important duties of instructing ambassadors and of advising the council in its determination of foreign policy. The office, in short, while it existed, was the keystone of Anglo-French relations.

Contemporaneously with the establishment of that organization occurred the revision and cataloguing of the diplomatic archives. Liber A and Liber B, the Gascon calendar, and Bishop Stapeldon's calendar were the results of that general house-cleaning of record repositories. With the composition of the last two registers the keeper of processes was intimately concerned, by virtue of his position as a technical expert in matters of diplomacy. All were eminently practical in their form and method, executed with the needs of the future clearly in mind.

These things represent efforts to cope with particular problems, but they are not divorced from the clarification of ordinary diplomatic organization that occurred at the same time. There was a delineation of activities in foreign affairs taking place within the ordinary governmental departments, a process in line with the general administrational changes and developments that were being made during this period. King and council retained the ultimate control of diplomacy; parliament as yet played an insignificant part, although the indications of future development were present. Chancery ceased to do more than to issue the formalized foreign correspondence, having abdicated many of its secretarial functions to the wardrobe. After a brief but important period during which the wardrobe handled the finances of diplomacy, the exchequer became the diplomatic accounting department with a set method of handling this business. When the smoke of realignment and reorganization cleared away, the wardrobe came out as the department most flexible

CONCLUSION

and satisfactory for diplomatic affairs, being both a mobile exchequer and a secretariat. When the privy seal left the wardrobe, it took with it the functions that the wardrobe had built up or acquired in foreign affairs and the methods and experience of the activities of the *custos*; these it combined and shared with the signet.

The course of later evolution, then, had been clearly laid out well before the end of the fourteenth century. Likewise the path had been marked for the development of the modern envoy from the technical expert who was always present at the Parlement de Paris and at the papal curia. All the elements were present: the step from medieval to modern administration and diplomatic representation was not a difficult one.

The diplomatic relations at the basis of those developments perhaps suggest an approach to yet another problem which, although not an essential part of administrative history, has some connection with it. It has to do with the subject of medieval international relations. While such thinkers as Bartolus of Sassoferrato were busy harmonizing the practical situation existing between the Empire and the *civitates* with a troublesome theory of world-wide *imperium*, difficulties of a not too dissimilar nature were being worked out on the western borders of Europe. Those difficulties hinged upon the dual role of the English king as a vassal of France and as a separate and distinct sovereign power. The core of the matter lies in the answer to the question of the extent to which the French king, in his relations with his vassal, was prepared to treat with the king of England as a political personage *sibi princeps*, an *imperator regni sui*. The problem, however, is much too comprehensive to be discussed in any detail here, and the following remarks must necessarily be no more than suggestions of a possible approach to an answer.

The king of France had always to recognize that the king of England was, as prince in his own land, a sovereign equal as well as a vassal. In letters to French seneschals in Gascony the expression was always 'rex Anglie, karissimus frater, et dux Aquitanie, fidelis noster'. Indeed, in correspondence not concerned with English possessions in France, the terms that indicated vassalage were often omitted. The same thing is borne out in treaty negotiations. In every instance, from 1259 to 1327, the preliminary discussions were always between the representatives of two sovereign equals: there is nowhere expressed the idea of a lord making peace with his vassal. Likewise, the forms treaties took implied a recognition of parity. In matters of diplomatic there was nothing to distinguish the treaty of 1259 from a treaty that might be contracted, for instance, between England and Norway. It was only with the execution of treaty terms that the note of inequality crept in, and this was inherent in the nature of those terms, for they almost invariably dealt with feudal relations. Once an agreement was drawn up, its fulfilment or non-fulfilment became a matter of keeping or of breaking a feudal contract, a question for litigation in the court of the overlord.

A line was drawn, then, between England and English possessions in France. On the one side was an individual recognized in his sovereign capacity—*imperator regni sui*; on the other, the same individual recognized in his inferior feudal capacity—*comes in regno Francie*. To a considerable extent the distinction was admitted *de facto* by the English king. *De iure* he might protest that his courts were independent and self-sufficient, but no small amount of his diplomatic relations with France was carried on in the position of litigant before the Parlement de Paris.

Neither monarch, however, was consistent in his attitude. In two notable instances the king of France allowed the settlement of claims to be attempted outside his court. The process of Montreuil and, to a greater degree, the process of Périgueux represent conferences of representatives of equal powers. The methods that were used on these occasions and the goal for which the parties were striving have in them the seeds of international law. A great many of Joneston's

CONCLUSION 191

documents reveal a preoccupation with the discovery and establishment of custom. The essence of law is custom, and when the representatives of England and France met for these conferences they endeavoured to arrive at a definite set of rules that could be used as a basis for adjusting claims and grievances. That their efforts came to naught does not detract from the significance of what they attempted. From the beginning failure was implicit in their undertaking, for the problems under debate had too much of a feudal character to admit of satisfactory and independent resolution.

An important relation had to be definitely settled before the time should be ripe for any system of law between the two countries. The question of that relation was beginning to emerge when Edward II pronounced a citation for homage to France invalid because it had been made to him in England as a definite sovereign power; it ran through the arguments of English proctors at the Parlement de Paris. Complete sovereignty of the English king in his relations with France had to be clearly established, and when Edward III threw down the gauntlet in 1339 the long war that followed was his method of establishing this sovereignty. Until it was achieved, even though eventually through the expulsion of the English from France, there could be no secure basis for any clearly defined law that would govern the relations of the two countries.

APPENDIX I

THE ACCOUNTS OF PHILIP MARTEL

1. *Brit. Mus. MS. Add. 7966 A, fo. 29 dorso.*

Martel

Magistro Philippo Martel, venienti ad mandatum regis usque Norhamptoniam et Lincolniam pro quibusdam negociis regnum Scocie tangentibus ordinandis, pro expensis suis per lxiiij dies mensibus Decembris et Januarii et Februarii; videlicet, per xxxviij dies per quos fuit extra curiam, veniendo et redeundo, percipienti per diem 6*s*. 8*d*., et per xxvj dies morando in curia ad loca predicta, percipienti per diem 3*s*. pro expensis et vadiis garcionis et equorum suorum et aliis minutis necessariis pro expensis hospicii sui, per compotum factum cum eodem apud Lincolniam xviij die Februarii—16 *li*. 11*s*. 4*d*.   (1300–1)

2. *Brit. Mus. MS. Add. 8835, fo. 12.*

Expense magistri Philippi Martel

Magistro Philippo Martel, eunti ad partes Francie in comitiva domini Roberti de Burghersh' ad inquirendum de dampnis datis supra mare per homines regis Francie de Calesia diversis mercatoribus Anglie, pro expensis suis a vij die Aprilis usque vj diem Maii, utroque computato, per xxx dies, percipienti per diem dimidium marce, 15 *mar*. Eidem, pro denariis per ipsum solutis pro custuma apud Dovorriam et Whytsand' eundo et redeundo, 3*s*. Eidem, misso per regem ad partes predictas pro quibusdam negociis specialibus regi Francie exponendis, pro expensis suis a v^{to} die Julii usque xxv diem Octobris, utroque computato, per cxiij dies per quos fuit circa negocia predicta, eundo, morando, et redeundo, percipienti per diem dimidium marce ut prius, 37 *li*. 13*s*. 4*d*. Eidem, pro passagio suo hominum et equorum suorum ad mare et custuma data apud Dovorriam et Whytsand' eundo et redeundo, 4 *mar*., per compotum secum factum apud Westmonasterium x° die Februarii anno xxxiij°. Summa—50 *li*. 9*s*. 8*d*.

(1304)

3. *Exch. Accts. 369/11, fo. 49 dorso.*

Expense P. Martel

Magistro Philippo Martel, eunti ad mandatum regis usque Lugdunum ad curiam domini pape pro quibusdam negociis ipsum regem tangentibus ibidem expediendis, pro expensis suis sic eundo, morando, et redeundo a xxiiij^{to} die Septembris anno xxxiij° usque x diem Aprilis anno presenti, utroque computato, per c iiij^{xx} xix dies, percipienti per diem dimidium marce, 66 *li.* 6 *s.* 8 *d.* Eidem, pro passagio suo hominum et equorum suorum, custuma data apud Douorriam et Whitsand sic eundo et redeundo, 4 *mar.* Eidem, eunti alia vice in negocio regis predicti usque Burdigaliam ad curiam domini pape predicti, pro expensis suis eundo et morando a xiij° die Julii anno presenti usque xxj diem Septembris anno eodem, quo die diem suum clausit extremum in curia predicta, utroque computato, per lxxj dies, percipienti per diem ut prius, 23 *li.* 13 *s.* 4 *d.* Eidem, pro passagio suo hominum et equorum suorum, custuma data sic eundo, 2 *mar.*, per compotum factum cum magistro Johanne Martel, fratre et executore eiusdem, London' mense Martii anno regni regis Edwardi filii regis Edwardi nono. Summa—94 *li.* (1305–6)

APPENDIX II

THE ACCOUNTS OF ELIAS JONESTON

1. *Exch. Accts. 309/17, 166/3* (8 July 1309–2 October 1336).

[*309/17, m. 1*] Particule compoti magistri Elie de Joneston', clerici, custodis quorumdam processuum et memorandorum regis ducatum suum Aquitanie tangencium, de receptis, misis, et expensis suis per ipsum factis circa custodiam et prosecucionem processuum et memorandorum predictorum ab octavo die Julii anno regni regis Edwardi tertio incipiente usque festum Sancti Michaelis anno vicesimo incipiente. Et ab eodem festo Sancti Michaelis usque xxv diem Februarii anno regni regis Edwardi tertii post conquestum vj^{to} incipiente.[1]

Expense ab viij die Julii anno regni regis Edwardi filii regis Edwardi tertio usque festum Sancti Michaelis proximo sequens

Idem computat in vadiis ejusdem Elie, continue intendentis negocijs memoratis ab viij° die Julii predicto anno tertio usque festum Sancti Michaelis proximo sequens per iiij^{xx} et iiij dies, capiente per diem in partibus cismarinis 12 *d.*—4 *li.* 4 *s.*

Summa vadiorum, 4 *li.* 4 *s.*

Recepta ejusdem Elie, anno tercio

Idem reddit compotum de 9 *li.* receptis de Ingelardo de Warle, custode garderobe dicti regis, de [presti]to super vadiis suis, ut patet in rotulo de prestitis dicte garderobe anni tertii predicti [regis, per] Ingelardum liberato in scaccarium.

S[umma recep]te, 9 *li.*

Idem computat in vadiis ipsius Elie, continue intendentis negociis memoratis per totum annum tercium predictum. De quibus in partibus transmarinis per ij vices; videlicet, prima vice missi per consilium cum processibus et memorandis predictis ad advocatos et procuratores causas dicti regis in parliamento Paris' regentes a die Lune in crastino

[1] Dip. Doc. Chan. 29/10/19–25 and E.A. 309/16 are drafts of this account.

Pasche, quo transfretavit versus partes predictas, usque diem Mercurii post octabas Pasche, quo rediit in Angliam, primo et non ultimo computato, per ix dies, capiente per diem 2 *s*., et secunda vice a vij° die Septembris usque ad ix diem Octobris per xxiij dies, qui faciunt in totum xxxij dies, capiente per diem 2 *s*.—64 *s*. Et in partibus cismarinis per cccxxxiij dies, capiente per diem 12 *d*.—16 *li*. 13 *s*.

Summa vadiorum, 19 li. 17 s.

Et in passagio et repassagio maris et custumis hincinde prima vice, 3 *s*. 4 *d*. Et in cariagio dictorum processuum a London' usque Dovorr' per ij dies, et redeundo a Dovorr' usque London' per ij dies, capiente per diem 6 *d*.—2 *s*. Et in passagio maris secunda vice versus partes Francie vij° die Septembris predicto pro dicto Elia cum uno equo, 2 *s*. Et in batello, portagio, pontagio, et custumis hinc inde, 14 *d*. Et in cariagio dictorum processuum de London' usque Dovorr' per ij dies, 12 *d*., capiente per diem 6 *d*. Et in ij robis per idem tempus, 40 *s*.

Summa necessariorum, 49 s. 6 d.

Recepta Elie, anno iiij^{to}

Idem reddit compotum de 13 *li*. 6 *s*. 8 *d*. receptis de predicto Ingelardo de prestito super vadiis suis anno iiij^{to}, sicut continetur in rotulo de prestitis garderobe anni quarti predicti, per dictum Ingelardum liberato in scaccarium.

Item, de 50 *s*. receptis ab Emerico de Friscumbaldo, constabulario Burdegalie, in partibus Vasconie anno iiij^{to} predicto mense Februarii.

Summa recepte, 15 li. 16 s. 8 d.

De quibus in vadiis ejusdem Elie, continue intendentis negociis memoratis a festo Sancti Michaelis anno dicti regis Edwardi iiij^{to} usque vij diem Julii proximo sequentem per cc iiij^{xx} et j diem. De quibus in partibus transmarinis a dicto festo Sancti Michaelis usque ad ultimum diem Octobris proximo sequentem per xxxij dies, missi per consilium cum dictis processibus et memorandis ad commissarios regis Anglie Paris'. Et secunda vice a xiij die Januarii, missi per consilium ad dictos commissarios in partibus Vasconie existentes, utroque die computato, per lxxix dies, qui faciunt in toto cxj dies, capiente per diem 2 *s*.—11 *li*. 2 *s*. Et in partibus cismarinis per clxx dies, capiente per diem 12 *d*.—8 *li*. 10 *s*.

Summa vadiorum, 19 li. 12 s.

Et in repassagio maris primo die Novembris sine equo. Et in batello, portagio, et custumis hinc inde, 18 *d*. Et in passagio maris versus partes

Francie xiij die Januarii pro dicto Elia cum uno equo, 6 *s*. Et in batello, portagio, pontagio, et custumis hinc inde, 20 *d*. Et in repassagio suo cum uno equo nichil, quia transfretavit magister Thomas de Cobham. Et in custumis hinc inde, 4 *d*. Et in cariagio dictorum processuum a Dovorr' usque London' redeundo. Et alia vice a London' usque Dovorr' et redeundo a Dovorr' London' per vj dies, capiente per diem pro cariagio 6 *d*.—3 *s*. Et in ij robis per idem tempus, 40 *s*.

Summa necessariorum, 52 *s*. 6 *d*.

De annis quinto et sexto nichil computat, sicut patet in libro dicte garderobe.[1]

[*m. 2*]   Recepta ejusdem Elie, anni vij

In primis, a domino Cantuariensi archiepiscopo in domo sua London' viij die Decembris, 10 *li*. De quibus idem oneratur in libro garderobe de unde respondebitur, anni viij [*sic*] predicti.

Idem apud Westmonasterium a thesaurario et camerariis mense Novembris, 30 *s*.

Item, a thesaurario et camerariis apud Westmonasterium viij die Februarii, 20 *s*.

Item, a dictis thesaurario et camerariis ibidem xx die Junii, 20 *s*. De quibus 70 *s*. fit mencio in rotulis de liberacionibus factis dicto domino Ingelardo in scaccario recepte, de terminis Michaelis et Pasche anni vij predicti. Et de 20 *s*. receptis de custode garderobe Isabelle regine apud Pontis' mense Maii, sicut continetur ibidem.

Item, a domino Johanne Van, London' xxiij de Junii, 20 *s*.

Item, de Petro Galeys, fratre dicti Johannis Van, Paris' xxviij die mensis predicti, 64 *s*.

Summa totalis recepte, 17 *li*. 14 *s*.

In vadiis ejusdem Elie, continue intendentis negociis memoratis a festo Sancti Michaelis dicti anni vij usque vij diem Julii proximo sequentem per cc iiij^{xx} et i diem, de quibus in partibus transmarinis per tres vices: prima vice, missi ad regem Bolonie cum litteris cancellarii et thesaurarii ordinatis per consilium ad impediendum quoddam arbitrium inter dominum regem prelocutum a xiiij die Decembris usque ad xxviij diem ejusdem mensis, utroque die computato, per xv dies; et secunda vice, missi ad parliamentum Paris' cum litteris regis directis Francorum regi et senescallo Vasconie et ceteris omnibus de consilio dicti regis Anglie ad predictum parliamentum venturis pro dicto

[1] *Infra*, no. 2.

arbitrio impediendo a xix die Februarii usque xvij diem Maii, utroque die computato, per iiij^{xx} et viij dies; et tercia vice, missi per ordinacionem consilii ad parliamentum predictum pro negocio predicto et pro responsionibus per Francorum regem factis ad peticionem dicte domine regine a xxviij die Junii usque vij diem Julii per x dies, cxiij dies, ipso capiente per diem 2 *s*.—11 *li*. 6 *s*. Et in partibus cismarinis per clxviij dies, capiente per diem 12 *d*.—8 *li*. 8 *s*.

Summa vadiorum, 19 *li*. 14 *s*.

Et in passagio maris versus partes Francie, xiiij die Septembris pro dicto Elia, 4 *s*. Et in batello, portagio, et custumis hinc inde, 10 *d*. De repassagio et custumis non computat, quia transivit cum familia regis. Et in passagio maris versus partes Francie xix die Februarii predicto pro dicto Elia et cum uno equo, 4 *s*. Et in batello, portagio, et custumis, 16 *d*. Et in passagio maris tercia vice, videlicet, xxvij die Junii pro dicto Elia, 8 *d*. Et in batello, portagio, et custumis, 10 *d*. Et in repassagio ejusdem, 6 *d*. Et in batello usque ad navem, portagium, et custumis, 8 *d*. Idem pro duabus robis suis de eodem anno, 40 *s*.

Summa necessariorum, 52 *s*. 10 *d*.

De anno viij et ceteris omnibus subsequentibus usque ad xix diem mensis Octobris anni xvij nichil computat, quia computavit in garderoba regis, prout apparet per libros garderobe de annis predictis.[1]

Recepta ejusdem Elie, anni xvij

In primis, de domino Adam de Lynberge, constabulario Burdegalie, in partibus Vasconie et Tholos' inter xxx diem Decembris et primum diem Aprilis per vices, 50 *li*. *turon*., qui valent 10 *li*. *sterlingorum*, ut patet in libro compoti dicti constabularii.

Item, in garderoba comitis Cancie, Paris' die Sabati in septimana Pasche, 13 *s*. 4 *d*.

Item, idem Elias recepit in garderoba patris domini nostri regis tempore quo dictus Rogerus de Norbourth' fuit custos garderobe predicte in denariis in quibus remanet in arreragiis anno xiiij, 79 *s*. Et computavit plene de vadiis suis cum eodem domino Rogero usque ultimum diem Aprilis anno xv.[2]

Summa recepte, 14 *li*. 12 *s*. 4 *d*.

---

[1] *Infra*, nos. 3 and 4.
[2] *Hale* is written in the margin opposite this sentence. Henry of Hale was Northburgh's attorney and later cofferer of the wardrobe.

APPENDIX II

In vadiis ejusdem Elie, continue intendentis negociis memoratis a xx° die Octobris anni xvij predicti usque ad festum Sancti Michaelis proximo sequens per cccxlv dies, de quibus in partibus transmarinis missi per ordinacionem consilii ad partes Vasconie pro facto bastide Sancti Sacerdotis et aliis terram Vasconie tangentibus a x die Decembris usque xxiiij diem Aprilis per cxxxvj dies, capiente per diem 2 *s*.— 13 *li*. 12 *s*. Et in vadiis suis in partibus cismarinis per cccx dies, capiente per diem 12 *d*.—10 *li*. 9 *s*.

Summa vadiorum, 24 *li*. 12 *d*.

Et in passagio maris versus partes Francie x° die Decembris predicto sine equo, 6 *s*. Et in repassagio xxv die Aprilis, 19 *d*. Et in equis conductis usque Paris' de ordinacione consilii London', facta pro celeriori expedicione nunciorum regis ad Francorum regem destinatorum et litteras regis Anglie Paris' expectancium, 12 *s*. Et in equis conductis redeundo London' a civitate Paris' infra quatuor dies, cum litteris domini Dublinensis et comitis Cancie predictorum super premunicione citacionis ad arma per Francorum regem facta, 10 *s*. Et in uno equo nigro empto Paris' et mortuo in partibus Caturcinii, 40 *s*. Et in duabus robis per idem tempus, 40 *s*.

Summa necessariorum, 109 *s*. 7 *d*.

[*m. 3*]   Recepta ejusdem Elie, anni xviij

In primis, recepit de thesaurario et camerariis scaccarii apud Westmonasterium iiij^{to} die Decembris de prestito super vadiis suis versus partes Francie, 60 *s*.

Item, ab eisdem thesaurario et camerariis loco predicto ix die Martii de prestito super vadiis ejusdem versus partes predictas, 20 *s*.

Item,[1] die Augusti de eisdem thesaurario et camerariis loco quo prius de prestito super vadiis suis versus partes predictas, 20 *s*. Ut patet in rotulis de prestitis scaccarii anni viij[2] predicti.

Item, recepit in garderoba regis a domino Roberto de Wodehouse, custode dicte garderobe, mense Septembris apud Langedon' et Bourne per duas vices de prestito super expensis versus partes Francie cum familia comitis Cestre, 60 *s*. Ut patet in rotulo de prestitis garderobe liberato in scaccarium per dictum dominum Robertum.

Summa recepte, 8 *li*.

---

[1] The scribe has omitted the day of the month. It is given as 16 August in E.A. 325/7, a list of prests made to Joneston.
[2] An error for *xviij*.

THE ACCOUNTS OF ELIAS JONESTON 199

In vadiis ejusdem Elie, intendentis negociis memoratis a festo Sancti Michaelis anni xviij predicti usque idem festum anno revoluto per ccclxv dies, de quibus in partibus transmarinis per iiij^{xx} xiij dies per tres vices; videlicet, prima cum dominis Norwycensi et Wyntoniensi episcopis ad ostendendum eis transcripta processuum et litterarum tangencium negocia eis injuncta ab viij die Decembris usque xxiij diem Januarii proximo sequentem, utroque die computato, per xlvij dies. Et secunda vice cum familia domine regine[1] ad idem quod supra a xiiij die Martii usque x diem Aprilis per xxviij dies; et tercia vice a xiij die Septembris, quo die transfretavit versus partes Francie cum familia comitis Cestre, usque festum Sancti Michaelis proximo sequens per xviij dies, qui faciunt in toto iiij^{xx} xiij dies, capiente per diem 2s.— 9li. 6s. Et in partibus cismarinis per cclxxij dies, capiente per diem 12d.—13li. 12s.

Summa vadiorum, 22li. 18s.

Et in passagio maris versus partes Francie viij die Decembris predicto cum uno clerico sine equo, 2s. Et in batello, portagio, et custumis, 14d. Et in repassagio xxiij die Januarii, 2s. 8d. Et in batello, portagio, et custumis, 18d. Et in passagio maris secunda vice xiiij die Martii predicto cum clerico suo sine equo, 2s. Et in batello, portagio, 6d.; et nichil in custumis propter transitum domine regine. Et in repassagio xj die Aprilis cum uno clerico sine equo, 2s. Et in batello, portagio, et custumis, 14d. Et tercia vice in passagio maris versus partes Francie cum duobus clericis custodientibus processus regis xiij die Septembris predicto, in quodam batello conducto in crastino passagii dicti comitis et in portagio, 3s.; de custumis non computat propter transitum comitis predicti. Et in duabus robis per idem tempus, 40s.

Summa necessariorum, 56s.

Summa totalis expensarum, 25li. 3s.

Recepta anni xix

In primis, recepit in garderoba comitis Cestre de domino Willelmo de Cusauns, custode garderobe predicte, Paris' mense Novembris, sicut continetur in libris dicte garderobe anni predicti, 40s.

Item, in eadem garderoba de domino Ricardo de Buri, custode garderobe predicte, Paris' inter dictum mensem Novembris et ultimum diem Januarii proximo sequentem de prestito super vadiis suis, 9li.

Summa recepte, 11li.

---

[1] MS., *reginne*.

De quibus, in vadiis ejusdem Elie per totum annum xix per ccclxv dies; videlicet, in partibus transmarinis missi per ordinacionem consilii in comitiva domini comitis Cestre pro custodia processuum et memorandorum predictorum a dicto festo Sancti Michaelis anni quarti predicti incipientis usque primum diem Februarii proximo sequentem[1] per cxxij dies, capiente per diem 2 s.—12 li. 4 s. Et in partibus cismarinis per ccxliij dies,[2] capiente per diem 12 d.—12 li. 3 s.

Summa vadiorum, 24 li. 7 s.

Et in repassagio ejusdem primo die Februarii cum duobus[3] clericis sine equis. Et in batello, portagio, et custumis hinc inde, 2 s. 10 d. Et in apparatu cariagii dictorum processuum, videlicet, in burgis de coreo, 7 s. Et in uno sacco de coreo, 3 s. 6 d. Et in cariagio dictorum processuum a villa Dovorrii usque London' per tres dies mense Februarii, capiendo per diem 6 d.—18 d. Et in cartis, litteris autenticis, et processibus originalibus transcribendis, 6 s. 8 d. Et in expensis cujusdam nuncii, missi a Paris' usque London' pro negociis regis ibidem in parliamento, per xviij dies, expectans responsum consilii regis, 16 s. Et in duabus robis per idem tempus, 40 s.

Summa necessariorum, 77 s. 6 d.

Pars anni xx[mi]

Idem Elias computat in vadiis suis, intendens continue negociis predictis in partibus cismarinis a festo Sancti Michaelis anno xx[mo] usque ad xxiiij diem Januarii proximo sequentem per cxvij dies, capiente per diem 12 d.–116 s. Et pro una roba yemali per idem tempus, 20 s.

Summa, 6 li. 17 s.

Pars anni primi

Idem Elias computat in vadiis suis, continue intendens negociis predictis a dicto xxiiij[to] die Januarii usque ad festum Sancti Michaelis proximo sequens, in partibus cismarinis per ccxlviij dies, capiens per diem 12 d.–12 li. 8 s. Et pro roba sua estivali per idem tempus, 20 s.

Summa, 13 li. 8 s.

[m. 4] Recepta anni secundi

In primis, de thesaurario et camerariis ad scaccarium recepte mense Decembris de prestito super expensis suis anni secundi predicti, sicut continetur in rotulis de prestitis scaccarii predicti anni ejusdem, 40 s.

Summa recepte, 40 s.

[1] MS., sequententem.
[2] The scribe has written s. instead of dies.
[3] MS., duobis.

De quibus, in vadiis eiusdem Elie, continue intendentis negociis memoratis per totum annum secundum per ccclxv dies, in partibus cismarinis sequendo regem cum dictorum processuum transcriptis ad parliamenta Eboraci et[1] Norhampton' et ad consilia ejusdem regis apud Wygorn' et alibi, capiendo per diem 12 *d*.—18 *li*. 5 *s*. Et in dictorum transcriptorum cariagio ad loca predicta per xl dies, capiendo per diem 6 *d*.—20 *s*. Et pro duabus robis per idem tempus, 40 *s*.

Summa totalis, 20 *li*. 5 *s*.

Recepta anni tercii

In primis, recepit a thesaurario et camerariis apud Westmonasterium mense Maii ad scaccarium recepte, 13 *s*. 4 *d*.

Item, a domino Ricardo de Buri, custode garderobe regis, apud Boloniam et Ambianis eodem mense, 60 *s*.

Summa recepte, 73 *s*. 4 *d*.

De quibus, in vadiis ejusdem Elie, continue intendentis negociis memoratis per totum annum tercium per ccclxv dies; videlicet, in partibus transmarinis sequendo regem usque Ambian' et redeundo in Angliam cum ejus familia cum dictorum processuum et memorandorum transcriptis, videlicet, a xxvj die Maii, quo transfretavit versus partes predictas, usque xij diem mense Junii, quo rediit in Angliam, primo die computato, per xvij dies, capiente per diem 2 *s*.—34 *s*. Et in partibus cismarinis per cccxlviij dies, capiente per diem 12 *d*.—17 *li*. 8 *s*.

Summa vadiorum, 19 *li*. 2 *s*.

Et in cariagio dictorum processuum a London' usque Dovorriam eundo versus partes predictas et a Dovorria usque London' redeundo per vj dies, et a London' usque Kenelleuorth' et a dicto loco redeundo London' per vj dies, capiente 6 *d*.—2 *s*. Et in batello et portagio usque ad navem pro dicto Elia et dictis processubus et duobus clericis dictos processus custodientibus, 12 *d*. De passagio maris et repassagio et custumis hinc inde non computat, quia transivit cum familia regis. Et in duabus robis per idem tempus, 40 *s*.

Summa necessariorum, 47 *s*.

Summa totalis, 21 *li*. 9 *s*. Et habet de superplusagio, 17 *li*. 15 *d*. 8 *s*.

Recepta anni quarti

In primis, de thesaurario et camerariis ad scaccarium recepte mense Februarii hoc anno de prestito super vadiis suis, 10 *li*.

[1] MS., *in*.

Item, de isdem thesaurario et camerariis loco quo prius mense Julii, 7 *s.*

Item, in garderoba regis de magistro Thoma de Garton', custode garderobe predicte, apud Kenellewourth' mense Decembris anni ejusdem, 33 *s.* 4 *d.*

Item, de dicto magistro Thoma in garderoba predicta inter mensem Marcii et mensem Septembris anni ejusdem, 19 *s.*

Summa recepte, 12 *li.* 19 *s.* 4 *d.*

De quibus, in vadiis ejusdem Elie, continue intendentis negociis memoratis per totum annum quartum per ccclxv dies; videlicet, in partibus transmarinis missi per consilium ad parliamentum Francorum regis cum processibus inter dictos reges pendentibus indecisis a primo [die] Lune quadragesime, quo transfretavit versus partes predictas, usque Dominicam in medio quadragesime, quo reddiit in Angliam, primo die computato, per xx dies, capiente per diem 2 *s.*—40 *s.* Et in partibus cismarinis per cccxlv dies, capiente per diem 12 *d.*—17 *li.* 5 *s.*

Summa vadiorum, 19 *li.* 5 *s.*

Et in passagio maris versus partes predictas Francie cum duobus clericis primo die Lune quadragesime predicte, 3 *s.* Et in batello, portagio, et custumis, 2 *s.* 6 *d.* De repassagio non computat, quia transivit cum familia comitis Lancastrie. Et in custumis, 12 *d.* Et in restauro unius equi badii mortui in servicio domini regis in partibus cismarinis hoc anno, 36 *s.* Et in duabus robis per idem tempus, 40 *s.*

Summa necessariorum, 4 *li.* 2 *s.* 6 *d.*

[*m. 5*]   Recepta anni quinti

In primis, de thesaurario et camerariis ad scaccarium recepte mense Octobris hoc anno de prestito ut supra, 10 *s.*

Item, de eisdem thesaurario et camerariis loco quo prius mense Decembris hoc anno, 12 *li.*

Item, de dictis thesaurario et camerariis mense Augusti loco et anno predictis de prestito super expensis suis versus partes Francie, 66 *s.* 8 *d.*

Item, de domino Johanne Vincent, receptore regis in comitatu suo Pontivi, mense Septembris hoc anno de prestito super expensis suis in partibus predictis, 50 *s.*

Summa recepte, 18 *li.* 6 *s.* 8 *d.*

De quibus, in vadiis ejusdem Elie, continue intendentis negociis memoratis per totum annum quintum per ccclx [*sic*] dies, de quibus in

THE ACCOUNTS OF ELIAS JONESTON

partibus transmarinis missi per ordinacionem consilii in comitiva domini Johannis Travers et magistri Johannis de Hildesle pro quibusdam litteris Francorum regis in Angliam portandis a xxvij die Julii, quo transfretavit versus partes Francie, usque xvj diem Septembris, quo rediit in Angliam, primo die computato, per lij dies, capiente 2 s.—104 s. Et in partibus cismarinis per cccxiij dies, capiente per diem 12 d.— 15 li. 13 s.

Summa vadiorum, 20 li. 17 s.

Et in passagio maris versus Franciam nichil computat, quia transivit in comitiva dictorum Johannis Travers et Johannis de Hildesle, et in batello, portagio, et custumis hinc inde, 2 s. 6 d. Et in repassagio maris redeundo in Angliam, 3 s. Et in custumis hincinde, batello, et portagio, 2 s. 6 d. Et in duabus robis per idem tempus, 40 s.

Summa necessariorum, 47 s. 11 d.
Summa totalis, 23 li. 4 s. 11 d.

Recepta anni sexti incipientis

Idem reddit compotum de 10 s. receptis de domino Norwycensi episcopo mense Januarii hoc anno de prestito super expensis anni ejusdem.

Summa recepte, 10 s.

De quibus, idem computat in vadiis ipsius Elie, continue intendentis negociis predictis in partibus cismarinis per cxlix dies, capiente ibidem pro vadiis suis per diem 12 d. per idem tempus; videlicet, a festo Sancti Michaelis anno vj^{to} predicto incipiente usque xxv diem Februarii proximo sequentem, 7 li. 9 s. Et pro roba sua yemali, 20 s.

Summa expensarum, 8 li. 9 s.[1]

[166/3, m. 1]. Particule compoti magistri Elie de Ioneston', clerici, nuper custodis quorumdam processuum et memorandorum regis ducatum suum Acquitanie tangencium, de receptis, misis, et expensis suis per eundem factis circa custodiam et prosecucionem eorumdem processuum et memorandorum a xxv° die Februarii anno regni regis Edwardi tertii post conquestum vj^{to}, usque quem diem alias computavit, usque secundum diem Octobris anno x° finiente.

Recepta anni vj^{ti}

Item, reddit compotum de 20 s. receptis de Johanne Vyncent, receptore Pontivi, apud Wytsand' mense Maii anno vj^{to} super

[1] The account is struck through to indicate enrolment (Pipe 6 Edw. III, m. 51).

expensis suis circa prosecucionem dictorum processuum in partibus transmarinis.

Summa recepte, 20 s.

De quibus computat in vadiis ipsius, continue intendentis negociis memoratis a xxv die Februarii anno vj^{to} predicto, usque quem ultimo computavit in scaccario predicto, usque ad festum Sancti Michaelis proximo sequente [*sic*], primo die computato, per ccxvj dies, de quibus in partibus transmarinis a xix die Maii, quo transfretavit versus partes Francie de ordinacione consilii, usque ad xxiij diem ejusdem mensis proximo sequentem, quo rediit in Angliam, primo die computato, per quatuor dies, capiendo per diem 2 *s*.—8 *s*.; et in partibus cismarinis per ccxij dies, capiendo per diem 12 *d*.—10 *li*. 12 *s*. Summa vadiorum, 11 *li*. Et in una roba per idem tempus, 20 *s*.[1] Et in passagio maris cum dictis processibus et duobus equis versus partes Francie, 9 *s*. 6 *d*. Et in batellis et portagio ad navem apud Dovorr' et a nave usque Wytsand', 14 *d*. Et in custumis apud Dovorr', 8 *d*., et apud Wytsand', 16 *d*. Et in repassagio maris cum dictis processibus et duobus equis, 6 *s*. 6 *d*. Et in batellis et portagio ad navem apud Wytsand' et a nave vsque Dovorr', 12 *d*. Et in custumis apud Wytsand', 16 *d*., et apud Dovorr', 8 *d*. Et in cariagio dictorum processuum a London' usque Dovorr' eundo versus partes Francie, et a Dovorr' redeundo London' per quinque dies, capiendo per diem pro hujusmodi cariagio 6 *d*.—2 *s*. 6 *d*. Item, mense Julii in scriptura processuum missorum de ordinacione consilii ad curiam Francie pro consilio habendo ab advocatis dicte curie super forma recuperandi terram Agenn' et alias terras per Francie regem occupatas, 33 *s*. Item, mense Septembris in scriptura processuum missorum ad curiam Francie et ad partes Vasconie per magistrum Henricum de Cantuaria pro consilio habendo super facto predicto, 15 *s*. Summa necessariorum, 4 *li*. 12 *s*. 8 *d*.

Summa totalis, 15 *li*. 12 *s*. 8 *d*.[2]

Recepta anni septimi

Idem reddit compotum de 20 *s*. receptis de thesaurario et camerariis ad scaccarium recepte xvij die Octobris anno vij° de prestitis super vadiis et expensis suis circa custodiam et prosecucionem processuum regis tangencium ducatum Acquitanie in custodia sua existencium. Et

---

[1] This item crossed out.
[2] *xv li.* has been crossed out and *xiiij* written above.

THE ACCOUNTS OF ELIAS JONESTON 205

de 100 s. receptis de eisdem thesaurario et camerariis ibidem super eisdem xv° die Aprilis anno vij°.

Summa recepte, 6 li.

De quibus computat in vadiis ipsius, continue intendentis negociis memoratis per totum annum septimum predictum; videlicet, a festo Sancti Michaelis anno septimo predicto usque idem festum anno revoluto per ccclxv dies, primo die computato, de quibus in partibus transmarinis de ordinacione consilii a xix die Aprilis, quo transfretavit versus partes Francie, usque xxiiij diem Junii proximo sequentem, quo rediit in Angliam, primo die computato, per lxvj dies, capiendo per diem 2 s.—6 li. 12 s. Et in partibus cismarinis per cc iiij^{xx} xix dies, capiendo per diem 12 d.–14 li. 19 s. Summa, 21 li. 11 s. Et in una roba estivali infra[1] idem tempus, 20 s.

Et in passagio maris versus partes Francie cum dictis processibus et tribus equis, 21 s. Et in batellis et portagio usque ad navem apud Dovorr' et a nave usque villam Calleti, 17 d., et in custumis apud Dovorr', 8 d., et apud villam Calleti, 20 d. Et in repassagio maris cum duobus clericis et dictis processibus sine equis, 3 s., et in batellis et portagio usque ad navem apud Wytsand' et a nave usque Dovorr', 14 d. Et in custumis apud Wytsand', 16 d., et apud Dovorr', 8 d. Et in cariagio dictorum processuum a civitate Eboraco usque Dovorr' eundo versus partes Francie, et a Dovorr' usque Eboracum redeundo, per xviii dies, capiendo per diem 6 d.—9 s. Et in cariagio dictorum processuum usque London' pro ipsis liberandis magistro Johanni Piers, per vi dies, 3 s. Item, mense Octobris London' et apud Westmonasterium in scriptura processuum missorum ad partes Francie per Norwycensem et Wygorniensem episcopos, 20 s. Item, mense Maii in curia Francie regis extra Paris' in scriptura processuum et in litteris sigillatis tangentibus castrum et castellaniam Blavie et alias causas domini nostri regis, 50 s. Et in scriptura Paris' eodem mense et mense sequenti, 15 s. Summa necessariorum, 8 li. 7 s. 11 d.[2]

Summa totalis, 28 li. 18 s. 11 d.

Recepta anni octavi[3]

De quibus computat in vadiis ipsius, continue intendentis negociis memoratis per totum annum octavum predictum; videlicet, a festo Sancti Michaelis anno viij° predicto usque ad idem festum anno

---

[1] Written above *per*, which is crossed out.   [2] This sentence struck out.
[3] A blank space is left for the receipts, but remains unfilled.

revoluto, primo die computato, per ccclxv dies, de quibus in partibus transmarinis a vj^{to} die Octobris, quo transfretavit versus partes [*m. 2*] Francie de ordinacione consilii, usque sextum diem Martii, quo rediit in Angliam, primo die computato, per clj dies. Et a quarto die Aprilis, quo transfretavit versus partes Francie de ordinacione consilii, usque quintum diem Septembris, quo rediit in Angliam, primo die computato, per cliiij dies. Et sic in partibus transmarinis cccv dies, capiendo per diem 2 *s*.—30 *li*. 10 *s*. Et in partibus cismarinis per lx dies, capiendo per diem 12 *d*.—60 *s*.

Summa vadiorum, 33 *li*. 10 *s*.

Et in duabus robis per idem tempus, 40 *s*. Et in passagio maris versus partes Francie dicto mense Octobris sine dictis processibus et sine equis, 12 *d*. Et in batellis et portagio usque ad navem apud Dovorr' et a nave usque Wytsand', 7 *d*. Et in custumis apud Dovorr', 2 *d*. Et apud Wytsand', 6 *d*. Et in repassagio maris dicto mense Martii sine dictis processibus et sine equis, 18 *d*., et in batellis et portagio ad navem apud Wytsand' et a nave usque Dovorr' 6 *d*. Et in custumis apud Wytsand', 6 *d*. Et apud Dovorr' 2 *d*. Item, in passagio maris dicto mense Aprilis cum dictis processibus et duobus equis, 9 *s*. 6 *d*. Et in batellis et portagio usque ad navem apud Dovorr' et a nave usque Wytsand', 13 *d*. Et in custumis apud Dovorr', 6 *d*., et apud Wytsand', 14 *d*. Et in repassagio maris dicto mense Septembris cum uno clerico et dictis processibus sine equis, 3 *s*. Et in batellis et portagio usque ad navem apud Wytsand' et a nave usque Dovorr', 11 *d*. Et in custumis apud Wytsand', 12 *d*., et apud Dovorr', 4 *d*. Et in portagio dictorum processuum a London' usque Dovorr' eundo versus partes Francie, et a Dovorr' usque Eboracum redeundo, per xij dies, capiendo per diem pro hujusmodi cariagio, 6 *d*.—6 *s*. Item, in scriptura processuum Paris' et alibi sequendo regem Francie per tempus predictum, 20 *s*. Summa necessariorum, 4 *li*. 8 *s*. 5 *d*.

Summa totalis, 37 *li*. 18 *s*. 5 *d*.

Recepta anni noni

Idem respondet de 13 *li*. 6 *s*. 8 *d*. receptis de thesaurario et camerariis scaccarii quarto die Januarii super consimilibus expensis suis memorandorum predictorum.

Summa recepte, 13 *li*. 6 *s*. 8 *d*.

De quibus computat in vadiis ipsius, continue intendentis negociis memoratis per totum annum nonum predictum; videlicet, a festo

THE ACCOUNTS OF ELIAS JONESTON

Sancti Michaelis anni noni predicti usque ad idem festum anno revoluto per ccclxv dies, de quibus in partibus transmarinis a xxxiiij^{to} [*sic*] die Januarii, quo transfretavit versus partes Francie de ordinacione consilii, usque secundum diem Aprilis, quo rediit in Angliam, primo die computato, per lxviij dies, capiendo per diem 2 *s*.—6 *li*. 16 *s*. Et in partibus cismarinis per cc iiij^{xx} xvij dies, capiendo per diem 12 *d*.—14 *li*. 17 *s*.

Summa vadiorum, 21 *li*. 13 *s*.[1]

Et in duabus robis per idem tempus, 40 *s*. Et in passagio maris cum dictis processibus et tribus equis, 21 *s*. Et in batellis et portagio ad navem apud Dovorr' et a nave usque Wytsand', 13 *d*. Et in custumis apud Dovorr', 8 *d*. Et apud Wytsand', 16 *d*. Et in repassagio cum uno clerico et dictis processibus sine equis, 3 *s*., et in batellis usque ad navem apud Wytsand' et a nave usque Dovorr', 14 *d*. Et in custumis apud Wytsand', 12 *d*. Et apud Dovorr', 4 *d*. Et in cariagio dictorum processuum ab Eboraco usque Dovorr' eundo versus partes Francie, et a Dovorr' usque Eboracum redeundo, per xix dies, capiendo per diem pro hujusmodi cariagio 6 *d*.—9 *s*. 6 *d*. Summa necessariorum, 79 *s*. 1 *d*.

Summa totalis, 25 *li*. 12 *s*. 1 *d*.

Recepta anni decimi

Idem reddit compotum de 46 *s*. 8 *d*. receptis de eisdem ibidem de prestito super expensis predictorum processuum ad parliamentum London' xxj° die Februarii anno x°.

Summa recepte, 46 *s*. 8 *d*.

De quibus computat in vadiis ipsius, continue intendentis negociis memoratis a festo Sancti Michaelis dicti anni decimi incipientis usque festum Sancti Michaelis proximo sequens et ab eodem festo usque ad secundum diem Octobris anni undecimi incipientis, primo die computato, per ccclxviij dies, capiendo per diem 12 *d*.—18 *li*. 8 *s*. Et in duabus robis per idem tempus, 40 *s*. Et in cariagio dictorum processuum ab Eboraco usque parliamentum mense Martii London' pro ipsis liberandis magistro Johanni Pieres per septem dies, capiendo per diem pro hujusmodi cariagio 6 *d*.—3 *s*. 6 *d*.

Summa totalis, 20 *li*. 11 *s*. 6 *d*.
Summa totalis recepte, 22 *li*. 13 *s*. 4 *d*.
Summa totalis expensarum, 127 *li*. 13 *s*. 7 *d*.
Et sic habet de superplusagio 105 *li*. 3 *d*.[2]

---

[1] This sentence struck out.
[2] The account is struck through to indicate enrolment (Pipe 11 Edw. III, m. 39).

2. *Brit. Mus. Cotton MS. Nero C. viii, fo. 65.*

Expense magistri E. de Joneston'

Magistro Elie de Joneston', clerico ad processus, memoranda, articulos treugarum et pacis inter dominos Anglie et Francie reges, necnon memoranda ducatum Aquitanie tangencia custodienda assignato, pro vadiis et expensis suis per totum annum presentem; videlicet, per ccclxvj dies, propter annum bisextilem, per quos continue fuit intendens negociis memoratis in partibus Anglie, percipienti per diem 12 *d.*—18 *li.* 16 *s.* Eidem pro robis suis hiemali et estivali anni ejusdem, 40 *s.*, per compotum secum factum London' v^{to} die Novembris anno decimo —20 *li.* 6 *s.* (1311–12)

3. *Exch. Accts. 375/9, fo. 19.*

Elias de Joneston'

Elie de Joneston', clerico, moranti Parisius per assignacionem regis ad prosequendum negocia sua in parliamento regis Francie terram Vasconie tangencia, de prestito super expensis suis per manus proprias apud Parisius xviij° die Aprilis—20 *s.* (1314)

4. *Brit. Mus. MS. Add. 17362, fo. 13.*

Expense Elie de Joneston', clerici

Magistro Elie de Joneston' clerico ad prosequendum negocia domini regis ducatum Aquitannie tangencia per ipsum dominum regem et consilium suum assignato, pro vadiis et expensis suis per totum annum presentem xiij; videlicet, per ccclxvj dies, propter annum bisextilem, per quos fuit intendens negociis predictis tam in partibus cismarinis quam transmarinis, percipiendo per diem 12 *d.*— 18 *li.* 6 *s.* Eidem percipienti per ordinacionem consilii predicti duas robas per annum, pro hujusmodi robis suis hiemali et estivali anni presentis, 40 *s.* Eidem pro stipendiis unius equi portantis processus et memoranda negociorum predictorum inter London' et Ambianos eundo et redeundo per xij dies mensibus Junii et Julii in comitiva domini regis, percipiendo pro dicto equo et uno garcione 6 *d.* per diem—6 *s.*; per compotum factum apud Odyham xv° die Dcembris anno xiiij. Summa, 20 *li.* 12 *s.* (1319–20)

THE ACCOUNTS OF ELIAS JONESTON 209

5. *Brit. Mus. MS. Stowe 553, fo. 32 dorso.*

Expense E. de Joneston', clerici, extra curiam
in negociis regis

Magistro Elie de Joneston', assignato per dominum regem et consilium suum ad prosequendum quedam negocia ipsius domini regis ducatum suum Aquitannie tangencia, pro expensis suis a primo die Maii anno quintodecimo usque vij^m diem Julii anno sextodecimo finiente, utroque computato, per ccccxxxiij dies, de quibus fuit in partibus transmarinis ad prosequendum eadem negocia in curia regis Francie per xxx dies mensibus Martii et Aprilis anno sextodecimo, percipiendo 18 *d.* per diem, et in partibus cismarinis per cccciij dies, percipiendo 12 *d.* per diem, per compotum inde factum—22 *li.* 8 *s.* (1322–3)

APPENDIX III

THE ACCOUNT OF ROGER STAUNFORD

Exch. Accts. 166/9

(6 October 1336–1 February 1339)

Compotus Rogeri de Staunford', clerici, custodis processuum et memorandorum domini regis de ducatu suo Aquitanie, a vj^{to} die Octobris anno regni regis Edwardi tercii post conquestum xj^o incipiente usque ad primum diem Februarii anno regni ejusdem regis terciodecimo.

Annus xj^{us}

Expense

Idem computat in vadiis suis pro custodia dictorum processuum et memorandorum a vj^{to} die Octobris anno xj^o incipiente usque ad festum Sancti Michaelis proximo sequens per ccclix dies, capiente per diem 12 d.—17 li. 19 s.

Et in robis suis yemali et estivali, 40 s. Et in cariagio dictorum processuum et memorandorum ad diversos tractatus apud Notyngham et Eboracum et alibi per ix dies, 4 s. 6 d., capiente per diem 6 d.

Summa expensarum, 20 li. 3 s. 6 d.

Annus xij^{us}

Recepta

Idem reddit compotum de 100 s. receptis ad receptam scaccarii per manus camerariorum eiusdem xxj^o die Julii anno xij^o super vadiis suis in officio p[redicto].

Summa recepte, 100 s.

Expense

De quibus idem computat in vadiis s[ui]s a d[icto] festo Sancti Michaelis anno xij^o incipiente usque ad idem festum proximo sequens per ccclxv dies, 18 li. 5 s., [capien]te per diem 12 d. Et in robis suis yemali et estivali, 40 s. Et in cariagio dictorum processuum et memorandorum de London' usque Norhampton' et deinde usque Staunford'

THE ACCOUNT OF ROGER STAUNFORD

et deinde usque London' et deinde usque Dovorr' sequendo archiepiscopum et de Dovorr' usque London' per xvj dies, 8*s.*, capiente per diem 6*d.*

Summa expensarum, 20 *li.* 13 *s.*

Prima pars anni xiij

Expense

Idem computat in vadiis suis a dicto festo Sancti Michaelis anno xiij° incipiente usque primum diem Februarii proximo sequentem per cxxv dies, ultimo die computato, 6 *li.* 5 *s.*, capiente per diem 12 *d.* Et in una roba, 20 *s.*

Summa, 7 *li.* 5 *s.*[1]

[1] The account is struck through to indicate enrolment (Pipe 12 Edw. III, m. 53).

APPENDIX IV

TABLE I

English Claims at Montreuil, 1306
(Based on D.D.C. 29/5/18 and 27/7)

1. *La Blacoge de Londres*

   Sailing from Winchelsea to Dieppe; plundered by Michel de Navarre in August 1301; taken to Calais and disposed of by same and Henri de Geneve.

   Cargo belonging to Richard Bush, of London:

	£	s	d	£	s	d
10,000 (pieces) of tin	67	0	0			
15 sacks of lead	12	0	0			
140 gold florins 'del premier coin du roi de France'	42	0	0			
80 *livres petits tournois noirs*	8	0	0			
9 weights of cheeses	6	0	0			
Cables, beds, &c.	15	0	0	150	0	0

   Claim, £20.

2. *La Blithe de Londres*

   Sailing from Brabant to London; plundered by Johan Pedroge off the North Foreland in July 1303; taken to Calais and disposed of by same and Odard de Maubusshon.

   Cargo belonging to Cecile atte More, of London:

	£	s	d	£	s	d
10 tuns of unpurified metal	10	0	0	10	0	0

   Claim, £2.

   Cargo belonging to William Bush, of London:

	£	s	d	£	s	d
40 tuns of unpurified metal	40	0	0	40	0	0

   Claim, £8.

3. *La Brume de Sandwiz*

   Sailing from Brabant to Sandwich; plundered by Johan Alsten, Johan Bay, Staci Beolf, Johan Huard, Odard de Maubusshon, and

TABLES

Guy Sodin at Orwell between 7 April and 29 September 1303; taken to Calais and disposed of by same.

Cargo belonging to Johan Drake, of Sandwich:

 £8 sterlings *coronez*   —   —   —
 Claim, £16.

Cargo belonging to Johan Lonerik, of Sandwich:

 185 *livres en ciseins, en torneis*
  doubles, et en gros torneis   23   2   6   23   2   6
 Claim, £3.

Cargo belonging to Berthelmeu Love, of Sandwich:

 Moneys and merchandise   4   0   0
 Armour   1   4   0   5   4   0
 Claim, £7.

4. *La Coqe Seinte Marie*

Sailing from Brabant to Sandwich; plundered by Johan Bay, &c. (as in no. 3); taken to Calais and disposed of by same.

Cargo belonging to Johan Arnais, of Sandwich:

 Cloths, &c.   25   4   8   25   4   8
 Claim, £1 10*s.*

Cargo belonging to Thomas de Bomenal, of Sandwich:

 Cloths, &c.   15   5   2   15   5   2
 Claim, £1 10*s.*

Cargo belonging to Geffrey Darundel and Johan Pece, of Sandwich:

 Cloths, &c.   277   16   4   277   16   4
 Claim, £30.[1]

Cargo belonging to Roberd Monin (Johan de Langedon, attorney), of Sandwich:

 1 scarlet cloth   6   0   0
 1 russet cloth   1   6   8   7   6   8
 Claim, £1 6*s.*

[1] Incomplete.

APPENDIX IV

5. *La Custance de Sandwiz* (William Berepak, master)

Sailing from Sandwich to Antwerp; plundered by Johan Pedroge at Oye, near Calais, between 7 April and 29 September 1303; taken to Calais and disposed of by same.

Cargo belonging to Custance, wife of Estevene Crawe, of Sandwich:

60 sums of grain			
2 measures of canvas	40	0	0
Claim, £10.			

6. *La Distaf de Haneford*

Sailing from Berwick to London; plundered by Johan Pedroge and men of Calais at Blakeney on 27 August 1303; taken to Calais and disposed of by same.

Cargo belonging to Gilbert de Asshendon, of London:

134 salmons	5	11	8			
1 bed with fittings	1	0	0			
1 coffer with various articles	1	0	0			
14 housings		18	8	8	10	4
Claim, £8 10s. 4d.						

Cargo belonging to Thomas atte Hurst, of London:

3 robes	3	6	8			
Iadas and cotton	2	0	0			
2 pails and 1 basin of metal		5	0			
1 bowl of mazer	1	6	8			
1 chalice	2	0	0			
2 vestments and 2 liveries	2	13	4			
Sheets and canvas		5	0	11	16	8
Claim, £11 16s. 8d.						

7. *Godefroi de Duffle*

Sailing from London to Brabant; plundered by Michel de Navarre and others of Calais off the North Foreland in May 1298; taken to Calais and disposed of by same and Henri de Geneve.

Cargo belonging to Thomas Cros, of London, executor of the will of Thomas Cros *père*, who was executor of the will of Henri Box, of London:

11 sarplers of wool	80	0	0	80	0	0
Claim—see no. 24.						

8. *La Halop Seint Johan de Bayone*

Sailing from Tonnay-Charente (*dép.* Charente-Inf., *arr.* Rochefort) to England; plundered by Reyner Grimaud and others and taken to Calais in August 1303.

Cargo belonging to James le Reue, fish-dealer of London:

4 wines		–	–	–			
6 tuns (of wine)		3	12	0			
6 pipes (of wine)		–	–	–	3	12	0[1]

Claim, ?

9. *La Hayne de Sandwiz*

Sailing from Sandwich to Newcastle; plundered by Johan Alsten, Staci Beolf, Simon Davyn, Johan Huard, Odard de Maubusshon, and Guy Sodin at Stackard[2] between 7 April and 29 September 1303; taken to Calais and disposed of by same; nine men killed.

Cargo belonging to Hamon Cundi and William Kyok, of Sandwich:

Goods and merchandise	30	0	0			
Value of ship	21	0	0	51	0	0

Claim, £10.

10. *Johan Atheland*

Sailing from London to Brabant; plundered by Michel de Navarre and others of Calais off the North Foreland in May 1298; taken to Calais and disposed of by same and Henri de Geneve.

Cargo belonging to Thomas Cros (see no. 7)

20 sarplers of wool	202	0	0	202	0	0

Claim—see no. 24.

11. *Johan Azelard de Mallins*

Sailing from London; plundered by Michel de Navarre, &c. (as in no. 10).

Cargo belonging to Watier le Hert de Mallins and Rose de Salisbery, of London:

2 sarplers and 1 sack of wool	18	6	0[1]			
9 pieces of worsted	4	1	0			
12 *guilliers de* ...		14	0[1]			
14 gold florins	5	4	0			
1 silver bowl without legs	–	–	–	28	19	2

Claim, £6.

[1] Incomplete.   [2] I have been unable to identify this place.

216   APPENDIX IV

12. *Johan le Chandeler*

Sailing from London to Brabant; plundered by Michel de Navarre, &c. (as in no. 10).

Cargo belonging to Cecile atte More, of London:

7 sacks and 6 cloths of wool	66	9	3	66	9	3
Claim—see no. 26.						

Cargo belonging to Thomas Cros (see no. 7):

12 sarplers of wool	102	0	0	102	0	0
Claim—see no. 24.						

13. *La Lechenard*

Sailing from Scotland to London; plundered by men of Calais and others between Kirkley and Harwich in 1298; taken to Calais and disposed of by same; one man killed.

Cargo belonging to Richer de Resham, citizen of London:

16 sacks of wool, 3 lasts and 6 dickers of leather, lead, metal vessel, pots, pails, cauldrons, tallow, and ointment	151	5	0	151	5	0
Claim, £151. 5s.						

14. *Margarete de Jernemuth*

Sailing to London; plundered by Johan Pedroge and men of Calais at Orfordness in 1302; ship taken to Calais by same; men killed.

Cargo belonging to Johan de Chelchethe, of London:

8 lasts of herring	5	6	8			
1 barrel of *halayn*	2	8	0			
1 silver bowl	1	3	0			
2 beds, 2 robes, 1 coffer	3	6	8			
1 pot . . .	—	—	—			
. . . of straw		8	0	39	5	8
Claim, £39 5s. 8d.						

Cargo belonging to Adam de Fulham, of London:

5 lasts of herring	20	0	0	20	0	0
Claim, £20.						

TABLES

Cargo belonging to Edmonde Lambins, of London:

3 lasts of herring	12	0	0	12	0	0

Claim, £12.

15. *La Mariote de Seland*

Sailing from Antwerp to London; plundered by Michel de Navarre, &c. (as in no. 10).

Cargo belonging to William Bush, of London:

1 load containing 18 russet cloths of Brabant	54	0	0			
5,000 salt fish	83	6	8			
300 boards	3	15	0			
36 barrels of oil	28	16	0			
2 packs of rabbit skins, containing 2,400	6	0	0	175	17	8

Claim, £20.

16. *Michel de Arwe* (owned by William Sare)

Sailing from London to Brabant; plundered on the high seas by Reyner Grimaud and others on 6 October 1303; taken to Calais and disposed of by same; sailors imprisoned at Calais.

Cargo belonging to Johan le Blund, Johan Gode, Richard le Goldsmith, Johan de Hetheye, William de Nesse, William le Sherman, Wauter Top, all of London:

9 sacks and 16 cloths of good wool in 9 sarplers	96	3	6			
10 sacks and 4 cloths of good wool in 9 sarplers and 6 lambskins	101	18	4			
5 sacks and 22 cloths of wool in 5 sarplers and 156 lambskins	88	15	0			
6 sacks and 42 cloths	86	3	4			
5 sacks and 4 cloths	51	11	4			
7 sacks and 4 cloths	71	11	4			
7 sacks and 26 cloths	80	0	0	576	2	10

Claim, £656 3s. 8d.

17. *Michel de Middelborgh*

Sailing from London to Brabant; plundered by Michel de Navarre and others of Calais off the North Foreland in May 1298; taken to Calais and disposed of by same and Henri de Geneve.

Cargo belonging to Thomas Cros (see no. 7):
    6 sarplers of wool   60 0 0   60 0 0
    Claim—see no. 24.

18. A ship owned by Nichol de Caich

Sailing from Scotland to Brabant; plundered by Odard de Maubusshon, Johan Pedroge, Johan de la Barge, Lani Jacop, Gusse Odin, Johan le Parker, Valseur le Mariner, Hirnolet le Mau, and Petre le Pottere at Kirkley in August 1304; ship and goods taken to Calais and disposed of by same; men killed.

Cargo belonging to Aleyn de Thornden, burgess of Lynn:
    2 lasts and 3 dickers of deerskin   8 0 0
    1,200 lambskins   8 0 0
    60 salmons   4 0 0
    51 pounds of pollards   40 0 0   133 0 0[1]
    Claim, £143.

19. *La Nicholas*

Sailing from Lynn to Scotland; plundered by Odard de Maubusshon, Johan Pedroge, Johan Buard, Gusse Odin, Simond Davyn, Johan Allestein, Clay Clinchamer, Vaaseur le Mariner, Johan Paye, and Pettre le Pottere at Scarborough in August 1303; taken to Calais and disposed of by same; a mariner killed.

Cargo belonging to William Quineberge, burgess of Lynn:
    Bread, ale, honey, meat, hard salt
        fish, &c.   35 15 8   35 15 8
    Claim, £45 15s. 8d.

20. *Tydman Mullard del Bek*

Sailing to Antwerp; plundered by Reyner Grimaud and other off the coast of Holland in August 1303; taken to Calais and disposed of by same.

Cargo belonging to Robert But, of Norwich:
    12 sarplers of wool   160 0 0   160 0 0
    Claim, £60.

[1] Must include value of ship.

21. *La Welifare de Sandwiz*

Sailing from Sandwich to Antwerp; plundered by Johan Alsten, &c. (as in no. 3), near the Isle of Thanet between 7 April and 29 September 1303; taken to Calais and disposed of by same.

Cargo belonging to Johan Peni and Wauter le Draper, of Sandwich:

20 tuns 6 pipes of wine	60	0	0	60	0	0
Claim, £10.						

22. *William B . . .*[1]

Sailing from London to Brabant; plundered by Reyner Grimaud on the high seas; taken to Calais and disposed of by same; shipper imprisoned for a year and six months.

Cargo belonging to Johan de Masseworthe:

Wool	100	0	0			
1 trunk	1	0				
1 blue robe	8	10^2		100	9	10^2
Claim, £175 13*s*.[2]						

23. *William de Douere*

Sailing from Antwerp to England; plundered by Johan Pedroge and Odard de Maubusshon and others at Dover in September 1303; taken to Calais and disposed of by same.

Cargo belonging to Adam Houson, of Gloucester:

Cloths, silver in bulk	220	0	0	220	0	0
Claim, £280.						

24. *William le Fitz Henri*

Sailing from London to Brabant; plundered by Michel de Navarre, &c. (as in no. 10).

Cargo belonging to Thomas Cros (see no. 7):

16 sarplers of wool	192	0	0			
3 sarplers of wool	36	0	0	228	0	0
Claims, £100.						

---

[1] Badly mutilated; this entry may form a part of no. 16.
[2] Incomplete.

APPENDIX IV

25. *William Henriessone de Seland*

Sailing from London to Brabant; plundered by Michel de Navarre, &c. (as in no. 10).

Cargo belonging to Cecile atte More, of London:
5 sacks and 36 cloths of wool   44 18 5   44 18 5
Claim—see no. 26.

26. *William Petersone de Seland*

Sailing from London to Brabant; plundered by Michel de Navarre, &c. (as in no. 10).

Cargo belonging to Cecile atte More, of London:
4 sacks and 56 cloths of wool   36 6 7   36 6 7
Claims, £20.

27. ———

Sailing from Newcastle to London; plundered by Michel de Navarre, Reyner Grimaud, and others at Margate; taken to Calais and disposed of by same.

Cargo belonging to Rauf de Gatesdene, of London:
... and 1 pipe of unpurified silver   30 15 0   30 15 0
Claim, £10.

28. ———

Sailing from Sandwich to Winchelsea; plundered by Johan Alsten, &c. (as in no. 3), between Sandwich and Dover between 7 April and 29 September 1303; taken to Calais and disposed of by same.

Cargo belonging to Lucas Clolle, of Sandwich:
———   18 0 0   18 0 0
Claim, £3.

Total value of cargoes on 28 ships   3,250 3 5
Total amount of claims by 40 persons   1,882 16 0

TABLE 2

Pipe Roll Accounts of Envoys

22 Edward I–4 Edward III

(Only one account—Pipe 27 Edw. I, m. 31—from the reign of Edward I is included in this table; the others are from the following reign, with the exception of one—E.A. 309/32, a part of which runs into the reign of Edward III.)

Receipts

Exchequer		26055	1	8
Direct payment	22453			
Through the Bardi	3302 : 1 : 8			
Through the collector of wool customs in London	200			
Through Hugh de Patryngton	100			
Other sources		302	14	8½
Receiver in Gascony	130			
Collector of wool customs in London	100			
Wardrobe	56			
Constable of Bordeaux	16 : 14 : 8½			
	Total	26357	16	4½

Expenses

Wages, travelling costs, &c.	Total	27344	17	5

TABLE 3
Pipe Roll Accounts of Envoys
1–14 Edward III

(Based on figures from the accounts published by MM. Mirot and Déprez and corrected by Mr. Larson.)

Receipts

Exchequer		6729	11	9
Other sources		27626	16	9
Miscellaneous	20036: 13: 10			
Bardi	5791: 15			
Other Italian merchants	911: 16: 3			
Constable of Bordeaux	561: 4: 4			
Wardrobe	182: 0: 8			
Collector of wool customs in London	143: 6: 8			
	Total	34356	8	6

Expenses

Wages, travelling costs, &c.	Total	55110	3	8

TABLE 4
Pipe Roll Accounts of Envoys
22 Edward I–14 Edward III
(A combination of Tables 2 and 3)

Receipts

Exchequer	32784: 13: 5			
Miscellaneous	20036: 13: 10			
Bardi	5791: 15			
Other Italian merchants	911: 16: 3			
Constable of Bordeaux	577: 19: 0½			
Collector of customs, London	243: 6: 8			
Wardrobe	238: 0: 8			
Receiver in Gascony	130			
	Total	60714	4	10½

Expenses

Wages, travelling costs, &c.	Total	82455	1	1
Balance in favour of accountants		21740	16	3½

TABLE 5

Wardrobe Accounts of Envoys

36 Henry III–15 Edward II

(Based on the Exchequer Accounts of all envoys travelling abroad from 36 Henry III, when this series of accounts begins, to 15 Edward II. Bishop Langton's account—E.A. 308/19—is omitted and discussed in detail below. One document—E.A. 308/21—is out of place in this series, belonging to the class of Wardrobe Debentures. A few accounts —E.A. 308/1–5, 10, 12, 26, 28—are accounts of payments to messengers and will be included under that title.)

Receipts

Wardrobe		676	12	6
Direct payment	401:19: 7			
Through the Bardi	170:16: 8			
Through the Scali	93:16: 3			
Through merchants of Lucca	10			
Italian merchants		262	18	11
Frescobaldi	128:18: 9			
Ballardi	116:16:10			
Lucca	16:13: 4			
Other sources		199	17	$8\frac{1}{4}$
Prests	63:13: 4			
Exchequer	60: 6: 4			
Great wardrobe	51: 3:$11\frac{1}{2}$			
Private persons	9: 6: 8			
Treasurer of Ireland	6			
Queen's wardrobe	5			
Receiver in Ponthieu	4: 7: $4\frac{3}{4}$			
	Total	1138	19	$1\frac{1}{4}$

Expenses

Wages, travelling costs, &c.	Total	9114	2	$1\frac{3}{20}$
Balance in favour of accountants		7975	2	$11\frac{9}{10}$

APPENDIX V

THE ACCOUNT OF WALTER LANGTON

A FEW remarks need to be made regarding the arrangement followed in printing the account. The book as it exists in the Public Record Office under the reference number E.A. 308/19 was bound up following an arrangement of the folios by Dr. Friedrich Bock. After some hesitation I have decided to regroup the folios roughly to correspond with the titles found in larger wardrobe books and, whenever possible, to fit them together in chronological order. This, I feel, has the merit of being a more serviceable if not a more logical arrangement. Fo. 7^v, which records payments to messengers, and fo. 8, which is written only on one side and which records repayments of loans from Italian merchants, are so badly mutilated that the results of transcription would be quite useless. Accordingly, I have omitted them and inserted in their place fo. 16 of Bodleian MS. Dodsworth 76. The order of contents within each folio has not been disturbed, and I have kept the original numbering of the folios, but their sequence is now as follows: fo. 1^v, *Titulus*; fos. 2, 14, *Confederaciones*: payments to allies, including a memorandum of money received from the Frescobaldi and paid into the wardrobe; fos. 16, 13, 10, 9, *Prestita*: imprests, arranged chronologically; fos. 3, 4, 16 MS. Dodsworth 76, *Necessaria*: payments for parchment, carriage of money, transportation, Langton's expenses, etc.; fos. 5, 11, 15, *Dona et elemosine*: gifts, alms, payments to Gascon hostages and refugees; fos. 6, 7, 12, *Nuncii*: payments to messengers, arranged chronologically; fos. 17, 18, *Recepta*: receipts.

fo. 1^v COMPOTUS DE DIVERSIS RECEPTIS, MISIS, ET LIBERACIONIBUS FACTIS PER VENERABILEM PATREM DOMINUM W[ALTERUM] DE LANGETON', COVENTRENSEM ET LICHFELDENSEM EPISCOPUM, THESAURARIUM REGIS EDWARDI, PRO NEGOCIIS IPSIUS REGIS IN PARTIBUS TRANSMARINIS PER LOCA DIVERSA, ANNIS REGNI REGIS EJUSDEM XXIIII° ET XXV^{to}, REDDITUS IN GARDEROBA DICTI REGIS DOMINO JOHANNI DE DROKENESFORD, CUSTODI EJUSDEM GARDEROBE, PER WILLELMUM DE ESTON' [QUI COM]PUTAVIT IN [NOMINE DICTI WALTERI IN] GARDEROBA PREDICTA APUD [CLIFTON', MENSE] JULII, ANNO REGNI REGIS [EDWARDI] PREDICTI XXVII°.

Domino Guidoni, comiti Flandrie et marchioni Namucensi, in fo. 2ʳ perpacacionem centum mil. *librarum tur. parvorum* sibi debitarum pro primo anno etc., quod continetur in magna littera confederacionum initarum inter dominum regem et ipsum comitem, per manus domini Jacobi de Doura, receptoris sui, in diversis particulis apud Bruges— 70,000 *li. tur. nigr.*, qui solvebantur in *st.* et aliis monetis conversis in *st.*, videlicet 24 *li. st.* solutis pro 100 *li. tur.*—16,800 *li.*

Et memorandum quod idem comes receperat prius super dicto pagamento de Elia Russel et Reginaldo de Thonderle, ut creditur in Brabantia—6,000 *li. tur.*, et apud Westmonasterium, mense Februarii, de thesaurario et camerariis, ut creditur super eodem pagamento etc.— 24,000 *li. tur.*

Domino Johanni de Cabilone, domino Darlay, Johanni de Burgundia, Gualtero de Monte Falcone, et Simoni de Mont Behard, domino de Montron, nomine nobilium Burgundie, confederatorum regis Anglie, pro medietate pagamenti 60,000 *li.* sibi debitarum pro primo anno confederacionis predicte, per manus dominorum J[ohannis] et J[ohannis], G[ualteri], et S[imonis] predictorum apud Bruxellam mense Maii, anno xxv—30,000 *li. tur. parvorum*. Eisdem, pro medietate 2,000 *li.* ejusdem monete eisdem nobilibus debite ultra dictam summam 60,000 *li.*, et pro eodem anno, per manus eorumdem ibidem, eodem mense—1,000 *li. tur.* Summa utriusque summe—31,000 *li. tur. nigr.*, qui valent, 4 *tur.* computatis ad unum denarium *st.* quia sic fit conversio in recepta etc.—7,750 *li.*

Domino Aymoni, domino de Faucoigny, de Burgundia, pro guerra contra regem Francie incipienda per se et eciam continuanda per confederacionem et convencionem cum ipso domino Aymone per dominum Ottonem de Grandissono pro rege Anglie initas in hac parte, per manus proprias ibidem eodem mense—2,000 *li. tur. nigr.*, qui valent—500 *li. st.*

Manton' Domino Johanni de Bar, cum quo conventum fuit per regem ad morandum in servicio ipsius regis in guerra sua contra regem Francie in comitiva domini H[enrici], comitis Barr', fratris sui, cum l equis ad arma per unum annum, percipiendo de rege 500 *li.* hujusmodi mora sua in denariis liberatis eidem . . .[1] 18,000 *li.*, quas Robertus de Segre recepit ad scaccarium ad duc[endum] . . .[2] Coventrensem et Lichfeldensem episcopum, mense Junii . . .[3]

Domine Blanche, regine Navarre, in denariis ei solutis in partibus fo. 2ᵛ

[1] Three words lacking.   [2] About five words lacking.
[3] Remainder of page, probably one line, lacking.

transmarinis per preceptum regem, videlicet per manus Homederii Bonfillol, valleti sui, apud Bruxellam in septimana Pasche anno xxv^to— 1,000 *mar. st.* Eidem domine regine, per manus ejusdem valleti sui, mense Julii in Flandria apud Bruges, in denariis solutis per manus ejusdem valleti in pluribus particulis solutis pro cera, vino, vinis, et aliis emptis pro ipsa domina contra transfretacionem suam in Angliam per Flandriam mense Junii, et in denariis liberatis eidem valleto per vices super expensis ejusdem domine ibidem ante passagium suum, sicut patet per litteram dicti valleti quam fecit de recepcione pecunie sic solute—900 *li. st.* Summa—1,566 *li.* 13 *s.* 4 *d. st.*

fo. 14^r *Dux Brabantie et dominus de Kuc* Dominis J[ohanni], duci Brabantie, et J[ohanni], domino de Kuc, de prestitis super solucione 40,000 *li. tur.* in quibus domini Eliensis, W[illelmus] de Valencia, H[ugo] le Despenser, et W[alterus] de Langeton' per litteram suam obligati existunt, per manus Elie Russel et Johannis de Burgundia, solvencium denarios H., capellano domini de Worthe—100 *li. tur.* Eisdem, super eadem solucione per manus ejusdem Elie, solventis denarios dictis . . duci et domino de Kuc—300 *li. tur. nigr.*

Arnaldo de Ramis, scutifero hospicii regis, moranti in partibus transmarinis in comitiva domini . . thesaurarii annis xxiiii et xxv per vices et eunti in nuncium pro negociis regis tam in Alemanniam quam Brabantiam, Hollandiam, Flandriam, et alibi per vices, de prestitis super expensis in denariis sibi liberatis per Eliam Russel, in—14 *s. tur. gr.*, 7 *li.* 7 *s. par.* Eidem, de prestitis super hujusmodi expensis suis in precio ii saccorum lane de lanis regis ei liberatis per eundem Eliam apud Andworp'—44 *li.* 8 *s.* 11 *d. par.* Summa—51 *li.* 15 *s.* 11 *d. par.*, qui valent in *tur.*—64 *li.* 14 *s.* 11 *d. tur.*

In denariis liberatis et solutis in garderoba per manus domini Radulphi de Manton', coffrarii, recipientis compotum eorumdem denariorum redditum in garderoba per dominum Thomam de Bynington', capellanum thesaurarii, quos denarios idem dominus Thomas receperat de Coppe Cotenne et sociis suis, mercatoribus de Friscombald', et inde respondit in garderoba, et sic remanet idem Radulphus inde oneratus, et de quibus denariis W[illelmus] de Eston' oneravit se infra quandam summam contentam in quadam dividenda facta inter eosdem mercatores et eundem Willelmum per visum dicti domini Radulphi apud Eboracum mense Julii anno xxvii—619 *li.* 7 *s.* 6 *d. tur. nigr.*, qui valent in *st.*, 4 *tur.* computatis ad 1 *st.*—154 *li.* 16 *s.* 10½ *d. st.*[1]

[1] This paragraph is struck through, with the notation in the margin: 'Cancellatum quia superius in uno rotulo anno xxiiii super Thoma de Bynington'.

Summa pagine, 464 *li.* 14 *s.* 11 *d. tur.*, qui valent 116 *li.* 3 *s.* 8½ *d.* qua *st.*
Item, pro particula tangente dominum Thomam de Bynington'—154 *li.* 16 *s.* 10½ *d. st.*

De Grandisono Domino Ottoni de Grandisono, moranti in partibus fo. 16ʳ Francie circa prosecucionem negociorum domini regis, in comitiva dominorum W[alteri] de Langeton', Coventrensis et Lichfeldensis tunc electi, thesaurarii, et comitis Sabaudie, coram cardinalibus Albanensi et Penestrensi, de prestitis super expensis suis in denariis sibi liberatis per Coppe Cotenne et socios suos, mercatores de Friscomb', mense Julii anno xxiiiiᵗᵒ, Parisius—400 *li. tur. nigr.* Eidem, super eodem, per manus monachi sui, xxº die Septembris apud Sovigniacum in Alvernia—100 *li. tur.* Et per manus ejusdem super eodem, viii die Octobris, Parisius—100 *li. tur.* Et per manus ejusdem, x die Octobris, ibidem—125 *li. tur.*

De Vikio Hugolino de Vikio, misso in nuncium ad regem Alemannie per dictos thesaurarium, comitem Sabaudie, et O[ttonem] de Grandisono ex parte domini regis, de prestitis super expensis suis in denariis sibi liberatis Parisius per mercatores de Friscomb' predictos, mense Julii—19 *li.* 13 *s.* 9 *d. tur. nigr.*

Eidem, misso ad eundem regem in nuncium ut prius de Molendinis in Alvernia xiiii die Septembris, de prestitis super vadiis et expensis suis—32 *li.* 16 *s.* 3 *d. tur.*

Ferrera Magistro Reymundo de Ferrera, misso per dictos nuncios regis Anglie de Parisius in Vasconiam pro quibusdam negociis ipsius regis exequendis, de prestitis super expensis suis per manus magistri Guillelmi, clerici sui, xxii die Julii—80 *li. tur.*

Selveston' Magistro Johanni de Selveston', redeunti de Parisius ad partes Anglie et usque in Scociam ad regem, de prestitis super expensis suis xxiiii die Julii—37 *li.* 10 *s. tur.*

Dogemerffeld, nuncius Willelmo de Dogemerffeld, nuncio regis, misso de Parisius versus partes Anglie cum litteris dictorum nunciorum directis ad regem, de prestitis super expensis suis xxvi die Julii, qui recessit de Parisius tercio die a recessu dicti magistri J[ohannis], per manus proprias—100 *s. tur.*

Ramis Arnaldo de Ramis, misso de Parisius ad partes Hollandie in nuncium per dictos nuncios, de prestitis super expensis suis xxiiii die Julii—20 *li. tur.*

Eidem, redeunti postea apud Molend' in Alvernia et misso ibidem ad partes Alemannie, de prestitis super expensis suis ix die Septembris, 19 *li.* 13 *s.* 9 *d. tur.*

APPENDIX V

Bynington' Domino Thome de Binington', capellano thesaurarii, de prestitis super quibusdam expensis ejusdem thesaurarii Parisius xxiii die Julii—57 *li.* 10 *s. tur.*

Hustwait Domino Johanni de Hustweit, de prestitis super officio suo per manus garcionis Johanni Vanne, recipientis denarios apud Whitsand' super cariagio pellure quam dominus thesaurarius venire fecit de Parisius, videlicet super cariagio ejusdem pellure de Dovoria usque Londonium mense Octobris—25 *s. tur.*

Summa pagine—998 *li.* 8 *s.* 9 *d. tur. nigr.*, qui valent 249 *li.* 12 *s.* 2 *d.* qua *st.*

fo. 16ᵛ *De Vico* Magistro Petro Arnaldi de Vico, de prestitis super expensis cujusdam clerici sui missi de Vasconia in Angliam[1] in nuncium ad regem in principio guerre Vasconie, per manus proprias apud Sovigniacum xxiii die Septembris—12 *li. tur.*

Albertinus Fulberti Albertino Fulberti, misso de Parisius ad curiam Romanam in nuncium regis per predictos thesaurarium, comitem Sabaudie, et Ottonem de Grandisono mense Julii, de prestito super expensis suis in denariis sibi liberatis per Coppe Cotenne et socios suos, mercatores de Friscombald', commorantes Parisius, 13 *li.* 2 *s.* 6 *d. tur.*

Ver Domino Hugoni de Ver, de prestito in denariis sibi missis per dominum Jacobum de Bello Campo et magistros Reymundum de Ferrera et P[etrum] Arnaldi de Vico, recipientes peccuniam apud Sovigniacum in Alvernia mense Septembris, in 17 *li.* 11 *s.* 8 *d. tur. gr.*, 28 *den. aur.* de moneta regis Francie, 2 *s.* 4 *d. obolorum novorum*, et 2 *d. tur. parvis*, per manus predictorum—266 *li.* 13 *s.* 4 *d. tur.*

Summa pagine—291 *li.* 15 *s.* 10 *d. tur. nigr.*, qui valent—72 *li.* 18 *s.* 11½ *d. st.*

Bynington' Domino Thome de Binington', capellano domini Coventrensis et Lichfeldensis episcopi, thesaurarii, de prestitis super expensis ejusdem thesaurarii, morando in partibus transmarinis pro negociis regis coram cardinalibus anno presenti xxiiii, in denariis eidem Thome liberatis per Coppum Cotenne et socios suos, mercatores de societate Friscomb' de Florencia, in Francia per vices inter primum diem Junii et ultimum diem Julii anno eodem, de quibus denariis W[illelmus] de Eston' oneratur infra quandam summam contentam in quadam dividenda facta inter eosdem mercatores et eundem Willelmum per visum dicti domini Radulphi de Manton' apud Eboracum mense Julii anno xxvii, 619 *li.* 7 *s.* 6 *d. tur. nigr.*, qui valent in *st.*, 4 *tur.* computatis ad 1 *st.*—154 *li.* 16 *s.* 10½ *d. st.*

[1] MS., *in Angliam* repeated.

Summa folii—1,290 *li*. 4 *s*. 7 *d*. *tur*., qui valent 322 *li*. 11 *s*. 1½ *d*. qua *st*.

Item, pro particula Thome de Bynington'—154 *li*. 16 *s*. 10½ *d*. *st*.

Quidam miles regis Alemannie Domino Robino de Covere, militi regis Romanorum et . . archiepiscopi Treverensis, misso per dominos Coventrensem et Lichfeldensem thesaurarium . . , comitem Sabaudie, Ottonem de Grandisono, Hugonem le Despenser, et Johannem de Berewyco, nuncios domini regis, de Cameraco ad dictum regem Romanorum in nuncium, de prestitis super expensis suis xv die Decembris—40 *li*. *tur*. *nigr*. fo. 13ʳ

Sandale Dominis Johanni de Sandale et Thome de Cantebrigg' de prestitis super solucione vadiorum existencium in obsequium regis in Vasconia, per manus magistri Petri Arnaldi de Vico, recipientis denarios apud Cameracum super expensis suis xviii die Decembris—70 *li*. *tur*. *nigr*.

Engolismo Domino Iterio de Engolismo, de prestitis super expensis suis per manus Robertini, scutiferi sui, ibidem xxiiii die Decembris—40 *li*. *tur*. *nigr*.

Eidem eunti de Cameraco versus partes Alemannie pro negociis regis, de prestitis super expensis suis xxviii die Decembris per manus proprias—35 *li*. *tur*. *nigr*.

Vescy Domino Willelmo de Vescy, de prestitis apud Cameracum per manus proprias xxiiii die Decembris ad instanciam domini Dunelmensis episcopi—200 *li*. *tur*. *nigr*.

Eidem, per manus Johannis Vanne ibidem, pro debito quod debuit eidem J[ohanni] per scriptum suum, ibidem eodem die—100 *li*. *tur*. *nigr*.

Hustwait Domino Johanni de Hustwait, emptori magne garderobe regis, de prestitis super officio suo per manus Jakomini Pilate de Doaco pro ii penis ad mantellum de minuto verro, vi penis de minuto verro de ix tiris ad supertunices, vi penis de minuto verro de viii tiris ad supertunices, et xii capuciis de minuto verro, provisis et emptis per ipsum Jakominum pro rege et pro quibusdam misis appositis circa eandem pelluram, sicut patet per quandam cedulam ipsius Jakomini quam liberavit domino thesaurario apud Cameracum xxiiii die Decembris—112 *li*. 12 *s*. *par*., qui valent in *tur*.—140 *li*. 15 *s*. *tur*.

Mercatores de Friscumbald' Taldo Ianiani et sociis suis de Friscombald', de prestitis in denariis solutis pro domino Henrico de Bodringham per manus Johannis Vanne apud Cameracum pro illis—40 *li*. *st*. quos dictus Talde recepit apud Sanctum Edmundum mense Novembris et quos denarios idem Talde solvisse debuit dicto domino H[enrico] per socios suos Parisius per preceptum . . thesaurarii—160 *li. tur. nigr.*

De Grandissono Domino Ottoni de Grandissono, de prestitis super expensis suis morando in Francia cum cardinalibus pro negociis regis, per manus Gaerii Bonacursi et Johannis Vanne apud Cameracum xxvii die Decembris—100 *li. tur. nigr.*

De Berewico et Monte Caniso Dominis Johanni de Berewyco et Willelmo de Monte Caniso, de prestitis apud Cameracum xxvii die Decembris, quos denarios idem dominus Johannes recepit ad opus ejusdem Willelmi et eos promisit solvere pro eodem W[illelmo]—40 *li. tur.*

Summa pagine—925 *li.* 15 *s. tur.*, qui valent 231 *li.* 8 *s.* 9 *d. st.*

fo. 13ᵛ   *De Ferrera* Magistro Reymundo de Ferrera, de prestitis super expensis suis morando in partibus Francie, Alemannie, Burgundie, et alibi in presencia cardinalium et absencia eorumdem per vices circa negocia regis, per manus proprias apud Cameracum xxviii die Decembris—30 *li. tur. nigr.*

De Grandissono Domino Ottoni de Grandissono, de prestitis super expensis suis morando circa negocia regis ut prius, in denariis sibi liberatis per Coppe Cothenne in Brabantia mense Januarii—400 *li. tur. nigr.*

Vescy Domino Willelmo de Vescy, de prestitis in denariis solutis magistro Giloni de Ayre de Cameraco pro expensis et custodia cujusdam equi quem idem dominus Willelmus dimiserat ibi infirmatum ad Natale in recessu suo de parliamento cardinalium, qui quidem equus extitit in custodia dicti Gilonis per lxv dies et postea moriebatur ibidem, et percepit per diem pro dicto equo 18 *d. tur.* per manus ejusdem Gilonis xv die Marcii—4 *li.* 17 *s.* 6 *d. tur.*

Ramis Arnaldo de Ramis, misso de Bruxella ad regem Alemannie in nuncium pro negociis regis, de prestito super expensis suis xxvii die Marcii—8 *li. tur.*

Dogmerffeld, nuncius Willelmo de Dogmerffeld, nuncio regis, misso de Bruxella versus Angliam ad regem cum litteris, de prestitis super expensis suis et passagio suo, per manus proprias ultimo die Marcii—10 *li. tur.*

Eidem nuncio, redeunti alia vice de Bruxella ad regem cum litteris thesaurarii, de prestitis super expensis suis et passagio ad mare xii die Maii, 6 *li. tur.*

Ramis Arnaldo de Ramis, misso cum litteris in nuncium ad regem

Alemannie primo die Maii, de prestitis super expensis suis apud Anwiorp—4 *li. tur.*

Dux Brabantie et dominus de Kuc Johanni, duci Brabantie, et . . domino de Kuc, de prestitis super solucione 40,000 *li. tur.* in quibus[1] dominus . . episcopus Elyensis, W[illelmus] de Valencia, H[ugo] le Despenser, et W[alterus] de Langeton' sibi per litteram obligantur, per manus ejusdem domini de Kuc apud Anuuers vii die Maii, 100 *li. tur. nigr.*

Eisdem duci et domino de Kuc, de prestitis super eadem solucione, per manus Henrici, capellani domini de Hamestell', xxvi die Junii apud Bruges—100 *li. tur. nigr.*

Eisdem, de prestitis super eadem solucione, per manus Terrici de Gelre, valleti Ottonis de Kuc, recipientis denarios de J[ohanne] de Sancto Odomaro apud Bruges xv die Julii—200 *li. tur.*

Eisdem duci et domino de Kuc, de prestito super eadem solucione, in denariis sibi liberatis per Coppe Cotenne in Brabantia—150 *li. tur.*

Summa pagine—1,012 *li.* 17 *s.* 6 *d. tur.*, qui valent 253 *li.* 4 *s.* 4½ *d. st.*

Summa folii—1,938 *li.* 12 *s.* 6 *d. tur.*, qui valent 484 *li.* 13 *s.* 1½ *d. st.*

R[eginaldus] Ferre et Haveringg' Domino Reginaldo Ferre et magistro Ricardo de Haveryng', transfretantibus in Hollandiam cum comite Hollandie et morantibus in partibus illis per aliquod tempus et postea redeuntibus in Angliam per Flandriam, de prestitis super expensis suis per manus Thome, garcionis dicti domini Reginaldi, et Willelmi le Walshe, garcionis magistri Ricardi, recipiencium pecuniam apud Bruges ad solvendum pro fretto cujusdam navis passantis equos eorumdem Reginaldi et Ricardi de Flandria in Angliam nono die Junii— 13 *li.* 6 *s.* 8 *d. tur. nigr.* fo. 10^r

Bon, nuncius Bon, nuncio regis, redeunti de Flandria in Angliam, de prestitis super expensis suis x die Junii apud Bruges—4 *li. tur. nigr.*, xxix die Julii.

Dogemerffeld, nuncius Willelmo de Dogmerffeld, nuncio regis, misso cum litteris ad regem Alemannie, de prestitis super expensis suis eodem die—40 *s. tur. nigr.*

S[imon] Loys, nuncius Eodem die Simoni Loys, nuncio regis, misso cum litteris regis ad comitem et comitissam Barri, dominum Ottonem de Grandissono, dominum Johannem de Cabilone, dominum Darlay, et ulterius ad comitem Sabaudie, de prestitis super expensis suis per manus proprias in *st.* et *tur.*—106 *s.* 8 *d. tur. nigr.*

[1] MS., written above *partibus,* struck through.

APPENDIX V

Eidem Simoni, per manus Dikoni de Hamelton', recipientis denarios pro uno hakeneio ab ipso empto ad equitaturam ejusdem nuncii pro itinere predicto, videlicet pro 17 s. st.—68 s. tur. nigr.

Hustwait vi die Augusti, domino Johanni de Hustwait, de prestitis super officio suo magne garderobe regis per manus Reginaldi de Thumderle, solventis denarios pro vi miliariis de canobo emptis ad opus regis et liberatis W[illelmo] de Carleton', clerico ejusdem domini J[ohannis], precii centi 17 s. 3 d. st.— 51 li. 15 s. st. Et per manus ejusdem Reginaldi, solventis denarios pro mmvi^c et dimidium c de canobo empto per eundem Reginaldum et penes ipsum remanente, ejusdem precii—23 li. 13 s. st. Et pro denariis per eundem Reginaldum solutis pro dicto canobo mensurando et plicando—5 s. st. Summa istarum particularum in st.—75 li. 13 s. st., qui solvebantur in par., marca de 10 s. st. computata ad 33 s. 4 d. par., et sic solvebantur pro dictis 75 li. 13 s. st.—252 li. 3 s. 4 d. par., qui valent in tur.— 315 li. 4 s. 2 d. tur., qui valent in st. 78 li. 16 s. ½ d., et sic ponuntur hic in exitu per 75 li. 13 s. st.—78 li. 16 s. ½ d. st. quia solvebatur eadem summa in moneta par. et ponitur in recepta pro dicta summa par. predicta summa—78 li. 16 s. ½ d. st.

Summa pagine, 28 li. 16 d. tur. nigr. Item, 78 li. 16 s. ½ d. st. Qui valent 85 li. 16 s. 4½ d. st.

fo. 10^v *P[etrus] de Dene* Magistris Petro de Dene et Petro Aymerici, missis ad curiam Romanam in nuncium regis in quadragesima anno presenti xxv, de prestitis super expensis suis in denariis sibi liberatis per mercatores de Friscombald' in Brabantia mense Marcii—100 li. tur.

Eidem magistro Petro de Dene, de prestitis super eodem, in denariis solutis Rogero de Meridene pro uno runcino sor[ello] ab ipso R[ogero] empto et liberato eidem magistro P[etro] pro itinere predicto, dicto mense—46 s. 8 d. st.

Prestita Maior de Sandwico Johanni de Hou, maiori de Sandwico, de prestitis super custibus navis que vocatur La Rose de Sandwico preparande pro passagio dominorum thesaurarii et J[ohannis] de Berewico versus Flandriam in principio quadragesime anno presenti xxv et super vadiis nautarum ejusdem navis, primo videlicet xxiii° die Februarii— 6 li. 13 s. 4 d. Item, eidem super eodem xxvii die Februarii—6 li. 13 s. 4 d. Item, eidem super vadiis W. Toly, magistri bargie de Winchelse, et sociorum ejusdem Toly, nautarum ejusdem bargie, pro eodem passagio, quorum nautarum vadia debent incipere xxv die Februarii, per manus ejusdem Toly et Gervasii Andree, naute ejusdem bargie—4 li. Eidem maiori de prestitis super eodem apud Bruges in Flandria x die

Marcii tunc proximo sequente, videlicet tam super vadiis nautarum dicte navis De La Rose quam in vadiis dictorum nautarum bargie predicte—20 *li. st.*

Ade Jori, magistro bargie que vocatur La Floyne de Sandwico, de prestitis super vadiis debitis ei et sociis suis, nautis bargie, de quibusdam passagiis que fecerunt in estate preterita, videlicet anno xxiiii pro negociis regis inter Dovoriam et Whitsand, pro quibus passagiis nondum est eis satisfactum de vadiis suis apud Bruges, viii die Marcii per manus proprias—20 *s. st.* Eidem Jori, passanti in Flandriam cum domino thesaurario mense Novembris anno presenti xxv finiente, de prestitis super vadiis et expensis suis morando in Flandria expectando reditum ejusdem thesaurarii dicto mense, quia idem Adam non fuit ad vadia inter ceteros nautas, per manus proprias apud Sclus' xviii die Novembris—20 *s. st.*

Johanni de Dele, magistro bargie que fuit bargia Toly, passanti eadem vice cum dicta bargia in comitiva ejusdem domini thesaurarii, de prestitis super vadiis suis et sociorum suorum apud Sclus' per manus Whitepese eodem die—20 *s. st.*

Summa pagine, pro 100 *li. tur.* 25 *li. st.* Item in *st.*—42 *li.* 13 *s.* 4 *d. st.*—67 *li.* 13 *s.* 4 *d. st.*

Summa folii tam *tur.* conversis in *st.* quam *st.*, etc., 153 *li.* 9 *s.* 8½ *d. st.*

Segre Domino Roberto de Segre, de prestitis super providenciis victualium faciendis in Flandria contra adventum regis ad partes illas per manus proprias xx die Junii—13 *li.* 10 *s.* 5 *d. st.* Eidem super eodem xviii die Julii—100 *li. st.* Eidem super eodem xxvii die Julii—500 *li. st.* Eidem super eodem ii⁰ die Augusti—200 *li. st.* Eidem super eodem ix die Augusti—100 *li. st.* Eidem domino R[oberto] et Andree le Treheur, de prestitis super eodem per manus Willelmi le White de Dam et Petri Vinne de eadem pro vinis emptis ab eis ad opus regis per dictos Robertum et Andream mense Julii—119 *li.* 10 *s.* 9 *d. st.* Eisdem super eodem per manus dicti Petri Vinne similiter pro vinis—40 *li.* 4 *s. st.* Eisdem super eodem per manus Petri de Desebur', Alemanni, pro vinis ab eis emptis per eosdem—78 *li.* 6 *s.* 2 *d. st.* Et ei[s]dem domino R[oberto] et Thome Brim super eodem per manus Evani de Markeni, Alemanni, pro bacone et carne bovis ab ipso emptis per eosdem—64 *li.* 14 *s.* 10 *d. st.* Eisdem super eodem per manus Johannis de Bassefeld de Bruges pro bacone similiter empto per eosdem ab eo—28 *li.* 14 *s.* 10½ *d. st.* Et per manus Saeri de Somer de Bruges pro bacone—12 *li.* 11 *s.* 6 *d.* Et per manus Johannis Heiwit' de Dan pro

fo. 9ʳ

bacone similiter—131 *li.* 11 *s.* 2 *d. st.* Eisdem super eodem per manus Willelmi Joef de Bruges similiter pro bacone—20 *li.* 19 *s.* 3 *d. st.* Et per manus Hanekini Fosse pro bobus, vinis ab eo emptis—24 *li.* 13 *s.* 10 *d. st.* Et per manus Willelmi Whitbard pro bacone—40 *li.* 7 *s.* 8 *d.* Eisdem super eodem per manus Johannis Bridel similiter pro bacone—36 *li.* 10 *s.* 5 *d. st.* Summa—1,511 *li.* 4 *s.* 10½ *d. st.*

Russel Elie Russel, de prestitis super empcione vinorum pro rege apud Andworp mense Julii per manus proprias—800 *li. st.*

Atte Gate et de Sancto Audomaro Johanni Atte Gate de London' et Johanni de Sancto Audomaro, morantibus apud Bruges pro vendicione lanarum regis, de prestitis super quibusdam solucionibus et mutuis per manus ipsorum per preceptum thesaurarii faciendis mense Junii—368 *li.* 7 *s.* 4 *d. st.*

Summa pagine—2,679 *li.* 12 *s.* 2½ *d. st.*

fo. 9ᵛ *Hustwait* Domino Johanni de Hustwait, emptori magne garderobe regis, de prestitis super officio suo per manus Johannis de Burlint, pelliparii de Gandavo, pro pellura ab ipso empta pro rege in principio mensis Augusti apud Bruges—100 *li. st.*

Eidem super eodem officio suo per manus Bernardi le Mercander ibidem xxx die Julii—25 *li. st.*

Eidem de prestitis super eodem per manus Burnetti Bulgarini et Johannis Vanne, mercatorum, recipiencium denarios ad scaccarium xviii die Maii anno xxv super debito quod eis debebatur ex officio ejusdem garderobe—300 *li. st.*

Summa pagine—425 *li. st.*

Summa folii—3,104 *li.* 12 *s.* 2½ *d. st.*

fo. 3ʳ *Necessaria ann*[*o xxv*]

Pro duobus forceriis de coreo emptis Londonii pro litteris directis ad partes transmarinas imponendis xix die Februarii—3 *s.* 6 *d. st.*

In pargameno empto ibidem tam per magistrum J[ohannem] Bosh' quam W[illelmum] de Eston', 2 *s.* 11 *d. st.*

Pro x paneris emptis ad 1,000 *li. st.* imponendas ad cariandum de Anuuers usque Bruxellam et pro cordis emptis pro eisdem paneris trussandis xxiii die Marcii—10 *s.* 4 *d. tur.* Et pro stipendiis unius carecte cariantis dictas 1,000 *li.* de Anuuers usque Bruxellam per convencionem 32 *s. tur. nigr.* Et in expensis quorumdam dictam pecuniam conducencium—10 *s. tur. nigr.*

Et in portagio et cariagio 2,000 *li. st.* apud Bruxellam de hospicio domini thesaurarii ad dominum Henricum le Lumbard—2 *s.* 3 *d. tur.*

THE ACCOUNT OF WALTER LANGTON 235

Willlemo de Dogemerffeld, misso de Cameraco versus partes Flandrie mense Marcii in nuncium secretum, pro expensis suis per v dies—14 *s. par.*, cum uno equo. Eidem, misso de Anuuers eodem mense Marcii usque Bruges pro 1,000 *li. st.* querendis et cariandis usque Bruxellam, pro expensis suis et pro expensis quorumdam hominum equitum assignatorum eidem Willelmo per receptorem Flandrie ad dictam pecuniam inter Bruges et Bruxellam conducendam, una cum expensis v hakeneyorum eandem pecuniam cariancium et garcionum eos sequencium ut in victualibus predictis conducentibus et feno et avena pro dictis hakeneis—52 *s.* 4 *d. par.* Et pro stipendiis dictorum hakeneyorum ex convencione pro dicto J[ohanne] pro quibus 12 *s. par.* preter custus eorum et in feno et avena superius computatis— 60 *s. par.* per manus ejusdem Willelmi. Summa—6 *li.* 6 *s.* [4 *d.*] *par.*, qui valent in *tur.* 7 *li.* 17 *s.* 11 *d. tur. nigr.*

In tribus duodenis pergameni emptis apud Bruges et una libra de cera rubea—16 *s.* 10½ *d. tur. nigr.*

Item in pergameno empto per vices mense Julii et Augusti apud Bruges, 25 *s. tur. nigr.*

Item in pergameno empto apud Insulam in Flandria et apud Bruxellam in xl^a preterita per Boush' et Eston'—19 *s.* 5 *d.* [*tur. nigr.*].

Item in stipendiis unius currus cariantis quandam pecunie summam de Bruges usque Anuuers xxviii die Junii—100 *s. tur.*

Summa pagine, 18 *li.* 13 *s.* 9½ *d. tur.* Item 6 *s.* 5 *d. st.*, qui valent 4 *li.* 19 *s.* 10 *d. st.*

Magistro Johanni Bush', misso per dominum thesaurarium usque Gandavum ad ducem Brabantie tempore quo idem dux fuit in municione ejusdem ville, pro quodam scripto obligatorio faciendo et expectando quod idem dux erat facturus domino regi Anglie de quadam pecunie summa sibi per ipsum dominum regem mutuate, pro expensis suis per xxiiii dies per quos morabatur ibidem mense Julii antequam dictum obligatorium haberet, ut in expensis oris sui, garcionum, et equorum—10 *li.* 20 *d. par.* Et in expensis ejusdem magistri J[ohannis] per quinque dies per quos mittebatur in nuncium per dominos thesaurarium et J[ohannem] de Berewic' de Insula in Flandria usque Doacum ad dominum Guillelmum de Flandria pro negociis regis in ultima ebdoma quadragesime preterite per manus proprias sicut patet per particulas—23 *s.* 10 *d. par.* Summa dictarum duarum summarum 11 *li.* 5 *s.* 6 *d. par.*, qui valent in *tur.*—14 *li.* 22 *d. tur.*, qui valent in *st.*—70 *s.* 5½ *d. st.* fo. 3^v

Summa pagine—70 *s.* 5½ *d. st.*

Summa folii—8 *li.* 10*s.* 3½ *d. st.*

fo. 4ʳ   Duobus minatoribus pauperibus venientibus ad dominum Coventrensem et Lichfeldensem, thesaurarium, apud Westmonasterium mense Decembris et petentibus vadia sibi debita de minera Devon', ad expensas suas redeundo versus mineram predictam per preceptum thesaurarii quia nichil receperunt de vadiis predictis ista vice—2*s. st.*

In pergameno empto contra passagium domini thesaurarii in Flandriam mense Octobris preterito—14*d. st.*

Johanni Jolif, naute de Sandwyco, qui venit lodmannus de Sandwico usque portum de Swine in quadam nave de Baiona que transfretavit Ricardum de Wynton' et Willelmum Klut, missos per dominum regem ad partes Flandrie mense Augusti preterito, pro lodmannagio suo per convencionem—20*s. st.*

Johanni Furnival, magistro navis que vocatur La Rose de Sandwico, habuit in comitiva sua in eadem nave i constabularium et xlviii nautas, et exeunti in obsequio regis passando in Flandriam cum domino Coventrensi et Lichfeldensi episcopo, thesaurario, mense Octobris et Novembris anno xxv, morando in partibus illis, et in Angliam redeundo, videlicet a xxvi die Octobris, quo die incepit tenere dictam familiam ad sumptus suos in nave, usque xxi diem Novembris anno xxvi incipiente, utroque computato, per xxvii dies, infra quod tempus dictus magister cum familia sua predicta fuit ad vadia et sumptum communitatis de Sandwyco per xxi dies racione servicii quarum navium domino filio regis per iii septimanas a communitate Quinque Portuum concessi, pro vadiis suis et dictorum nautarum vi dierum residuorum, percipienti per diem pro se, constabulario, et quolibet nauta vadia consueta per manus proprias apud Dovoriam xx die Novembris—78*s. st.* Eidem magistro, uni constabulario, et xxxi nautis, transfretantibus in eadem nave de Sandwyco in Flandriam in comitiva domini R[oberti] filii Pagani circa festum Sancti Michaelis proximo preteritum et existentibus in veagio predicto post diem exitus vadiorum sibi pro illo passagio solutorum per duos dies pro arreragiis vadiorum suorum illorum duorum dierum de quibus non fuerunt ante nunc soluti, per manus ejusdem magistri ibidem—20*s. st.*

Petro Mony, naute de Tengemuth', venienti London' mense Decembris anno xxvi et petenti arreragia quorumdam vadiorum sibi debitorum de mora sua in Vasconia in obsequio regis, ad expensas suas redeundo versus partes suas quia nondum satisfiebat ei de petitis nec habuit quid expenderet, xi die Decembris—10*s. st.*

Johanni Jolif, naute de Sandwico, qui fuit lodmannus in predicta nave De La Rose in predicta transfretacione domini thesaurarii in Flandriam mense Octobris et Novembris ut predicitur, pro lodmannagio suo passando et repassando et pro expensis quas fecit morando in Flandria illa vice, per manus proprias—40 *s. st.*

Pro stipendiis iii hakeniorum portancium 1,000 *marc.* de Roffa usque Sandwicum per ii dietas in comitiva domini thesaurarii mense Marcii te[m]pore quo dominus rex rediit de Flandria et applicuit apud Sandwicum—3 *s. st.*

In denariis solutis per vices pro pergameno empto pro compoto isto et rotulo ejusdem compoti scribendo et pluries transcribendo—8 *s.* 7 *d. st.*

Et in denariis solutis duobus clericis transcribentibus aliquos rotulos istius compoti, pro labore suo nomine stipendii cuilibet 3 *s.*—6 *s. st.*

Summa pagine—9 *li.* 8 *s.* 9 *d. st.*

In expensis domini W[alteri] Coventrensis et Lichfeldensis episcopi, fo. 4ᵛ thesaurarii, et aliorum militum, clericorum, et valletorum diversorum in comitiva ejusdem existencium, morando in Francie, Flandrie, Cameraci,[1] et Brabantie partibus circa prosecucionem diversorum negociorum regis coram cardinalibus Albanensi et Penestrensi et alibi inter xxiii diem Julii anno xxiiii et finem anni xxvᵗⁱ, sicut patet per duos rotulos de eisdem expensis in garderoba liberatos apud Clifton' juxta Eboracum mense Julii anno xxvii—1,233 *li.* 12 *s.* 7 *d. st.*

Summa pagine patet.

Summa folii—1,243 *li.* 16 *d. st.*

In cariagio argenti de Campser usque Midelburg' et deinde usque fo. 16 galliam de Gernemeuwe per preceptum episcopi Dunelmensis, 5 *s. st.* MS. Dodsworth 76

In cariagio predicti argenti de gallia de Gernemeuwe existenti in portu de Campser usque Berewesand' in terra ducis Brabantie, 24 *s. st.* In discartacione dicti argenti ibidem, 10 *s.* 8 *d.*; pro quolibet barillo 4 *d. st.* In cartacione xvi carectarum ibidem, 16 *s.*; pro quolibet barillo 6 *d. st.* In cariagio dicti argenti de Berewesome usque Anwers, 4 *li.* 16 *s.*; precium carecte 6 *s. st.* In discartacione dicti argenti ibidem, 10 *s.* 8 *d.*; pro quolibet barillo 4 *d. st.* In reparacione et emendacione dictorum barillorum cum circulis emptis, 10 *s. st.* Item ibidem in cartacione dicti argenti, 16 *s.* Item in cariagio dicti argenti deinde usque Malines per xvi carectas, 16 *s.*, quia dux acquietabat residuum cariagii illius diete. Item in cariagio dicti argenti deinde usque Lovayn per xvi carectas, 4 *li.*; pro qualibet carecta 5 *s. st.* In discartacione dicti argenti ibidem, 10 *s.* 8 *d.* In remocione dicti argenti de una domo usque aliam cum reparacione et emendacione dictorum barillorum quando dominus

---

[1] MS., *Cameracum.*

dux recepit custodiam dicti argenti in castro suo de Lovayn, 17 s. 4 d. Summa, 15 li. 12 s. 4 d.

Item portagium et cariagium xvi carectarum quando dominus thesaurarius recessit versus Hollandiam, 32 s. 6 d., cum clavis et cerculis emptis ad emendacionem dictorum barellorum cuidam querenti cariagio 18 d., cariagio de Lovayn usque Malines, 4 li. st. Item cariagium de Malines usque Lere, 4 li.; deinde usque Honstrete, 8 li.; deinde usque Montem Sancti G[e]retrud, 8 li. Summa, 25 li. 13 s. 6 d.

In gentaculo armigerorum ducencium argentum apud Lovayn, 10 s. Item in hospicio nostro et expensis nostris apud Malines, 27 s. 6 [d.] Item in hospicio nostro et expensis armigerorum apud Lere, 34 s. Item in hospicio n[ostro] et expensis armigerorum conducencium thesauriam apud Honsttrete, 57 s. 10 d. Item in crastino apud Breda[m] in expensis dicto[rum] armigerorum pro gentaculo, 17 s. Item in expensis dictorum armigerorum apud Montem Sancti Geretrud, 52 s. 5 d. Item in stipendio dictorum armigerorum revertencium apud Lovayn et Anuers, 72 s.

Summa, 13 li. 10 s. 9 d.

Item conductio argenti de Monte Sancti Geretrud usque Durdracum cum allocacione barillorum, 23 s. 6 d. In [discar]tacione et portagio dictorum barillorum apud Dordracum, 33 s. 8 d. Summa, 57 s. 2 d.

Item apud Durdracum in factura et emendacione i turris ibidem pro argento imponendo per ballivum de Dur[draco], 8 li. st. In i serura empta, 12 d. In i lampadario et oleo emptis, 8 d.; cuidam pond[eran]ti de dono, 20 s. st. Summa, 9 li. 20 d.

Summa totalis, 69 [li.] 12 s. 7 d.

fo. 5ʳ Fuxino, valleto domine regine Navarre, venienti ad regem in Anglia de partibus Vasconie in nuncium ipsius domine, de dono regis ad unum runcinum sibi emendum ex precepto ipsius regis, per manus proprias apud Whitsand ix die Decembris—70 s. st.

Dominis A[rnaldo] de Gavaston', R[eymundo] de Caupenne, et Bertrando de Panissals, qui nuper fuerunt in prisona regis Francie et evaserunt, in denariis sibi liberatis ad expensas suas faciendas eundo per Brabantiam et passando in Angliam—30 li. tur. nigr., qui valent in st. —7 li. 10 s.

Magistro Roberto de Leyset, qui fuit in prisona regis Francie et evasit, venienti ad dominum thesaurarium apud Bruges in Flandria, in denariis sibi liberatis ad expensas suas factas in Flandria et faciendo, transfretando, et eundo in Angliam ad regem acquietandum, per manus proprias vii die Marcii apud Bruges—100 s. st.

Quindecim piscatoribus de Schorham, captis in mari per naves Hispanie et ductis in Flandriam per eosdem Hispanie et liberatis apud Bruges per comitem Flandrie, presente domino Coventrensi, thesaurario, cuilibet ad expensas suas redeundo in navibus Anglie, 12 *d. st.*—15 *s. st.*

Reymundo de Marquesii, existenti in prisona regis Francie, in denariis sibi mis[sis] in subsidium sustentacionis sue, per manus Guillelmi de Pojolo, vallecti sui, apud Bruges viii die Junii—30 *li. tur.*, qui valent in *st.*—7 *li.* 10 *s.*

Arnaldo Guillelmi Marquesii, existenti similiter in prisona predicta, de denariis sibi eodem modo missis, per manus ejusdem et eodem die—20 [*li.*] *tur. nigr.*, qui valent in *st.*—100 *s.*

Guillelmo de Poilo predicto, pro expensis quas fecit veniendo ad dominum thesaurarium pro negocio dictorum obsidum et redeundo ad eosdem, eodem die ibidem—4 *li. tur. nigr.*, qui valent in *st.*—20 *s.*

Fr[atr]ibus de Monte Carmeli celebrantibus capitulum suum generale apud Bruges in Flandria in festo Pentecostes, pro putura sua unius d[iei] Martis in eodem festo de elemosina regis presentibus dominis Coventrensi et Lichfeldensi, thesaurario, et J[ohanne] de Berewico 45 *li.* 16 *s.* 5 *d. par.* Eisdem, pro putura sua unius alterius diei de elemosina regis ut prius, per manus Fratris Michaelis de Ardenbourg'—40 *li. par.* Summa, 85 *li.* 16 *s.* 5 *d. par.*, quo valent in *tur.* 107 *li.* 5 *s.* 6 *d. tur. nigr.* Et memorandum quod iidem fratres pascebantur tercia die pro anima regine consortis, per dominum J[ohannem] de Berewico.

Summa pagine, 191 *li.* 5 *s.* 6 *d. tur.*, qui valent 47 *li.* 16 *s.* 4½ *d. st.* Item summa particularum istius pagine in *st.*, 9 *li.* 5 *s. st.* Summa, 57 *li.* 16½ *d. st.*

Bush' Magistro Johanni Bush', misso de Paris' ad unam dietam ad cardinalem Penestrensem pro litteris de conductu pro nunciis domini regis Anglie sigillo suo signandis, pro expensis suis duorum dierum mense Julii—12 *s.* 6 *d. tur. nigr.* Eidem moranti alia vice retro thesaurarium cum dicto cardinale pro littera regis Francie de conductu pro ducissa Brabantie expectanda, pro expensis suis v dierum sic morando mense Octobris, 28 *s.* 5 *d. tur. nigr.* Summa, 40 *s.* 11 *d. tur.*, qui valent. fo. 11ʳ

In pergameno empto apud Paris' et Sovigniacum per magistrum Johannem Bush' et W[illelmum] de Eston' per vices in estate et autumpno—8 *s.* 9 *d. tur. nigr.*

Lovetot Magistro Nicholao de Lovetot, misso de Castellion usque

Paris' pro quibusdam negociis regis secretis sibi per dictos nuncios injunctis, pro expensis suis per x dies eundo, morando, et redeundo, per manus proprias apud Nivers—4 *li. tur. nigr.*

Summa pagine—6*li.* 9*s.* 8*d. tur.*, qui valent 32*s.* 5*d. st.*

fo. 11ᵛ *Obsides Vasconie* Domino Augerio Mote, militi de Vasconia, existenti in prisona regis Francie inter alios obsides quod dominus rex Anglie fecit liberari regi Francie tempore quo ducatum Aquitanie liberavit in manum regis Francie, in subsidium sustentacionis ipsius domini Augerii in dicta prisona, per manus Willelmi Reymundi de Comis, recipientis pecuniam Parisius xx die Julii—40*li. tur. nigr.* Eidem existenti ut prius, in subsidium sustentacionis sue ut supra, per manus Guillelmi Elot apud Cameracum xvii die Septembris—30*li. tur. nigr.*

Domino Arnaldo de Gavaston', existenti similiter in prisona predicta, in subsidium expensarum suarum, per manus Arnaldi de Seni eodem die—40*li. tur.*

Domino Reimundo de Capenna, existenti in prisona ut prius, in subsidium ut supra, per manus Johannis de Perger eodem die—50*li. tur.*

Domino Bertrando de Panisales, existenti ibidem, in subsidium ut prius, per manus Guillelmi de Roffinak' eodem die—35 *li. tur. nigr.*

Eisdem dominis Arnaldo, Reymundo, Bertrando, existentibus ut prius, in denariis sibi liberatis in subsidium ut prius, per manus Johannis de Perger apud Sanctum Dionisium x die Octobris—80*li. tur. nigr.*

Magistro Roberto de Leyset, existenti ibidem, in denariis sibi liberatis eodem modo per manus Guillelmi Vivent, clerici sui, dicto xx die Julii Parisius, 35 *li. tur. nigr.* Eidem existenti ut prius, in denariis sibi liberatis eodem modo per manus dicti Guillelmi apud Cameracum xvii die Decembris, 25 *li. tur.*

Reymundo Marquesii, existenti ibidem, in denariis sibi liberatis eodem modo per manus Guillelmi de Pogio Parisius dicto xx die Julii—35 *li. tur. nigr.* Eidem, per manus Willelmi de Pogio apud Cameracum xvii die Decembris predicto—25 *li. tur. nigr.*

Arnaldo Guillelmi Marquesii, existenti ibidem, in denariis sibi liberatis ut prius per manus Johannis de Saduic—30 *li. tur. nigr.* apud Parisius. Eidem eodem modo apud Cameracum per manus W[illelmi] de Pogio dicto xvii die Decembris—20*li. tur. nigr.*

Guillelmo de Bovis Villa, existenti ibidem, in denariis sibi liberatis ut prius per manus Marcialis Parisius xx die Julii—35 *li. tur. nigr.*

THE ACCOUNT OF WALTER LANGTON

Eidem, per manus dicti Marcialis apud Cameracum xvii die Decembris in subsidium ut prius—30 *li. tur. nigr.*

Gerardo de Monte Olivo, existenti ibidem, in denariis sibi liberatis ut prius per manus Johannis de Perger Parisius dicto xx die Julii— 25 *li. tur. nigr.* Eidem, per manus Petri de Gavo Monte apud Cameracum in subsidium ut prius dicto xvii die Decembris—20 *li. tur. nigr.*

Summa pagine—555 *li. tur.*, qui valent 138 *li.* 15 *s. st.*

Summa folii—561 *li.* 9 *s.* 8 *d. tur.*, qui valent 140 *li.* 7 *s.* 5 *d. st.*

Frater Nicholaus quondam abbas Sancti Augustini Cantuariensis fo. 15^r
Fratri Nicholao, quondam abbati Sancti Augustini Cantuariensis, existenti in domo ordinis Cartusiensis prope Parisius, in denariis sibi liberatis nomine regis de elemosina ipsius regis—100 *s. tur. nigr.*

Serviens regem Francie ad arma Johanni Felice, servienti regem Francie ad arma, conducenti dominum Coventrensem, thesaurarium, de Lusarches usque Wythsand et moranti cum ipso thesaurario per viii dies mense Octobris, pro expensis suis veniendo et morando ut in equis et garcionibus suis—51 *s.* 10 *d. par.* Eidem pro expensis suis redeundo de Wythsond ad curiam regis Francie, 100 *s. par.* Qui valent in *tur.* 9 *li.* 9 *s.* 9½ *d. tur. nigr.*

Summa pagine, 14 *li.* 9 *s.* 9½ *d. tur.*, qui valent 62 *s.* 5 *d.* qua *st.*

Willelmo de Dogemerffeld, nuncio regis, misso ad curiam Romanam fo. 15^v
in nuncium ipsius regis, ad expensas suas xxvii die Septembris apud Pully juxta Boveyam per manus proprias—4 *li. tur. nigr.*

Guilloto de Doveria, garcioni domini Roberti de Borwassh, venienti cum litteris de partibus Scocie et Anglie et passanti inter Dovoriam et Bononiam de nocte et sic transeunti per regnum Francie versus partes Alvernie ad dominum . . thesaurarium, in denariis sibi liberatis in recompensacione laboris sui et pro periculo quod assumpsit sic transfretando et veniendo, per manus proprias apud Sovignimacum xxii die Septembris in 40 *s. st.*— 8 *li. tur. nigr.* Eidem, redeunti de Soviniaco dicto xxii die Septembris ad deferendum litteras cardinalium de conductu pro magistro Johanne de Selveston', veniente de Anglia ad partes Francie, pro expensis suis et conductione batelli de Whitsand' usque Doveriam—100 *s. tur. nigr.*

Cuidam valetto equiti misso in nuncium de Monte Argi ad ducem Brabantie pro negociis regis, ad expensas suas primo die Augusti, in 50 *s. par.*—62 *s.* 6 *d. tur. nigr.*

Cuidam garcioni dicti ducis Brabantie venienti ad dominum . . thesaurarium cum litteris, pro expensis redeundo cum litteris thesaurarii ad dictum ducem de Castellione ii die Augusti—7 *s.* 6 *d. tur. nigr.*

Johanni Dornn, garcioni Elie Russel et Gilberti de Cestreton', venienti cum litteris eorumdem et reportanti litteras thesaurarii ad eosdem, ix die Augusti pro expensis suis—25 *s. tur. nigr.*

Nuncio comitis Sabaudie, venienti cum litteris domini sui usque Molyns in Alvernia et redeunti cum litteris . . thesaurarii, xvii die Augusti pro expensis suis 6 *s.* 6½ *d. tur. nigr.*

Garcioni episcopi Convenarum venienti apud Molend' cum litteris domini sui et redeunti cum litteris thesaurarii, ultimo die Augusti ad expensas suas, 3 *s.* 9 *d. tur. nigr.*

Reymundo Barde venienti apud Molins in Alvernia de partibus Blavie et Burgi cum litteris domini Radulphi Basset' et aliorum nobilium Anglie existencium in municione dictorum locorum et redeunti cum litteris thesaurarii, iii die Septembris ad expensas suas—7 *li.* 10 *s. tur. nigr.*

Eidem venienti alia vice cum litteris dictorum Radulphi et aliorum, pro expensis suis redeundo xxvii die Septembris—4 *li. tur. nigr.*

Garcioni domini Iterii, misso per dominum thesaurarium et socios suos in quodam nuncio secreto, xxvi die Septembris pro expensis suis—20 *s. tur.*

Garcioni domini cardinalis Albanensis venienti de Sancto Odoeno cum litteris domini sui ad thesaurarium apud Regalem Montem, ad expensas suas redeundo xiiii die Octobris—2 *s. tur. nigr.*

Cuidam garcioni deferenti litteras thesaurarii Choro Picti, mercatori de Friscumbald', apud Nivers, pro expensis—2 *s. tur. nigr.*

Summa pagine—34 *li.* 19 *s.* 3½ *d. tur. nigr.* qui valent 8 *li.* 14 *s.* 9½ *d.* qua *st.*

Summa folii in *tur.*—49 *li.* 9 *s.* 1 *d. tur.*, qui valent 12 *li.* 7 *s.* 3 *d.* qua *st.*

fol. 6ʳ Reymundo Barde dicto le Haster venienti apud Cameracum de Vasconia cum litteris dominorum Radulphi Basset et aliorum magnatum Anglie existencium apud Burgum et Blaviam et redeunti ad eosdem cum litteris domini Coventrensis et Lichfeldensis episcopi, thesaurarii, pro expensis suis et labore, xxvii die Decembris apud Cameracum—8 *li. tur. nigr.*

Garcioni domini Ottonis de Grandisono venienti de Cameraco usque Tyrewane cum litteris ejusdem domini sui directis domino . . thesaurario, pro expensis suis redeundo ultimo die Decembris in 6 *tur. gr.*—6 *s.* 6½ *d. tur. nigr.*

Maykyno, garcioni Albertini Fulberti, deferenti litteras dominorum Coventrensis et Lichfeldensis thesaurarii et Ottonis de Grandissono ad dominum P[etrum] de Columpna, cardinalem, pro negociis regis, ad expensas[1] suas eodem die in 50 *tur. gr.*—54 *s.* 8 *d. tur. nigr.*

Willelmo de Dogmersfeld, nuncio regis, misso de Whytsand' in Flandriam per thesaurarium, pro expensis suis primo die Januarii—40 *s. tur.*

David, garcioni, deferenti litteras thesaurarii de Chelmersford' usque Doveriam ad dominum R[obertum] de Burgwash pro negociis regis xi die Januarii pro expensis suis—12 *d. st.*

Guilleto de Doveria, nuncio regis, deferenti litteras thesaurarii de London' usque Herewycum ad regem, pro expensis suis et hakeneio conducendo xiiii die Januarii—2 *s. st.*

Cursori Albertini Fulberti, deferenti litteras ad regem de London' versus partes Suffolicie cum festinacione ad expensas suas xviii die Januarii—2 *s. st.*

Willelmo Toly de Wynchelese, deferenti litteras regis de privato sigillo dominis Willelmo de Leyburne, constabulario Doverie, maiori et baronibus de Sandwyco et maiori ac baronibus de Wynchelse, pro expensis suis vii die Februarii apud Walsingham—10 *s. st.*

Hugoni de Wyteby, cursori, deferenti litteras . . thesaurarii de Bruges in Flandria usque Parisius ad Johannem Vanne pro negociis regis, pro expensis suis iiii die Marcii, in 6 *s. tur. gr.*—17 *s.* 6 *d. tur. nigr.*

Henrico, cursori, deferenti litteras thesaurarii ad comitem Hollandie pro negociis regis, pro expensis suis v die Marcii, in 6 *tur. gr.*—6 *s.* 6½ *d. tur. nigr.*

Hugoni de Cameraco, valletto domine regine Navarre, misso de Bruges in Flandria ad cardinales existentes in partibus Cameraci cum litteris dominorum thesaurarii et J[ohannis] de Berewyco, pro expensis suis eundo, morando, et redeundo per v dies, per manus Roberti de Ipre apud Cameracum xv die Marcii—47 *s.* 6 *d. tur. nigr.* Et pro denariis per ipsum solutis duobus garcionibus deferentibus dictas litteras de Doaco ad cardinales existentes apud Cameracum eo quod idem Hugo non erit ausus illuc accedere propter guerram jam inceptam inter Flandrenses et Gallicos, per manus ejusdem ibidem—15 *s. tur. nigr.* Summa, 62 *s.* 6 *d. tur.*

Antonio, valleto comitis Hanonie, venienti per vices in Flandriam ad dominos thesaurarium et J[ohannem] de Berwyk in nuncium domini sui mense Marcii, pro expensis quas fecit sic veniendo et redeundo et in equis conductis pro eodem, per manus proprias xiiii die Marcii—4 *li. tur. nigr.*

[1] MS. contains an extra *ex.*

Thome Wyneband, misso in Angliam cum litteris thesaurarii ad regem, ad expensas suas xv die Marcii—40 *s. tur. nigr.*

Reymundo Barde dicto le Haster venienti usque Cameracum de partibus Vasconie cum litteris dominorum comitis Lincolnie, J[ohannis] de Britannia, Radulphi Basset, et aliorum magnatum et redeunti cum litteris . . thesaurarii ad eosdem magnates de Cameraco, xvi die Marcii pro expensis suis et labore, 8 *li. tur. nigr.*

Summa pagine, 31 *li.* 7 *s.* 9 *d. tur.* Item 15 *s. st.*, qui valent 8 *li.* 11 *s.* 11 *d.* qua *st.*

fo. 6ᵛ Guillelmo de Pojolio de Vasconia, misso cum quibusdam litteris per dominum . . thesaurarium de Cameraco in Vasconiam, pro expensis suis xvi die Marcii, 50 *s. tur.*

Marciali, valleto Guillelmi de Bovis Villa, incarcerati, pro expensis suis redeundo, 10 *s. tur.*

Nuncio Arnaldi Guillelmi Marquesii, incarcerati ibidem, venienti eodem modo, ad expensas redeundo dicto xvi die Marcii—10 *s. tur.*

Cuidam valleto comitis Barr', venienti apud Bruxellam ad dominos thesaurarium, O[ttonem] de Grandissono, et J[ohannem] de Berewyk in nuncium ipsius comitis et comitisse, pro expensis suis redeundo xxv die Marcii, 4 *li. tur. nigr.*

Hugoni de Whyteby, deferenti litteras thesaurarii de Br[uges a]d comitem Flandrie, pro expensis suis xxvii die Marcii—5 *s. tur.*

Fratri Gilberto de ordine Alemannorum, venienti apud Cameracum in nuncium regis Alemannie ad diem constitutum per cardinales, videlicet primum diem Marcii jam proximo preteritum, et eunti de Cameraco usque Bruxellam et moranti ibidem per aliquos dies pro quodam tractatu ibi habito inter nuncios domini regis Anglie et comitis Hanonie et alios quosdam, in denariis ei liberatis ad expensas suas redeundo ad dictum regem Alemannie xxvii die Marcii—20 *li. tur. nigr.*

Simoni, cursori, deferenti litteras thesaurarii de Bruxella usque Andworp' ad Coppe Cotenne, pro expensis suis xxviii die Marcii—2 *s. tur. nigr.*

Henrico, cursori, deferenti litteras thesaurarii usque Parisius ad Johannem Vanne. . . .[1] Anglicum, pro expensis suis vi die Aprilis—10 *s. tur. nigr.*

[Hu]goni, cursori, eunti de Insula in Flandria usque portum de Swyne et deinde usque Gravelinge et Dunkirke ad inquirendum de passagio Dogmersfeld, [nuncii regis, et] pro aliis rumoribus explorandis, vii die Aprilis ad expensas—7 [*s.* 6] *d. tur.*

---

[1] Two words lacking.

Cuidam garcioni deferenti litteras thesaurarii ad Elyam Russel de Curtraco usque Andworp', pro expensis suis viii die Aprilis—2 *s.* 6 *d. tur.*

Hugoni, cursori, deferenti litteras thesaurarii de Bruxella usque Andworp' ad E[lyam] Russel, in crastino Pasche ad expensas—2 *s. tur.*

Nuncio comitis Barri, venienti cum litteris domini sui ad dominos.. thesaurarium, O[ttonem] de Grandisono, J[ohannem] de [Berew]yk apud Bruxellam, ad expensas suas redeundo dicto die—30 [*s. tur*].

Cuidam valleto domini Johannis Sauvage, venienti de Anglia usque Bruxellam ad thesaurarium cum litteris regis, ad expensas suas redeundo die Martis in ebdomada Pasche—40 *s. tur.*

Henrico, cursori, deferenti litteras thesaurarii Elye Russel, ad [expensas suas] dicto die—14 *d. tur.*

Garcioni Iterii, deferenti litteras thesaurarii de Andworp' . . .[1] [ad] Arnaldum de Ramis, [pro] expensis suis pri[mo die] Maii—12 [*d. tur.*]

Nuncio comitisse Flandrie, venienti ad thesaurarium cum litteris domine sue, pro expensis suis redeundo dicto die—12 *s.* 6 *d. tur.*

Hugoni, cursori, deferenti litteras thesaurarii comiti et comitisse Flandrie, iiii die Maii ad expensas suas—6 *s.* 3 *d. tur.*

Henrico, cursori, deferenti litteras thesaurarii de Andworp' [usque] Solon' ad ducem Brabantie, a[d e]xpensas suas v die Maii—12 *s. tur.*

Wyneband, deferenti litteras thesaurarii de Andworp' usque Bruges ad dominum J[ohannem] de Berewyk', pro expensis suis eodem die et pro conductione hakeneyorum—19 *s.* 5 *d. tur.*

Honte, deferenti litteras thesaurarii domino W[illelmo] de Monte Caniso de Anuuers [in] Flandriam, pro expensis suis eodem die— 3 *s.* 9 *d. tur.*

Cuidam garcioni domini de Kuc, venienti ad thesaurarium cum litteris domini, pro expensis [suis eundo et re]deundo e[odem] die— 2 *s. tur.*

Henrico, cursori, deferenti litteras thesaurarii de Andworp' in Selandiam ad dominum Wolfardum de [ ]ersele, pro expensis suis xv die Maii—14 *s. tur.*

Garcioni ducis Brabantie, venienti ad thesaurarium cum litteris domini sui et redeunti ad eundem ducem cum litteris dicti thesaurarii, pro expensis suis eodem die—4 *s.* 8 *d. tur.*

Summa pagine, 36 *li.* 5 *s.* 9 *d. tur.*, qui valent 9 *li.* 17 *d.* qua *st.*

Summa folii, 67 *li.* 13 *s.* 6 *d. tur.* Item 15 *s. st.*, qui valent 17 *li.* 13 *s.* 4½ *d. st.*

---

[1] Two or three words lacking.

fo. 7ʳ   Duobus garcionibus missis de Andworp' in Flandriam in nuncium dominorum thesaurarii et J[ohannis] de Berwyco, in denariis sibi liberatis per Johannem Abel pro expensis suis a festo apostolorum Philippi et Pauli—12 *s. tur.* [*nigr.*]

Cuidam garcioni venienti de curia Romana et portanti rumores de magistro Petro de Dene eunte versus curiam eandem, in denariis liberatis ad garcionem per dominum J[ohannem] Abel eodem die—20 *s. tur.*

Wyneband, misso de Anuuers in Angliam cum litteris thesaurarii ad regem, pro expensis suis et passagio suo ad mare xvii die Maii—6 *li. tur.*

Hugoni, cursori, deferenti litteras [thesaurarii] de Gandavo ad dominum de Kuc, pro expensis suis xviii die Maii—[7 *s.*] 6 *d. tur.*

Cuidam scutifero regis Alemannie venienti cum litteris ipsius regis ad dominos thesaurarium, O[ttonem] de Grandisono, et J[ohannem] de Berwyk, pro expensis suis redeundo xviii die Maii, 50 *s. tur. nigr.*

Cuidam garcioni deferenti litteras thesaurarii duci Brabantie et domino de Kuc, pro expensis suis xxi die Maii apud Bruges—10 *s. tur.*

Hugoni, cursori, deferenti litteras thesaurarii ad ducem Brabantie et dominum de Kuc, pro expensis suis xxiiii die Maii—10 *s. tur.*

Johanni Bouch [et . . .]no Spinatit de Wynchelse passanti Bon, nuncium, de Anglia in [Flandriam], venienti apud Bruges et redeunti in Angliam [de] domino . . .[1] de comitissa Barr', ad expensas suas et sociorum suorum, nautarum . . .[2] barchie, redeundo cum dicta domina dicto die—6 *li. tur.*

Nuncio comitisse Barri, redeunti de Bruges versus dominam suam, pro expensis suis iii die Junii—20 *s. tur.*

Hugoni, cursori, deferenti litteras thesaurarii de Bruges ad dominum Ottonem de Grandissono in partibus Brabantie existentem, pro expensis suis et conductione hakeneyorum viii die Junii apud Bruges—12 *s.* 10 *d. tur.*

Hugoni, [cursori], misso pluries in nuncium pro negociis regis per dominos thesaurarium et J[ohannem] de Berewyk' ad partes diversas tam Alemannie, Brabantie, et Holandie quam Flandrie et Francie per vices, ad unam cobam sibi emendam apud Gandavum . . .[3] [die] Junii — . . .[3] *s. tur.*

Hugoni, cursori, deferenti litteras thesaurarii de Bruges usque Andworp' ad comitem Barri et Elyam Russel, ad expensas xii die Junii —6 *s.* 3 *d. tur.*

---

[1] Three words lacking.   [2] One word lacking.   [3] Figure lacking.

THE ACCOUNT OF WALTER LANGTON 247

Henrico, cursori, deferenti litteras thesaurarii domino Ottoni de Grandissono et Elye Russel ad partes predictas eodem die pro expensis —7 *s.* 6 *d. tur.*

Garcioni [It]erii, misso cum litteris thesaurarii ad ducem Brabantie xv die Junii [pro expensis suis]—2 *s.* 6 *d. tur. nigr.*[1]

Garcioni ducis Brabantie, venienti cum litteris domini sui ad thesaurarium apud Crael, pro expensis suis redeundo cum litteris thesaurarii directis ad ducem xiiii die Octobris—7 *s.* 6 *d. tur.* fo. 12ʳ

Duobus garcionibus, missis de Paris' ad curiam Romanam pro negociis regis mense Junii, pro expensis suis in denariis sibi liberatis per Coppe Cotenne ibidem, in 160 *tur. gr.*—8 *li.* 15 *s. tur.*

Cuidam garcioni misso similiter de Paris' ad eandem curiam pro negociis regis eodem mense, in denariis sibi liberatis ad expensas per Gaerium Bonacursi, mercatorem de Pistor', ibidem, in 60 *tur. gr.*— 65 *s.* 7½ *d. tur.*

Bon, nuncio regis, deferenti litteras regis thesaurario post reditum ejusdem thesaurarii de Francia ad partes Anglie de Roffa ad regem versus partes Leycestrie mense Novembris, ad expensas suas— 2 *s. st.*

Summa pagine—12 *li.* 8 *s.* 1½ *d. tur.* Et 2 *s. st.*, qui valent—64 *s.* qua *st.*

De garderoba predicta, in denariis liberatis dicto W[illelmo] de Eston' et magistro Reymundo de Ferrera, q[uo]s idem magister Reymundus r[ecep]it nomine domini It[erii] de Engolisma pro 10 *li. par.* liberatis eidem It[erio] per Eliam Russel [in Br]abantia anno eodem xxvᵗᵒ super expensis ejusdem Iterii morando in partibus [predic]tis pro negociis regis, unde garderoba oneratur ex compoto dicti Elie in eadem reddito 105 *li. par.*, qui valent in *st.*, 4 *par.* computatis ad [5 *tur.*] et 4 [*tur.*] ad 1 *st.*—32 *li.* 16 *s.* 3 *d.* fo. 17ʳ

De eadem garderoba per [manus] Johannis Atte Gate de London' [nomi]nati ad quasdam lanas regis vendendas in Flandria, solventis [pre]dicto Willelmo, unde garderoba oneratur super diversis solucionibus faciendis in Brabantia [et] Flandria pro negociis regis anno eodem xxvᵗᵒ—353 *li.* 17 *s.* 4 *d. par.*, qui valent in *tur.*, 4 *par.* computatis ad [5] *tur.*, 442 *li.*[2] 6 *s.* 8 *d. tur.*, qui valent in *st.*, computatis 4 *tur.* pro 1 *st.*—110 *li.* 11 *s.* 8 *d.*

De eadem garderoba per manus ejusdem J[ohannis], solventis denarios dicto Willelmo, unde garderoba oneratur super consimilibus

---

[1] Remainder of page, possibly twenty lines, lacking.
[2] MS., *c*[*c*]*ccxlij*.

248   APPENDIX V

solucionibus factis in partibus predictis anno eodem, 10 *li*. 18 *d.st.*
crocarde, qui solvebantur pro tot *st.*—10 *li*. 18 *d*.

De eadem garderoba per manus ejusdem J[ohannis], solventis denarios domine Blanche, regine Navarre, apud Bruges mense Junii anno eodem xxv in partem solucionis cujusdam summe quam dominus rex precepit solvi eidem domine per manus thesaurarii, unde garderoba oneratur per compotum ejusdem Johannis redditum in eadem— 95 *li*. 8 *s.*

De eadem garderoba per manus ejusdem J[ohannis], solventis denarios unde garderoba oneratur receptori Flandrie in partem solucionis 1,000 *li. st.* quas idem receptor mutuaverat dicto thesaurario pro negociis regis in Flandria anno xxv eodem, mense Julii—35[8] *li*. 6 *s*. 8 *d*. *par.*, qui valent in *st.*, 35 *s. par.* computatis ad marcam de 10 *s. st.*— 102 *li*. 7 *s.*[1] 7½ *d*.

De Duracone Huberto et sociis, mercatoribus de societate Pullicum et Rembertinorum, de mutuo facto pro negociis regis per manus dicti thesaurarii in Brabantia anno eodem xxv, mense Aprilis—1,000 *li. tur. nigr.*, qui valent in *st.*, 4 *tur.* computatis ad 1 *st.*—250 *li. st.*, unde iidem mercatores habuerunt litteram thesaurarii ad denarios recipiendos in Anglia—250 *li.*

De Coppo Cotenne et sociis suis, mercatoribus de societate Friscombaldorum de Florencia, in denariis per eosdem mutuatis pro negociis regis, per manus dicti thesaurarii, recipientis denarios in Francie, Flandrie, Cameraci, [et] Brabantie partibus infra annos xxiiii et xxv— 18,845 *li.*[2] 16 *s. tur. nigr.*, de qua summa recipiebantur ab eisdem mercatoribus per manus domini Thome de Bynington', capellani dicti thesaurarii—619 *li*. 7 *s*. 6 *d. tur. nigr.*, de quibus idem Thomas plene computavit in garderoba regis; et totum residuum recipiebatur per manus Willelmi de Eston' predicti, et tamen idem W[illelmus] onerat se pro se et dicto Thoma predicto de totali summa predicta per quandam dividendam factam inter eosdem mercatores et eundem Willelmum; et valet predicta summa totalis recepta a mercatoribus predictis, 4 *tur.* computatis ad 1 *st.*—4,71[1] *li*. 9 *s.*

fo. 17ᵛ   De Terrico le Vileyn, burgense de Gandavo, mutuante 200 *li. st.* ad [ro]gatum thesaurarii predicti ad pagamentum comiti Flandrie debitum faciendum mense Maii anno xxv, qui quidem Terricus habuit litteram thesaurarii directam locum suum tenenti in Anglia ad dictam summam in Anglia recipiendam; et tamen idem Terricus istam summam 200 *li. st.* ad scaccarium non recepit, nec constabat thesaurarium

[1] MS., *v*[*ij*].   [2] MS., *xviij mill. dc*[*ccxl*]*v.*

THE ACCOUNT OF WALTER LANGTON

nec alium camerariorum de scaccario tempore confectionis et reddicionis istius compoti, a quo aut per cujus manus dictus Terricus summam illam recepit—si sit ei inde satisfactum aut non—200 *li*.

De domino Jacobo de Doura, receptore . . comitis Flandrie, in denariis per ipsum mutuatis pro negociis regis in partibus Flandrie ad rogatum dicti domini thesaurarii mense Julii, et de quibus denariis satisfactum est eidem domino Jacobo per manus Elie Russel, Johannis Atte Gate, et aliorum venditorum lanarum regis in partibus illis eodem anno—1,000 *li*.

De Johanne Peny de Sandwyco, de denariis per ipsum receptis de custuma regis lanarum et coriorum in eadem villa—30 *li*.

De denariis receptis de avantagio cambii, computando cum domino Guidone, comite Flandrie, in persolucione et perpacacione pagamenti 70,000 *li. tur. nigr.* quas idem comes recepit mense Junii in Flandria secundum formam confederacionum inter dominum regem et ipsum comitem initarum, pro cambio 6,000 *li. st.* quos idem comes receperat in Anglia per manus receptoris sui mense Februarii proximo preterito pro pagamento 24,000 *li. tur.* [*nigr.*] sibi tunc debitarum per confederaciones predictas. De quibus 6,000 *li. st.* computabatur cum domino comite quia sic convenit inter ipsum et dominum Coventrensem et Lichfeldensem episcopum, thesaurarium regis, [quod] recipere debuit, et recepit 24 *li. st.* pro 100 *li. tur. nigr.*, et sic computato cum ipso comite et satisfacto eidem de 5,760 *li. st.* de dicta summa 6,000 *li. st.* pro dicto pagamento 24,000 *li. tur. nigr.* sunt computandi hic de avantagio cambii—240 *li. st.* qui postea computati et allocati fuerunt in dicta solucione pagamenti 70,000 *tur. nigr.*—240 *li.*

De denariis receptis de avantagio cambii 1,000 *li. tur. nigr.* receptarum de mercatoribus de soci[etate] Mozorum in Brabantia ut patet superius, quia recipiebantur ab eis 1,050 *li. tur. nigr.*, pro quibus iidem mercatores receperunt in Anglia per litteram dicti thesaurarii 250 *li. st.* tantum qui computantur ad valorem 1,000 *li. tur.*, et sic computantur dicte residue 50 *li. tur.* in avantagio cambii, qui valent in *st.*, 4 *tur.* computatis ad 1 *st.*—12 *li.* 10 *s.*

Summa folii ex utraque parte—6,795 *li.* 4 *s.* ½ *d.*, probatur.

De denariis receptis in avantagio cambii 2,000 marcarum *st.* diversimodorum [c]ambiatorum in Brabantia ultra 54 *s.* 4 *d. tur. nigr.* receptos pro marca de 13 *s.* 4 *d. st.*, 481 *li.* 2 *s.* 6 *d. tur. nigr.*, qui valent in *st.*, 4 *tur.* computatis ad unum *st.*—120 *li.* 5 *s.* 7½ *d. st.*

Item, de denariis receptis de avantagio cambii de quibusdam minutis

fo. 18ʳ

particulis *st.* et *tur. gr.* cambiatorum per vices in Brabantia anno xxv presenti—12 *li.* 7 *s.* 4 *d.*

De denariis receptis de vino vendito, videlicet de duobus doliis vini de stauro ante proviso apud Cameracum pro adventu nunciorum domini regis de partibus Anglie, Vasconie, Brabantie, Alemannie, et aliunde, pro tractatu habito ibidem coram cardinalibus de negocio pacis reformande inter reges Anglie et Francie mense Decembris anno xxv, quod quidem vinum remanebat in recessu eorumdem nunciorum de ibidem, et continebant dicta duo dolia x modios iii sexteria et dimidium, minus dificiens in gaugia, pro quo defectu subtrahebantur 6 *s.* 3 *d. tur.*, precii cujuslibet modii 28 *s. tur.*—13 *li.* 13 *s.* 10 *d. tur.* Et de quodam remanenti unius dolii vini venditi ibidem per Johannem Abel—32 *s.* 11 *d. tur.* Summa, 15 *li.* 6 *s.* 9 *d. tur.*, qui valent in *st.*, 4 *tur.* computatis ad 1 *st.* ut prius—76 *s.* 8 *d.*

Memorandum de 10,000 *li. st.* quas dominus J[ohannes] de Berewyk recepit de thesaurario et camerariis de scaccario super lib[eracion]e W[alteri] de Langeton' de tempore quo fuit custos garderobe regis, et eosdem [den]arios transduxit in Flandriam mense Julii anno xxv^{to}, qui denarii liberabantur integraliter domino G[uidoni], comiti Flandrie, per preceptum regis, unde littera ejusdem comitis obligatoria ep[iscopo] in garderoba regis, [de] qua summa Johannes de Drokenesford, custos garderobe predicte, oneratur infra unam summam de 35,056 *li.* 7 *s.* 3 *d.*, de qua summa tota dictus W[alterus] de Langeton' eundem J[ohannem] de Drokenesford oneravit in compoto ipsius W[alteri] de custodia dicte garderobe de anno xxiii, tempore reddicionis ejusdem compoti ad scaccarium.

Et memorandum quod littera obligatoria comitis Flandrie de predictis 10,000 *li. st.* sibi ut premittitur liberari, liberata fuit domino Radulpho de Manton', cofrario, apud Eboracum mense Julii anno xxvii^o ad deferendum in garderobam regis et liberandum domino Johanni de Benstede, contrarotulatori.

Summa pagine—136 *li.* 9 *s.* 7½ *d.*
Summa totalis recepte—34,726 *li.* 17 *s.* 3 *d.*, probatur.

BIBLIOGRAPHY

(1) MANUSCRIPT RECORDS

THE Dodsworth MS. 76 in the Bodleian Library contains a folio relating to Bishop Langton's diplomatic mission of 1296–7. Of the collections in the British Museum, Additional MSS. 7965, 7966A, 8835, 9951, 17362, 35292, 37655, Cottonian MS. Nero C. viii, and Stowe MS. 553 are wardrobe accounts. They constitute a source, as yet unexhausted, that is rich in administrative details bearing on foreign relations. Information under the title of *necessaria* is particularly full, and records of many early embassies are to be found here. The wardrobe accounts are the most important manuscript materials outside the Public Record Office. Cottonian MS. Julius E.i is one of the five Gascon registers compiled during the reign of Edward II. The second half of the manuscript contains the proceedings of the process of Périgueux.

The real treasure-house of material, practically none of which has either been used or printed, is contained in the collection of Diplomatic Documents, Chancery (C 47), preserved in the Public Record Office. Unlike the Diplomatic Documents, Exchequer (E 30), a great many of which were used by Rymer in his *Foedera*, it is of modern constitution and arises from the sorting of chancery records formerly preserved in the Tower that took place about 1890. It includes the so-called 'state papers' and all documents dealing with foreign affairs or persons that are neither letters, petitions, nor warrants. Besides these there are some that are of a political rather than a diplomatic nature. The whole collection might be said to consist of 'informal' diplomatic documents. A manuscript list was made in 1896, but further reclassification began in 1908 and the complete list was not published until 1923. Additions since that date are catalogued in a small typescript kept in the Literary Search Room of the Public Record Office. Supplementary material of the same nature is scattered through the classes of Ancient Correspondence (SC 1), Ancient Petitions (SC 8), Chancery Miscellanea (C 47), Papal Bulls (SC 7), Parliamentary and Council Proceedings, Chancery (C 49) and Exchequer (E 175), Scottish Documents, Exchequer (E 39), and the Treaty Rolls (C 76).

The technical and financial aspects of diplomacy are especially illustrated in the large group of Exchequer Accounts (E 101), which contain the *particule compoti* of ambassadors as well as some wardrobe books. These were usually enrolled in an abbreviated form on the Pipe Rolls (E 172) and the duplicate Chancellor's Rolls (E 352). Additional wardrobe records are to be found in Enrolled Accounts, Wardrobe and Household (E 361), and among Wardrobe Debentures (E 404). The Issue Rolls, Exchequer of Receipt (E 403), and

BIBLIOGRAPHY

Liberate Rolls, Chancery (C 62), yield many details of a financial and secretarial nature. Chancery Warrants (C 81) furnish information on the issue of certain types of diplomatic documents. The class of Miscellaneous Books, Exchequer Treasury of Receipt (E 36), contains various calendars and registers of instruments relating to foreign affairs.

(ii) PRINTED SOURCES

Annales Londonienses, edited by William Stubbs. Chronicles of the Reigns of Edward I and Edward II, vol. i. Rolls Series. London, 1882–3.

Annales Paulini, edited by William Stubbs. Chronicles of the Reigns of Edward I and Edward II, vol. i. Rolls Series. London, 1882–3.

Les Archives historiques du département de la Gironde. 58 tomes. Paris and Bordeaux, 1859–1932.

AVESBURY. *Robertus de Avesbury, De gestis mirabilibus regis Edwardi tertii*, edited by E. M. Thompson. Rolls Series. London, 1889.

BÉMONT, CHARLES, editor, *Recueil d'actes relatifs à l'administration des rois d'Angleterre en Guyenne au xiiie siècle (Recogniciones feodorum in Aquitania)*. Documents inédits sur l'histoire de France. Paris, 1914.

BLISS, W. H., and JOHNSON, C., editors, *Calendars of Entries in the Papal Registers relating to Great Britain and Ireland*, vols. i, ii. London, 1894–7.

BREUIL, GUILLAUME DU, *Stilus curie parlamenti*, edited by Félix Aubert. Collection des textes pour servir à l'enseignement de l'histoire. Paris, 1909.

BROWN, RAWDON, editor, *Calendar of State Papers and MSS. relating to English Affairs, existing in the Archives of Venice, and in Other Libraries of Northern Italy*, vol. i. London, 1864.

BURTON. *Chronica monasterii de Melsa, a fundatione ad annum 1396, auctore Thoma de Burton, abbate*, edited by E. A. Bond, vol. ii. Rolls Series. London, 1867.

Calendar of Chancery Warrants preserved in the Public Record Office. London, 1927.

Calendar of the Close Rolls. London, 1892–1934.

Calendar of the Patent Rolls. London, 1891–1914.

Catalogue of Additions to the Manuscripts in the British Museum in the Years 1854–1875, vol. ii. London, 1877.

CHAMPOLLION-FIGEAC, editor, *Lettres de rois, reines et autres personnages des cours de France et d'Angleterre depuis Louis VII jusqu'à Henri IV tirées des archives de Londres par Bréquigny.* 2 tomes. Documents inédits sur l'histoire de France. Paris, 1839.

CHAPLAIS, PIERRE, editor, *Some Documents regarding the Fulfilment and Interpretation of the Treaty of Brétigny (1361–1369).* Camden Miscellany, vol. xix; Camden Third Series, vol. lxxx. London, 1952.

—— *The War of Saint-Sardos (1323–1325); Gascon correspondence and diplomatic documents.* Camden Third Series, vol. lxxxvii. London, 1954.

Chronicon Angliae, ab anno Domini 1328 usque ad annum 1388, auctore monacho quodam Sancti Albani, edited by E. M. Thompson. Rolls Series. London, 1874.

Chronique des quatre premiers Valois (1327–1393), edited by Simeon Luce. Société de l'Histoire de France, tome xlii. Paris, 1862.

CUTTINO, G. P., 'A Memorandum Book of Elias Joneston'. *Speculum*, xvii (1942).

—— 'Another Memorandum Book of Elias Joneston'. *English Historical Review*, lxiii (1948).

—— *The Gascon Calendar of 1322.* Camden Third Series, vol. lxx. London, 1949.

—— *Gascon Register A (Series of 1318–1319).* Oxford University Press for the British Academy (in press).

—— *Le Livre d'Agenais.* Cahiers de l'Association Marc Bloch de Toulouse: Documents d'histoire méridionale, No. 1. Toulouse, 1956.

DENHOLM-YOUNG, N., editor, *The Liber Epistolaris of Richard de Bury.* Roxburghe Club. Oxford, 1950.

Flores historiarum, per Matthaeum Westmonasteriensem collecti, edited by H. R. Luard, vol. iii. Rolls Series. London, 1890.

FRANCISQUE-MICHEL, BÉMONT, CHARLES, RENOUARD, YVES, editors, *Rôles gascons.* 4 tomes. Documents inédits sur l'histoire de France. Paris, 1885–1906 (tomes i–iii); Paris and London, 1962 (tome iv).

FROISSART. *Œuvres de Froissart publiées avec les variantes des divers manuscrits*, by Baron Kervyn de Lettenhove. Chroniques, tome ii. Brussels, 1867.

Gesta Edwardi de Carnarvon auctore canonico Bridlingtoniensi, edited by William Stubbs. Chronicles of the Reigns of Edward I and Edward II, vol. ii. Rolls Series. London, 1882–3.

HALL, HUBERT, editor, *The Red Book of the Exchequer*, part iii. Rolls Series. London, 1897.

HEMINGBURGH. *Chronicon domini Walteri de Hemingburgh, de gestis regum Angliae*, edited by Hans Claude Hamilton, vol. ii. The English Historical Society. London, 1849.

HRABAR, VLADIMIR E., editor, *De legatis et legationibus tractatus varii.* Dorpat, 1905.

Istore et croniques de Flandres, d'après les textes de divers manuscrits, edited by Baron Kervyn de Lettenhove, tome i. Académie Royale de Belgique. Brussels, 1879.

KNIGHTON. *Chronicon Henrici Knighton, vel Cnitthon, monachi Leycestrensis*, edited by J. R. Lumby, vol. i. Rolls Series. London, 1889.

LANGTOFT. *Chronicle of Pierre de Langtoft; in French Verse, from the Earliest Period to the Death of Edward I*, edited by T. Wright, vol. ii. Rolls Series. London, 1868.

LARSON, ALFRED, 'English Embassies during the Hundred Years' War'. *English Historical Review*, lv (1940).
LE BEL. *Chronique de Jean le Bel*, edited by Jules Viard and Eugène Déprez, tome i. Société de l'Histoire de France. Paris, 1904.
LESCOT. *Chronique de Richard Lescot, religieux de Saint-Denis (1328–1344)*, edited by Jean Lemoine. Société de l'Histoire de France, tome xciii. Paris, 1896.
Liber quotidianus contrarotulatoris garderobe; anno regni regis Edwardi primi vicesimo octavo, A.D. MCCXCIX & MCCC. Society of Antiquaries. London, 1787.
MARSDEN, REGINALD G., editor, *Select Pleas in the Court of Admiralty*, vol. i Selden Society, vol. vi. London, 1894.
Memoranda de parliamento: Records of the Parliament holden at Westminster 28 February, 33 Edward I (A.D. 1305), edited by F. W. Maitland. Rolls Series. London, 1893.
MIROT, LÉON, and DÉPREZ, EUGÈNE, editors, *Les Ambassades anglaises pendant la guerre de Cent Ans: catalogue chronologique (1327–1450)*. Bibliothèque de l'École des Chartes, tome lix. Paris, 1898.
MURIMUTH. *Adae Murimuth, Continuatio chronicarum*, edited by E. M. Thompson. Rolls Series. London, 1889.
PALGRAVE, SIR FRANCIS, editor, *The Antient Kalendars and Inventories of the Treasury of H.M. Exchequer*. 3 volumes. Record Commission. London, 1836.
—— *Documents and Records illustrating the History of Scotland; preserved in the Treasury of H.M. Exchequer*, vol. i. Record Commission. London, 1837.
—— *The Parliamentary Writs and Writs of Military Summons*. 2 volumes in 5 parts. Record Commission. London, 1827–34.
PARDESSUS, J. M., *Us et coutumes de la mer; ou Collection des usages maritimes des peuples de l'antiquité et du Moyen Âge*. 2 tomes. Paris, 1847.
PARIS. *Matthaei Parisiensis Chronica majora*, edited by H. R. Luard, vol. v. Rolls Series. London. 1880.
PERROY, ÉDOUARD, editor, *The Anglo-French Negotiations at Bruges, 1374–1377*. Camden Miscellany, vol. xix; Camden Third Series, vol. lxxx. London, 1952.
—— *The Diplomatic Correspondence of Richard II*. Camden Third Series, vol. xlviii. London. 1933.
PRYNNE, WILLIAM, *The History of King John, King Henry III, and the most illustrious King Edward the I*. London, 1670.
Public Record Office Lists and Indexes:
  No. I. *Index of Ancient Petitions of the Chancery and of the Exchequer*. London, 1892.
  No. XI. *List of Foreign Accounts enrolled on the Great Rolls of the Exchequer*. Henry III–Richard III. London, 1900.

No. XV. *List of Ancient Correspondence of the Chancery and the Exchequer.* London, 1902.

No. XXXV. *List of Exchequer Accounts.* Henry III–George III. London, 1911.

No. XLIX. *List of Diplomatic Documents and Scottish Documents and Papal Bulls.* London, 1923.

Return of the Members of Parliament, part i and index. London, 1878–91.

RICHARDSON, H. G., and SAYLES, GEORGE, editors, *Rotuli parliamentorum Anglie hactenus inediti,* MCCLXXIX–MCCCLXXIII. Camden Third Series, no. li. London, 1935.

RISHANGER. *Willelmi Rishanger, quondam monachi S. Albani, Chronica et annales,* edited by H. T. Riley. Rolls Series. London, 1865.

Rotuli parliamentorum; ut et petitiones in parliamento tempore Edwardi R. III, vols. i, ii. n.p., n.d.

Royal Commission on Historical Manuscripts:
Fourth Report, part i. London, 1874.
Fifth Report. London, 1876.
Eleventh Report: the Manuscripts of the Corporations of Southampton and King's Lynn. London, 1887.
Various Collections. London, 1901.

RYMER, THOMAS, editor, *Foedera, conventiones, litterae, et cuiuscunque generis acta publica,* vols. i–iii. Record Commission. London, 1821.

TRIVET. F. *Nicholai Triveti, de ordine fratrum praedicatorum, Annales sex regum Angliae,* edited by Thomas Hog. The English Historical Society. London, 1845.

TWISS, SIR T., editor, *Black Book of the Admiralty, with Appendices.* 4 volumes. Rolls Series. London, 1871–6.

WALSINGHAM. *Thomae Walsingham, quondam monachi S. Albani, Historia anglicana,* edited by H. T. Riley, vol. i. Rolls Series. London, 1863.

(III) BOOKS AND ARTICLES

AUBERT, FÉLIX, *Histoire du parlement de Paris de l'origine à François Ier, 1250–1515.* 2 tomes. Paris, 1894.

BALDWIN, JAMES FOSDICK, *The King's Council in England during the Middle Ages.* Oxford, 1913.

BEHRENS, B., 'Origins of the Office of English Resident Ambassador in Rome'. *English Historical Review,* xlix (1934).

—— 'Treatises on the Ambassador written in the Fifteenth and Early Sixteenth Centuries'. *English Historical Review,* li (1936).

BLACK, J. G., 'Edward I and Gascony in 1300'. *English Historical Review,* xvii (1902).

BOCK, FRIEDRICH, 'Some New Documents illustrating the Early Years of the Hundred Years War (1353–1356)'. *Bulletin of the John Rylands Library. Manchester,* xv (1931).

BOCK, FRIEDRICH, 'Englands Beziehungen zum Reich unter Adolf von Nassau'. *Mitteilungen des Oesterreichischen Instituts für Geschichtsforschung*, xi (1933).

CHAPLAIS, PIERRE, 'English Arguments concerning the Feudal Status of Aquitaine in the Fourteenth Century'. *Bulletin of the Institute of Historical Research*, xxi (1948).

—— 'The Making of the Treaty of Paris (1259) and the Royal Style'. *English Historical Review*, lxvii (1952).

—— 'Règlement des conflits internationaux franco-anglais au XIVe siècle'. *Le Moyen Âge*, lvii (1951).

CHEYETTE, FREDRIC L., 'The Sovereign and the Pirates, 1332'. *Speculum*, xlv (1970).

CHEYNEY, EDWARD P., 'The dawn of a New Era, 1250-1453'. *The Rise of Modern Europe*, edited by William L. Langer, vol. i. New York, 1936.

CHRIMES, S. B., *English Constitutional Ideas in the Fifteenth Century*. Cambridge, 1936.

CHURCHILL, IRENE JOSEPHINE, *Canterbury Administration: the Administrative Machinery of the Archbishopric of Canterbury illustrated from Original Records*. 2 volumes. London, 1933.

COKE, SIR EDWARD, *The Fourth Part of the Institutes of the Lawes of England; concerning the Jurisdiction of Courts*. London, 1669.

COVILLE, A., L'Europe occidentale de 1270 à 1380, Deuxième Partie, de 1328 à 1380'. *Histoire générale: histoire du Moyen Âge*, edited by Gustave Glotz, tome vi. Paris, 1941.

CUTTINO, G. P., 'An Unidentified Gascon Register'. *English Historical Review*, liv (1939).

—— 'The Archives of Gascony under English Rule'. *The American Archivist*, 25 (1962).

—— 'Henry of Canterbury'. *English Historical Review*, lvii (1942).

—— 'Historical Revision: the Causes of the Hundred Years War'. *Speculum*, xxxi (1956).

—— 'The Process of Agen'. *Speculum*, xix (1944).

—— 'A Reconsideration of the *Modus tenendi parliamentum*' in *The Forward Movement of the Fourteenth Century*, edited by Francis Lee Utley. Columbus, Ohio, 1961.

DAVIES, JAMES CONWAY, *The Baronial Opposition to Edward II: a Study in Administrative History*. Cambridge, 1918.

DAVIS, H. W. C., editor, *Essays in History presented to Reginald Lane Poole*. Oxford, 1927.

DELACHENAL, R., *Histoire des avocats au parlement de Paris, 1300-1600*. Paris, 1885.

DENHOLM-YOUNG, N., 'The Cursus in England'. *Essays presented to H. E. Salter*, no. iii. Oxford, 1934.

—— 'Richard de Bury (1287–1345)'. *Transactions of the Royal Historical Society*. Fourth Series, xx (1937).

DÉPREZ, EUGÈNE, *Les Préliminaires de la guerre de Cent Ans; la papauté, la France, et l'Angleterre (1328–1342)*. Bibliothèque des Écoles françaises d'Athènes et de Rome, 86° fascicule. Paris, 1902.

—— 'Le Trésor des chartes de Guyenne sous Édouard II'. *Mélanges Bémont*. Paris, 1913.

—— 'La Conférence d'Avignon (1344); l'arbitrage pontifical entre la France et l'Angleterre'. *Essays presented to T. F. Tout*, no. xxiii. Manchester, 1925.

DESIMONI, CORNELIO, 'I conti dell'ambasciata al chan di Persia nel MCCXCII'. *Atti della Società Ligure di Storia Patria*, xiii, fascicolo 3. Genoa, 1879.

DIBBEN, L. B., 'Secretaries in the Thirteenth and Fourteenth Centuries'. *English Historical Review*, xxv (1910).

Dictionary of National Biography, edited by Sidney Lee and Leslie Stephen. 63 volumes. London, 1885–1921.

FAWTIER, ROBERT, *Les Capétiens et la France; leur rôle dans sa construction*. Paris, 1942.

—— 'L'Europe occidentale de 1270 à 1380, Première Partie, de 1270 à 1328'. *Histoire générale: histoire du Moyen Âge*, edited by Gustave Glotz, tome vi. Paris, 1940.

FOSS, EDWARD, *The Judges of England*, vol. ii. London, 1851.

FULTON, THOMAS WEMYSS, *The Sovereignty of the Sea*. Edinburgh and London, 1911.

GALBRAITH, V. H., 'The *Modus tenendi parliamentum*'. *Journal of the Warburg and Courtauld Institutes*, xvi (1953).

—— 'The Tower as an Exchequer Record Office in the Reign of Edward II'. *Essays presented to T. F. Tout*, no. xviii. Manchester, 1925.

GAVRILOVITCH, MICHEL, *Étude sur te traité de Paris de 1259 entre Louis IX, roi de France, & Henri III, roi d'Angleterre*. Bibliothèque de l'École des hautes études, 125° fascicule. Paris, 1899.

GIUSEPPI, M. S., *A Guide to the Manuscripts preserved in the Public Record Office*, vol. i (Legal records, &c.). London, 1923.

GUILHIERMOZ, P., *Enquetês et procès; étude sur la procédure et le fonctionnement du parlement au xive siècle*. Paris, 1892.

HALL, HUBERT, *Studies in English Official Historical Documents*. Cambridge, 1908.

—— *A Formula Book of English Historical Documents*, part i (Diplomatic documents). Cambridge, 1908.

HIGOUNET, CH., 'Bastides et frontières'. *Le Moyen Âge*, liv (1948).

HILL, MARY C., *The King's Messengers 1199–1377: a Contribution to the History of the Royal Household*. London, 1961.

HOLDSWORTH, SIR WILLIAM, *A History of English Law*, vol. ii. London, 1936.

JENKINS, HELEN, *Papal Efforts for Peace under Benedict XII, 1334–1342.* Philadelphia, 1933.
JOHNSON, CHARLES, 'The Homage for Guienne in 1304'. *English Historical Review,* xxiii (1908).
—— 'The Keeper of Papal Bulls'. *Essays presented to T. F. Tout,* no. x. Manchester, 1925.
KANTOROWICZ, ERNST. *Frederick the Second, 1194–1250.* London, 1931.
KERN, F., *Die Anfänge der französischen Ausdehnungspolitik bis sum Jahre 1308.* Tübingen, 1910.
KINGSFORD, C. L., 'John de Benstede and his Missions for Edward I'. *Essays Essays presented to R. L. Poole.* Oxford, 1927.
LARSON, ALFRED, 'The Payment of Fourteenth-century English Envoys'. *English Historical Review,* liv (1939).
LITTLE, A. G., and POWICKE, F. M., editors, *Essays in Medieval History presented to Thomas Frederick Tout.* Manchester, 1925.
LOWE, WALTER I., *The Considerations which induced Edward III to assume the Title King of France.* Annual Report of the American Historical Association, 1900, vol. i. Washington, 1901.
LUBIMENKO, INNA, *Jean de Bretagne comte de Richmond: sa vie et son activité en Angleterre, en Écosse et en France.* Lille, 1908.
LUCAS, HENRY S., *The Low Countries and the Hundred Years' War, 1326–1347.* University of Michigan Publications, History and Political Science, vol. viii. Ann Arbor, 1929.
—— 'The Machinery of Diplomatic Intercourse'. *The English Government at Work, 1327–1336,* vol. i, no. vii. Cambridge, Mass., 1940.
MAITLAND, FREDERICK WILLIAM, 'The History of the Register of Original Writs'. *The Collected Papers of F. W. Maitland,* edited by H. A. L. Fisher, vol. ii. Cambridge, 1911.
MAXWELL-LYTE, SIR H. C., *Historical Notes on the Use of the Great Seal of England.* London, 1926.
Mélanges d'histoire offerts à M. Charles Bémont par amis et ses élèves. Paris, 1913.
MOLLAT, G., *Étude critique sur les Vitae paparum Avenionensium d'Étienne Baluze.* Paris, 1917.
Oxford Essays in Medieval History presented to Herbert Edward Salter. Oxford, 1934.
PERROY, ÉDOUARD, *La Guerre de Cent Ans.* Paris, 1945.
PIRENNE, HENRI, 'The Place of the Netherlands in the Economic History of Medieval Europe'. *Economic History Review,* ii (1929).
POWICKE, F. M., *King Henry III and the Lord Edward: the Community of the Realm in the Thirteenth Century.* 2 volumes. Oxford, 1947.
—— *The Thirteenth Century 1216–1307.* The Oxford History of England, edited by G. N. Clark, vol. vi. Oxford, 1953.

QUELLER, DONALD E., *The Office of Ambassador in the Middle Ages*. Princeton, 1967.
RAMSEY, J. H., *A History of the Revenues of the Kings of England, 1066–1399*, vol. ii. Oxford, 1925.
ROUND, J. H., 'The Barons' Letter to the Pope'. *The Ancestor*, nos. vi, vii (1903), viii (1904).
SALT, MARY C. L., 'List of English Embassies to France, 1272–1307'. *English Historical Review*, xliv (1929).
SCHULZ, H. C., 'Thomas Hoccleve, Scribe'. *Speculum*, xii (1937).
SELDEN, JOHN, *Mare clausum, seu de dominio maris*. London, 1636.
STRAYER, JOSEPH R., 'Defense of the Realm and Royal Power in France'. *Studi in onore di Gino Luzzato*. Milan, 1949.
—— 'The Laicization of French and English Society in the Thirteenth Century'. *Speculum*, xv (1940).
—— and TAYLOR, CHARLES H., *Studies in Early French Taxation*. Harvard Historical Monographs, xii. Cambridge, Mass., 1939.
STURLER, J. DE, *Les Relations politiques et les échanges commerciaux entre le duché de Brabant et l'Angleterre au Moyen Âge*. Paris, 1936.
TARDIF, ADOLPHE, *La Procédure civile et criminelle aux xiiie et xive siècles, ou procès de transition*. Paris, 1885.
TEMPLEMAN, G., 'Edward III and the Beginnings of the Hundred Years War'. *Transactions of the Royal Historical Society*. Fifth Series, ii (1952).
TOUT, T. F., *Chapters in the Administrative History of Mediaeval England*. Manchester Historical Series, nos. xxxiv, xxxv, xlviii, xlix, lvii, lxiv. 6 volumes. Manchester, 1928–37.
—— *The History of England from the Accession of Henry III to the Death of Edward III (1216–1377)*. The Political History of England, edited by William Hunt and Reginald L. Poole, vol. iii. London, 1930.
—— *The Collected Papers of Thomas Frederick Tout with a Memoir and Bibliography*. Manchester Historical Series, nos. lxiii, lxv, lxvi. 3 volumes. Manchester, 1932–4.
—— *The Place of the Reign of Edward II in English History*. Second edition, revised throughout by Hilda Johnstone. Manchester Historical Series, no. xxi. Manchester, 1936.
TRABUT-CUSSAC, J.-P., 'L'Administration anglaise en Gascogne sous Henri III et Édouard Ier de 1252 à 1307'. *École Nationale des Chartes: Position des Thèses* (1949).
—— 'Les Cartulaires gascons d'Édouard II, d'Édouard III et de Charles VII'. *Bibliothèque de l'École des Chartes*, cxi (1953).
—— 'Les Coutumes ou droits de douane perçus à Bordeaux sur les vins et les marchandises par l'administration anglaise de 1252 à 1307'. *Annales du Midi*, lxii (1950).
ULLMANN, WALTER, 'The Development of the Medieval Idea of Sovereignty'. *English Historical Review*, lxiv (1949).

UNWIN, GEORGE, editor, *Finance and Trade under Edward III*. Manchester Historical Series, no. xxxii. Manchester, 1918.
—— *Studies in Economic History: the Collected Papers of George Unwin*, edited by R. H. Tawney. London, 1927.
UTLEY, FRANCIS LEE, editor, *The Forward Movement of the Fourteenth Century*. Columbus, Ohio, 1961.
WILKINSON, B., *The Chancery under Edward III*. Manchester Historical Series, no. li. Manchester, 1929.
WILLARD, JAMES F., and MORRIS, WILLIAM A., editors, *The English Government at Work, 1327–1336*, vol. i. Cambridge, Mass., 1940.

INDEX

Abbas, Henricus, 141 n. 1
Abbeville (*dép.* Somme), 35
Abbeville, dean of, 35, 85 n. 1
Abbots, 33 n. 6, 125
Accounts, allowances, 167, 169
— assignments, 169
— audit of, 169, 173
— auditors of, 78, 169
— bills, 168, 172, 173
— debentures, 40, 116, 185
— enrolment of, 119, 168 and n. 1
— exchequer of, *see under* Exchequer
— quittances, 7, 118, 124, 126
— vouchers, 173
— *see also* Envoys, *and under various departments*
Acera (Italy, prov. Caserta), 176
Administration, *see* Diplomacy *and under various departments*
Admirals, 65, 68, 73, 137, 140
Admiralty, Court of, 68 n. 2, 83
Adolf of Nassau (king of the Romans), 12, 171, 180, 181, 185 n. 2
Advocates, 35, 42 n. 2, 57 n. 4, 80, 81. *See also under* Parlement de Paris
Agen (*dép.* Lot-et-Garonne), 105, 124
— process of, *see under* Processes
Agenais (France), 4, 7, 8, 15, 22, 42, 44 n. 1, 45 n. 1, 53, 119, 124
— seneschal of, 111
Aimeri, Pierre, 118
Airmyn, Adam, 154
— William, bishop of Norwich, 136
Albano, cardinal bishop of, 180
Ale, 115
Alexander IV (Rainaldo da Segni), 28
Alfonso X (of Castile), 3, 17, 19, 45, 124
Allowances, *see under* Accounts
Almonds, *see under* Food
Alps, 178
Ambassadors, *see under* Envoys
Amiens (*dép.* Somme), 15, 48, 52, 75
— bailiff of, 77
— bishop of, *see* Fouilly
— treaty of, *see under* Treaties
Anagni (Italy, prov. Rome), 176
Angelo, Master, 185
Animals, gerfalcons, 175

— horses, 40, 131, 134, 174, 185
— leopards, 175
— oxen, 175
— squirrels, 175
— wolves, 175
Anjou (France), 5, 7
Anjou, Charles of, 3
Antwerp (Belgium), 138, 178 n. 1, 183
Apostolic chamber, *see under* Papacy
Appellants, 41, 142. *See also under* Parlement de Paris
Aquapendente (Italy, prov. Rome), 176
Aquitaine (France), 5, 16, 21, 23, 26, 27, 32, 37, 42, 45 n. 1, 50, 51, 79, 90, 107, 117, 119, 121, 124, 125, 143 n. 3, 146, 150, 160
— dukes of, *see* England, kings of
Aragon, 12, 113, 126
— king of, 31 n. 3
Arbitration, 82–3, 86
— papal, 10–11, 33, 34, 35, 50, 51, 63, 64, 82–3, 93, 97, 98, 124, 180
— royal, 11, 12, 63, 64, 82–3, 101, 114
Arbitration, Permanent Court of, 66
Archbishops, 18 n. 1, 32, 33, 38 n. 3, 40, 44 and n. 1, 58, 125, 133, 137, 148, 153 and n. 4, 170, 182
Archdeacons, 185 n. 2
Arches, dean of the, 55 n. 1
Archives, 30–2, 60, 87 n. 3, 104, 112, 126, 187, 188. *See also* Records *and under various departments*
Archives Nationales (Paris), 5 n. 1
Arjish (Turkey), 176
Arles (France), 12
Armagnac (France), 11 n. 2, 124
Arrabloy, Jean d', 92
arrêts, *see under* Parlement de Paris
Arson, 68
Artois, Robert d', 19
aspri, *see under* Currency
Assignments, *see under* Accounts
Astley, Thomas, 104 n. 1
Atteyo, Jean de, 170
Attorney, 134, 136, 139, 180
— letters of, *see under* Records
Aubeterre (*dép.* Dordogne), 89
Aubeterre, Marie of, 125

INDEX

Audit, *see under* Accounts
Auditors, 55 *n.* 1, 69, 74, 75, 81, 83
— of accounts, *see under* Accounts
Audley, Hugh, earl of Gloucester, 135
Aumale, Denis d', 75 n. 4
Auvillar (*dép.* Tarn-et-Garonne, *arr.* Castelsarrasin), 124
— viscount of, 119
Avenza (Italy, prov. Tuscany), 176
Avignon (*dép.* Vaucluse), 35, 92, 129 n. 1
— papacy at, 17, 144. *See also* Papacy

Bags, *see under* Receptacles
Baiburt (Turkey), 176
Bailiffs, 74, 75 n. 4, 77
Bakewell, Sir John, 34, 35, 64 and n. 5, 79, 81, 82, 85 n. 1, 143
Balance of power, 17–19
Baldock, Robert, 122 and n. 5
Baldwin, J. F., 55, 56, 152, 165
Balliol, John (of Scotland), 21
Bankers (Lee, co. Kent), 64 n. 5
Bankers, *see* Loans, Merchants
Bannerets, *see* Knights
Banquets, 132, 174
Bar, 13, 126
— counts of, *see* Henri III, Jean
Barber, 175
Bardi, the, 16 n. 4, 120, 171
Bardney, abbot of, 33 n. 6
Barentino, William de, 136
Barletta (Italy, prov. Apulia), 176
Barons, 4, 5, 6, 13, 67, 88, 132
— of Cinque Ports, *see under* Cinque Ports
— of exchequer, *see under* Exchequer
Barrels, *see under* Receptacles
Bar-sur-Seine (*dép.* Aube, *arr.* Troyes), 174
Baskets, *see under* Receptacles
Basset, Ralph, 133
Bastides, 14, 22, 23 and n. 2, 42, 45 n. 1, 88, 89, 93, 119, 124
Battles, *see* Sluys
Bautersem, Henri de, 16
Bayonne (*dép.* B. Pyrénées), 10, 63 n. 3, 73 n. 4, 75 n. 4, 114, 124
— mayor of, 64 n. 3
— process of, *see under* Processes
Bazas (*dép.* Gironde, *arr.* Langon), 124
— bishop of, 97 n. 5
Béarn, 124, 125

Béarn, Gaston de, 9, 124, 125
Beaucaire, castellan of, 134
Beaulieu (France), 12
Beaumanoir, Philippe de, 24
Beauvais (*dép.* Oise), 15
Beds, 175
Belvès (*dép.* Dordogne, *arr.* Sarlat-la-Canéda), priory of, 125
Belvèze (*dép.* Tarn-et-Garonne, *arr.* Castelsarrasin, *c.* Lauzerte), parish of, 94 n. 1
Bench, King's, *see under* Justices
Benedict XII (Jacques Fournier), 17, 18 and n. 1, 134
Benefices, 18 n. 1, 36, 139
Benstead, John, 147
Béraud (Beraudi), Vital, 44 n. 1, 45 n. 1
Bergerac (France), 124
Bertrand, cardinal, 18 n. 1
Berwick (co. Berwick), 35 n. 1
Besançon, archbishop of, 18 n. 1
Bexwell, church of, 36
Bicknor, Alexander, 87
Bigorre (France), 125
Bills, *see under* Accounts
Biscay, Marie of, 17
Bishops, 7, 11 n. 1, 33 n. 6, 36 and n. 3, 38 n. 3, 40, 44 n. 1, 45 n. 1, 47, 52, 53, 56, 57, 63, 85 n. 1, 91, 95 n. 2, 96, 97 and n. 5, 98, 100, 118, 125, 129, 133, 135, 136, 137, 147, 148, 149, 160, 170, 173, 180, 182
Black Hall (Tower of London), 31
Blanche (of Navarre), 178
Blanot, Jean de, 24
Blanquefort (*dép.* Gironde, *arr.* Bordeaux), 111
Boats, *see* Ships
Boisset (*dép.* Dordogne, *arr.* Périgueux, *c.* Neuvic, *cne.* St-Aquilin), parish of, 94 n. 1
Bon, Arnold, 183
Boniface VIII (Benedetto Caetani), 10–11, 21, 28, 44 n. 1, 50, 63, 93, 97, 98, 124, 182
Boniface, Bertrand, 103
Books, *see under* Records
Bordeaux (*dép.* Gironde), 35, 37, 38, 48, 49, 75, 97, 109, 116, 117, 120, 121 n. 2, 125
— archbishop of, 125
— castle of, 97, 118. *See also* Ombrière, L'

INDEX

— church of, 97
— constable of, 37, 40, 42 n. 2, 100, 102, 116, 117, 137, 145 n. 1
— dean of, 125
Bosco, Gaufridus de, *see* Dubois, Geoffroi
Bosse, 116
Boston (co. Lincs.), 72 n. 2
Boulogne (*dép.* Pas-de-Calais), 44 n. 1
— count of, *see* Robert VI
Bourbonnais (France), 180, 181
Bourdeilles (*dép.* Dordogne, *arr.* Périgueux, *c.* Brantôme), lord of, 94, 95, 96
Bourret (*dép.* Tarn-et-Garonne, *arr.* Montauban, *c.* Verdun-sur-Garonne), 64 n. 7
Bourret, Étienne de, 64, 74 n. 2
Bousserit, Jean, 75 n. 4
Boxes, *see under* Receptacles
Brabant, 12, 126, 170, 180, 182
— dukes of, *see* Jean I, Jean II, Jean III
Brabant, Giles of, 134
Brabazon, Sir Roger, 63
Bradelby, Hugh of, 154
Branketre, John, 153 n. 4
Brantôme (*dép.* Dordogne, *arr.* Périgueux), 93, 94, 95, 96
Braughton, Richard, 41 n. 3, 143
Braunton, R. de, 47
Brayton, Thomas, 139
Bread, *see under* Food
Bréda (Holland), 183 n. 1
Bretagne, Jean de, earl of Richmond, 36, 85 n. 1, 89, 90, 96, 97, 99, 118, 158, 160
Breuil, Guillaume du, 47, 143 n. 2, 170
Brindisi (Italy, prov. Apulia), 175
Bristol (co. Glos.), 72 n. 2
Brittany (France), 76, 80
Brown, Rawdon, 128
Bruges (Belgium), 16, 71, 138, 178 n. 1, 183
Brunswick, dukes of, 121 n. 3
Brussels (Belgium), 178 n. 1, 183
Buetin, Jean de, 75
Bulls, papal, 31, 35, 38 n. 3, 41, 64, 75, 78, 80, 81, 85 n. 1, 124, 126, 142–3, 169, 181, 182, 183, 184
— keeper of, *see* St. Denis, John of
Burghersh, Bartholomew lord, 132 n. 1, 137–8, 140
— Henry, bishop of Lincoln, 42 n. 2, 132–3, 137

— Sir Robert, 34, 154, 159
Burgundy, 12, 126, 178, 180, 181. *See also* Franche-Comté
Burton, Richard, 118, 122
Bury, Richard, bishop of Durham, 136–7
Bury St. Edmunds (co. Suff.), 181
Bush, John, 122
— Richard, 69–70
Butter, 115

Cahors (*dép.* Lot), 44 n. 1, 93
— bishop of, 7, 97 n. 5
— diocese of, 4, 7, 9, 93
Cahorsin (France), 88
— seneschal of, 92
Calais (*dép.* Pas-de-Calais), 34, 70, 71, 80
— bailiff of, 74
— captain of, 73
Calendars, *see under* Records
Cambrai (*dép.* Nord), 181
— siege of, 18 n. 1
Cambrésis (France), 180
Cambridge (co. Cambs.), 36, 38, 143
Camineriis, de, fief in Agenais, 94 n. 1
Campsall, church of, 139
Canche river, 62
Canons, 33 n. 6, 139
Canterbury (co. Kent), 42 n. 2, 43, 173
— archbishop of, 32, 40, 58, 148. *See* Offord, Winchelsea
— archbishopric of, 55 and n. 1, 83
— diocese of, 36, 75 n. 4
Canterbury, Henry of, 41 n. 3, 43, 52, 53, 59, 91, 119, 121, 122, 123, 126, 143
Canvas, 179
Capua (Italy, prov. Campania), 176
Capuanus, Peter, 141 n. 1
carati, see under Currency
Cardinals, 18 n. 1, 169, 180
— College of, 64
Careron, Vincent de, 75 n. 4
Cargoes, 66, 69, 71, 73
Carmelites, 111
cartarii, 131
Carts, 179
Cartularies, *see under* Records
Castanède (*dép.* Tarn-et-Garonne, *arr.* Montauban, *c.* Montpezat-de-Quercy, *cne.* Montalzat), parish of, 94 n. 1

Castelsagrat, (*dép.* Tarn-et-Garonne, *arr.* Castelsarrasin, *c.* Valence-d'Agen), 97 n. 4, 98
Castenet, Raymond de, 125
Castile, 4, 12, 126
— kings of, *see* Alfonso X
Castile, Blanche of, queen of Louis VIII, 3
Castillon-la-Bataille (*dép.* Gironde, *arr.* Libourne), 125
Catalonia, 68
Caucasus mountains, 176
Cause-de-Clérans (*dép.* Dordogne, *arr.* Bergerac, *c.* Lalinde), parish of, 94 n. 1
Causton, John, 139
Cazes, Guillaume de, 93, 118, 143 n. 2
Censures, ecclesiastical, 18 n. 1, 134
Ceprano (Italy, prov. Campania), 176
Chaise-Dieu, La (*dép.* Hte-Loire, *arr.* Brioude), monastery of, 97 n. 5
Chamber, receiver of, 137
Chamberlains, 137
— of exchequer, *see under* Exchequer
Chambéry (*dép.* Savoie), 174
Chambre des Comptes, 95, 121 n. 3
Chancellor, *see under* Chancery
Chancellor's rolls, *see under* Exchequer
Chancery, 39 n. 1, 60, 68 n. 2, 114, 116, 127, 145, 183, 186
— archives, 30, 31, 152, 187
— chancellor, 35, 38, 43, 46, 86 n. 4, 137, 140, 148, 152, 153
— — of France, *see under* France
— clerks, 30, 32, 54, 116, 139, 140, 152, 153, 154, 165, 184
— close rolls, 30, 31, 52, 133, 136, 152, 164
— hanaper, 31
— issue of letters by, *see* Records
— keeper of rolls of, 136
— masters in, 30, 54
— of Ireland, *see under* Ireland
— papal, *see under* Papacy
— patent rolls, 30, 52, 152, 164
— prothonotary, 164
— treaty rolls, 52, 152, 164
— *see also under* Diplomacy
Channel Islands, 97, 98, 102
Chantries, 136
Chapel of the Pyx (Westminster), 31
Chaplains, 38 n. 3, 115, 174, 175
Chaplais, Pierre, 27, 120 n. 7

Chapter House (Westminster), 31
Charente river, 4
Charles IV (of France), 15–16, 19 n. 2, 21, 23, 24, 45 n. 1, 108, 111
Charters, 40, 50, 119, 160
Chartres, Fulbert of, 110
— Nicholas of, 175, 176
Châtelet, the, *see under* Paris
Chauvet, Jean, 92
Chester, bishop of, 147
— earl of, 40, 52
— justice of, *see under* Justices
Chester, Thomas, 119
Chests, *see under* Receptacles
Chichester (co. Sussex), 55
Chichester, bishop of, *see* Langton
— canon of, 33 n. 6
Chigwell, Robert, 153 n. 4
Chronicles, 1, 114, 129, 181
Church, the, 5, 7, 67, 83, 134
Churches, 36 and n. 4, 40, 62, 93, 103, 119, 139, 158
Chiny, count of, 16
Cinque Ports, 34, 72 n. 2, 73 n. 4
— barons of, 154
— warden of, 137, 159
— *see also* Romney, Hythe, Dover, Sandwich, Rye, Winchelsea
Civil law, *see under* Law
Civil service, 61, 140–1
Clare, Margaret of, countess of Cornwall, 135
Clarendon (co. Wilts.), 154
Clement V (Bertrand de Got), 35, 38 n. 3, 41, 54, 64, 75, 79, 81, 84
Clergy, 29–30, 65 n. 2, 91, 100, 134, 136, 139, 146, 181, 182. *See also under* Parliament
Clerks, 27, 30, 58, 59, 75 n. 4, 103, 111, 114 n. 1, 115, 116, 119, 120, 122, 129 n. 3, 132 n. 1, 134, 135, 140, 174, 175, 179, 187
— king's, 39, 40, 54, 58, 102, 132 n. 1, 139, 153
— *see also under various departments*
Cleves, count of, *see* Lof
Clifton (co. Yorks.), 180
Clinton, William, 104 n. 1
Cloaks, *see under* Clothing
Close rolls, *see under* Chancery
Cloth, 175
Clothing, cloaks, 175
— covers, 175

INDEX

Clothing, furs, 175
— robes, 41, 153
— skins, 175
— tunics, 175
Cluny (*dép.* Saône-et-Loire, *arr.* Mâcon), monastery of, 97 n. 5
Cobham, Sir Reginald, 138
— Thomas, 36, 48, 58, 85 n. 1, 91, 143
Codico, Arnaud de, 88, 89
Cœur, Jacques, 138
Cofferer, *see under* Wardrobe
Coffers, *see under* Receptacles
Coins, value of, *see* Currency
Coke, Sir Edward, 68 and n. 2
cokini, 131
Collectors, *see under* Customs
Colle, Robertus de, 116
Cologne, archbishop of, 18 n. 1, 170, 182
— archdeacon of, 185 n. 2
— dean of, 170, 182
Comminges, bishop of, 181
Commissions, 11 n. 4, 34, 35, 41, 42 n. 2, 44 n. 1, 50, 52, 55, 57, 62 ff., 89 ff., 102 ff., 118, 130 n. 4, 153
— *See also under* Parlement de Paris
Committees, *see under* Council
Common Pleas, *see under* Justices
Commons, *see under* Parliament
Comterel, Jean, 75 n. 4
Conques, Guillaume, 93
Conservator of truces, *see under* Truces
Constables, 34, 37, 40, 42 n. 2, 102, 116, 117, 118, 123, 133, 137, 145 n. 1, 159
Constantinople (Turkey), 175, 176
contestatio negativa, *see under* Procedure, legal
Controller, *see under* Wardrobe
Convents, 55, 94, 125, 136
Cooks, 175
Copper, *see under* Metals
Corbie (*dép.* Somme, *arr.* Amiens), 75, 77, 78
Cords, 184
Corme-Royal (*dép.* Charente-Mar., *arr.* Saintes, *c.* Saujon), 93 n. 5
Cornwall, county of, 182
— countess of, *see* Clare
— earl of, *see* Eltham
— John, earl of, 17
— Richard, earl of, 4, 5, 6
Cottingham, Robert, 115
Cotton, 184
Cottonian MS., 121

Council, 10, 25 n. 5, 27, 33, 35 and n. 1, 36 n. 6, 37, 43, 47, 52, 60, 63, 68 n. 2, 86, 91, 92, 100, 103, 118, 119, 126, 136, 144–7, 152, 153, 167, 168 187
— clerks of, 55, 56 n. 2
— committee of, 146, 147, 149
— French, *see under* France
— great and administrative, 144–5, 146, 147
— petitions to, 36, 37, 38, 39 n. 3, 103, 118, 119, 145
— relations of, with exchequer, 36, 165–6
— relations of, with keeper of processes, 33, 46, 53–9, 60, 145, 187–8
— *see also under* Diplomacy, Parliament
Cour, Raymond de la, 125
Court, French, *see* Parlement de Paris
— papal, *see* Papacy
Courtissien, Simon le, 133
Courtrai (Belgium), 183
Coutances (*dép.* Manche), bishopric of, 98
Coventry, bishop of, *see* Langton
— diocese of, 38 n. 3, 75 n. 4
Covers, *see under* Clothing
Coville, A., 20
Credence, letters of, *see under* Records
Crek, Ricardus de, 158
Croix-Saint-Leufroy (*dép.* Eure, *arr.* Les Andelys, *c.* Gallion), 77, 84
Cros, Thomas, 70
Cross-bows, 175
Crusades, 3, 17, 22, 149
Cullier, Hugues, 92 and n. 3, 95
Curia, *see* Papacy
Currency, 178
— *aspri*, 176 and n. 1
— *carati*, 176 n. 1
— florins, 176 and n. 1
— *lire genovine*, 176 and n. 1
— *perperi*, 176 and n. 1
— sterling, 174, 176 n. 1
— *tournois gros*, 174
— — *noirs*, 182
— — *petits*, 174
Cursus, the, 164–5, 184
Cusancia, Gerardus de, 158
Customs, 41, 168
— collector of, 169
— pilotage, 168

INDEX

Customs (*cont.*):
— pontage, 41, 168
— portage, 41, 168
custos processuum, *see* Processes, keeper of
Cuyk, lord of, *see* Jean

Dampierre, Guy de (of Flanders), 115, 178, 182
Dante Alighieri, 22
Darlington, John, 119
Dartmouth (co. Devon), 72 n. 2
Daurade, La, de Toulouse (*dép.* Hte-Garonne, *arr.* Toulouse), monastery of, 97 n. 5
Davin, Simon, 74 n. 2
Dax (*dép.* Landes), bishop of, 97 n. 5
Deans, 35, 55 n. 1, 56, 65, 85 n. 1, 125, 170, 182
Deans of the Arches, *see* Arches
Debentures, *see under* Accounts
Debts, 4, 78, 119, 167, 169
— release from, 135
— respite for, 33, 158 n. 1
Decretals, papal, 127, 181
Defendants, 69, 70, 71, 72, 73, 74, 75, 79, 80, 106, 142. *See also* Procedure, legal
Deliveries of records, *see under* Processes, keeper of, Records
Dene, forest of, 33
Denmark, 68
Déprez, Eugène, 18 n. 1
Derby, John of, 116, 154 n. 2, 184
Despenser, Hugh, 135
Destriers, *see* Horses
Déville (*dép.* Dordogne), parish of, 88
Devon, county of, 182
Dictamen, *see* Cursus
Diplomacy, administration of, 1, 29–30, 60–1, 187
— by chancery, 151 ff., 187
— by council, 53 ff., 144–51, 188
— by exchequer, 165 ff., 188
— by keeper of processes, 50 ff., 145, 187–8
— by parliament, 147–51, 188
— by small seals, 186, 189
— by wardrobe, 12–13, 166, 167, 171 ff., 188–9
— *see also under various departments*
Diplomatic, *see* Records, Treaties
Documents, *see* Records

Dogmersfield, William, 178 n. 1
Domme (*dép.* Dordogne, *arr.* Sarlat-la-Canéda), bastide of, 89
Dordrecht (Holland), 13, 170, 171, 183 n. 1
Dorturer, William, 185
Dover (co. Kent), 42 n. 2, 43, 58
Dover, constable of, 34, 133, 137, 159
Draghton, 116
Droxford, John, 115, 117, 147, 177, 183, 184 n. 7
Dublin, archbishop of, 38 n. 3
Dubois, Geoffroi (Gaufridus de Bosco), 44 n. 1, 45 n. 1
Dunwich (co. Suff.), 72 n. 2
Dunwich, John, 119
Durandus, Guilelmus, 24, 128
Durham, bishop of, 147. *See* Bury
Durham, Ives of, 154 n. 2
Dymmere, Richard, 180

Edinburgh (co. Midlothian), 151 n. 1
— treasury at, 114
Edward I (of England), 7–13, 14, 18, 21, 22, 26, 28, 31 n. 3, 32, 33, 34 and n. 3, 35, 38, 41, 43, 44 n. 1, 48, 54, 57, 58, 62, 63, 72, 75, 78, 79, 83, 84, 85, 86, 87, 90, 113, 114, 116, 120, 124, 144, 145, 147, 166, 167, 170, 172, 175, 177, 179, 180, 181, 182, 183
Edward II (of England), 11, 13–15, 19 n. 2, 24, 26, 33, 37, 38, 43, 46, 48, 49, 57, 84, 87, 88, 89, 90, 91–2, 100, 102, 113, 123, 136, 137, 138, 140, 147–8, 166, 174, 177, 191.
Edward III (of England), 6, 7 n. 2, 15–20, 21, 27, 28, 30, 37, 38, 39, 52, 56, 84, 85, 86, 100, 101, 110, 111, 128 n. 3, 133, 134, 135, 136, 138, 140, 145, 148–9, 153, 167, 172, 177, 178, 187, 191.
Edwards, Sir Goronwy, 114 n. 1.
Eltham, John of, earl of Cornwall, 17
Ely, bishop of, 173.
— diocese of, 36
Embassies, 29–30, 128, 131 ff., 156, 177, 178, 187. *See also* Envoys, *and under names of countries*
Empire, Holy Roman, 4, 6, 12, 13, 17, 68, 180, 182, 189
— kings and emperors of, *see* Adolf of Nassau, Lewis of Bavaria

INDEX 267

England, 8, 16, 18 and n. 1, 23, 25, 26, 27, 34 n. 3, 37, 40 n. 3, 49, 63 n. 3, 67, 68, 76, 77, 80, 82, 91, 92, 93, 94, 95, 96, 97, 98, 99, 100, 101, 104, 105, 107, 108, 109, 110, 111, 113, 114, 117, 118, 124, 147, 149, 153, 158, 173, 179, 181, 183, 185
— kings of, *see* Henry II, Richard I, John, Henry III, Edward I, Edward II, Edward III, Richard II, Henry IV, Henry V, William III
England, Joan of, 4
English Channel, 3, 63, 174
English Sea, admiralty of, 47, 50, 54, 68 and n. 2
Enrolment, *see under* Accounts, Chancery, Exchequer, Records, Treaties, Wardrobe
Envoys, 24, 29, 30, 32, 35, 50, 51, 52, 60, 64, 124, 125, 127 ff., 149, 152, 154 ff., 184, 189.
— accounts of, with exchequer, 166, 167 ff.
— — with wardrobe, 166, 172 ff.
— ambassadors, 24, 29, 43, 48, 124, 128, 129–30, 131, 141 ff., 155, 177
— itineraries of, 172, 174–6, 180–3
— legates, 127, 128, 129
— messengers, 77, 129, 131, 148, 149, 153, 160, 169, 170, 171, 172, 177, 179, 185 n. 2
— *nuncii speciales*, 129
— reports of, 160, 168, 181
— wages of, 168, 169, 170, 179
— *see also under* Processes, keeper of
Eriom, R., 45 n. 1
Erzerum (Turkey), 176
Eschamat, W., 125
Espagne, Giles d', 131
Esquires, *see* Squires
Eston, William, 178 n. 1, 180
Evessent, Jean d', 76 n. 4
— Guillaume d', 76 n. 4
Ewenny, prior and convent of, 55
Exceptions, *see under* Procedure, legal
Exchange, *see* Currency
Exchequer, 35, 39, 48, 49, 60, 119, 122, 127, 145, 178
— accounts, 36–8, 40, 166–70, 172, 188
— archives, 30, 31, 43, 120, 122, 187, 188
— barons, 35, 37, 38, 64 n. 5, 138, 165, 167, 169

— chamberlains, 39 and n. 1, 41, 42 n. 2, 43, 122, 150, 169
— chancellor's rolls, 50
— clerks, 126, 168
— issue rolls, 168
— marshal, 31
— of account, 168, 169
— of receipt, 169
— pipe rolls, 167
— treasurer, 35, 36, 37, 38, 39 and n. 1, 41, 42 n. 2, 43, 44 and n. 1, 119, 122, 136, 150, 167, 168, 169, 177, 181, 183
— treasury of, 31–2, 42 n. 2, 55, 112, 115, 118, 120, 121, 122, 126, 152, 165
Excommunication, *see* Censures, ecclesiastical
Exeter, bishop of, 45 n. 1, 170. *See* Stapeldon
Extradition, 131
Eymet (*dép*. Dordogne, *arr*. Bergerac), parish of, 94 n. 1
Eyr, William le, 119

Falconers, 131, 175
Farms, 136
Fastolf, Laurence, 139
Fawtier, Robert, 20
Feasts, *see* Banquets
Feed, 174
Ferrand, Bertrand, 104 n. 1
Ferre, Guy, 89, 99
Fezensac (France), 11 n. 2, 119, 124
Fézensaguet (France), 119
Figeac (*dép*. Lot), monastery of, 97 n. 5
Fines, *see under* Procedure, legal
Fish, *see under* Food
Fissaco, de (dioc. Périgueux), parish of, 94 n. 1
Flanders, 11 and n. 4, 12, 13, 18 n. 1, 25, 34 n. 3, 48, 114, 133, 138, 146, 175, 180, 183
— counts of, *see* Guy de Dampierre, Robert III
— — receiver of, 178
Flanders, Marguerite of, 3
Flares, 174
Fleets, 65 n. 4
Flisco, Sir Nicolin de, 133
Flitcham, Roger Baroun of, 74
Florence (Italy), 139, 174

INDEX

Florent V (of Holland), 13, 147, 170, 180, 182, 184
Florins, *see under* Currency
Flour, *see under* Food
Foix (France), 17, 25
— count of, 25
Fonte, Bertrandus de, 44 n. 1
Food, 179
— almonds, 174
— bread, 115, 174
— fish, 115, 174
— flour, 174
— fruit, 174
— meat, 115
— pastry, 174
— potage, 174
— powder, 174
— prices, 115, 174
— sauce, 174
Forest, justices to perambulate the, *see under* Justices
Forfeitures, 135
Fouilly, Robert II de, bishop of Amiens, 89, 92, 96, 97, 99
Fournier, Jacques, *see* Benedict XII
Fraisse (*dép.* Dordogne, *arr.* Bergerac, *c.* La Force), parish of, 94 n. 1
France, 8, 16, 17, 18 n. 1, 19, 20, 25, 26, 28, 48, 50, 63, 68, 91, 92, 93, 94, 95, 96, 97, 98, 99, 101, 103, 105, 106, 107, 108, 109, 110, 111, 113, 117, 118, 124, 125, 135, 141–2, 145, 146, 148, 154, 170, 179, 187, 189, 190, 191
— chancellor of, 77, 78, 81
— council of, 77–8, 80, 160
— kings of, *see* Philip I, Philip Augustus, Louis VIII, Louis IX, Philip III, Philip IV, Louis X, Philip V, Charles IV, Philip VI
France, Blanche of, 124
— Isabella of, queen of Edward II, 13, 15–17, 36 n. 6, 40, 43, 52, 136
Franche-Comté, 178. *See also* Burgundy
Frederick II, Emperor, 141 n. 1
Frescobaldi, the, 178, 185 n. 2
Friars Minor, chapter of, 81, 92
— guardian of, 64, 81, 85 n. 1
Friars Preachers, chapter of, 81, 105, 117
— priors of, 64, 81, 85 n. 1
Friesland, 68
Froissart, Jean, 129, 132

Fronsac, viscount of, *see* Raymond
Fruit, *see under* Food
Fuel, 174
Fumel, Gausbert, 125
Furs, *see under* Clothing

Gaillard, abbot of Figeac, 8
Gaillon (*dép.* Eure), treaty of, *see under* Treaties
Galeto, *see* Goulet, Le
Galeys, Peter, 40
Galleys, *see* Ships
Gallion, *see* Gaillon
Galmanes (*dép.* Dordogne), parish of, 88
Garçon, Nicholas de, 75 n. 4
Gardelle (*dép.* Lot-et-Garonne, *arr.* Marmande, *c.* Lauzun), parish of, 94 n. 1
Garton, Thomas, 135
Gascony, 3, 9, 13, 19, 20, 21, 22, 23, 24, 25, 26, 27, 28, 36, 39, 42 and n. 2, 43, 45, 46, 47, 48, 50, 51, 55, 57, 87, 88, 92, 97, 101, 102, 103, 116, 117, 118, 119, 121, 124, 125, 146, 148, 174, 179, 180, 181, 184
— council in, 118, 146, 148, 150
— seneschal of, 9, 39, 42 n. 2, 111, 120, 138, 189
— *see also* Guyenne
Gavrilovitch, M., 2
Geertruidenberg (Holland), 183 n. 1
Geneve, Henri de, 70
Genoa (Italy), 68, 133, 139, 175, 176
Gerard, 175
Gerard, Master, 185 n. 2
Gerfalcons, *see under* Animals
Germany, *see* Empire, Holy Roman
Ghent (Belgium), 138, 178 and n. 1, 183
Gloucester, earl of, *see* Audley
Gloucester, R. de, 44 n. 2
Got, Bertrand de, *see* Clement V
Goulet, Le (*dép.* Eure), treaty of, *see under* Treaties
Gourdon, Pons de, 8
Gournay, Thomas, 131
Gower, Henry, bishop of St. David's, 58
Grace, letters of, *see under* Records
Grandselve (*dép.* Tarn-et-Garonne, *arr.* Castelsarrasin), abbot and convent of, 125

INDEX

Grandson, Otton de, 90
Grants and subsidies, 16 n. 4, 115, 119, 135, 138, 170, 181
Gravesend, Richard of, bishop of London, 63
Great seal, *see under* Seals
Great wardrobe, *see under* Wardrobe
Greece, 82
Greenfield, William, 63
Gregory VII (Ildebrando Aldobrandeschi), 101
Grimaud, Reyner, 68, 69, 70, 73, 85 n. 1
Grooms, 131, 174
Grymesby (Grimsby), Edmund, 139, 153 n. 4
Gueldres, counts of, *see* Renaud I, Renaud II
Guildford (co. Surrey), 36
Guildhall (London), 138
Guillaume IV (of Holland, II of Hainault), 132
Guyenne, 8, 9, 27, 33, 37 n. 3, 56, 87, 91, 94, 123. *See also* Gascony

Hainault, counts of, *see under* Flanders and Holland
— Jean of, 16
— Philippa of, queen of Edward III, 16
Hale MS., 67 n. 1
Hamilton, William, 35 n. 1
Hamlake, *see* Ros
Hanaper, *see under* Chancery
Harwich (co. Essex), 72 n. 2
Haverhulle, J. de, 116
Havering, John, 32, 117
Havonte, 116
Henri III (of Bar), 171, 178 n. 1
Henry II (of England), 114
Henry III (of England), 3–7, 11, 18, 21, 22, 23, 25, 28, 32, 65, 113, 116, 124, 165, 177
Henry IV (of England), 66 n. 1
Henry V (of England), 65
Henry, dean of St. Wulfram's, 35
Hereford, bishop of, 169
Herle, Sir William, 138
Hervey, John, 82
Hethe, Hamo de, bishop of Rochester, 36 n. 4
Hetheye, Johannes de, 85 n. 1
Higounet, Ch., 23 n. 2
Hildesle, John, 102, 103, 119, 120, 121

Holland, 12, 13, 68, 126, 170
— counts of, *see* Florent V, Jean I, Guillaume IV
Holland, Bertha of, queen of Philip I, 62
Holy Land, 3, 8, 17
Homage, 15, 18 n. 1, 30, 50, 119, 126, 185
— of English kings to France, 5, 6, 8, 10, 14, 15–16, 33–4, 43, 45, 47, 48–9, 52, 56, 84, 100, 101, 146, 160, 191
— respite of, 158 n. 1
Homicides, 68, 135
Hoogstraeten (Holland), 183 n. 1
Horses, *see under* Animals
Hostages, 179
Hostels, 132
Hôtel-Dieu (Montreuil), 62
Hotoft, John de, 180
Household, *see* Privy seal, Signet seal, Wardrobe
Hubert, 175
Hues, Petre, 74 n. 2
Hythe (co. Kent), 72 n. 2

Indentures, *see under* Records
Inge, William, 89, 92, 99, 100
Ingham, Sir Oliver, 138
Inns of Court, 30
Inquisitions, 42, 125, 126
Instruments, notarial, *see under* Records
International law, *see under* Law
Ireland, 63 n. 3, 80, 126, 173, 185
— chancery of, 139
Ireland, John of, 154 n. 2
Isle, Jourdain de l', 125
— R. de l', 184
Issigeac (*dép.* Dordogne, *arr.* Bergerac), diaconate of, 97 n. 5
Issue rolls, *see under* Exchequer
Italy, 19, 134, 140, 174, 176
Itinerant justices, *see under* Justices
Itineraries, *see under* Envoys

Jernemue (Gernemuth, Jeremuta), Adam, 116 and n. 1
— Hugh, 116 and n. 1
— John, 116 and n. 1
Jewels, 16 n. 4, 178 n. 1
Jews, 42 n. 2, 97
Jean (of Bar), 12, 178, 179, 180, 182
Jean I (of Brabant), 12
Jean II (of Brabant), 178, 180, 182, 183

INDEX

Jean III (of Brabant), 16, 18 n. 1
Jean (of Cuyk), 147, 178
Jean I (of Holland), 178 n. 1
John (of England), 3, 7, 44 and n. 1
John, 175
Johnson, Charles, 36 n. 4, 55 n. 1
Joinville, Sir Geoffroi de, 64
Joneston, Elias, *see* Processes, keeper of
Jourdain, Austence, 45 n. 1, 47, 59, 143 n. 2
Jülich, 18 n. 1
Justice, letters of, *see under* Records
Justices (Judges), 82, 83, 134, 142
— of Chester, 138
— for common pleas, 138
— of forest, 64 n. 5
— itinerant, 64 n. 5
— of King's Bench, 139
— of oyer and terminer, 135, 136, 139

Keeper, *see under* Wardrobe
— of great seal, *see under* Seals
— of papal bulls, *see* St. Denis, John of
— of privy seal, *see under* Seals
— of processes, *see* Processes, keeper of
— of realm, *see* Regents
— of rolls, *see under* Chancery
Keleseye, Robert, 139, 153 n. 4
Kent, earl of, 40
Khoi (Turkey), 176
Killerby, John of, 154 n. 5
King's Bench, *see under* Justices
King's clerks, *see under* Clerks
Kingston-on-Hull (co. Yorks.), 138
Kingston, Jacob of, 154
Knights, 5, 6, 89, 102, 103, 118, 132, 134, 174
— respite of service of, 158 n. 1

Lacy, Henry de, earl of Lincoln, 10, 90
La Floyne de Sandwich, *see under* Ships
Lancaster, Edmund, earl of, 10, 124, 180, 182
— Henry, earl of, 132 n. 1
— Thomas, earl of, 135, 138, 140
Landes (France), 125
Langele, G., 175–6
Langetoft, John, 153 n. 4
Langon (*dép*. Gironde), 97, 111
Langtoft, Pierre de, 181
Langton, John, bishop of Chichester, 54
— Thomas, 183

— Walter, bishop of Coventry and Lichfield, 38 n. 3, 170, 177–83
Larceny, 135
Laroque-Timbaut (*dép*.Lot-et-Garonne, *arr*. Agen), 105
La Rose de Sandwich, *see under* Ships
Laudunaco, Ives de, 92
Law (Laws), 9, 42, 50, 56, 60, 65 and n. 2, 66, 68, 70, 73, 76, 78, 79, 80, 82, 96, 124, 125, 143–4
— canon, 82, 96
— civil, doctors and professors of, 32, 143, 144, 153
— international, 190–1
— Roman, 82, 143
League of Nations, 144
Leather, 66, 175, 183
Le Bel, Jean, 138
Lectoure (*dép*. Gers, *arr*. Condom), viscount of, 119
Legates, *see under* Envoys
— papal, 15, 128, 133, 180
Legore, Thomas de, 64
Leicester, countess of, *see* Montfort
— earl of, 5
Leisseth, Robert, 117
Leopards, *see under* Animals
Letters, *see under* Records
Lewis of Bavaria (Emperor), 18 n. 1
libellus, *see under* Procedure, legal
Libourne (*dép*. Gironde), 42
Libraries, 136
Licences, *see* Grants and subsidies.
Lichfield, bishop of, *see* Langton
Liége, bishop of, 182
Lierre (Belgium), 183 n. 1
Lille (Belgium), 183
Limoges (*dép*. Hte-Vienne), 93
— bishop of, 7
— countess of, *see* Marguerite
— diocese of, 7, 9, 93
Limousin (France), 9
Lincoln, county of, 136
Lincoln (co. Lincs.), 136
— bishop of, 33 n. 6, 129. *See* Burghersh
— canon of, 139
— earl of, 63, 147. *See* Lacy
lire genovine, *see under* Currency
Lisle (*dép*. Dordogne, *arr*. Périgueux, *c*. Brantôme), 89
Litelburs, Sir Robert, 134
Littlehampton (co. Sussex), 72 n. 2
Livings, *see* Benefices

INDEX

livres tournois, see under Currency
Llandaff, diocese of, 55
Loans, 16 n. 4, 126, 139, 171, 178, 179, 181, 182
Lof (of Cleves), 171, 180
London, 58, 59 n. 4, 64, 69, 72 n. 2, 74 n. 2, 79, 132, 134, 138, 139, 171
— alderman of, 64 n. 5
— bishop of, 63. *See* Gravesend
— canon of, 139
— collector of wool customs in, 139
— sheriff of, 139
— Tower of, 31, 42 n. 2, 43, 115, 116, 119
— — warden of, 137
Looz, count of, 16
Lorraine, duke of, 182
Louis VIII (of France), 7
Louis IX the Saint (of France), 3–6, 7, 11, 14, 23, 28
Louis X, the Quarreler (of France), 19 n. 2
Louvain (Belgium), 178 n. 1, 183 n. 1
Lovel, John, 64
Low Countries, 12, 13, 16, 17, 19, 128 n. 3, 132, 137, 170, 178, 179, 182. *See also* Bar, Brabant, Chiny, Flanders, Gueldres, Hainault, Holland, Juliers, Looz, Zeeland
Lubimenko, I., 2
Lucca (Italy, prov. Tuscany), 174, 176
Luzarches (*dép.* Seine-et-Oise, *arr.* Montmorency), 181
Lynn, King's (co. Norf.), 58, 72 n. 2, 74
Lyoart, Regon', 170
Lyon (*dép.* Rhône), 174

Magnates, 146, 184. *See also under* Parliament
Maitland, F. W., 54, 147
Maldon, William, 118, 185
Malines (Belgium), 13, 171, 178 n. 1, 183 n. 1
Manfred, 175
Manton, Ralph, 178 n. 1
Marand (Persia), 176
March, earl of, *see* Mortimer
Marche, La, count of, 45 n. 1, 124
Marguerite (of Limoges), 9
Maritime disputes, 10, 20, 26, 34–5, 62 ff.
Marmon (*dép.* Tarn-et-Garonne, *arr.* Castelsarrasin, *c.* Lauzerte, *cne.* Montagudet), parish of, 94 n. 1

Marque, letters of, *see under* Records
Marriages, 13, 16, 17, 149
Marshal, *see under* Exchequer
Martel, Jean de, 93
— John, 35 n. 3
— Philip, *see* Processes, keeper of
Masters in chancery, *see under* Chancery
Masworth, Johan de, 71–2
Maubusshon, Odard de, 71, 73, 85 n. 1
Mayors, 64 n. 3, 75 n. 4
Meat, *see under* Food
Melasgird (Turkey), 176
Melton, William, archbishop of York, 44 and n. 1
Memoranda, *see under* Records
Men-at-arms, 168, 175, 179
Mende, bishop of, 25
Merchants, 179 n. 1, 182
— English, 35 and n. 1, 63, 64, 67, 74 n. 2, 134, 138, 146, 147, 154 n. 5, 166, 171
— Flemish, 35 n. 1, 147, 166
— French, 15, 35, 62, 63, 75, 77–8
— Italian, 16 n. 4, 120, 134, 139, 140, 167, 171, 176, 178, 185 n. 2
Merenbergh, Hartrad of, 170
Messane, *see* Messina
Messengers, *see under* Envoys
Messina (Sicily), treaty of, *see under* Treaties
Metals, copper, 175
— silver, 175
— tin, 182
Michel de Arwe, *see under* Ships
Middleton, Gilbert, 55 n. 1, 85 n. 1, 91
Mignano (Italy, prov. Campania), 176
Ministers, 45 n. 1, 49, 145
Miniver, *see* Clothing
Minstrels, 132
Modus tenendi parliamentum, 136
Moissac (*dép.* Tarn-et-Garonne, *arr.* Castelsarrasin), monastery of, 97 n. 5
Monasteries, 97 n. 5, 114
Moncessou (*dép.* Tarn-et-Garonne), parish of, 94 n. 1
Money, 71, 134, 170, 178 n. 1, 181, 182. *See also* Currency
Monflanquin (*dép.* Lot-et-Garonne, *arr.* Villeneuve-sur-Lot), 105.
Monnier, Piere le, 72 n. 3
Montagnac-d'Auberoche (*dép.* Dordogne, *arr.* Périgueux, *c.* Thenon), parish of, 88

INDEX

Montagudet (*dép*. Tarn-et-Garonne, *arr*. Castelsarrasin, *c*. Lauzerte), parish of, 94 n. 1
Montague, Simon, bishop of Worcester, 135
— William, earl of Salisbury, 132 n. 1, 135
Mont-Cenis pass, 174
Montefiascone (Italy, prov. Rome), 176
Montesarchio (Italy, prov. Campania), 176
Montfaucon (France), 12
Montfort, Bertrade de, 62
— Eleanor de, countess of Leicester, 5
Montguyard (*dép*. Dordogne, *arr*. Bergerac, *c*. Eymet, *cne*. Serres-et-Montguyard), parish of, 94 n. 1
Montjoi (*dép*. Tarn-et-Garonne, *arr*. Castelsarrasin, *c*. Valence), 98
Montpezat (*dép*. Lot-et-Garonne, *arr*. Agen, *c*. Prayssas), bastide of, 45 n. 1, 107 n. 2
— lord of, 14
Montreuil-sur-Mer (*dép*. Pas-de-Calais), 62, 74, 75, 76, 80, 85 n. 1, 145 n. 2
— mayor of, 75 n. 4
— peace of, *see under* Treaties
— process of, *see under* Processes
Morant, Jordan, 122
Mortimer, Roger, earl of March, 16 n. 4, 135, 136, 138, 140
Motis, Arnaldus de, 44 n. 1, 45 n. 1
Mountbouch, Bertrannus de, 158
Moustier (*dép*. Lot-et-Garonne, *arr*. Marmande, *c*. Duras), parish of, 94 n. 1
Multon, Simon, 153 n. 4
Muniments, *see* Records
Murimuth, Adam, 1, 55 n. 1
Mussidan (*dép*. Dordogne, *arr*. Périgueux), castle of, 88

Naples (Italy), 176
Naples, Berard of, 184
Navarre (France), 113
— queen of, *see* Blanche
Navarre, Michel de, 70
necessaria, 41, 173, 178
Netherlands, *see* Low Countries
Newark, John, 119
Neuwerk, Sir H. de, 31 n. 3
Newcastle-upon-Tyne (co. Northumberland), 72 n. 2

Nobles, 29, 39, 67, 134–6, 140–1, 178. *See also* Magnates
Normandy (France), 5, 7, 8 n. 1, 76, 80, 98
Normans, the, 10, 63 n. 3, 73 n. 4
Northampton (co. Northants.), 32, 58
Northampton, county of, 136
— earl of, 132 n. 1
Northburgh, Roger, 119,
North Sea, 17, 178
Norway, 19, 68, 114, 190
— Maid of, 115
Norwich (co. Norfolk), 75 n. 4
— bishop of, 40, 44 n. 1, 52, 53, 118, 160. *See* Airmyn, Salmon
— diocese, 36
— taxation, 32
Notaries, 57 n. 4, 75, 82, 114, 118, 122, 137, 153 n. 4, 164–5, 169, 170, 184–6. *See also under* Wardrobe
Notre Dame, cathedral of (Paris), 81
Nottingham (co. Notts.), 58
Nottingham, Roger, 119
nuncii, *see* Messengers
— *speciales*, *see under* Envoys.

Oaks, 33
Oaths, 5, 8, 48, 51, 64, 79, 80, 81, 106, 108, 130, 142. *See also under* Procedure, legal
Officials, *see under various departments*
Offord, Andrew, 41 n. 3, 153
— John, archbishop of Canterbury, 55 n. 1, 153
Ofgrendik, Henri, 74 n. 2
Oil, 174
Oléron, island of (France), 117, 118, 124
Olmières (*dép*. Tarn-et-Garonne, *arr*. Castelsarrasin, *c*. Beaumont-de-Lomagne, *cne*. Belbès), parish of, 94 n. 1
Ombrière, L', castle (Bordeaux), 116, 117
Orange, bishop of, 133
Ordinances, 41, 42, 50, 51, 54, 68, 75, 78, 80, 97, 154, 166, 182
— of Westminster (1324), 37, 166, 167
— Walton (1338), 167
— *see also under* Parlement de Paris
Orwell (co. Suff.), 72 n. 2
Osney (co. Oxford), council at, 56
Ostrevant (France), 12

Otranto (Italy, prov. Apulia), 176
Oxen, see under Animals
Oxford, John of, 104 n. 1
Oyer and terminer, justices of, see under Justices

Palaces, 81, 144. See also Westminster
Palestrina, cardinal bishop of, 180
Papacy, 6, 26, 32, 34, 35, 38 and n. 3, 55 n. 1, 57, 87, 124, 127, 128, 134, 142–3, 144, 169, 173, 184, 189
— apostolic chamber of, 143
— chancery of, 143, 164
Parchment, 115, 123, 129, 168, 171, 179, 184
Parcoul (dép. Dordogne, arr. Périgueux, c. Saint-Aulaye), bastide of, 93
Pardons, 135
Paris (France), 22, 64, 81, 84, 91, 92, 100, 103, 121 n. 2, 124, 174, 180
— Châtelet, 142
— Parlement de, see Parlement de Paris
— Temple, 7
— treaties of, see under Treaties
— University of, 160
Parlement de Paris, 22, 82, 83, 85, 87, 91, 92, 95, 110, 130, 187, 189
— advocates and proctors at, 42 n. 2, 44 n. 1, 47, 48, 52, 53, 57, 86 n. 4, 101, 103, 122, 143–4, 170, 189, 191
— appeals to, 9–10, 42, 44 n. 1, 45 and n. 1, 93
— arrêts of, 9, 42 and n. 2, 45 and n. 1, 48
— cases in, 2, 9, 30, 37, 39, 45, 47, 51, 56, 57, 59, 122, 150
— commissions of, 65 n. 2, 81 n. 1, 83, 143 n. 2
— ordinances of, 42
— procedure of, 82, 142
— proctor of, 130
Parliament, 54, 59
— clergy in, 16 n. 4, 56 n. 2, 148, 149
— commons in, 134, 138, 147, 148, 149
— council in, 119, 147, 148, 149
— magnates in, 148, 149
— petitions in, 46, 119
— reports to, 59, 150
— rolls of, 147, 148, 149, 150, 151 n. 1
— speeches in, 148
— See also under Diplomacy
Parma (Italy, prov. Emilia), 174

Passano, Antonio di, 139
Pastry, see under Food
Patent rolls, see under Chancery
Pavia (Italy, prov. Lombardy), 174
Pavilions, see Tents
Pavilly (dép. Seine-Mar.), 62
Payne, Arnold, 104 n. 1
Peaces, see Treaties
Peckham (co. Surrey), 54 n. 5
Pedroge, Johan, 70–1, 75 n. 4, 85 n. 1
Pelet, Bernard, 92
Pembroke, earl of, see Valence, Aymer of
Penne-d'Agenais (dép. Lot-et-Garonne, arr. Villeneuve-sur-Lot), 105, 106
Pensions, 126, 184
Pereres, Ricardus de, 158
Périgord (France), 7, 9, 45, 88, 89, 97, 124
— count of, 7, 8, 88
— seneschal of, 14, 24, 48, 92, 93, 94
Périgueux (dép. Dordogne), 7, 92, 93, 97, 125
— bishop of, 7, 94, 95, 96, 97 n. 5
— diocese of, 4, 7, 9, 93, 95 n. 2
— process of, see under Processes
perperi, see under Currency
Perroy, Édouard, 27
Persia, khan of, 175, 176
Peter, cardinal, 18 n. 1
Petier, Petre, 74 n. 2
Petitions, 50, 52, 125, 142
— See also under Council; Parliament; Procedure, legal
Petrarch, 137
Philip I (of France), 62
Philip Augustus (of France), 3, 7
Philip III the Bold (of France), 6, 8, 9, 21, 44 n. 1, 124
Philip IV the Fair (of France), 8, 10–11, 12, 13–14, 21, 23, 28, 31 n. 3, 34 and n. 3, 35, 41, 48, 58, 62, 63, 64, 72, 78, 89, 90, 91, 92, 93, 94, 95, 96, 97, 98, 99, 100, 124, 179, 180, 182.
Philip V the Tall (of France), 14, 47, 56
Philip VI of Valois (of France), 15–20, 21, 24, 27, 28, 52, 53, 84, 100, 101, 110, 111, 128 n. 3, 129, 149
Physicians, 175
Piacenza (Italy, prov. Emilia), 174
Piers, John, 39, 43, 53, 59 and n. 4, 85 n. 1, 143, 144, 150
Pilotage, see under Customs
Pipe rolls, see under Exchequer

INDEX

Piracy, 63, 65, 66, 68, 73 n. 4, 82
Pistoja (Italy, prov. Tuscany), 176
Pizou, Le (*dép.* Dordogne, *arr.* Périgueux, *c.* Montpon-Ménestérol), 88
Plaintiffs, 66–7, 69, 70, 71, 72, 73, 74, 75, 76, 80, 105, 106, 142
— *See also* Procedure, legal
Pleas, Common, *see under* Justices
Plumstock, Richard, 36, 48, 58, 91, 129 n. 1, 143, 144
Poitiers (France), sub-dean of, 65, 74 n. 2
Poitiers, Alphonse de, 4, 7, 8, 44 n. 1, 119, 124
— Jeanne de, 4
Poitou (France), 5, 7, 45 n. 1, 76, 80, 97, 98, 99
— count of, 93
Pole, William de la, 138, 140
Policy, *see* Diplomacy
Pollard, Willelmus, 158
Pomayo, Sir Robert de, 134
Pontage, *see under* Customs
Pontefract (co. Yorks.), 88, 136
Ponthieu (France), 10, 111, 126
— receiver in, 40
— seneschal of, 64 n. 5, 83
Pont-l'Abbé-d'Arnoult (*dép.* Charente-Mar., *arr.* Saintes, *c.* Saint-Porchaire), 93 n. 5
Pont-Sainte-Maxence (*dép.* Oise), 101
Pont-Saint-Mamet (*dép.* Dordogne), parish of, 88
Poole (co. Dorset), 72 n. 2
Popes, *see* Alexander IV, Boniface VIII, Clement V, Benedict XII
Portage, *see under* Customs
Port-d'Envaux (*dép.* Charente-Mar., *arr.* Saintes, *c.* Saint-Porchaire), 93 n. 5
Porte St. Martin (Paris), 81
Portinari, Andrea de', 139
Portland (co. Dorset), 72 n. 2
Portsmouth (co. Hants), 72 n. 3
Potage, *see under* Food
Pouches, *see under* Receptacles
Pound sterling, *see under* Currency
Poveray, John, 115
Powder, *see under* Food
Powicke, Sir Maurice, 21, 22
Preston Bisset (co. Bucks.), church of, 139
Prests, *see under* Wardrobe
Prices, *see* Food

Prime, Gile, 74 n. 2
Principalities, *see* Aquitaine
Priors, 55, 64, 81, 85 n. 1, 125
Prisoners, 49, 66–7, 69, 71, 134, 160
Prisons, 62, 71, 179
privilégiés, see under Vassals
Privy seal, *see under* Seals
Procedure, legal, 60, 74–5, 82–3, 105–7, 141–2
— *contestatio negativa*, 70, 75, 76
— exceptions, dilatory, 47, 49, 70–1, 73 n. 3, 75, 108, 142
— — peremptory, 47, 56, 142
— fines, 81
— *libellus* (claim), 66–7, 69–70, 75
— oaths, 70, 142
— petitions, 67–8, 72, 76, 80, 85 n. 1, 101
— proof of ownership, 66, 73, 106
— *repplicatio*, 67, 70–1, 72–3, 75, 76, 85 n. 1
— witnesses, 66, 75, 81, 105, 106, 142
— *See also* Defendants, Plaintiffs, *and under* Parlement de Paris
Processes, 39, 42 n. 1, 47, 49, 50, 52, 53, 65–6, 114, 122, 124, 125.
— of Agen, 45, 100 ff.
— of Bayonne, 41, 42
— of Montreuil, 2, 11, 17, 34, 41, 42 n. 2, 43, 45, 47, 48, 49, 51, 53, 57, 62 ff., 87, 111, 124, 187, 190
— of Périgueux, 2, 14, 17, 36, 42 and n. 2, 44 and n. 1, 45, 49, 53, 57, 85 n. 1, 87 ff., 111, 118, 124, 187, 190
Processes, keeper of, 1, 32, 187–8
— accounts of, 33 n. 1, 34 n. 3, 35 n. 3, 36–8, 40–1, 188
— archives of, 41–9, 60, 188
— clerks of, 40, 74
— deliveries of documents by, 48, 52–3, 188
— duties, 46–7, 49–50, 187–8
— instructions from, to envoys, 50–2, 188
— Joneston, Elias (keeper), 35–9, 40, 41–4, 46–9, 50, 52–3, 55–8, 59 and n. 4, 75 n. 4, 79, 86, 91, 118–19, 122, 123, 125, 126, 133, 143, 145, 150, 187, 190
— Martel, Philip (keeper), 1, 32–5, 36, 38 n. 3, 40, 41, 47, 49, 50, 51, 54–5, 60, 64, 74, 77–81, 83, 84, 85 n. 1, 143, 187

INDEX

— relations of, with council, 33, 53–9, 60, 145–6, 188
— Staunford, Roger (keeper), 39–40, 41, 44, 49, 58, 59, 104, 143, 187
Proctors, 35, 41, 42 n. 2, 47, 50, 57, 67, 68, 74, 75, 76, 80, 92, 101, 103, 105, 106, 124, 129, 130, 144, 153, 170
— See also under Parlement de Paris
Procuration, letters of, see under Records
procurator, see Proctors
Promulgation of treaties, see under Treaties
Proof of ownership, see under Procedure, legal
Protection, letters of, see under Records
Prothonotary, see under Chancery
Provence (France), 12
Provence, Eleanor of, queen of Henry III, 7
Provisions, 179. See also Food
Prynne, William, 68
Public Record Office (London), 16 n. 2, 46, 104, 117
Pujols (*dép.* Lot-et-Garonne, *arr.* and *c.* Villeneuve-sur-Lot), 106
Puy, bishop and chapter of, 125
Puy, Gérard de, 59
Puymirol (*dép.* Lot-et-Garonne, *arr.* Agen), 105
Pyn, Haime, 74 n. 2
Pyrenees mountains, 181

Quercy (France), 4, 8, 22, 97
— seneschal of, 14, 94
Queyzaguet (*dép.* Lot-et-Garonne, *arr.* Marmande, *c.* Lauzun), parish of, 94 n. 1
Quittances, see under Accounts

Rabastens, Pierre Raymond de, 103
Raceborgh, Martin de, 85 n. 1
Rapallo (Italy, prov. Liguria), 176
Rasen, William of, 154 n. 2
Ratification of treaties, see under Treaties
Ravignan, Bernard de, 125
Raymond IV (of Fronsac), 8, 124–5
Raymond IV (of Turenne), 8
Raymond VI (of Toulouse), 4
Raymond VII (of Toulouse), 8
Razac-d'Eymet (*dép.* Dordogne, *arr.*

Bergerac, *c.* Eymet), parish of, 94 n. 1
Rebellions, 97
Receipt, exchequer of, see under Exchequer
Receptacles:
— bags, 119
— barrels, 178 n. 1
— baskets, 42 n. 2, 113, 125, 179
— boxes, 42 n. 2, 43, 183
— chests, 113
— coffers, 42 n. 2, 45 n. 1, 113, 119, 120, 125, 184
— pouches, 42 n. 2, 43, 45 n. 1, 119, 125, 169, 179, 184
— vessels, 175
Records, 22, 27, 30, 40, 87 n. 3, 104
— books, 46–51, 113, 152, 173, 177 n. 1
— calendars, 42, 121–6
— — Gascon, 42 n. 2, 43, 48, 113, 121–5, 188
— — Stapeldon's, 113, 125–6, 188
— cartularies, 125
— deliveries of, 41–4, 125
— indentures, 39, 42 and n. 2, 44, 125
— letters, 40, 41, 42, 43, 45 and n. 1, 48, 52 n. 5, 56 and n. 6, 66, 71, 78, 85 n. 1, 86 n. 4, 89, 90, 91, 102, 103, 110, 113, 121, 124, 126, 128, 129, 134, 142, 145 n. 1, 149, 153, 154, 167, 169, 177, 186
— — 'blanks', 159
— — close, 129, 156
— — enrolment of, 164, 183
— — of attorney, 157, 158 and n. 4
— — of credence, 33 and n. 6, 34 n. 3, 156–7, 158, 181, 182
— — of grace, 113, 124
— — of justice, 113
— — of marque, 65–6
— — of procuration, 74, 154–6, 157, 182
— — of protection, 33, 36 n. 3, 157–8, 180, 181
— — of request, 65–6
— — of safe conduct, 126, 133, 180, 181
— — patent, 35, 74 n. 2, 129, 155, 158, 161, 162, 163, 164
— memoranda, 39, 41 n. 3, 42 n. 2, 44 n. 1, 47, 49, 52, 55, 86 n. 1, 104, 107, 108, 118, 124, 125, 126, 146, 168, 184, 186

INDEX

Records (*cont.*):
— notarial instruments, 41, 42 and n. 1, 44, 45, 75, 82, 85 n. 1, 114, 121, 124, 125, 126, 184–6
— registers, 45 n. 1, 50, 55, 69, 72, 112–21, 125
— — Gascon, 103, 113, 119–21
— — Liber A, 113–16, 154, 188
— — Liber B, 113–16, 154, 188
— rolls, 1, 42, 44 n. 1, 45 n. 1, 50, 56 n. 6, 69, 72 n. 3, 73 n. 1, 75 n. 4, 85 n. 1, 104, 114, 116, 118, 119, 120 n. 3, 121, 124, 125, 126, 184
— schedules, 34, 44 n. 1, 45 n. 1, 56 n. 6, 85 n. 1, 108, 124, 125, 168
— transcription of, 40, 41, 42, 43, 45 n. 1, 53, 90, 113, 115, 116, 117, 118, 120, 122, 125, 146 n. 1, 150, 154, 184–6
— transportation of, 40, 41, 52
— writs, 37, 38, 39, 48, 58, 74, 84, 116, 119, 143 n. 3, 146, 150, 154, 157, 167, 169, 170, 173, 184
— *See also under various departments*
Regents, 15–17, 135, 136, 137
Reginald, 38 n. 3
Registers, *see under* Records
Renaud I (of Gueldres), 180
Renaud II (of Gueldres), 16
Réole, La (*dép.* Gironde, *arr.* Langon), 148
— abbey of, 97
— prior of, 125
Reports, *see under* Envoys, Parliament
repplicatio, *see under* Procedure, legal
Request, letters of, *see under* Letters
Reve, Jeme le, 74 n. 2
Rhine, states of, *see* Empire, Holy Roman
Rhône river, 174
Riccardi, the, 171, 176
Richard I (of England), 4, 44 and n. 1, 50
Richard II (of England), 186
Richard, 175
Richmond, earl of, *see* Bretagne, Jean de
Robbery, 31, 68, 134, 135
Robert I (of Scotland), 151 n. 1
Robert III (of Flanders), 147
Robert VI (of Boulogne), 89, 92, 99
Robes, *see under* Clothing
Rochelle, La (*dép.* Charente-Mar.), 72 n. 3
Rochester (co. Kent), 36 n. 4
— bishop of, *see* Hethe

Rolls, *see under* Parliament, Records
— keeper of, *see under* Chancery
Roman Empire, 82
Rome (Italy), 33, 174, 176, 186
— court of, *see* Papacy
Romney (co. Kent), 72 n. 2
Ronhale, Richard, 153
Ros, William, baron of Hamlake, 136
Roumagne (*dép.* Lot-et-Garonne, *arr.* Marmande, *c.* Lauzun), parish of, 94 n. 1
Ruilly, Richard de, 174
Rumell, Jean de, 75 n. 4
Russel, Elias, 179 n. 2
Rutland, sheriff of, 135
Rye (co. Sussex), 72 n. 2
Rymer, Thomas, 131

Saddles, 175
Safe conduct, letters of, *see under* Records
Sailors, 9, 20, 26, 66, 179
Saint-Agnan (*dép.* Lot, *arr.* Cahors, *c.* Montcuq, *cne.* Valprionde), parish of, 94 n. 1
Saint-Aignan (*dép.* Lot-et-Garonne, *arr.* Villeneuve-sur-Lot, *c.* Penne-d'Agenais), 106
Saint Albans (co. Herts.), 31 n. 3
Saint-Amans-du-Pech (*dép.* Tarn-et-Garonne, *arr.* Castelsarrasin, *c.* Montaigu-de-Quercy), parish of, 94 n. 1
Saint Andrew, Holborn, parish, 102
Saint-Antoine (*dép.* Dordogne), hospital of, 88
Saint-Ayr-de-Vaudreuil (France, *dép.* Eure), treaty of, *see under* Treaties
Saint David's, bishop of, *see* Gower, Thoresby
Saint Denis, John of, 32
Sainte Austreberthe, 62
Sainte-Marthe (*dép.* Dordogne, *arr.* Bergerac, *c.* Eymet), parish of, 94 n. 1
Saintes (*dép.* Charente-Mar.), bishop of, 97 n. 5
— castle of, 93 n. 5
Saint-Étienne (*dép.* Lot-et-Garonne, *arr.* Marmande, *c.* Seyches, *cne.* Puymiclan), parish of, 94 n. 1
Saint-Eutrope de Saintes (*dép.* Charente, *arr.* Angoulême, *c.* Montmoreau-Saint-Cybard), priory of, 93 n. 5

INDEX

Saint-Front-d'Alemps (*dép*. Dordogne, *arr*. Périgueux, *c*. Brantôme), parish of, 88
Saint-Germain (*dép*. Lot-et-Garonne, *arr*. Marmande, *c*. Tonneins), parish of, 94 n. 1
Saint-Hilaire-sur-Garonne (*dép*. Lot-et-Garonne, *arr*. and *c*. Agen), parish of, 94 n. 1
Saint-Jean-de-Duras (*dép*. Lot-et-Garonne, *arr*. Marmande, *c*. Duras), parish of, 94 n. 1
Saint-Julien-de-Bourdeilles (*dép*. Dordogne, *arr*. Périgueux, *c*. Brantôme), parish of, 88
Saint-Louis-en-L'Isle (*dép*. Dordogne, *arr*. Périgueux, *c*. Mussidan), bastide of, 88, 89
Saint-Lupin, Jacques de, 92
Saint-Macaire (*dép*. Lot-et-Garonne, *arr*. Marmande, *c*. Lauzun), parish of, 94 n. 1
Saint-Martial de Limoges (*dép*. Hte-Vienne), monastery of, 97 n. 5
Saint Mary's, church of, Cambridge, 36
Saint-Nazaire (*dép*. Lot-et-Garonne, *arr*. Marmande, *c*. Lauzun), parish of, 94 n. 1
Saint Nicholas, church of, Guildford, 36
Saint-Omer (*dép*. Pas-de-Calais), 145 n. 1
Saintonge (France), 4, 8, 14, 93, 97, 99, 119, 124
— seneschal of, 14, 125
Saint-Pardoux-Isaac (*dép*. Lot-et-Garonne, *arr*. Marmande, *c*. Lauzun), parish of, 94 n. 1
Saint-Pastour (*dép*. Lot-et-Garonne, *arr*. Villeneuve-sur-Lot, *c*. Monclar), parish of, 94 n. 1
Saint-Paul, Peter de, 75 n. 4
Saint Peter, church of, Stamford, 40
Saint-Rémy (*dép*. Tarn-et-Garonne, *arr*. Castelsarrasin. *c*. Lauzerte, *cne*. Montagudet), parish of, 94 n. 1
Saint-Romain de Blaye (*dép*. Gironde, *arr*. Blaye), monastery of, 97 n. 5
Saint-Sardos (*dép*. Lot-et-Garonne, *arr*. Agen, *c*. Prayssas), War of, 14, 48, 56, 107 n. 2, 160
Saint-Saulve, church of, Montreuil, 62
Saint-Sauveur (*dép*. Gironde, *arr*. Blaye), monastery of, 97 n. 5

Saint-Sernin (*dép*. Lot-et-Garonne, *arr*. Marmande, *c*. Duras), parish of, 94 n. 1
Saint-Sornin (*dép*. Charente, *arr*. Angoulême, *c*. Montbron), 93 n. 5
Saint-Sornin de Toulouse (*dép*. Hte-Garonne, *arr*. Toulouse), monastery of, 97 n. 5
Salisbury, diocese of, 75 n. 4
— earl of, *see* Montague
Salmon, John, bishop of Norwich, 36, 89, 90, 91, 96, 97, 99
Salt, 115, 174
Sampson, Henry, 33 n. 3
— Thomas, 59
San Casciano (Italy, prov. Tuscany), 176
Sancta Marsa, de (dioc. Agen), parish of, 94 n. 1
Sancto Claro, John de, 33 n. 3
Sandall, John, 36
Sandwich (co. Kent), 69, 72 n. 2, 178 and n. 1
Sandwich, Henry of, 115
Sapiti, Andrew, 170
Sardene, William de, 47, 55 n. 1
Sarlat-la-Canéda (*dép*. Dordogne), 7, 89
— monastery, 97 n. 5
Sassoferrato, Bartolus of, 189
Sauce, *see under* Food
Sauvage, Roger, 34 n. 3
Sauve-Majeure, La (*dép*. Gironde, *arr*. Bordeaux, *c*. Créon), monastery of, 97 n. 5, 125
Sauvetat (*dép*. Dordogne), parish of, 88
Savoy, 12, 113, 174, 180
Savoy, Amédée of, 182
— Lewis of, 170
Schedules, *see under* Records
Scoihe, John de, 75 n. 4
Scotland, 10, 11, 14, 16, 17, 20, 21, 32, 39, 45, 49, 54, 58, 67, 88, 90, 114, 115, 124, 125, 145, 151 n. 1, 182, 183, 185
— kings of, *see* Balliol, Robert I
Scrope, Sir Geoffrey, 139
Scutifer, 175
Seals, 68, 74, 119, 158, 160, 184
— great, 66 n. 1, 129, 145 n. 1, 151, 183
— —, keeper of, 136
— privy, 66 n. 1, 119, 121, 129, 145 n. 1, 151, 152, 153, 154, 164, 167, 172, 173, 183, 186

INDEX

Seals, privy (cont.):
— — bills and writs of, 157, 169, 173
— — keeper of, 122, 136
— signet, 151, 152, 186
Secretary, king's, 54
Sees, vacant, 167
Segre, Robert, 170–1, 178 n. 1, 179 n. 2
Seinte Marie de Castre Enordiales, see under Ships
Selden, John, 68
Seneschals, 9, 14, 24, 39, 42 n. 2, 48, 64 n. 5, 83, 92, 93, 94, 103, 111, 125, 138, 189
Sens, Eudes de, 143 n. 2, 170
Sept Arbres (*dép.* Tarn-et-Garonne, *arr.* Castelsarrasin, *c.* Beaumont-de-Lomagne, *cne.* Belbès), parish of, 94 n. 1
Sergeants, 181
Serjeants, 138
Servants, 168, 175
seurté, see Oaths
Sheen (co. Surrey), 122 n. 1
Sheffeld, Roger, 41 n. 3, 122, 126, 143
Sherborne, William, of, 74, 75 n. 4
Sheriffs, 135, 139
Ships, 48, 58, 63, 66, 68 and n. 1, 69, 71, 146, 168
— hire of, 41
— *La Floyne de Sandwich*, 179
— *La Rose de Sandwich*, 179
— *Michel de Arwe*, 71
— *Ste. Marie de Castre Enordiales*, 72 n. 3
Shordich, John, 52, 153
Shoreham (co. Sussex), 72 n. 2
Sicilian affair, 4, 22
Sicily, 12, 19, 113, 126, 131, 141 n. 1
Sieges, *see* Cambrai
Siena (Italy, prov. Tuscany), 174, 176
Signet seal, *see under* Seals
Silver, *see under* Metals
Skins, *see under* Clothing
Skirlaw, Walter, 153
Sluys, battle of, 68 n. 2
Sodin, Guy, 74 n. 2
Sourzac (*dép.* Dordogne, *arr.* Périgueux, *c.* Mussidan), 89
Southampton (co. Hants), 57, 72 nn. 2, 3, 171
Spain, 68, 131
Speculum Judiciale, 24
Speculum legatorum, 124

Speeches, *see under* Parliament
Squires, 132, 174
Squirrels, *see under* Animals
Stables, 174
Stamford (co. Lincs.), 29, 58
Stanes, Simon, 53, 143
Stapeldon, Walter, bishop of Exeter, 42 n. 2, 43, 113, 119, 121, 122, 125–6
Staple, the, 13, 138, 171
Star Chamber, 166
Statutes, *see* Law
Staunford, *see* Stamford
Staunford, Roger, *see* Processes, keeper of
Stephen, 175
Sterling, *see under* Currency
Steward, papal, 134
Stone (co. Kent), church of, 36 n. 4
Stores, *see* Provisions
Stowe, John, 116 n. 1
— Walter, 116 n. 1
Stratford, John, 52, 139, 169
Strayer, J. R., 25
Sturler, J. de, 171
Subsidies, *see* Grants and subsidies
Summons, 10, 14, 15, 191
— writs of, 74
Sumpters, 131, 174
Susa (Italy, prov. Piedmont), 174
Sutri (Italy, prov. Rome), 174
Swinfen, Robert, 134
Switzerland, 17
Sword Room (Tower of London), 119

Tabriz (Persia), 175
Tailors, 131
Tallies, 169
Tange, Andrew de, 45 n. 1, 185
Teignmouth (co. Devon), 72 n. 2
Temple, *see under* Paris
Templeman, G., 20, 21
Temporalities, *see* Sees, vacant
Tenth, papal, 18 n. 1, 32, 185
Tents, 175
Thames river, 137
The Hague (Holland), 66
Theology, professors of sacred, 143
Thoresby, John, bishop of St. David's and Worcester, archbishop of York, 137, 153 n. 4
Thorp, Walter, 55 n. 1, 91
Thynden (Finedon), church (co. Northants.), 103

INDEX

Tin, *see under* Metals
Tiran, Gombald de, 125
Toulouse, counts of, *see* Raymond VI, Raymond VII
Touraine (France), 5, 7
Tour de la Reine, la (Montreuil), 62
tournois, livres, see under Currency
Tournon d'Agenais (*dép.* Lot-et-Garonne, *arr.* Villeneuve-sur-Lot), 105, 106
Tout, T. F., 1, 19, 29, 61, 165, 167
Trabut-Cussac, J.-P., 23 n. 2
Tractatus de Actionibus, 24
Transcription of records, *see under* Records
Transportation of records, *see under* Records
Travers, John, 37, 102
Treasurer, *see under* Exchequer, Wardrobe
Treasury, *see under* Exchequer, Wardrobe
Treaty rolls, *see under* Chancery
Treaties, 30, 42, 43, 44, 50, 56, 58, 82, 86, 87, 89, 90, 92, 93, 94, 95, 96, 98, 99, 100, 103, 113, 114, 123, 124, 131, 137, 148, 149, 151, 154, 186, 187, 190
— enrolment of, 164
— forms of, 160-4
— of Amiens (1279), 8, 14, 44 n. 1, 87, 93, 97
— of Gaillon (1195), 44 n. 1
— of Le Goulet (1200), 44 n. 1
— of Messina (1191), 44 n. 1
— of Montreuil (1299), 44 n. 5, 50
— of Paris (1259), 3-6, 8, 14, 15, 16, 19, 22, 23, 25, 26, 27, 28, 44 n. 1, 51, 60, 78, 87, 93, 94, 95, 96, 98, 99, 141, 163-4, 187, 190
— of Paris (1286), 8, 14, 87, 93, 95, 96, 97
— of Paris (1303), 11, 13, 48, 63-4, 74 n. 2, 87, 93, 99, 184
— of Paris (1325), 15, 161
— of Paris (1327), 15, 44 n. 1
— of Saint-Ayr-de-Vaudreuil (1195), 44 n. 1
— promulgation and ratification of, 151 and n. 1, 162, 163, 164
Trebizond (Turkey), 176
Trevisa, La (*dép.* Dordogne), parish of, 88
Trials, 138
Troja (Italy, prov. Apulia), 176

Truces, 35, 50, 58, 63, 72, 74 n. 2, 78, 85 n. 1, 86, 102, 124, 131, 147, 180
— conservator of, 65
Trussel, Sir William, 58
Tumbe, 116
Tunics, *see under* Clothing
Tunis, 141 n. 1
Turenne, viscounts of, *see* Raymond IV
Turin (Italy), 174
Tutors, 137

Ufford, Andrew, 39, 143, 150
— John, 104 n. 1
Ullmann, W., 25
Ulnager, king's, 139
University of Paris, *see under* Paris
Utrecht, bishop of, 182

Valence, Aymer of, earl of Pembroke, 90, 147
Valence, diocese of, 134
Valenciennes (*dép.* Nord), 132
Valets, 131, 132 n. 1, 174, 179 n. 1
Vallem Rodolii, *see* Saint-Ayr-de-Vaudreuil
Valois, Charles, count of, 108
Valprionde (*dép.* Lot, *arr.* Cahors, *c.* Montcuq), parish of, 94 n. 1
Vane, John, 40
Varlicou (*dép.* Tarn-et-Garonne, *arr.* Castelsarrasin, *c.* Beaumont-de-Lomagne, *cne.* Belbès), parish of, 94 n. 1
Vassals, 5, 8, 189-91
— *privilégiés*, 7, 8
Vauban, Sébastien de, 62
Venice, doge of, 128 n. 3
Ver (*dép.* Oise), 65 n. 1
Ver, Hugh de, 124, 173-4
— Sir Jean de, 65, 74 n. 2, 81.
Verneuil (*dép.* Eure), 47.
Vessels, *see under* Receptacles, Ships
Veyrines (*dép.* Gironde, *arr.* Bordeaux), castle of, 111
Vienne, archbishop of, 133
Vigier, Pierre, 48
Villefranche-de-Saint-Louis, *see* Saint-Louis-en-L'Isle
Villeneuve-sur-Lot (*dép.* Lot-et-Garonne), 105, 106
Villeréal (*dép.* Lot-et-Garonne, *arr.* Villeneuve-sur-Lot), 105
Viterbo (Italy, prov. Rome), 174, 176

INDEX

Viviers (France), 12
Vouchers, *see under* Accounts
Vow of the Heron, The, 19
Vyne, Pieres de la, 72 n. 3

Wadenho, Roger, 36, 46, 91
Wages, 40, 41, 115, 154, 167, 168, 169, 170, 171, 179, 184–5. *See also under* Envoys
Waldershare (co. Kent), church of, 36
Wales, 11, 22, 126, 185
Walewayn, John, 153
Walter, 170
Waltham, Roger, 119
Walton ordinances, *see under* Ordinances
War, 5, 10, 13, 14, 15, 17, 19, 21, 22, 24, 27, 28, 39, 78, 79, 86, 87, 89, 107 n. 2, 117, 124, 134, 149, 153, 167, 172, 177 n. 1, 181, 187, 191
Wardcope, Robert of, 154
Wardrobe, 40, 41 n. 3, 59, 114, 118, 119, 121, 123, 125, 127, 145, 152, 153–4, 167
— abroad, 13, 171–2, 177 n. 2, 178 n. 1
— accounts of, 32, 34 nn. 1, 3, 35 n. 3, 37–8, 40, 115, 153, 166, 172–4, 177–80, 188
— archives of, 30, 31, 115, 118, 119, 121, 126, 184–6, 187
— clerks of, 173, 186
— cofferer, of, 137, 173
— controller of, 31, 114, 115, 117, 135, 147, 177, 184, 186
— great, 171
— keeper of, 31, 37, 118, 119, 135, 137, 147, 173
— notaries in, 122, 184–6
— prests, 166, 178
— rolls of, 164, 183
— seals of, 172, 186
— treasurer of, 31, 35, 118
— treasury of, 31, 119, 121
— *see also under* Diplomacy
Warrants, 121, 145 n. 1, 152, 158, 167, 183
Wassingborough, church (co. Lincs.), 158

Wax, 184
Weapon Room (Tower of London), 119
Wellesworth, Edmund of, 75 n. 4
Westminster, 35, 42, 43, 46, 54, 59, 64 n. 3, 100, 115, 116, 136, 148, 164, 171, 178 n. 1
— ordinance of, *see under* Ordinances
Weston, William, 153
Weymouth (co. Dorset), 72 n. 2
White Friars, 117
White Tower (Tower of London), 31, 119
Wickford, Robert, 153 n. 4
William III (of England), 18
Winchelsea (co. Sussex), 72 n. 2
Winchelsea, Thomas, archbishop of Canterbury, 33, 180, 181
Winchester (co. Hants), 72 n. 3
Winchester, bishop of, 11 n. 1, 52, 56, 148, 160
— diocese of, 36
Winchester, John of, 184
Wines, 72 n. 3, 115, 174, 178, 179
Wissant (*dép*. Pas-de-Calais, *arr.* Boulogne-sur-Mer, *c.* Marquise), 174, 175, 181
Witnesses, *see under* Procedure, legal
Wodehouse, John, 153 n. 4
Wolfenbüttel MS., 121 n. 3
Wolves, *see under* Animals
Wool, 66, 71, 72 n. 3, 140, 171, 178, 179, 182
Worcester, bishop of, 47, 53, 57, 135, 137
Writs, *see under* Records, Summons

Yarmouth (co. Norf.), 72 n. 2, 171
York, county of, 136
York (co. Yorks.), 58, 148, 150, 154 n. 5
York, archbishop of, *see* Melton, Thoresby
— dean of, 56
Ypres (Belgium), 16, 138, 175

Zeeland, 35 n. 1, 68, 170
Zouch, William de la, 132 n. 1